Leo Hickman is a journalist and editor at the *Guardian*, and writes a weekly column on ethical living. He is also the author of *A Life Stripped Bare: My Year Trying to Live Ethically* and *How to Buy*, and editor of *A Good Life: The Guide to Ethical Living*. Leo lives in Cornwall with his wife, Jane, and their three children.

THE FINAL CALL

'We have got to find a way to shift to a slow-travel culture. Our very survival as a species could well hinge on it. I very much hope this important book helps to awaken people, and make them want to join the debate.'
Jeremy Leggett

'Hickman has hit on an important subject and it deserves to be taken seriously.'
John Humphrys

'*The Final Call* is a thought-provoking call to action. Leo Hickman offers a comprehensive assessment of the future towards which today's tourism industry is driving us. I recommend this book to all who travel – whether for work or play – and hope that together we can make this world a more sustainable and peaceful place for all living things.'
Jane Goodall, Ph.D., DBE, founder of the Jane Goodall Institute and UN Messenger of Peace

'Despite the polemic, there is plenty of interest here, not least in [the book's] accessible description of how the travel industry works and the structures in place around the globe . . . Hickman acknowledges the increasing acceptance of environmental standards . . . But the argument he presents is a stark one – travel is damaging the world, and if we don't act soon, it may be too late. Sobering stuff.'
Travel Weekly

'A fascinating and harrowing read. I doubt anyone has spelt out the inherent dangers of mass tourism so clearly before. The publication of this could well prove to be a 'tipping point'.'
Jason Webster, author of *Guerra*

'Leo Hickman's enthralling book *The Final Call*, ventures into the dark underbelly of mass tourism, illuminating the reality beyond the cheesy tour rep smiles, and focusing on the astonishing price of tourism on local culture as well as on the environment. *The Final Call* is a book that should be read by politicians, students and, most of all, by every would-be package tourist standing in a travel agent with a glossy brochure in his hand.'
Tahir Shah, author of *The Caliph's House*

THE FINAL CALL

Investigating Who Really Pays for Our Holidays

Leo Hickman

TRANSWORLD PUBLISHERS
61–63 Uxbridge Road, London W5 5SA
A Random House Group Company
www.rbooks.co.uk

First published in Great Britain
in 2007 by Eden Project Books
an imprint of Transworld Publishers
in association with Guardian Books,
an imprint of Guardian News and Media Ltd

This paperback edition published in 2008

This book is a work of non-fiction based on the experiences and recollections of the author. In
some limited cases names of people have been changed to protect their identity or the privacy of
others. The author has stated to the publishers that, except in such minor respects not affecting
the substantial accuracy of the work, the contents of this book are true as at January 2008.

A CIP catalogue record for this book
is available from the British Library.

ISBN 9781905811069

Addresses for Random House Group Ltd companies outside the UK
can be found at: www.randomhouse.co.uk
The Random House Group Ltd Reg. No. 954009

Penguin Random House is committed to a sustainable future for
our business, our readers and our planet. This book is made from
Forest Stewardship Council® certified paper.

Typeset in Minion by Falcon Oast Graphic Art Ltd
Printed and bound in Great Britain by Clays Ltd, Elcograf S.p.A.

2 4 6 8 10 9 7 5 3

Every effort has been made to obtain the necessary permissions with reference to copyright
material, both illustrative and quoted. We apologize for any omissions in this respect and
will be pleased to make the appropriate acknowledgements in any future edition.

In loving memory of
Jessica Pearl Joy Ward
1960–2006

www.cancerbackup.org.uk

Contents

Acknowledgements

My foremost thanks go to the many people who gave their time – some at considerable personal sacrifice or risk – to be interviewed for this book. Many are quoted directly within these pages, but there are a number of silent voices that none the less guided me throughout each destination.

There are also a number of people who generously opened their contact books for me. I was particularly fortunate to be able to call on the *Guardian's* unrivalled network of foreign correspondents. Special thanks go to John Aglionby, Angelique Chrisafis, Rory McCarthy, Giles Tremlett and Jon Watts. Thanks, too, go to: Tricia Barnett and Guyonne James at Tourism Concern; Erika Harms and Amy DiElsi at the UN Foundation; Diaa Hadid at *Gulf News*; Kevin Thrussell and Ian Ledlie at Sanya China Travel; Chris Beddoe at ECPAT; Supreeya Rungnobhakhun; Stephen Armstrong; Teri Shore at the Bluewater Network; Kathy Loretta at the *Miami Herald*; Ron Mader at Planeta.com; Penny Guy at NATS; Montserrat Gasco Alcoberro at Benidorm City Council; and Kyra Cruz at ACTUAR in Costa Rica.

The logistics of researching a book such as this seemed overwhelming to me at times. I would like to thank sincerely all the following people for oiling the wheels of my transit: Louise Oram and David Tarsh at the WTTC; Benedict Fisher and Michela Chiappa at Nakheel; Anne Bleeker at Jumeirah; the staff at the Hong Kong Tourism Board; Irene Chan, Glendy Chu and Donn Walker at Disney; Surinder Manku at Royal Caribbean; Irina Svidlov and Tiina Kiibus at the Tallinn City Tourist Office; Raimo Poom at the British Embassy in Estonia; and Fiona O'Farrell at Emirates.

And this book would simply not have happened without the

support, advice and understanding of the following people: Susanna Wadeson, Sarah Emsley, Kate Samano, Manpreet Grewal, Steve Mulcahey and Geraldine Ellison at Transworld; Lisa Darnell at Guardian Books; Roger Field at New Media Law LLP; and Andy Pietrasik, Chris Elliott, Kath Viner, Leslie Plommer and Lucy Clouting at the *Guardian*.

Special mention, naturally, goes to my wife Jane, and our daughters Esme and Jessie, who had to accommodate what was at times my obsession to complete this long, long journey.

Permission to use copyright material is gratefully acknowledged:

pp. 14–15, 'Seven Steps to Preserving the Mountain' supplied by Ski Club of Great Britain, www.respectthemountain.com

pp. 115–16, extract from *(Hetero)Sexual Politics*, copyright © J. O'Connell Davidson, 1995.

p. 117, extract from 'Dollars are a Girl's Best Friend? Female Tourists' Sexual Behaviour in the Caribbean' in *Sociology*, copyright © Jacqueline Sánchez Taylor, 2001.

p. 139, *The Beach*, by Alex Garland (Viking, 1996), copyright © Alex Garland, 1996. Reproduced by permission of Penguin Books Ltd.

pp. 148–50, extract from 'Why Destination Areas Rise and Fall in Popularity: An Update of a Cornell Quarterly', copyright © Dr Stanley Plog, 2001. Reprinted by permission of SAGE Publications, Inc.

pp. 172–3, extract from a paper, 'Chinese Tourists' Behaviour in "Elsewhereland"', copyright © Wolfgang Arlt, 2006.

p. 249, *'Like An Alien In We Own Land'*, by The Mighty Pep, © Desmond Long/Pitton Music Productions, 1994. Lyrics reproduced by kind permission.

pp. 279–80, extract from 'Ecotourism as a Western Construct' from the *Journal of Ecotourism*, copyright © E. Cater, 2006.

p. 280, extract from 'Ecotourism: A Consumption Perspective' from the *Journal of Ecotourism*, copyright © R. Sharpley, 2006.

pp. 280–81, extract from *A Trip Too Far: Ecotourism, Politics and Exploitation*, copyright © Rosaleen Duffy, 2002.

Introduction

To tell which way the wind is blowing, all you need to do in my home is lie still in bed and listen. The first clue comes at about four thirty a.m., when a low, distant drone slowly becomes audible – but only when there's a westerly wind.

This isn't the sound of the wind rustling the leaves on the cherry trees, or a neighbour's washing twisting on the line in the breeze. It's the first plane of the day – typically a Boeing 737 – passing at around four thousand feet over my home in south London on its approach to Heathrow airport. It still has eight minutes and twenty miles to fly before it touches down to disgorge its passengers into one of what will soon be five terminals, but by the time it passes overhead the whine of its jet engines is responsible for the forty-eight decibels of aircraft-related sleep disturbance that the law allows. Just a few minutes or so later, another aircraft will follow in its wake. And another, and another, until late evening, when flights into Heathrow are once again suspended for the 'night', a period determined to be from eleven thirty p.m. to six a.m. That Heathrow is allowed special dispensation for sixteen flights a night to land between this period explains why the six a.m. deadline is broken almost daily. According to HACAN ClearSkies, a campaign group formed by residents living under Heathrow's flightpath, some areas of south London experience almost five hundred planes flying overhead per day.

In total, the airport – the world's busiest – manages a daily average of nearly 1,300 aircraft movements. Like all airports, it uses the direction of the wind to determine which way aircraft will approach its runways, as it is safer for a plane to descend into a head wind. Unfortunately, residents of south London are cursed by the fact that the UK's prevailing winds are westerly. This means that we are forced to list descending aircraft alongside car alarms and police sirens as some of our many sources of noise pollution. The only saving grace is that I don't live any nearer to Heathrow – residents of Barnes, Richmond, Twickenham, East Sheen, Kew and Hounslow are so close that some claim they can even make eye contact with the pilots.

Sometimes, as I lie awake at night counting planes instead of sheep, I wonder where each passenger passing over me has just come from. Are they returning from a holiday? Is this their first time visiting Britain? Are they, like me when I go somewhere for the first time, both apprehensive and excited about arriving in a new country and new city? Where will they be sleeping tonight? Is someone coming to meet them?

And then I move on to the consequences of all these journeys. How much fuel is needed to fly sixty tonnes of aircraft through the air for many hundreds, if not thousands, of miles? What effect is the resulting pollution having on the environment? Is flying hundreds of millions of people around the world each year for their holidays really sustainable? Can our skies handle this load? And what of the destinations and the people who live there? What impact are all these arrivals having on them? It's enough to keep you awake at night, even if the planes' roar wasn't already doing so.

My angst is only deepened when I mull over the forecasts for how much international travel is set to boom within the next few decades – people who live under flightpaths tend to have a keen eye for such data – as flying becomes increasingly accessible and, it would seem, ever cheaper.

In 2005, Britons made 66.4 million visits abroad – an all-time record and three times the amount in 1984 – with 81 per cent of those journeys made by air, according to the Office of National Statistics. That's broadly an average of one international trip a year per person, with Spain and France between them accounting for 38 per cent of all destinations. In the other direction, travellers from overseas made 30 million visits to the UK in 2005, again the highest total ever and double the amount in 1984. Two-thirds of all those journeys were made by people going on holiday, the rest being either business trips or so-called VFRs (visits to friends and relatives).

But the figures just seem to keep expanding exponentially as you gaze into the future. When the UK government published a white paper in 2003 aiming to set out the country's aviation needs for the next thirty years, it predicted that the UK's airports would need to be able to handle between 350 and 460 million passengers by 2020. That's two to three times the amount in 2002 and at least ten times the 1970 figure. Incredibly, it estimated that one-fifth of the world's international passengers are on flights to or from a UK airport. When a 'progress report' into the white paper was published in late 2006 by the Department for Transport, the number of passengers using the UK's airports had already risen by 14 per cent since 2003. Aviation demand is not just taking off, it's soaring out of sight.

The bulk of this future demand is, of course, going to be driven by tourists. It's our growing desire for two-week holidays in the sun, visits to the ski slopes, or short weekend city breaks that will exacerbate this rush to the skies. But shouldn't we be debating whether this is really such a sensible way to proceed, especially in the light of increased concerns about the environmental legacy of flying? Not according to the United Nations. Its tourism division, known as the World Tourism Organization (UNWTO), thinks that tourism is one of the best industries for developing nations to turn to because it leads to 'prosperity and peace'. High hopes, indeed, but it's worth hearing its views in detail:

At the start of the new millennium, tourism is firmly established as the number-one industry in many countries and the fastest-growing economic sector in terms of foreign-exchange earnings and job creation.

International tourism is the world's largest export earner and an important factor in the balance of payments of most nations.

Tourism has become one of the world's most important sources of employment. It stimulates enormous investment in infrastructure, most of which also helps to improve the living conditions of local people. It provides governments with substantial tax revenues. Most new tourism jobs and business are created in developing countries, helping to equalize economic opportunities and keep rural residents from moving to overcrowded cities.

Intercultural awareness and personal friendships fostered through tourism are a powerful force for improving international understanding and contributing to peace among all the nations of the world.

Impressive. It is certainly not lacking in hope and ambition. Tourism, if you believe the UNWTO, is the knight on a charger that could ride forth to save the underprivileged peoples of the world, who should be taking full advantage of the fact that many of them live in places where the world's rich want to holiday – either sun-drenched, pristine environments such as palm-lined beaches, or countries offering that sought-after cultural 'other'. In short, there is a sustainable, healthy living to be made by helping foreign tourists gain temporary sanctuary from the mundane routines of their day-to-day lives: the stress of the office, the supermarket check-out queues, the school run, the credit-card bills.

This all sounds wonderful in theory, but is tourism really such a global force for good? Can we all just keep on going on more and more trips abroad each year – 15 per cent of the UK population now go on three or more flights abroad each year – as all the predictions seem to suggest? And what of the emerging demands of international tourists from countries such as India and China? Can all the host destinations cope? The UNWTO, while it lauds tourism's potential, does accept that there can sometimes be problems:

> The UNWTO recognizes that tourism can have a negative cultural, environmental and social impact if it is not responsibly planned, managed and monitored. The UNWTO thus encourages governments to play a vital role in tourism, in partnership with the private sector, local authorities and non-governmental organizations.

But one of the main problems with the mass rush to tourism by many nations around the world is that, somewhat mysteriously, it barely registers on the to-do lists of their governments. It is rare for any government to have, say, a secretary of state for tourism. At best, nations will have a minister for tourism, someone who is far down the pecking order of influence. Instead, governments tend to focus on the traditional matters at hand – health, education, the economy. As yet, few countries have acknowledged that tourism, if it is to be invested in as a key industry, is intrinsically tied up with all of these.

The net result of this widespread lack of governmental recognition is that tourism is currently one of the most unregulated industries in the world, largely controlled by a relatively small number of Western corporations such as hotel groups and tour operators. Are they really the best guardians of this evidently important but supremely fragile global industry?

And what of our role as tourists? Are we really just passive lumps of flesh and bone, being transported across the globe for our pleasure without a care in the world? Or can we change the impact of our holidays on each destination for the better? Perhaps some of our favourite holiday spots are simply too vulnerable and sensitive to sustain the growing volume of visits? Or are their residents now so reliant on tourism that they would struggle to survive without us?

In early 2006, I grew tired of these questions revolving in my head night after night as I lay in bed listening to the planes pass by. I decided to pack my bags and attempt to find some answers. Where I should go was determined by many factors – financial and logistical considerations being principal among them – but most importantly, I wanted to try to visit a spread of popular destinations that would represent the various trends and pressures of global tourism today: climate change, demographic shifts, the maturation and sophistication of holidaying tastes, the widening partition between the world's wealthy and poor, and globalization.

It has often struck me that I live in one of the world's leading tourist destinations, a place that attracts twelve million tourists a year – more than New York, Sydney and Las Vegas combined. Tourism is clearly hugely important to London's economy – it is the city's second-largest and fastest-growing industry, accounting for 8 per cent of its GDP and 13 per cent of its workforce, according to the Government Office for London, and I see tourists wandering the streets every day, clutching their guidebooks and maps. It is evident that vast volumes of tourists can be absorbed by cities such as London without a noticeable impact on its citizens. But what effect do we as tourists have on places where our arrival greatly swells the population? What effect does our footfall have on places that are both environmentally and ecologically sensitive? And just how much do the resident communities really have to gain economically from our stay?

This book is but one person's journey through a handful of the destinations we all love to visit, from the Alpine mountainsides and the deserts of Dubai to the corals of the Caribbean and the costas of Spain, but at each port of call two key questions hover above all others: just where as tourists are we heading, both literally and metaphorically? And are we content with the implications?

1

Two Degrees from Meltdown

Chamonix, France

E VERY DAY SINCE 1936, meteorologists have been making the long climb up to the Weissfluhjoch test station that sits high up on a Swiss mountainside overlooking the village of Davos to read the thermometer and measure snow levels. Only once in seventy years has the weather contrived to beat them back. Scientists from across the Alps now meet up annually to study this vital archive, to share other data collated from test sites across the mountain range, and to mull over the implications of their findings. Each year the frowns of concern deepen.

Throughout the Alpine region there is now increasing evidence – both anecdotal and scientific – of melting glaciers, less and later snow, higher mean temperatures and snowlines retreating up the mountains. Bergit Ottmar of the Swiss Federal Institute for Snow and Avalanche Research in Davos, which maintains the Weissfluhjoch test station – in large part to issue accurate avalanche warnings for the area – speaks as a true scientist when she says that the institute's job is only to provide accurate data. It is for others to act on it. 'At lower and middle altitudes there has been a decrease in snow over this seventy-year period that is statistically relevant.' In other words, something is definitely happening. 'But it is very hard to differentiate between natural changes and climate change,' she adds, refusing to be drawn on whether she instinctively agrees with the fast-hardening consensus among scientists that anthropogenic – man-made – global warming is overwhelmingly to blame for the rapid changes now taking place in the Alps.

Take avalanches, she says to explain her position. The institute has a huge database that records avalanches that have caused deaths, or destroyed buildings or forests. 'But we haven't noticed a steady increase – just variations. For example, over this seventy-year period there have only been two "avalanche years", as we call them – 1951 and 1999. These are loosely described as years in which people were killed in their own homes by avalanches, such were their ferocity. Most avalanche deaths are caused by skiers going off-piste: 90 per cent of the avalanches that kill skiers are caused by the skiers themselves. In Switzerland, we have between ten and forty of these avalanche deaths a year.'

An unseasonably rapid and deep snowfall across the Alps in early March 2006, combined with an extreme cold snap, led to that year's ski season being labelled one of the worst on record for avalanche deaths. By mid-March more than eighty people participating in winter sports across the Alps had died in snow slides. The French authorities in particular have become increasingly exasperated at the growing trend for 'free-riding', in which skiers and snowboarders chase the virgin snows that lie tantalizingly beyond the poles that mark out the congested pistes. The French government has demanded 'zero tolerance' for skiers found disobeying the largely ignored by-law that says they must keep to defined tracks. But for many, the chance to glide through the powder, leaving solitary tracks behind them, is still a prize worth risking death for.

Bergit Ottmar is not keen to pass judgement on skiers' actions. In fact, she points out that avalanches can have a positive impact on

Alpine flora and fauna. 'Alpine forest is rather poor in biodiversity, because it's dominated by one or two native trees which don't allow much light on to the ground. When the trees are destroyed there is more variation in biodiversity. "Avalanche alleys" keep knocking over the trees. It's just part of nature.' What does impede this natural cycle, though, are piste building, the increasing use of artificial snow, and man-made avalanche screens aimed at protecting skiers and buildings. 'The worst impact of winter sports is the creation of very flat, wide pistes, using heavy vehicles. The flattening of the ground destroys the vegetation underneath. It has taken millions of years in some areas of the Alps to create just a few millimetres of soil. If this is destroyed or disturbed, it is very hard for vegetation to grow back. In the summer, when the snow melts, you can really see where the pistes were.'

Other people are prepared to be much more damning about the impact that humans are having – both through climate change and, more directly, through winter sports – not just on the Alps but across all the world's mountain ranges. In January 2007, for example, the *Journal of Applied Biology* published findings by researchers at the University of Turin which showed that there was a marked decline in bird life around pistes compared to natural mountain grasslands. 'Winter sports represent a potentially serious threat to the conservation of wildlife habitat in the Alps,' said Professor Antonio Rolando, the lead researcher. 'Bulldozers and power shovels are used to remove soil and provide suitable slopes for skiers. To a lesser extent, vegetation may also be damaged by skiing and ski-piste preparation by snow-grooming vehicles. The ski pistes that we sampled were devastated environmental patches, from which shrubby and herbaceous native vegetation had been removed and/or severely damaged, and artificial seeding – if any – had produced very poor grass cover.' The researchers found fewer arthropods (insects and spiders) on the ski pistes they studied in the Western Alps, suggesting that a shortage of food may be responsible for the reduced presence of birds. A study published in March 2007 by researchers at the University of Bern showed that stress levels in black grouse are raised by disturbance from skiers. They said it could also be a factor affecting other species such as snow hare, ibex and red deer. Sergio Savoia, the director of the World Wildlife Fund (WWF)'s Alpine programme, says that the skiing industry is impacting on the Alps in a 'big, big way'. He draws up a long list of reasons that includes increased traffic, the damage caused by artificial snow, the threat to wildlife, and rubbish dumped on mountainsides.

'It's the sheer size of it that worries me', he explains from his office in Bellinzona, Switzerland. 'Around eighty million tourists visit the Alps every year. It used to be as many as a hundred million. Compare that with the resident population of about sixteen million. This means there is five times the amount of tourists to residents. According to the World Tourism Organization (UNWTO), 12 per cent of all the world's tourists each year come to the Alps. But there's virtually nowhere left to develop now, and as the snow keeps retreating higher up the mountains, so the pressure on the remaining space and resources increases.'

Savoia says he doesn't need scientists and their data to tell him that the Alps are changing: he can see it with his own eyes. He seems mournful about the Alps' chances of overcoming the problems brought on by winter sports and, much more so, by climate change. 'I was born in the mountains and have lived here all my life. I have seen less and less snow. Yes, we've had good snow this year. But my eldest daughter, who is fourteen, had never seen snow like this before. The last time I saw it was twenty years ago. This doesn't say much because it is just a human lifespan, but look at the pictures of glaciers a hundred years ago and you can see the dramatic retreat. Some are saying that there won't be glaciers in Switzerland – the heart of the Alps – in another hundred years. It's not the first time in history that this has happened, but it has never happened so fast. I don't think there is much, to be honest, that we can do to halt the retreat of the glaciers. All we can do is try not to make it worse. If we stop emissions right now, the glaciers would still retreat because the climate has a long inertia. It's like trying to stop a ship. The consequences for slope stability and water supply are going to be huge. If you think that the Alps supply hydropower – not to mention drinking water – to most of the surrounding area of Europe, you can see that this is going to have major strategic, economic and even political ramifications. We are literally the water reservoir for much of Europe. I see the potential for catastrophe here. I don't want to paint a doom-and-gloom picture, but this is what is happening before our eyes.'

WWF says the Alps are one of the world's biodiversity 'hotspots', with more than thirty thousand animal species and thirteen thousand plant species. Some of Europe's last remaining pristine areas are found within the Alps, but they are under increasing threat. In a report published in 2006, WWF said that snowfall in the Italian Alps has decreased by 20 per cent over the past thirty years.

'We are trying to make people realize that it's economic suicide to ignore the environment in the Alps,' says Savoia. 'People in the Alps say they are very environmentally conscious now. But they see what's happening both as a problem and as an opportunity. The mountains are their livelihood, after all. In Austria, most of the ski stations are mid- to low-level, and in thirty to fifty years they will all be out of business because the snow will be gone. Well-intentioned Austrian legislators won't authorize the building of snow cannons that make artificial snow in these lower areas. Instead, they are only allowing the higher-level resorts to be saved. The Swiss cantons have also said they will not finance low-lying ski resorts. But this just forces people further up the mountain.'

Going ever higher, he says, brings with it obvious problems, such as increased transport and infrastructure demands, as well as placing further pressure on once-pristine areas. In an effort to reduce this impact, some ski-resort owners are calling for 'ski highways' to link various resorts with a far-reaching network of cable cars and lifts that would carry skiers up and over mountains to neighbouring valleys, which previously would have required a journey by car, bus or train. Rather than skiing all the pistes of one mountain over a day, skiers would instead move much more easily between mountains, before returning to their hotel or chalet in the evening. Savoia dismisses this idea, pointing out that it would be a highly damaging, short-term measure that might not even recoup the huge financial outlay of the developers, simply because the snow could all be gone by the time it was built. 'There are only three options now available to the ski industry,' he says. 'Use artificial snow; go ever higher; or start adapting to summer tourism and forget about chasing the snow. I believe the last option is the only truly sustainable way forward.'

My route to Chamonix valley will be familiar to the vast majority of the 2.5 million people who visit the Alps' busiest winter sports area each year. The A40 toll road – more commonly called the *route blanche* because of the mighty Mont Blanc that looms over it – connects Geneva to Chamonix. It carries the many thousands of tourists who arrive at the busy lakeside airport each day, as well as the heavy freight trucks – as many as 2,500 a day – that also travel up to the entrance of the Mont Blanc tunnel. Whereas the truckers pass into the tunnel, heading south towards Italy, the tourists generally turn left into Chamonix or continue further up the thin valley towards the other resorts that lie along its fifteen-mile-long, half-mile-wide floor.

But before reaching the valley's narrow entrance, I take a diversion midway along the A40 at Cluses and journey up the steep hairpin bends and across the Giffre valley's pastures, fast reappearing in the springtime thaw, to the popular village resort of Samoëns that sits beneath the Grand Massif ski area. I am meeting Clare Simon, the

French *chargée de mission* of the International Commission for the Protection of the Alps (CIPRA). Founded in 1952, CIPRA has long studied the direct impact of tourism on the Alps. Its aim is to 'oversee economic and environmental balance' in the mountains through its network of regional branches, one in each of the seven Alpine nations – Switzerland, Liechtenstein, France, Germany, Austria, Slovenia and Italy. It was the driving force behind the signing of the Alpine Convention in 1991 that saw these nations all agree, in principle at least (some nations have yet to formally ratify the convention), to a series of measures aimed at better protecting the mountain range. CIPRA has also lobbied the International Olympic Committee not to grant the winter Olympics to a new destination every four years – the jamboree was first held in Chamonix in 1924 – since this inevitably leads to major development and upgrading of facilities. Instead, it wants two or three areas to be chosen to share the games permanently.

We meet in a bar in a side street leading off Samoëns' exquisite medieval square. Over hot chocolate and accompanied by the loud soundtrack of a television showing a fast-edit montage of daring snowboarding mountain descents, Clare explains the effects winter sports are having on the region. She starts by pointing out of the window at the near-vertical face of the imposing Criou mountain that seems to lean over Samoëns.

'Can you see that plane flying over the mountain?'

I can just make out a small speck moving above its summit.

'That is a sightseeing flight,' she says. 'Some areas now get fifteen of these flights a day passing overhead. There's hardly any relief from the low whine of their engines, and the noise can carry for miles across these mountains. In the summer, we get quad bikes, and motorbikes going off road, too: the politicians here just seem to allow it.' This is just one example, she says, of the creeping influence tourism is having on this former wilderness.

Echoing Sergio Savoia's concerns about the plans for ski high-ways, Clare produces a map of the French *département* of Haute-Savoie and points to Samoëns. 'There's the Grand Massif Express, a brand-new high-capacity lift that took four years to build and now carries skiers from here up 1,600 metres to the Saix plateau in eight minutes. Along with the lift came the inevitable new car park and buildings. It was financed in part by the Compagnie des Alpes, the largest private lift operator in the world -- the company has a near monopoly on the lifts operating in the Chamonix valley, as well as in many other popular areas such as La Plagne, Tignes, Les Arcs, Meribel and Les Menuires. There is also a big project at the moment called the Espace Mont Blanc, which aims to link up all the pistes in the area, including over to Italy. The tour operators are demanding 150 kilo-metres of new pistes for the whole area.'

I ask her how strict the planning regulations are here in the Alps. Presumably there are exacting rules about what can and cannot be built in such a landscape?

'Sure, building a new ski lift is in theory hard, due to the planning requirements and the attention that needs to be paid to the environ-ment; but in practice there is little imagination here and projects get passed quite easily. After all, local politicians are elected every six to seven years, so everything is for the short term.'

Most of the pistes in the French Alps, she explains, are now managed by private companies who are 'only interested in pleasing their shareholders'. Few are controlled by the local town hall or mayor, as they once were. The only notable exception Clare can think of are the community-owned ski lifts in the village of Valloire in the Maurienne valley, which lies further south between the Trois Vallées and the Italian border.

This transfer of power has its roots in the 1960s and 1970s when, under President Charles de Gaulle's so-called *Plan Neige*, the French government invested heavily in the ski infrastructure in the region to promote tourism. A number of mega ski resorts were built at high altitude, including Flaine, Avoriaz, Les Menuires, Val d'Isère, Val Thorens and Les Arcs. Leading French architects, including pupils of Le Corbusier, were invited to apply their often modernist hands to the mountainsides to herald a new era for the region and bring with it much-needed income as the traditional agrarian economy receded. To provide a better quality of service for skiers, resorts were encouraged to offer private ski-lift firms long management licences – up to thirty years, in some cases – so that they could build modern, fast lifts up to the pistes. Clare says that many locals now regret this handing over of control, as they lack any real ability to influence these often Paris-based firms. In desperation, some communities have even tried to buy back the contracts. But the companies are now very much the gatekeepers to the Alps and can increase prices and dictate developments largely as they choose. 'In neighbouring Savoie, there are plans to build a brand-new ski resort in a pristine area. It was refused permission once and is awaiting another hearing at the moment. There is always a pressure to build here. These companies just wait for the politicians to change before they try again. Eventually, they seem to succeed, as they did here in Samoëns.'

But surely the local people must benefit from the huge number of tourists that visit this region each year, I ask. Clare smiles ruefully.

'Tourists here are called "wallets" by the locals. People can't wait for them to leave each year. They are really disliked. They don't try to know anything about the place – they just treat it like Disneyland and come here to play. More and more people are starting to question whether tourism in its current form is such a wonderful thing. The bottom line is that it's harder to make money, and fewer and fewer people are doing so. The Dutch, Swiss and British are buying lots of second homes here and pricing the locals out. It is causing a lot of resentment as these homes then stay empty for many months.'

According to Clare, the problem of 'cold beds', as this phenomenon is known, is being exacerbated by the number of new residential resorts being built by large developers. Local environmentalists were alarmed at the announcement in 2000 that Intrawest Corporation, the giant Canadian resort developer that has a huge portfolio of ski, golf and beach resorts across North America and Canada, including Whistler in western Canada, was to build its first European project at Les Arcs. The development of seven hundred residential units called 'Village Arc 1950' opened in late 2007, to be followed in 2008 by a 550-unit development at Flaine, which, like Samoëns, lies on the Grand Massif. About 70 per cent of the units at Les Arcs are understood to have already been bought by British investors. Tellingly, one of Intrawest's key demands when it was searching for development sites was that they should be at a high enough altitude to have guaranteed snow, given fears about retreating snowlines. It was no surprise that it sought a partnership with the Compagnie des Alpes. It, too, is now a leading resort developer as well as ski-lift operator, with plans to buy resorts in central Switzerland above 1,500 metres in order to have guaranteed snow. In June 2002, Compagnie des Alpes sold 13,700 square metres of building rights at Les Arcs to Intrawest and their partnership was literally cemented.

I ask Clare how she sees the future of the Alps, and whether she believes there is anything that tourists can do to help, or whether we will only ever aggravate the problem.

'It's simple,' she says. 'Development must be limited. The Alps must be kept a wilderness area. Tourists need to think about their actions and what they demand in the way of resources and facilities. During high season, the volume of waste water and sewage grows tenfold in Chamonix valley. Lots of infrastructure is required to clean up the water, but isn't needed for the rest of the year. On the pistes there is rubbish everywhere, but it is quickly covered by snow so tourists don't think about it. The locals can help themselves too. Only half the people visiting the area in the winter actually ski or snowboard every day. It is important to offer other activities. We have a unique landscape and culture that are not explained to visitors. About fifteen years ago, St Martin in the Swiss canton of Valais was refused permission to build more ski lifts, so instead it went into nature tourism and it has been a huge success. There's also a resort in Austria that markets itself as being car-free.'

I look up at the TV screen still showing snowboarders whooping and punching the air as they tear down sheer slopes and wonder just how attractive this will ever be to the adrenaline junkies that are drawn to Chamonix's playground.

It is another hour on from Samoëns to reach my hotel. Gîte Le Belvédère hugs the main road leading into Argentière, the second most popular destination in the valley after Chamonix itself. This small town offers direct access to Les Grands Montets, the valley's largest ski area, as well as easy access to the slopes above the village of Le Tour, which lies a couple of miles further up the valley on the border with Switzerland. It is particularly popular with more serious skiers wanting to escape the younger crowds and lively *après ski* at Chamonix.

By the time I arrive, it is already dark and the only indication I have of the mountains penning me in on either side are the roaming headlights of the 'piste-bashers' high above, which work from five p.m. to three a.m. each night, busily preparing the slopes for the next day's skiing.

The gîte is managed by Patti, who first came to the valley as a 'ski bum' from her native Canada in 1981. At full capacity, it can sleep fifty-two guests in four-bed dorms, with a further thirty-two able to stay at the sister establishment, Hôtel de Savoie, further up in the town opposite the railway station. At thirteen euros a night, Patti boasts that, bar camping, the gîte offers the cheapest bed in the valley. After dumping my bags, I join her in the large breakfast room that doubles up as a communal room for the guests. Talk, as always in the valley, immediately turns to the snow conditions.

'January is much colder now than when I first came to the valley – about -15C. April is still a consistent snow month, but there is less snow now overall, I believe, than back then. The snow season is now from 20 December to 10 May. And in January we tend to have almost exclusively ice climbers staying here.'

Patti says that concern among the local hoteliers about the changing environment has really increased in the past three to five years. The most notable signs of change, she says, are the melting glaciers and the low-lying smog caused by all the valley's traffic. As this attitude shift increases, so too does antipathy towards the visitors.

'Last year there were a few articles in the local newspapers about the bad vibes between the French and English in the valley. Tourism here is changing. Skiing here is now a luxury sport. There's far less budget accommodation than before, and lots of private land is now owned by Brits and Swedes. Primary schools have 25 per cent foreign children.'

One of the main problems – and causes of resentment – is rising prices, driven by the influx of wealthier visitors. Just take a glance in any of the valley's many estate agents' windows and you can see chalets priced far above a million euros. A studio in Argentière can cost €110,000.

'The Compagnie du Mont Blanc [part of the Compagnie des Alpes group] controls everything – the lifts, the restaurants. It's a mountain monopoly. Some locals hate the blandness of what's on offer here, particularly the restaurants, and now go skiing in Cormayeur in Italy because there are far more locally owned restaurants there. From time to time we do all try to get together and demand change, but nothing seems to happen. We once lobbied for Argentière to make a pedestrianized area to improve the town's identity and appeal, but the commerce board here just said "No." The one area of change is a small move back to farming and a blossoming of interest in local traditions. For example, there's more interest in local cheeses than ever before.'

Talk of food sends me out into the freezing night in search of a restaurant. About five minutes' walk up the road in the centre of Argentière I find a busy, small bar and restaurant called Stone Bar. There are between twenty and thirty hungry skiers inside, consuming restorative volumes of carbohydrates in the form of pizza or pasta, washed down with beer. I sit at the bar, order a huge pizza overloaded with bresaola ham, cheese and rocket, and chat to Marco, the bar's young Italian owner. As we talk, it occurs to me that everyone else around me seems to be English. 'EasyJet has really changed the clientele in Chamonix,' Marco says, looking around the room. 'Before five years ago people came here for the week – now they can come for just a few days. The locals really don't like this. The fire in the Mont Blanc tunnel in 1999 stopped all the Italians from coming. Now it's mainly the English. The locals don't like the English as they've made everything expensive. The pound is strong, too. "He's just an English," I sometimes hear locals say about people in shops.'

The number of budget airlines that fly into Geneva during the winter months from the UK is, indeed, phenomenal. For example, easyJet's website offers twenty flights from London's airports alone to Geneva every Saturday throughout January. At full capacity, that's around three thousand people a day arriving from London – and that's just with easyJet. And, of course, dozens of other airlines ferry skiers in each day from cities across Europe. The busiest slope in the whole of the Alps is that of aircraft descending over Lake Leman into Geneva.

Skiers place a huge premium on being the first in the queue for the ride up on to the mountain each morning. The prize on offer is the chance to be the first to scar the slopes with their own tracks. Breakfast, therefore, is usually a functional affair, akin to a fuel stop at a petrol station. Bread, butter and jam, accompanied by juice and a coffee, are followed speedily by the race to the boot room to collect skis, boots and polls.

But today low-lying cloud has depleted the usual early-morning enthusiasm to rush out of the door at Gîte Le Belvédère. Instead guests are taking their time, busying themselves with chat about where best in the valley to head to claim the best day's skiing.

I find a place at a long table by the window that, if the clouds weren't obscuring the view, would offer a chance to look up at the Argentière glacier that sits adjacent to the north-east of the Grands Montets ski area. On a shelf by the table I find a magazine article about the launch by the Ski Club of Great Britain of its 'Respect the Mountain' campaign. This includes a number of initiatives, such as raising awareness and funds through the sale of Respect the Mountain wristbands, T-shirts and hoodies, as well as donating fifty pence from each member's subscription fee to a tree-planting scheme. But the campaign is centred on the promotion of 'seven steps to preserving the mountain':

1 **Be aware of your environmental impact as skiers and boarders**
Educate yourself about your environmental impact on the mountains, and what you can do to minimize it.

2 **Do not leave litter on the slopes**
When the snow melts, the litter will still be there. Bin it or take it home. Orange peel takes up to two years to break down, and cigarette ends up to five years. If you find litter on the slopes, do the right thing – pick it up.

3 **Respect the natural habitat of mountain animals and plants**
If you ski through trees, you can damage them by knocking off branches and killing young shoots under the snow. Take

care. Many areas are out of bounds to protect the natural habitat of animals and plants – not just for safety reasons.

4 **Choose a resort which uses environmentally friendly practices**
Many resorts now use bio-diesel fuel in piste-bashers, solar panels for heating, hydroelectricity/wind energy for power and a host of other initiatives. Some resorts use the International Organization for Standardization (ISO) 14001 as a mark of their environmental credentials. (The Ski Club website, www.respectthemountain.com, now offers a Green Resort Guide.)

5 **Encourage tour operators to adopt green policies**
Find out if your tour operator offers train travel as an alternative to flying; if they use paper from sustainable forests for their brochures; if they use, for example, low-wattage light bulbs in their chalets and biodegradable detergents.

6 **Do your bit to reduce global warming on holiday and at home**
Reuse your towels each day, recycle household waste and switch off electrical appliances when not in use.

7 **Reduce CO_2 emissions**
By flying fewer miles, or switching from air to rail, you can help reduce the volume of greenhouse gases that contribute to climate change. When possible, use your bike instead of your car.

From across the table, Matt, a skiing instructor from upstate New York visiting Europe for the first time, offers to pour me a much-needed coffee. Having already taken in the day's weather reports pinned to the noticeboard, he's decided not to bother heading out and is going to spend the day reading. I'm interested to know from him how the Alps compare to the skiing on offer in the US. 'Skiing here seems very different,' he says. 'The vertical rise is steeper here and you ski through fewer trees. Actually, I prefer it in the US, but maybe it's just because that's what I know. But you can really see the air pollution here. It is far worse than in the US. Mountain valleys really trap pollution as the cold air sinks and gets trapped. I guess the worst place I've seen for this is Salt Lake City – it really suffers from "inversion" [when the cold, polluted air sits underneath the warmer air above].'

Matt believes European skiers are far more cavalier and undisciplined than those across the Atlantic. 'Safety is much tougher in the US. The ski patrol will fine you if you go off-piste – up to a thousand dollars. A few places are starting to allow an 'open gate' policy, where you can go off-piste in certain areas, but most of the land is still owned by the US Forest Service and the rules are strict and rigidly applied.'

He says there are the same concerns about the changing climate in the US. 'The snow just isn't consistent any more. The best skiing is from late January to March nowadays. Like here, they're trying to fight nature with artificial snow. But the snow guns are really expensive to run. I know that in Taos valley in New Mexico, where I've skied a lot, it costs about a thousand dollars just to start them up then another thousand an hour to keep them running. In general, I feel that skiers do care about the environment, because they're there in the middle of nature. But having said that, no one drives more SUVs than US skiers.'

It's true that US ski resorts have broadly led the way in promoting environmental best practice. In 2000, the US National Ski Areas Association (NSAA) launched its 'Sustainable Slopes' scheme, which encourages individual resorts to publish environmental reports, as well as a 'Keep Winter Cool' campaign aimed at raising awareness of the threat of climate change among skiers. This has triggered similar campaigns in Australia and Canada. Water and energy conservation are among the key goals, as well as the protection of wildlife habitats. But the annual summary of US resorts' collective efforts, published on the NSAA website, only provides figures for their total savings of water and energy. Without the overall consumption figures to set these statistics against, they are virtually meaningless. For example, in 2006, US resorts each saved on average five million gallons of water in their production of artificial snow, but it would be much more interesting to know the total water consumption for each resort. Furthermore, in 2006 only 29 per cent of the 180 participating resorts bothered to supply NSAA with that year's data.

It takes less than five minutes to travel the 720 vertical metres in the cable car from Argentière up to Lognan, the first station of the vast Grands Montets ski area. From here skiers have access to almost thirty-one kilometres of pistes, including a perilous run down parts of the Argentière glacier. The cloud is still low, but starting to break up, and I can see across to the pistes of La Flégère on the other side of the valley. Sadly, the much-heralded view over to Mont Blanc and the Vallée Blanche, the world-famous, seventeen-kilometre glacial descent from the needle-like 3,842-metre Aiguille du Midi station down to the valley floor, is obscured.

Most skiers usually carry straight on up the mountainside, by cable car or on the various chairlifts, to the higher pistes, leaving Lognan's restaurants behind until returning for a lunchtime stop. However, I choose to visit one of the army of *pisteurs* that maintain and patrol these slopes. Their main office is located underneath Lognan's large self-service restaurant. It also acts as Les Grands Montets' main medical facility, and as I enter, an injured skier strapped to a 'blood wagon' is carried in through a side door.

Inside I'm greeted by Christophe Boloyan, who has worked as a *pisteur* at Les Grands Montets for nine years, but has been skiing the valley for fifteen. He beckons me in to the treatment room, where he introduces me to the injured skier – he has a heavily sprained ankle caused by a fall near Bochard station, eight hundred metres higher up. He is in obvious discomfort, although he might be grimacing at another source of anguish: Christophe has just broken the news that his rescue is going to cost him, or his insurers, €321.

'We get about ten injuries a day coming in here,' Christophe says. 'Les Grands Montets is north-facing so we get lots of avalanches. These are the biggest and most popular pistes in the whole valley. We get an average of three thousand people a day on the slopes; if it gets up to eight thousand we have to close the area off to restrict any more arriving.'

There are twenty-four *pisteurs* at Les Grands Montets – seventy across the whole valley – and all of them work for the Compagnie du Mont Blanc. Christophe explains to me how the team prepares the runs each day. Where necessary, the *pisteurs* will dynamite the slopes to clear any dangerous build-ups of snow. About four or five stay behind each summer to remodel the slopes and break or blow up the stones that have fallen on to the slopes over the winter.

'We are the first to ski the slopes each morning and we have to decide if they are safe. We start at eight a.m. and in the evening we have to scour each run to make sure no one is left up here on the mountain overnight. There are about fifty deaths a year in the French Alps area and one or two here at Les Grands Montets, although we had four last year. In fact, there is still one person missing from a few weeks ago. We have stopped looking. It's futile to keep searching for more than a few days. We might find him in the summer when the snow has all gone.'

During his nine years working at Les Grands Montets, Christophe says that he's seen many changes, both in terms of the weather and the way the slopes are managed and used.

'We are getting fewer skiers because other resorts are cheaper, especially the ones lower down that are desperately cutting prices to keep the business. Snowboarding is less popular now, too. But other activities are coming up such as snow-shoeing, where you walk through forests. This resort has been here for forty years; there's no more room for development on these slopes – just upgrading of the current facilities.'

Christophe becomes noticeably downbeat when I ask him about the coming decades. He looks at me and gives a Gallic shrug. 'Who knows? The glaciers here have certainly shrunk in the last three years. This year the Glacier d'Argentière is a lot steeper than last year. The top of the glacier has dropped about five metres in the last seven to eight years. The *rimayes* [cracks at the top of the glacier] are certainly lower now. I rock-climb off the Aiguille du Midi every year. It used to be a two-metre drop from the station down to the top of the glacier. Now it is more like thirty metres. There is even talk of putting out adverts for tourists that say: "Quick, come and see the glaciers before they all go." In Switzerland they have started putting covers on the glaciers in the summer to stop them melting. It's very sad.'

In May 2005, vast sheets of polythene were laid out across the Gurschen glacier at Andermatt in Switzerland. In all, 2,500 square metres of the glacier were covered to help stop the sun's ultraviolet radiation from melting the ice. In neighbouring Austria, nearly sixteen hectares of covers were also spread across glaciers in the Tyrolean areas of Stubaital, Oeztal, Kaunertal and Pitztal. In total, about 5 per cent of the area's ski slopes were covered that summer. A handful of protestors from Greenpeace made their objections known, waving banners saying, 'Tackle the cause, not the symptom', but in general the local population was pleased that something was at last being done – particularly after the big melt during the record hot summer of 2003 – to slow down the shrinking of the glaciers. The Tyrolean government had already relaxed a previous ban prohibiting any further building of ski lifts on the region's glaciers, due to pressure from the industry to help secure the 1.2 million jobs that skiing in the Tyrol provides. Tellingly, it was only two generations ago that the same population used to send its priests up to the glaciers to pray to God to stop them encroaching further down into the valleys.

Skiers will have to become accustomed to the sight of man's desperate and, no doubt, ultimately futile attempts to halt the fate of these vast tongues of ice. In 2006, the World Glacier Monitoring Service, based in Zurich, said that the Alps could lose three-quarters of its glaciers during the coming century due to climate change. Summers in the area will be on average 3C warmer at the end of the century than now. According to the research group's data, nearly 4,474 square kilometres of the Alps were glaciated in 1850; by 2000, that figure had fallen to 2,272. This chimes with a United Nations Environment Programme report published in 2003, which predicted that the snowline in the Alps could rise by three hundred metres over the next five decades. And in mid-December 2006 – just as Alpine communities were frantically wondering if the snow would ever arrive, after the warmest November on record – the Organisation for Economic Co-operation and Development (OECD) published the 'first systematic cross-country study of ski areas in the Alpine arc', which said that the number of viable ski resorts in the Alps could fall from 666 to 400 by 2050 if average temperatures rose by 2C, as is predicted.

'Germany is most at risk,' said the OECD, 'with the 1C warming scenario leading to a 60 per cent decrease in the number of naturally snow-reliable ski areas. Austria (where half the tourism income, or 4.5 per cent of the national economy, is from winter tourism) is slightly more sensitive than the average. France is about average, Italy slightly above average, and Switzerland would suffer the least, though even there a 1C increase would reduce natural snow by 10 per cent and 4C would halve the number of snow-reliable slopes.'

Such studies tend to focus on the impact on winter tourism, but the wider effects could be huge, too: the Alps' glaciers are the source for the Rhône, the Rhine and the Po, as well as a number of the Danube's tributaries.

Rather than fight, some regions of the Alps have decided simply to retreat. In recent summers, a succession of ski resorts have 'suspended' – although surely it would be more honest to say 'for ever abandoned' – summer skiing on their glaciers. In Italy, popular summer skiing destinations such as Alagna, Bardonecchia, Arabba Marmolada, Passo Tonale and Val Senales have shut off access to the glaciers. Alpe d'Huez in France has suspended summer skiing for the 'foreseeable future', as have St Moritz and Verbier in Switzerland. In 2003, the summer heat even closed off much of Mont Blanc and the Matterhorn to climbers, due to dangerous rockfalls caused by the melting of the mountains' permafrost.

But climate change is not the only pressure now facing the Alps' beleaguered glaciers. In 2002, a special taskforce was set up by the Italian police to investigate the theft of snow from glaciers. So poor was the snowfall that year that there were reports that thieves were being paid up to €900 by ski resorts to deliver each truckful of snow taken illegally from the region's glaciers.

Desperate times call for desperate measures: cue the advent of the snow cannon.

'Artificial snow has only been used here since 1996,' says Christophe, pointing at all the snow-cannon locations on a wall-mounted map of Les Grands Montets in his office. 'But now we have fifty snow guns here. This is nothing, though. At Courcheval there are four hundred. In November and December we start to use the guns, as long as it's cold enough.' (In late 2006, many resorts across the Alps said it was too warm even to use their cannons.) 'We get the water from under the glacier. We pump it to a reservoir that sits behind a dam high up on the Swiss–French border.'

Christophe says that the temperature needs to be about -2C for the cannons to work well in dry air. But if the air is 'wet' then it needs to be -10 to -15C. 'One cubic metre of water makes about two cubic metres of snow. Artificial snow is good because it can add as much as a month to the life of a piste each season.'

Of all the ways that ski companies are trying to combat the effects of climate change, none is as controversial as the use of snow cannons. Put simply, these machines work by forcing water droplets at high pressure up into the cold night air over the pistes. As the droplets fall, they freeze and land as snow. The process requires huge amounts of energy as well as vast volumes of water. So much so that the industry is notoriously cagey about talking numbers.

However, according to Mountain Wilderness, a French conservation group that has described skiing as 'the cancer of the Alps', around four thousand cubic metres of water are required to generate enough snow to cover one hectare of piste for a season. (To put this in context, a hectare of corn requires 1,700 cubic metres of water during its growing season.) It says that during the 1999–2000 season, ten million cubic metres of water were used to make artificial snow across France's slopes, including those in the Pyrenees. This was equal to the water demands of the entire population of Grenoble, a town with a population of 170,000 people. But demand had risen to thirteen million cubic metres by 2004–5 as more and more resorts invested in snow cannons for their pistes. Across the entire Alpine range, it is estimated that artificial snow now consumes the same amount of water as 1.5 million people each year.

About half of the water for snow cannons in the Alps comes from purpose-built mountain reservoirs, as is the case at Les Grands Montets. A further third is taken directly from rivers, and the rest from local drinking-water supplies. Unlike natural snowfall, none of this water is 'pure'. When sediment in the river water, for example, gets pumped high up on to the mountainside, well above where it would normally be found, it can introduce a source of nutrients for plant life that then acts to destabilize the natural ecosystem. Also, additives are frequently mixed into the water: a bacterium called *Pseudomonas syringae* is often added as a nucleating agent (trademarked and sold under the name Snomax), to help the water molecules form crystals at a higher temperature than normal. It can increase the amount of snow produced by a snow cannon by as much as 50 per cent. It also helps to produce lighter, drier flakes, which are, of course, prized by skiers. Another popular product is called Drift, produced by Aquatrols, which is an 'organo-silicone surfactant' that acts at concentrations of three to five parts per million to allow the water to freeze more quickly. Little is known about the long-term effect of such additives on the mountain environment. CIPRA reports that there have been protests downstream of some Alpine resorts about the adverse effect artificial snow has on river water quality – although the manufacturers of the additives insist their products are safe to use.

With water resources becoming increasingly threatened and depleted across the world, some resorts are now trying to reduce the amount of water they take from natural sources for snow-making. In the winter of 2008, Mount Hotham in Victoria, Australia, will become the first ski resort in the world to use purified waste water to feed its snow guns. It will recycle 110 megalitres of sewage and waste water from the resort for use on the slopes. The water will be cleaned to 'Australian class A standard', meaning that it would be clean enough to irrigate vegetable crops which might be consumed raw. But it will still be dirtier than natural snow.

The other drawback of artificial snow is that it requires huge amounts of power. Mountain Wilderness says that about 25,000 kilowatt-hours of electricity, costing about €150,000, are needed to cover just one hectare of piste with snow for a season. Therefore, the more snow guns are used to counteract climate change, the more pollution enters the atmosphere as a result of electricity generation. A truly vicious circle. And with some resorts now using hundreds of snow cannons each – Méribel has more than six hundred, Alpe d'Huez almost eight hundred – it's no surprise to learn that the French ski resorts spent sixty million euros on artificial snow in 2004. No wonder there are so many complaints about the rocketing price of ski passes – a six-day family Chamski pass cost € 558 in 2006.

'Artificial snow is not the root of all evil,' says Sergio Savoia of WWF, 'but it is very close. One of the biggest problems is psychological: snow cannons give tourists the idea that it is business as usual; but we don't actually have much snow. We're just not facing up to the consequences of our behaviour.'

Perhaps the ultimate act of folly came in 2005. When snow was blown off a high-altitude piste at the French resort of Valloire-Valmeinier, helicopters were used to carry up replacement snow. Around three hundred flights were made, according to Mountain Wilderness, each carrying about one cubic metre of snow; meaning that, at best, no more than five hundred square metres of piste were repaired. It seemed to inspire others to follow suit: in January 2007 a lack of snowfall threatened the famous Hahnenkamm World Cup ski race at the Austrian resort of Kitzbühel, so the organizers flew in over 4,500 cubic metres of snow by helicopter at a cost of € 300,000.

The thrill of the slopes is clear to see. Watching wave after wave of skiers and snowboarders thread their way in alternating arcs down the pistes at Les Grands Montets is almost hypnotic. Some choose to stop for a hot drink or a plate of *tartiflette* – a warming mass of ham, cheese and potatoes served at all the mountain restaurants in the valley – but most join the queue to be carried straight back up the mountain for another descent. A group of three Frenchmen skid to a halt just in front of me, release the bindings on their skis with their polls, and join the growing line for the restaurant at Lognan.

'The snow is always good in Chamonix. We come here every year,' one of them tells me, when I ask why they choose to ski here. 'Sure, the glacier is getting thinner, but it doesn't affect our skiing. I've skied all my life. I would never want to stop. My legs will make that decision for me.'

Behind them stands Joseph from Dortmund. He tells me he has just flown in on German Wings, a budget airline, and is only here for a couple of days. 'I heard about the heavy snowfalls and couldn't resist jumping on the plane and coming out here as fast as possible.'

Next to him is Arne from Norway, an old friend who's decided to join him for some impulse skiing. 'Skiing in Norway is easily as good as here, but I like to have a change of scenery now and again. We aren't really seeing the changes in the snow in Norway that there are here. There's certainly not less snow, that's for sure, but I suppose the snow is getting later.'

A skier's instinct is always to hunt for new challenges and explore new terrain. It is this urge which drives some skiers away from the pistes and off into the 'backcountry'. Back down in Argentière, I meet one of the Alps' most experienced backcountry guides. Neil McNab is one of the world's leading snowboarders and is the chief trainer to the British Association of Snowboard Instructors. He has been British champion four times, and is the only British professional snowboarder qualified as a mountain guide in Europe; he also writes guidebooks. Such is his reputation among snowboarders that he is sponsored by streetwear labels such as Oakley, Salomon and Billabong. Up a short track muddied with slush leading off the main road is his handsome chalet, where he hosts groups of snowboarders, each of whom pay up to a thousand pounds a week for the privilege of being taken by him up on to the expansive, wide mountain plateaux that are rarely seen by the masses that ski the busy pistes. He explains to me how expectations are changing among his guests.

'People are now wanting to enter an environment after just a year of snowboarding that I spent twenty years getting used to. We are being pushed by clients to go to extremes. The media is really promoting extreme sports now. People's goals are changing. We used to always say to leave the mountain alone for two days after new snow, but now you see tracks within a few hours.'

Neil says this demand is forcing him to take clients to new, previously untouched areas. 'I'm going to Greenland next year. And we will go to the Himalayas, too. We take out groups of six with a guide into the backcountry. Heliboarding in Russia for ten days, for example, would cost £2,500–£3,000 and we'd take twelve people with two guides. We get lots of return business now. In Russia you are allowed to jump out of helicopters anywhere. In France, where would you land? It's so developed here – there's a chairlift everywhere. In Greenland we heli in then set up a base camp. It's amazing.'

Neil rejects the notion that he is part of the problem. He repeats his claim that it's the media's fault for relentlessly pushing extreme winter sports. This, he says, is what drives demand. But, like most other people in the valley, he agrees that the weather conditions are changing.

'I was climbing in Alaska last year and it was very noticeable that it's melting there, too. Thousands of years ago, the glaciers here used to go all the way down to Lyons. There is a natural ebb and flow with glaciers, for sure, but I believe we are changing things. The prevailing winds used to come from the north-west, but now all the weather comes from the south or south-west. I saw something the other day that I've never seen before – someone paragliding on to the actual summit of Mont Blanc, which must mean the thermals are now large enough to carry people up that high.'

It was the allure of Mont Blanc that first drew tourists to the valley in the late 1700s. In fact, the concept of tourism itself is said to have been born when two Englishmen, William Windham and Richard Pocock, entered the 'Vallée de Chamouny' in 1741 on an expedition of leisure from Geneva to the base of the mountain at Montenvers. It was Windham's recounting of the trip in a subsequent book that fuelled further interest in the valley and inspired other visitors from England to make the journey. The first accommodation offered exclusively to tourists was opened by Madame Coutterand in 1770. With remarkable foresight, she named it Hôtel d'Angleterre.

Today, the British make up the biggest portion of foreign visitors to the valley – 27 per cent, according to the Chamonix tourism office. And France remains the most popular nation for British skiers. According to the Ski Industry Report 2006, published by the UK's largest ski operator, Crystal Ski, of the 1.15 million ski holidays bought in 2005–6 by British skiers, 36 per cent were in France. Austria was the second most popular destination with 20 per cent of the market. Italy and Andorra were third and fourth, but with a declining share of the market compared to previous years.

But it's the emerging destinations that signal that many skiers are starting to seek the often cheaper alternatives to the increasingly distressed slopes of the Alps. Finland, Serbia, Bulgaria and Lebanon (halted by the war in 2006) have all seen an increase in skiers from Britain in recent years. Long-haul flights do not seem to be a barrier either, with the US and Canada still fast-growing destinations. Japan is becoming popular, too. But there are also signs that there is a growing appetite to defy nature's impertinent unpredictability and just bring the mountain to Mohammed. Indoor ski centres are now being built everywhere from the desert of Dubai to the sun-blessed coast of Perth, Australia. Developers planning to build a 'SnOasis' ski resort in a disused quarry at Great Blakenham, in Suffolk, boast that it would be the biggest such scheme in the world, attracting 820,000 visitors a year. If granted permission, they aim to open in 2009: the main piste would be up to seventy metres wide and 475 metres long, with a drop of a hundred metres.

Other such snowdomes, as they are sometimes called, have been criticized for using huge amounts of energy and water – after all, they rely on snow cannons operating in what, in essence, is a huge refrigerated room. Their evident popularity throws up an interesting question. Do they reduce the number of people flying off to distant mountain ranges to ski, therefore offering an environmental positive in the long term by sating people's desires closer to home? Or do they stimulate further interest in skiing and thereby increase the likelihood of people wanting to make a trip to a real piste? One thing is certain: while such slopes are a huge experiential leap forward compared to dry-slope skiing, such an artificial and ultimately unrewarding environment will never satisfy keen skiers. The call of the mountain will always be there.

2

A Line in the Sand
Dubai, United Arab Emirates

'WELCOME TO THE EIGHTH wonder of the world. This is what the tourists really want to come and see – more than any museum.'

Imad Haffar is a proud man. He is one of the twenty-thousand-strong workforce building Palm Jumeirah, a vast palm-shaped network of artificial islands off the coast of Dubai. Palm Jumeirah has quickly become a defining symbol of this small emirate's bold vision of becoming not just a major tourist destination in the Middle East, but a world-class destination. The islands, which have created 560 hectares of new land mass since reclamation started in August 2001, can already be seen from space.

Haffar, the Palm's research and development manager, invites me to step on to his launch, and we are soon cutting through the calm waters sheltered by the Palm's 11.5-kilometre-long outer crescent, which acts as a giant breakwater, towards the most developed of the seventeen 'fronds'. Once complete, these fronds will be home to the islands' 1,500 luxury private villas. As the boat picks up speed, we both greedily suck in the cooling sea breeze that offers some relief from the 40C heat.

A pair of dolphins soon appears alongside the bow of the boat. I raise my camera to take a picture of them, set against a backdrop of the Palm's so-called Golden Mile – a stretch of nearly complete shops and residential units lining the ten-lane highway that forms the Palm's two-kilometre link to the mainland – but I'm stopped by one of Haffar's staff.

'Sorry, we don't allow any unauthorized pictures here,' she says. 'Not even helicopters are allowed to fly over without our permission.' It's my first taste of Dubai's famously disciplined and, some say, autocratic culture.

As if the sight of a town being built in the sea (predictably, some have labelled the development the 'Venice of the Middle East') isn't enough to mangle one's sense of reality, Haffar is keen to dazzle me with his armoury of statistics. He tells me of the 154 million cubic metres of sand, rock and earth (which I later calculate is fifty-nine times the volume of stone used to build the Great Pyramid of Giza) that have been brought by truck and dredger on to the Palm to enable it to rise up out of reach of the Gulf's lapping waves; how each of the 2.5 million rocks used in the breakwater is stamped with its own GPS coordinate; how the Palm is adding 78.6 kilometres of new shoreline to Dubai's current seventy kilometres of natural coast; and how when the Palm was originally formed with sand – taken from within the United Arab Emirates' waters in the Gulf and from the vast Jebel Ali port further down the coast – the volume of sand sprayed from a flotilla of dredgers was equal to the workload of a thousand trucks a day over two years. Everything about the construction of the Palm is an engineer's fantasy.

'There will be nothing industrial-looking on the Palm at all – only residences, hotels, theme parks and shops. Even the mobile-phone masts will be disguised behind plastic palm trees,' says Haffar, pointing at an incongruous-looking object he explains is a test palm that he is so far unhappy with. 'It looks too straight, too unnatural, don't you think?'

It's easy to forget, given the island's epic scale, that everything I can see is, in fact, unnatural. The electrical cables and sub-stations will be disguised as villas, as will three sewage treatment plants. 'We will have fresh water from the mains supply, of course,' says Haffar, 'but we are also installing the largest privately owned desalination plants in the world, which will supply the Palm with 64,000 cubic metres of fresh water a day. To help save water, we are installing an irrigation system that reuses treated waste water to feed the Palm's plants, all of which will have their roots contained to save more water.'

After about ten minutes, we reach one of the furthest fronds from the shoreline. All the way down its length are villas; from a distance, each seems to be covered in flies, which on closer inspection reveal themselves to be workers, busy cleaning pools, painting walls or fitting tiles, windows and TV aerials. 'The first wave of owners will be moving into these villas in just a few months,' says Haffar, pointing out that this will be just over five years from when the Palm was started.

He is cagey about who is moving in, other than to say 'actors, singers and politicians'. But in 2003 the Palm made headlines around the world when it was revealed that at least eleven members of the England football squad, including David Beckham, Michael Owen and Ashley Cole, had purchased villas there during a stopover on their way to the 2002 World Cup in Japan and South Korea. No doubt such publicity boosted demand: it has also been reported that the villas all sold out within seventy-two hours of going on the market. 'Some have now even been sold on two or three times by investors and are said to be worth up to five million dollars. And they're not even finished yet,' says Haffar, smiling.

I ask him why there are two identical villas positioned next to each other when all the others seem so unique. 'Each buyer had sixty-five designs to choose from when they bought off-plan,' he says. 'As long as they chose one of these designs, they could have what they wanted.' I wonder, however, whether buyers were informed which design would be going up next door.

Looking out of the boat into the becalmed water below, it strikes me that it's not exactly what you would call a blue lagoon. The waters seem murky and unnaturally still. What has the development done, I wonder, to the currents and wave patterns that would have existed naturally here before construction started? And what of the sea life that must surely have been displaced by such an epic project?

'We monitor the water here constantly,' explains Haffar. 'We even – at great expense – opened up two huge gaps in the crescent to increase the flow of water into the inner lagoons when we noticed it wasn't flushing away fast enough. This has helped a lot. And there was nothing really in the sea here before we started building. Now we are finding that fish are being attracted to these artificial islands.'

This point is made again to me later by James Wilson, the CEO of Nakheel Hotels and Resorts, the developer responsible for Palm Jumeirah, who is obviously sensitive to the charge that the islands are an environmental menace. 'Ninety-six per cent of the seabed was just mud or sand before the Palm. Now there's a huge amount of marine life there. It's creating a new ecosystem.'

But not everyone agrees. Dr Frederic Launay, director of WWF's office in the United Arab Emirates, has expressed his displeasure at the building of the artificial islands. 'It has been detrimental for the natural environment of the Dubai coast,' he told Reuters in 2005. 'That is a little bit of a shame because there were very good habitats there. There were possibilities of recovery and protection, and there were possibilities of using that natural asset to make something. This opportunity has been lost and now we are only talking about remediation and mitigation.'

In another 2005 interview, this time with the *Salt Lake Tribune*, Launay complained that the new land masses off Dubai's coast had buried coral reefs, oyster beds and sea grasses, and disturbed sea-turtle nesting grounds. Local divers have also reported that up to two inches of silt have settled on some coral reefs due to round-the-clock dredging along the coast. 'If you build stretches of five-star hotels with landscaped gardens, you're transforming a wild environment into an urban environment. There will be different species. It's an artificial system,' said Launay, adding that the islands have re-routed currents, thereby helping to erode beaches on Dubai's natural shore-line.

It is true that Palm Jumeirah will be home to a number of inter-national hotel chains, including a forty-eight-storey Trump hotel, and a two-thousand-room resort and water park built by Kerzner International. Haffar is adamant, though, that the Palm's influence on the coastline – both good and bad – is manageable, and that in time, once the construction phase has finished, a natural equilibrium will be restored. 'We have even sunk the remains of fighter jets and a jumbo jet off the coast to create ideal diving sites for the future.' (Probably not what WWF had in mind when it spoke of 'remediation and mitigation'.) 'And thinking further ahead into the future, we have checked with World Bank climate-change data to see how high sea levels may rise and have allowed for a two-metre safety zone. Due to how hard we compacted the sand for the foundation, the Palm could withstand a 5.5 Richter scale earthquake, too.' The confidence felt in Dubai is as steadfast as its building projects.

As the boat turns to head back to the shore, a siren sounds loudly close by. We look over to an adjacent frond to see an ambulance racing past half-finished villas, followed by two 4×4s, towards a group of construction workers that has gathered by a cement-mixer. Haffar looks rather embarrassed by all the commotion. With exquisite timing we pass a huge sign saying 'Safety First'. Are those Nakheel's workers gathering by the ambulance, I ask with concern.

'No,' responds Haffar, to my surprise. 'Nakheel doesn't employ any staff here as such. All of them are employed by contractors.'

It's a point later confirmed by James Wilson. 'We're just a devel-oper. We tender the building contracts,' he explains. 'Al Naboodah

Laing O'Rourke, for example, is one such contractor. They will hire their own labour force.'

It's not the last time I will need to concentrate in order to understand who owns or controls what and how in Dubai. Take Nakheel itself, for example. It is currently overseeing about thirty billion dollars' worth of property developments in Dubai, making it the Middle East's largest such company. Hard as it is to imagine, the Palm is just the iconic figurehead of a company that is behind over a dozen similarly ambitious construction projects. In fact, the Palm has now been joined by four other offshore developments, which together will add an incredible 1,500 kilometres of new shoreline to Dubai's coast. Dwarfing Palm Jumeirah will be the Palm Deira, an island similar in design to Palm Jumeirah but, with a trunk fourteen kilometres long, bigger than Manhattan. It will be positioned offshore from Dubai's old port area. Thirty-five kilometres down the coast, past Palm Jumeirah and close to both Jebel Ali port and the six-runway Dubai World Central International airport that is still under construction, will be Palm Jebel Ali, again shaped like a palm but also including islands that spell out in the sea a poem in Arabic written by Sheikh Mohammed Bin Rashid Al Maktoum, the current ruler and architect of modern Dubai, that includes the line: 'It takes a man of vision to write on water.' It would seem that modesty is not a commodity that commands a great price in Dubai.

This Palm will itself quickly be dwarfed by the proposed Dubai Waterfront project – 51 per cent of which will be owned by Nakheel – which will push into the sea by wrapping around the western side of Palm Jebel Ali, as well as reaching far inland to form the first phase of the Arabian Canal, a seventy-five-kilometre waterway lined with various developments that will wind its way through what is now the desert heart of Dubai, ultimately connecting back with the sea near Palm Jumeirah. The Dubai Waterfront project will include a new downtown marina area called Madinat Al Arab, home to half a million people, with its defining landmark being the Al Burj, one of three buildings currently under construction in Dubai all vying for the title of World's Tallest Building. (None of them is willing to disclose its intended height for fear that one of the others will push that little bit higher to claim the title.)

Viewing the plans on paper, it can all seem like a 1950s science-fiction movie's vision of how man might have colonized Mars (once we'd seen off those Martians with our superior laser guns). Certainly, nowhere else on Earth – not even in China – is anything being built on this scale. (A popular sport among locals seems to be boasting to visitors what percentage of the world's cranes are currently in Dubai: the highest figure I hear is 70 per cent, although 15–25 per cent seems to be what the crane industry itself believes.)

But the development that has captured most people's imagination is 'The World', Nakheel's attempt to re-create Earth in the form of three hundred artificial islands four kilometres out to sea, which together will form a map of the world when seen from the air. The development allows investors to buy an island, say 'Great Britain' or 'Iceland', for around ten million dollars, and then build what they want there (within certain planning constraints). There will be residential, commercial and hotel zones, and the islands will only be accessible by boat or helicopter, making it one of the most exclusive destinations on the planet – or so says its developer.

Nakheel's projects are just a fraction, however, of Dubai's 'build it and they will come' vision, first laid out by Sheikh Rashid Bin Saeed Al Maktoum, Sheikh Mohammed's father, who governed Dubai from 1958 until his death in 1990. It was Sheikh Rashid who created the spark that transformed Dubai from a sleepy port to a major world city, after he realized that the emirate could not survive on its relatively modest oil reserves (discovered 120 kilometres off the coast in 1966) and needed to diversify rapidly, making finance, commerce and tourism the cornerstones of its economy instead. Knowing that the oil could one day run dry, his mantra was said to be: 'My grandfather rode a camel, my father rode a camel, I drive a Mercedes, my son drives a Land Rover, his son will drive a Land Rover, but his son will ride a camel.'

Today, after more than three decades of rapid, often frenzied construction and investment, oil accounts for just 6 per cent of Dubai's economy, with tourism responsible for more than 20 per cent. Sheikh Mohammed was made crown prince of Dubai in 1995 and ever since has been labelled the 'CEO of Dubai', due to his unflagging ambition to push on with his father's vision. Following the death of his immediate predecessor and brother Sheikh Maktoum Bin Rashid Al Maktoum, he has ruled Dubai since January 2006, and is now credited with turning Dubai into the region's leading tourism destination.

Within months of becoming crown prince, he announced the creation of the Dubai Shopping Festival, which quickly gained worldwide fame, largely because its centrepiece was the Dubai World Cup, the world's richest horserace (in the 2006 race, the prize fund stood at six million dollars), and because shopping was tax-free. His other early achievements were to increase greatly the capacity of Dubai's airport, home to Dubai's hugely successful Emirates airline (which itself has played a massive role in attracting visitors to the region), and to market Dubai aggressively to potential tourists with the worldwide 'Destination Dubai' campaign.

Then in 1999 his most famous project opened its doors for the first time – the Burj Al Arab hotel. Sitting on its own artificial island, the 321-metre-high, dhow-shaped building has come to define its location as much as Sydney's Opera House or Bilbao's Guggenheim Museum, and is now probably the world's most instantly recognizable hotel.

Dubai's government, headed by Sheikh Mohammed, now either controls or has a huge stake in much of the development within the emirate through a handful of giant holding companies. For example, Nakheel is completely government-owned, as is Dubai Holding, another company with a mind-numbingly large number of grand-scale investments in Dubai that include free-trade business parks, luxury residences, energy companies, shopping malls, theme parks and golf courses. Dubai Holding also owns the Jumeirah hotel and resorts group, which in turn owns the Burj Al Arab hotel. Outside Dubai, its assets include the Travelodge hotel chain and a significant share in DaimlerChrysler. Then there's Emaar, by its own definition the 'world's largest real estate company by market realization', 32.5 per cent of which is owned by the Dubai government; as well as owning a number of property developments in Dubai itself, such as the Burj Dubai tower (another contender for World's Tallest Building when it's finished), Emaar has investments across much of the Middle East, India and the US. A portfolio of publicly owned investments like this goes some way to explain why no one needs to pay capital gains or income tax in Dubai.

James Wilson of Nakheel is keen to offer me his view on how all this government activity has helped to make Dubai one of the most talked-about tourist destinations in the world. 'The government in Dubai is run like a private company,' he explains. 'People often talk about "Dubai Incorporated", because there are a number of large companies here – Emirates and Nakheel, for example – that are effectively government-owned and are all swimming broadly in the same direction. There is a desire to succeed at all levels, so we will help each other if necessary. The government is sometimes more efficient than the private sector. Not many countries can say that. Plus, it has guaranteed sunshine and is an extremely safe place to live and work.'

But I want to see what's on offer for tourists today, not just tomorrow. Dubai currently has one of the highest average room tariffs and occupancy levels anywhere in the world, due to the fact that most of the accommodation on offer to tourists is classified as luxury and, despite all the hotel construction going on, most rooms get filled each night. There is little opportunity to visit Dubai on the cheap, although discounting is practised at slower times of the year such as the unbearably hot summer months.

Given Dubai's reputation for luxury, it is fitting that my 'room' for the night is at the 'seven-star' Burj Al Arab (a superlative invented by an entranced journalist, not the hotel itself); many claim it to be the world's most expensive hotel, with prices ranging from $1,000–$28,000 a night. I say 'room', but the Burj Al Arab doesn't actually have any single rooms. It offers what it calls duplexes – suites that extend over two floors. And I must add that I come as a guest of the hotel – few journalists could afford afternoon tea here, let alone the cost of a duplex.

It is rare for any tourist to come to Dubai without standing on the causeway that leads to the Burj Al Arab and taking a photo of this landmark building. From my ceiling-to-floor window on the thirty-fourth floor I can see for many miles. Out at sea on the horizon, huge arcs of sand are being sprayed into the air from dredgers; in time these will form the islands of The World. I can also see the tangle of cranes that are constructing the Burj Dubai tower, and through the sandy haze and band of smog in the far distance stands the old port district of Deira. Between us runs the arrow-straight Sheikh Zayed Road, Dubai's main drag that runs parallel to the coast and which locals call 'Refrigerator Row' due to the number of skyscrapers that hug its side like a line of vast appliances standing in the sand.

My duplex may be among the most luxurious hotel accommodation the world has to offer, but I confess that to me it seems gaudy and kitsch. Gold, mosaic, marble or mirror seem to embellish every surface. Once my eyes have adjusted to this, I begin to notice details such as the thirteen-option pillow menu and a personal-butler service that includes, for the eye-watering fee of 2,500 UAE dirhams (about

£360), the option of having a scented-oil-filled bath run for you, with caviar and champagne left beside the pile of pressed towels.

Upstairs in the Al Muntaha restaurant on the fifty-fourth floor I join Luc Delafosse, the hotel's general manager and former general manager of the Ritz in London, for lunch. As we sit down, a helicopter takes off from the helipad on the roof behind us to sweep past the restaurant's panoramic windows on a sightseeing tour – this is the helipad that became famous when Tiger Woods fired a golf ball from it into the sea and when Andre Agassi and Roger Federer used it to play a game of tennis. From this great height of about two hundred metres you can clearly see Nakheel's various developments underway down the coastline, and in particular a clutch of half-built skyscrapers that will form the Madinat Al Arab marina.

'Since I joined the hotel in December 2003, I have seen incredible growth from this window down towards Jebel Ali port,' Luc tells me.

Doesn't he worry about all this competition being built around him?

'We can't get complacent about being in a building like this. Knowing the vision that His Highness has for Dubai, there should be enough demand for the hotels being built. We shouldn't be afraid of competition. Dubai is so well organized and developed. For example, we know there will be enough airport capacity in, say, twenty years' time to bring people here. That is an incredible advantage and is unique to Dubai.'

I ask him what kind of person comes here; who can afford to visit such a hotel. 'Our number-one market is the UK, which accounts for about 22 per cent of our guests. This can go up to 25 per cent at some points of the year. Then it's the Germans at about 12 per cent, then visitors from the local region, and then the Russians – the number of weekly flights between Dubai and Russia grew to 38 in 2005, up from just six in 2002.

'But remember that Emirates alone has ninety-one flights a week going into the UK. The UK will remain our number one for a long time. There is an historic association between the UK and the UAE, of course. Dubai is becoming one of the leading choices, even for the weekend-break market. A growing market for us at the moment is Asia – it's growing at about 2 per cent a year. Some days now I meet ten different nationalities.'

And is a hotel such as this always full? 'We are enjoying 90 per cent occupancy at the moment, but 83 per cent is the annual average, with 22 per cent being repeat guests. And we have one of the highest staff–guest ratios in the world; with 1,600 staff, we have about eight members of staff per suite.'

I later meet Gerald Lawless, Jumeirah Group's CEO, in his expansive office within the grounds of Jumeirah's Madinat Hotel, which is situated amid a network of artificial waterways set back behind a stretch of beach in the shadow of Burj Al Arab. He doesn't seem to be concerned about the number of hotels being built in Dubai, either. 'There are six million visitors a year now coming to Dubai, but the infrastructure being built demands fifteen million. And when this fifteen-million target was announced three years ago we were only at two million visitors a year. There are so many other markets still to come here. The American market still hasn't taken off – currently Americans make up only 3–4 per cent of our visitors. Ten years ago travelling from the UK to Dubai was considered long haul, but today we call it the 'long short-haul'. A seven-hour journey ten years ago was pretty much the limit, but now people think fourteen hours is the mental limit. We haven't begun to tap India and China.

'The biggest advertiser of Dubai must be Emirates airlines. Without them it would have been very hard for us to have done what we've done in the tourism industry. They bring everyone here. It also makes a huge difference that we have an open-skies policy, meaning that any airline can land here without restriction. Without sounding too big-headed about it, the centre of gravity has shifted east a bit, away from Europe, with the rise of Dubai. We have the most strategic-ally advantageous position in the world, situated here between Europe and Asia. And we have the infrastructure.'

There are moments when I feel as if I am being lured into a cult, such is the self-belief that seeps from everyone's lips in Dubai. And it's a faith that Lawless is keen to export, judging by his expansion plans for the Jumeirah Group. 'Our goal is to have forty Jumeirah hotels around the world by the end of 2009. We will continue to expand greatly here. We want to be in China and in places such as Jakarta, Bali, the Maldives and Thailand. In Europe we'd like some more key cities, plus some gateway cities in the US. Our parent company has a lot of investments in Morocco and Turkey, so we will go there too. Then the Caribbean. The world is very small.

'But when you go to China it's just the size of the market that grabs you. We will cut our teeth in Shanghai and Beijing, then hope to go to Hainan Island and places like that. We've already signed a management agreement with a hotel in Shanghai.'

Dubai is famous for its service culture: it's one of the things that always rates highly in visitor surveys. Hotel staff can even appear on the beach, asking if you need your sunglasses wiped. But how does Dubai afford to employ its vast army of service staff, from the cleaners and waiters through to the chefs and pool attendants? And what of the even larger number of construction workers who are busy building Dubai's swelling tourist infrastructure? The subject is fast becoming a burr on Dubai's highly polished gold.

'We have a recruitment team who scour the world looking for staff,' explains Lawless. 'Out of ten thousand people, we have a hundred nationalities working with us here. We expect this figure to have doubled in five years. It is important for us that we become an employer of choice. I would hope that we deal with our staff in an enlightened way. We put a lot of effort into recognizing staff here. We have a much lower turnover rate here than, say, in the UK. A lot of them are young, but the hospitality industry offers a far more varied career than it did twenty years ago.

'We have a purpose-built village which houses seven to eight thousand staff. In that village there are supermarkets, restaurants, housing, internet cafés, etc. It's about twenty minutes away by bus. We try to create a nice environment with three-floor housing, like a military academy. Most junior staff sleep three to a bedroom. The new phase will have two to a room. We realize that our staff have to be happy to make our guests happy. It's not rocket science.'

The hiring process interests me: how, for example, does he ensure that people seeking work in Dubai from within their own homelands aren't subject to dishonest local recruiting agencies, which might charge jobseekers huge fees in order to secure them interviews with a Jumeirah representative?

'We try to make sure that they don't have to pay a local agent to get an interview with us,' insists Lawless. 'We pay the agents, so they shouldn't charge the interviewees. If we find out that they are doing this, we stop using them. We do our best to make sure that people are treated fairly. But it's not Dubai's fault that this can happen. In India and Pakistan, for example, people are exploited. Dubai gives them a living and it provides a start for so many people. When I was growing up in Ireland in the 1950s and 1960s, a big contributor to the GDP was the remittances from people working in the UK and the US. It's the same for many of the workers here.'

Earlier, Luc Delafosse had also suggested that Dubai should harbour little guilt about the wellbeing of its immigrant workforce, despite the number of strikes among construction workers that have recently started to plague the area. 'It is better in Dubai than in most places in the world today,' he said. 'That is a fact. We do not see any people sleeping rough outside. Other countries should look at their own challenges before criticizing others. Ninety-nine per cent of the people here are properly treated. If there's a one per cent exception, let's say, we have to be very open and talk about it. We are an open country and extremely democratic. When people are given the vote it doesn't necessarily achieve a lot.'

Delafosse's words hang in the air as I travel by taxi down Sheikh Zayed Road for a meeting with Dr Mohamed Al Roken, one of Dubai's leading human-rights lawyers and law professor at UAE University. Al Roken has been a persistent critic of the country's labour laws and, more widely, of the lack of political rights for citizens and, especially, the huge immigrant population. As a result of his outspoken views, in recent years he has been discouraged from writing articles in the local press and barred from making speeches in public.*

Dr Al Roken's passionate response to the injustices he believes exist within his country soon surfaces as we talk. 'The problem is there are no political rights here,' he explains. 'There are no elections. No political parties. No active legislator. Which means there is no accountability; no transparency of the policies. I have applied to establish the first human-rights organization here in the UAE. But they have so far declined my application. I'm not allowed to set it up without the government's permission. Everything depends on the will of those running the country. They can develop whatever projects they like.'

Officially, all the federal, executive and legislative powers within the United Arab Emirates fall to the Federal Supreme Council (FSC), a body that consists of the hereditary rulers of the country's seven

*Two months after I met Dr Al Roken, he was arrested twice in quick succession by members of Amn Al-Dawla, the UAE's security service. On the first occasion he was held for twenty-four hours for giving an interview to an Arab television station about the war between Israel and Lebanon, and the second time he was arrested during a meeting with a German human-rights conference convener. Amnesty International immediately wrote to the UAE government, saying it considered Dr Al Roken to be a prisoner of conscience who should be released immediately. He was detained for three days. The authorities confiscated his passport, effectively banning him from travelling abroad.

emirates – Abu Dhabi, Ajman, Dubai, Fujairah, Ras Al-Khaimah, Sharjah and Umm Al-Quwain. The FSC then elects – from its own members – a president and vice president. In November 2004, it elected Sheikh Khalifa Bin Zayed Al-Nahyan, the ruler of Abu Dhabi, as its president for a five-year term. He, in turn, appointed a prime minister and cabinet.

A 2006 report by the US government's Bureau of Democracy, Human Rights and Labor stated that the UAE government's 'respect for human rights remained problematic'. It also published a list of areas where it believed human-rights problems 'exist or were reported'. These included:

- No citizens' right to change the government and no popularly elected representatives of any kind
- Flogging as judicially sanctioned punishment
- Arbitrary detention
- Incommunicado detention permitted by law
- Questionable independence of the judiciary
- Restrictions on civil liberties – freedom of speech and of the press, and of assembly
- Restrictions on the right of association, particularly for human-rights groups
- Restrictions on religious freedom
- Domestic abuse of women, sometimes enabled by police
- Trafficking in women and children
- Legal and societal discrimination against women and non-citizens
- Corruption and lack of government transparency
- Abuse of foreign domestic servants
- Restrictions on and abuses of workers' rights.

Without the option of a ballot box, the only way for citizens to express their views to their leaders is through a traditional *majlis* or open consultative meeting. A consultative body called the Federal National Council (FNC) also exists. It consists of forty advisers who are appointed by the FSC for a two-year term. In 2005, it was announced that the FNC would soon become partially elected for the first time in its history. This will be the only opportunity for a UAE citizen to cast any form of vote.

'Some people have said this is not the right way to run affairs, but they soon fall silent,' says Dr Al Roken ominously. 'I think there are many amazing things going on here with people enjoying their lives and being happy, but it's just for the time being in my view. What will happen in the future, I don't know. There could be problems. Dubai is a very confusing experience, even for people who live here.'

I ask Dr Al Roken what he thinks about the recent strikes by foreign construction workers. Is this a sign, perhaps, of the discontent about the lack of representation and rights among many workers?

'Workers striking is a new phenomenon that has started in the past two or three years,' he explains. 'It has developed because these workers have come from the Indian subcontinent and they have a good union background there. It is deeply rooted. Some of the conditions for workers here – housing, transportation, food – are not up to acceptable standards. The government is trying to make conditions better. Their intentions and law-making are good, but the executive power lacks the administration and manpower to enforce the labour laws here. For example, there are two million foreign construction workers now in the UAE, out of a total population of 4.2 million, but only seventy labour-law inspectors.'

With such a disproportionately large community of foreign workers come predictable tensions, even if for now they remain largely suppressed. 'The influx of construction workers started here in the early 1990s when the huge projects started. The official line is that they are temporary workers just here to build the sites. They are considered to be immigrants. But many UAE nationals have been very worried that these immigrants may be granted nationality in time and that their own language and culture will become diluted. UAE nationals only represent about 20 per cent of the population now. There are those who say we have to curtail this trend, but actually our society is tolerant to an extent that most people outside would not believe. You will never find a racist movement against a group of foreigners. We are used to seeing foreigners here.

Dr Al Roken seems concerned that continued strikes could ramp up the underlying tensions; at the same time he feels that many of the workers' grievances are fully justified. 'We don't have a minimum wage here for foreigners at the moment, for example, which is what a lot of people are campaigning to change. There is a minimum wage for UAE nationals working in the private sector, which is 3,000AED a month for a single person and 4,500AED for someone who's married. (1000 UAE dirhams – AED – are equivalent to about £146.) But in the construction sector an Indian worker, for example, will only earn about 600AED for unskilled labour, rising to 1,200AED for skilled work. This is a net earning as housing, transportation and food are paid for. Usually, about 90 per cent of this will be sent back home to their families. Waiters, gardeners and cleaners will get around 2,000–3,500AED a month net. And their working conditions are much better.

'Under UAE labour law, each labourer is entitled to annual leave, which most want to use to go home to see family. But most companies only supply a plane ticket to Dubai, then one back home again when the contract – usually for three years – ends. A return ticket home could cost the equivalent of £150–300 depending on the season. The law also stipulates that there must be cool water available, first aid, and a doctor on call for a workplace with over a hundred workers. But every summer people are brought to hospital with heat exhaustion.'

But, I ask, if they all signed up willingly to all this, what's the problem?

'Some workers don't get paid for three to six months.' Dr Al Roken cites Al Hamed Development and Construction as an example. It's an Abu Dhabi-based construction firm that was contracted by Nakheel to help build the luxury villas on Palm Jumeirah. According to an Agence France Presse report, in September 2005 about a thousand Asian workers employed by Al Hamed blocked Sheikh Zayed Road near to the Palm for two hours, causing huge traffic jams, in protest at not having been paid for four months.

'Al Hamed is owned by a very influential family in Abu Dhabi and such bad publicity is very embarrassing for people in this society. The government ordered them to pay all the dues within forty-eight hours, otherwise they would be blacklisted. So they paid.'

The Minister of Labour granted the company a two-month extension to pay the unpaid wages after it said it wouldn't be able to raise the sums required in such a short period of time. The Indian government, however, did later blacklist the company from employing Indian workers.

Al Hamed's administration manager promised the local press in the days after the strike that the 'workers will receive their wages as promised', but was angered by comments made to the media by some of the striking workers about the quality of accommodation provided by the company: 'The workers are lying. They are angry and so they are talking nonsense. These workers who protested . . . are from one of our work sites in Jumeirah. The Dubai Municipality team was here for inspection. Officials from the Dubai Human Rights Department are also making rounds and so are the officials from the labour ministry.'

Dr Al Roken believes this high-profile case will encourage other companies 'to behave': 'Until it explodes like this, it doesn't get noticed. But with increased building in coming years, there still does not seem to be an increase in government inspectors. I am astonished that this isn't happening.'

Another of the firms involved with the building of the Palm, Al Naboodah Laing O'Rourke, was the subject of Dubai's highest-profile strike to date. In March 2006, 2,500 workers downed tools for two days at the site of Emaar's Burj Dubai – one of the three towers trying to claim the 'world's tallest' status – that will be home to, among other things, a 160-room Giorgio Armani hotel and spa. Some workers attacked security staff, ransacked offices and damaged cars. It also sparked a sympathy strike by 2,500 Al Naboodah Laing O'Rourke workers at the site of the new terminal building at Dubai International Airport, which is under construction. At the time, the BBC reported that the workers were demanding better wages, over-time pay, improved medical care and better treatment from their foremen.

Dr Al Roken stresses that it's not just the construction workers who can suffer in Dubai. He says that domestic staff are notoriously badly treated – in 2002, India banned women under the age of thirty from working as housemaids in the Gulf states due to the persistent reporting of violent and sexual abuse – and until the law was recently changed following an international outcry, boys were trafficked from countries such as Pakistan and made to ride as jockeys in camel races. 'They now have robot jockeys,' he smiles.

He also considers prostitution to be a growing concern. 'The trafficking of women for prostitution is a problem, especially from the Eastern bloc: Ukraine, Belarus, Armenia and Kazakhstan. It's mainly for the tourists. The government now says that no single women under the age of thirty-five can come from these countries. But then women who were clearly in their early twenties started arriving with passports saying they were over thirty-five. It is a big problem, but no one talks about it. It really threatens the social fabric here, too, as it is an Islamic state. To have pleasure with such a lady costs about the equivalent of thirty pounds for an hour. It is very cheap. They are brought here by gangs and passed over to local gangs. Some of them escape and run to the police, but the problem is they are trapped because they are in debt to the gangs. Some of them come having been promised that they will be hotel receptionists or whatever, and pay the gangs for the opportunity, but I think most know why they are coming here. Their passports are seized by the gangs as soon as they arrive, and they face the threat of being punished by the gangs at home if they don't comply. If they go to the police they will be deported straight away without any judicial process.'

Another person working hard to better the lives of foreign workers in Dubai is K.V. Shamsudheen, an Indian stockbroker and resident of the UAE for thirty years. In 2001 he founded the Pravasi Bandhu Welfare Trust to help fellow Indians who 'suffer problems here'. Somewhat incongruously, given the subject of our discussion, I meet him in the lobby of the Burj Al Arab. Amid the sound of the cascading water feature and the bustle of passing millionaires, he begins by explaining why his countrymen are attracted to Dubai in such huge numbers.

'Anyone coming here is agreeing to the contract, of course, but in reality they don't understand the likely problems. One dirham is equal to twelve Indian rupees. It sounds a lot to them over there to be earning, say, 7,000 rupees a month, but they don't realize how much it costs to live here. They simply get trapped. To live at all comfortably in Dubai you must be earning at least 1,500 dirhams a month. But the recruiting agents are sending people to work here for about 400 dirhams a month. Indian agents are coming to Dubai and promising the companies they can get them cheap workers. I really blame the agents: these are their own people they're hurting, after all.

'But the biggest problem is that most of the workers are having to pay a hefty service charge back home. The agencies recruiting workers in India will demand between 100,000 and 250,000 rupees in fees. It can take years to pay back this kind of charge. Many workers have to take out loans back home to pay these charges and the interest rates are very high – as much as 120 per cent per annum.'

Shamsudheen tells me that there are an estimated 1.3 million Indians in the UAE, at least half of whom are classified as 'unskilled'. About half of the Indian workers originate from the southern state of Kerala. 'There has long been a culture in Kerala of going abroad for work. During British rule, the British were taking our people to Africa, then to Burma and Malaya. Since the oil money started here, it has attracted Keralans. We have five million jobless people in Kerala out of a population of thirty-three million. Kerala is now a very developed state within India, but only because of the money being earned abroad. Every day, it is said that 600 million rupees come into Kerala from workers abroad.'

But at what cost, he wonders. Not only do these workers face financial pressure but they also have to deal with huge emotional pressures too. Shamsudheen says that in 2005 there were eighty-four known suicides among Indian workers in Dubai, a figure that is rising year on year. 'These poor people here can be working fifteen-hour days sometimes. Furthermore, the families will spend all the money sent home. They might build a house, for example, and start to live lavishly. The family then gets angry with the worker when he goes home, and wants him to go back and carry on earning. So he must return and live in a single room with six to eight people so that his family can maintain their new lifestyle . . . If the worker loses his job or gets sick he has to go back home. Most companies give sick leave but they often don't supply medical insurance. I come across workers with diabetes, ulcers and hypertension who don't go for treatment because they can't afford to. It might cost them half their salary. They will often wait until they go back to India before they get medicine.'

Pravasi Bandhu Welfare Trust now offers a free helpline to workers and can also put them in touch with psychiatrists and sociologists to provide counselling. Shamsudheen says, 'I want to help train people to know how to ask for a better salary. Striking is not the right way – it creates a bad image. We try to educate our people, show them how to improve themselves – goal setting, time management, etc. We try to tell them how to save for the future by putting aside some money each month. We want them to create some kind of asset for the future. They mustn't keep falling into this trap. I always say that they are like candles – giving light to others, but melting themselves.'

Sonapur is an unhappy place in so many ways – even its name cruelly teases its residents. The name of Dubai's largest labour camp means 'city of gold' in Hindi, and it also sounds very similar to the local slang word for a female orgasm. Khaled, my translator, who has driven us the hour's drive into an area of Dubai that is about as far off the tourist map as it is possible to get, seems to rejoice in telling me this, but I'm sure that few of the 150,000 male workers who live here – some claim it's as many as 500,000, but there's little official head-counting going on – still smile at the irony of living in a place that's so evidently empty of both wealth or women.

As we pass the large cemetery on the road into Sonapur, a long convoy of buses heads in the opposite direction towards the hundreds of building sites across Dubai. Each contains forty or so workers with helmets and flowing scarves lodged high on their heads. Curtains to screen the workers from the fierce sun flap violently in the open windows as each driver moves up through the gears, spewing a dirty diesel puff from the back of his bus at every shift.

On entering the huge settlement – 'town' doesn't seem the right term as there's no sign of cinemas, libraries, restaurants, or even any landscaping – we pass block upon block of concrete walls, some topped with barbed wire and all fronted by large metal gates. Inside, Khaled says, are housing units, some of which are home for up to five hundred workers, owned by the dozens of contractors that feed Dubai's construction boom.

After ten minutes looking for the right street, we park in front of a gate. Khaled tells me to stay in the car until he's sure he's in the right place. As I wait, I watch three boys playing cricket in the street, with a feral dog watching on. It's the only sense I have of anyone being at play the whole afternoon we're in Sonapur.

Khaled soon beckons me to jump out of the car and urges me to pass quickly through the gate and into the compound, explaining that any Westerner seen here might arouse suspicion among the owners. The compound's security guard greets us – Khaled has possibly slipped him some money to gain access – and shows us into his office cum bedroom. Inside the musty box-room there is just enough space for a desk, a bed, a TV and a fan. After a few minutes, three workers enter the room after kicking off their shoes. We all perch rather tentatively on the bed.

The men are friends who live together, sharing a room with five others. None of them, though, work together on the same construction site. Rahmatula, a truly giant twenty-seven-year-old Afghan whose pumice-rough hands are in sharp contrast to his disarmingly soft green eyes, gives me a picture of his typical day. It starts, he says, at five thirty a.m. when he quickly gets up and, without having breakfast, boards a bus. By six he is at the building site, where hundreds of luxury villas are being constructed, and immediately starts work, moving bricks around by hand. 'I have fifteen minutes for my lunch "hour",' he says. 'I always eat roti bread with vegetable curry made the night before, which I bring with me.' He says that he's not allowed to stop again, even if he's hot and needs water. If he does, pay will be deducted from his salary. 'I've been working here for five years and my salary is now eight hundred dirhams a month, but with overtime I get it up to eleven hundred. I send home six hundred dirhams a month,' he says with evident pride.

I can't help looking at his sweat-stained shirt and thinking of the bath-and-caviar service at the Burj Al Arab. It would take Rahmatula over three months of picking up bricks, I calculate, to earn enough money to pay for such a bath.

'I finish at five p.m. and get back here each day at about six, due to the traffic,' he says. After a shower and a rest, he eats his dinner at nine, goes to pray, and is in bed by ten o'clock. This is his life for six days a week: he gets Friday off work, but spends much of the day cleaning clothes or cooking. 'It's like a prison sentence, I suppose,' he says. 'I haven't seen my wife for five years, but I'm going home to Khost [a region on the Afghan–Pakistan border] next month.' His emerald eyes moisten at the thought.

Dharmindar, who is twenty-nine, has been at this labour camp for ten years. He is a carpenter and therefore commands a marginally better wage of 810AED a month, 1,300AED with overtime. He sends 800–900AED home to his family in Bihar, India, each month. He tells me that he's working on a hotel at the moment, and has worked on many others before this.

'Yes, life is tough for us,' he adds. 'Some of us here sleep twelve to a room, and there are thirty baths and six kitchens for 350 people. All of us friends put in two hundred dirhams a month to buy food together, because it's cheaper in bulk. We buy enough rice and flour to last us twelve days, then take it in turns to cook. It's easier that way. If we get sick it costs about eighty dirhams for a check-up at the private clinic by the shop at the end of the road, otherwise the government hospital is thirty minutes away. This gets paid for by the company, but you have to be really sick to qualify.'

Mohammed, a twenty-seven-year-old painter from Bangladesh who's worked here for three years, earning just 680AED a month, also complains about the high costs of living in Dubai, saying that he can only afford to send home up to 400AED a month. 'I try to call home once a fortnight, but that costs two and a half dirhams per minute. And it costs fifteen dirhams a month to wire home my money.'

In November 2006, Human Rights Watch published a strongly

worded report into the plight of migrant construction workers in Dubai. It contained interviews with workers describing very similar working conditions and pay to those of Rahmatula, Dharmindar and Mohammed. The report's recommendations included advice to the governments of the source countries for the workers, as well as to Western countries and companies that trade with the UAE. But above all, it listed a wide range of areas in which the UAE government could make significant improvements, including: proper use of the many labour laws that already exist in the country; ratifying a series of International Labour Organization conventions; allowing NGOs to operate freely in the country; significantly increasing the number of site inspectors; aggressively prosecuting firms that break labour laws; prohibiting the widespread seizure by construction firms of workers' passports upon their arrival; and establishing an independent commission to investigate grievances by migrant workers.

Following the publication of an earlier report by Human Rights Watch, the Dubai labour minister announced in March 2006 that a law was to be drafted to allow construction workers to form trade unions and pursue collective bargaining. But the later report criticized the minister for not moving beyond this announcement: 'As of early October [2006] the government has not published any details of this law or of proposed mechanisms for its implementation. Instead, in September the Ministry of Labor issued a resolution banning striking migrant workers from further employment in the country for at least one year. (The government had deported workers suspected of organizing strikes on several occasions prior to this resolution.)'

Until these measures were adopted, the Human Rights Watch said that migrant workers in the UAE would continue to present a picture of 'wage exploitation, indebtedness to unscrupulous recruiters, and working conditions that are hazardous to the point of being deadly'.

We step back out into the heat and walk down one of the long alleyways that divide the housing units. Clothes hang drying from lines attached to every available eave. The men show me a bathroom with a long line of open-sided baths and, further along, a filthy kitchen with over twenty gas stoves but no sign of any refrigerators. Khaled says that he's been to other camps in Sonapur with even worse conditions. At some camps, workers are prevented from cooking their own food and instead are made to pay 200AED a month for a canteen service, which they complain is overpriced and, worse, of highly questionable quality and hygiene. There are neighbouring camps where the workers have to pay about 30AED a month for water and electricity and regularly complain about restrictions: in some extreme cases, the owners only switch on the services for an hour a day.

In Dubai, where as a tourist you rarely part company with air conditioning, be it in the car, the mall, the hotel or the restaurant, it's easy to forget that not everyone can take it for granted. More importantly, it's also easy to forget that Dubai today – and tomorrow – simply wouldn't exist without these workers, nor would the hotels, pools, shopping malls and holiday homes that the millions of tourists who visit Dubai each year all enjoy.

Before leaving Dubai I take two final diversions: one to a snow-covered 'mountainside', and the other to the heart of the desert. Each offers a very different vision of what Dubai could offer tourists in the future.

Visitors enter Ski Dubai, a 25-storey-high, 400-metre-long indoor skiing centre, through the Mall of the Emirates, the largest shopping mall outside the US. After passing the St Moritz Café, which serves fondue and hot chocolate, you pay your 115AED for a two-hour pass, collect your skis, boots, jacket and salopettes, then step on to the escalator up to the nursery slope, where you collect your poles. As you do so, you pass a large advertisement for the Emirates Hospital.

'There are kamikaze skiers everywhere,' says Jon, an ex-pat New Zealander working in 'Dubai's film industry', with whom I share a chairlift up to the highest run. 'When it first opened I came here just to watch the accidents. The slopes were totally full of first-time skiers. It was hilarious. Amazingly, they still let anyone go down from the top, even though it is a red run in places.' We both watch a group of young men, still wearing their traditional *dishdashas* under their insulated jackets, slide unsteadily down the slope beneath us on their skis.

It is certainly a strange experience stepping from the 40C-plus heat outside into what is in effect a huge freezer with temperatures hovering at -2C. Around thirty tonnes of snow are created each night when chilled water is sprayed from the twenty-one snow-makers attached to the roof; the temperature indoors is lowered further to -8C to aid the process. In total, there are about six thousand tonnes of snow on the slopes at any one time, to a depth of one metre. You don't need to be an engineer to work out that this process must require huge volumes of water, as well as energy.

Ski Dubai points out that a heat exchanger is used to reuse the freezing air to help air-condition the mall next door. The thirty tonnes of snow that are removed from the bottom of the slopes each day, pushed down by the action of the skiers, are also reused to help irrigate the landscaped gardens that surround the mall and the Kempinski hotel, with its 395 rooms and fifteen 'ski chalets'. But these are only acts of recycling. They don't address the resource consumption that allows Dubai to offer that most unnatural of mirages: deep snow in a desert.

Given the emirate's booming rate of growth, could Dubai be playing a potentially catastrophic game with its natural resources? A United Nations report published in 2006, 'Global Deserts Outlook', noted that the UAE is now one of the most 'water-imperilled' nations in the world, with less than 250 cubic metres of renewable fresh water per person per year, and supplies are predicted to dwindle further. To put that in context, the world average stands at about 7,000 cubic metres and the 'water poverty line' is considered to be 1,000 cubic metres.

Yet the UAE is also one of the most water-hungry nations in the world, with a current consumption rate of 570 litres a day per capita – roughly three times the world average. The thinking to date has been to fill this huge gap between supply and demand with desalination plants. Of course, this process is hugely energy-intensive, but if you're blessed with wells full of oil, why not use them to create wells of water?

Recognizing the huge energy and water demands that the construction boom must inevitably create, the state-controlled Dubai Electricity and Water Authority (DEWA) announced in October 2006 that it planned to triple Dubai's present power gener-ation and water desalination capacity over the next ten years. At an estimated cost of fifty-five billion AED, DEWA would increase its electricity capacity to 13,250 megawatts, and with a 13 per cent growth in demand for water in 2005 alone, it would increase water production to 575 million gallons of water a day.

The UAE is not exactly blessed with hordes of environmentalists pointing out that this kind of resource consumption is likely to come at a very high cost, both financially and environmentally. Habiba Al Marashi, chairperson of the Emirates Environmental Group, one of the few NGOs operating within the UAE, said in an interview with Gulf News in 2006 that her country has one of the world's largest ecological footprints, at 9.9 hectares per person. She said, 'What this means is that it will take 9.9 global hectares of land and sea area to sustain an average individual residing in the UAE. This area is necessary to generate all the resources he or she needs to live and absorb his or her wastes. This is not sustainable in the long term and has serious consequences for the envir-onment. In the UAE, the problem is complex because resources are not available locally. They are imported and thus add to the overall foot-print. This could have a negative impact on the ecological assets on which the economy depends.' She was referring, of course, to the very desert and sea that is being pushed aside to make way for Dubai's future.

*

If you drive south-east away from Ski Dubai and head along the Al Ain highway towards the mountain range on the horizon that marks the border with Oman, you enter what remains of Dubai's desert. But before you do so, you pass mile after mile of signs marking the location of what will soon be known as Dubailand. Once completed, this will be the world's largest theme park, twice the size of Florida's Disney World. Scheduled to open between 2015 and 2018, it aims to be the centrepiece of Dubai's tourism infrastructure, attracting up to 200,000 visitors a day. Dubai Holding, which is building the mega-project, says that at 278 square kilometres it will include the world's largest shopping mall, the world's largest observation wheel, twenty-nine square kilometres of themed worlds, including 'Women's World', and seventy-five square kilometres of 'Eco-tourism World', including a safari park, a vast sporting complex and a snowdome six times bigger than Ski Dubai. Standing as awkwardly in the desert as early arrivals at a party, the Dubai Autodrome racing track and Global Village are already completed; the latter, with its replica Taj Mahal and Eiffel Tower, looks like a hallucination one might have if stumbling through the desert gasping for water.

To house the visitors, the Bawadi hotel zone inside Dubailand will have nearly 30,000 rooms spread across thirty-one hotels, including one called 'Asia-Asia' which, with 6,500 rooms, will become the world's largest hotel upon completion in 2010. Dubai is unchallenged, it seems, in claiming the world record for the largest number of 'world's largest' building projects. (The emirate of Ras Al-Khaimah, just an hour's drive north of Dubai, intends to reach even higher: in 2006 a company called Space Adventures announced that the emirate is to be home to a $265 million space port which will carry tourists – albeit rich ones – on suborbital space flights.)

But if you drive on beyond all this, you finally reach the Dubai Desert Conservation Reserve, which at 225 square kilometres (5 per cent of Dubai's total land area) is the largest remaining area of preserved desert in the emirate. And at its centre lies the Al Maha desert resort, which many hail as one of the best examples of conservation tourism anywhere in the world. It has been lavished with awards by the likes of *National Geographic*, Conservation International, *Condé Nast Traveller* and the World Travel and Tourism Council (WTTC), which describes itself as 'the forum for global business leaders, comprising the presidents, chairs and CEOs of one hundred of the world's foremost [travel and tourism] companies.' Owned by Emirates airline, the resort opened in 1999 and now offers forty 'villa suites' throughout its twenty-seven square kilometres, each costing about $1,300 a night. The villas, styled liked Bedouin tents from the outside but fully air-conditioned within, each has its own plunge pool facing on to an uninterrupted desert vista. Its unique location has attracted George Clooney, Matt Damon and Victoria Beckham in recent years. One of its attractions, to some guests at least, may be its policy of excluding children under the age of twelve.

It occurs to me to question how air conditioning and individual plunge pools (which have to be emptied every time there's a sandstorm) in this kind of environment can be an example of 'conservation tourism', but instead I ask Greg Simkins, Al Maha's South African conservation manager, to explain how tourism can be used to protect a wilderness area and its endangered flora and fauna.

As we head out into the dunes in his 4×4, he says that this land was originally set aside as a reserve in the 1960s by Sheikh Rashid to protect it from hunters. But it's only in recent years, since camel farming was restricted and the resort was opened, that the area has started to return to its natural state.

'There are now 250 Arabian oryx in the reserve,' he tells me, all of which were donated by Sheikh Mohammed (who owns a villa at Al Maha, which is cleaned daily by four staff members on the off-chance that he may show up unannounced). 'There's also a pair of wild eagle owls, 350 gazelles, and sand foxes. We wanted to introduce lynx, but the culture here is that there should be no predators of this kind. Coming from South Africa, I believe that hunting and conservation are compatible, but tourism is the best form of conservation for here. Believe me, we had a scare when we heard a rumour they were going to come here looking for oil.'

We soon move off the dunes and on to a flat gravel plain. Greg is careful to follow the tracks in the sand exactly. 'The grasses on these gravel plains can take seven years to recover from car-track damage. We now restrict the number of desert tour operators that can enter the reserve to just four. Before the resort opened there were up to nineteen companies driving in tourists and there were no rules about where they could go.'

'Desert-bashing' is a popular activity for tourists in Dubai, with nearly every hotel offering such trips. They usually entail a day spent driving 4×4s or quad bikes across the desert, ending with a picnic, with accompanying belly dancers, in the dunes.

'The ones we allow in here are restricted to forty kilometres per hour. In other places, it's not desert, but just a series of tracks in the sand. Here, they must take all their waste out and follow road corridors marked out by GPS. But the culture in Dubai is that you can drive anywhere you want, so we've had to explain to locals that this reserve is restricted. You have to be sensitive, though, when telling them.'

So, I ask, does the resort provide all the funds to protect the reserve?

'The visiting tour groups now provide about half of the funds. And, yes, the other half comes from Emirates airline. But Emirates is now exporting this conservation model to a hotel called Wolgan Valley in Australia's Blue Mountains which it is opening in late 2007. The WTTC are using it as a model for conservation, too.'

It's hard to know just how viable this could ever be in a country that doesn't have Dubai's own unique brand of state-funded autocratic willpower, but Al Maha is a vision of how a small volume of tourists paying huge sums can fund a conservation scheme that would, in truth, be unlikely to survive without them.

Sadly it doesn't come without niggles. My last memory of Dubai before departing is of riding with a train of camels carrying hotel guests out on to a nearby dune to watch the sun go down. It was tranquillity itself until I noticed that a 4×4 had been sent out ahead of us, carrying a cooler box laden with champagne and fruit. Once we arrived, it had all been laid out on a table dressed with a crisp cloth. The honeymooners were thrilled by such decadence, but I couldn't drag my eyes from the cigarette butts lying in the sand around us. Like so much of Dubai, beneath the alluring veneer lay something altogether more uncomfortable.

3

The Model State

Kerala, India

THERE ARE INDIANS WHO LOOK to Kerala in the far south of their country with more than a tinge of envy. 'God's own country', as her citizens describe her, has one of the most progressive and complete health and education systems in all of India, meaning Keralites are highly literate and boast a high life expectancy. Kerala's child mortality rate is also as low as that of the US, and Kerala is almost unique in the developing world in having a population that consists of more women than men. The state has been officially recognized by the UN as having the highest Human Development Index – a universally acknowledged method of measuring social well-being – in India, one that is on a par with most Western nations.

Yet Kerala remains one of the poorest Indian states of all. This apparent paradox has led many to refer to the so-called 'Kerala Model' – a rare form of development that sees high levels of wellbeing achieved despite continued economic underdevelopment. It is studied by sociologists and demographers around the world. But it doesn't make sense, surely. Why hasn't this tremendous social wealth translated into material wealth? Are the state's firebrand politics – Kerala was one of the first places in the world democratically to elect a communist government in the 1950s, and has a rich heritage of unions and cooperatives – to blame for not nurturing the kind of entrepreneurial spirit that seems to flow freely from states such as Gujarat and Punjab to the north, or for not creating the sort of high-tech boom witnessed in neighbouring Karnataka, particularly in its capital Bangalore? And why have such a disproportionate number of Keralites chosen to leave the country and work abroad in the places such as the UAE?

Or is this entirely the wrong way to view Kerala? Perhaps it should be seen as an example of how success isn't always best measured solely in terms of Gross Domestic Product, or in terms of how many washing machines or cars each household owns. Perhaps Kerala illustrates how an economy seemingly operating in first gear, without the high-octane fuel of frenzied consumerism so cherished around the world, can still place its people very much in the fast lane in terms of the things that really count – health, education, wellbeing. Is Kerala a vision of sustainability in its truest sense?

It is worth bearing these questions in mind when looking at the development of tourism in the region. Again, people talk of the 'Kerala model of tourism' and cherish the way the state – as some see it, at least – has become a beacon of both sustainable and eco-tourism. Since the state's government launched a formal tourism policy in 1995, visitors have flocked to the nature reserves, backwaters and beaches set between the rugged crags of the Western Ghats to the east and the tropical Indian ocean to the west. So much so, in fact, that in 2003 the WTTC declared in a report examining the state's industry that Kerala had the fastest-growing tourism industry anywhere in the world. It forecast that Kerala would record an annual growth rate of 11.6 per cent up to 2012, and that the number of people employed in tourism there would nearly triple from 693,000 in 2003 to two million in 2012.

Other Indian tourist hotspots such as Rajasthan and Goa soon sought to learn more about the 'Kerala model of tourism', as did destinations further afield. What was it, they asked, that Kerala was getting so right? After all, this was a place now listed by *National Geographic* as among the fifty 'must-see' destinations in the world. The WTTC issued its own view: the 'first major step for tourism development', it said, was Kerala's drafting of the policy in 1995, at a time when India had only recently liberalized its economy and opened it up to direct foreign investment. 'The 1995 tourism policy remains the basis for much of the state's progress over the last eight years . . . New beaches and backwater resorts have been opened up by the [state-run] Kerala Tourism Development Corporation (KTDC), which also operates budget hotels, restaurants and cafés, as well as managing central reservation systems and conducting tours. Other projects undertaken by the KTDC include the development of Ayurveda [an alternative medicine] as a unique selling point and the development and promotion of nature-based and heritage tourism. The government is also taking measures to create an investment-friendly atmosphere and to generate confidence among non-resident Indians and other prospective investors.' Kerala was, in other words, very much dancing to the WTTC's tune of internationalized modern tourism, after decades of failing to exploit its undoubted potential. This was a report, it is worth noting, that was endorsed by various WTTC-member companies, including Abercrombie and Kent, American Express, Air India, Avis, Emirates, Thomas Cook, and several major Indian hotel companies such as the Oberoi and Taj groups.

Reading the state government's 1995 policy document today, it certainly scores highly on focus, vision and ambition: 'In this era of globalization we can say with confidence that tourism will grow at a very fast pace in the decades to come . . . It is liberalization rather than controls that create a proper atmosphere for the growth of tourism. We cannot afford to overlook the capacity of tourism to generate employment. We should also be able to take maximum advantage of the possibilities of tourism, aptly described as "invisible export", to bring in foreign exchange.

'We will follow a marketing strategy aimed at the markets with the highest potential. Western Europe is now the largest market for Kerala. The marketing will therefore be concentrated in Germany, England, France and Italy. At the same time we cannot afford to ignore the economically developed nations of East Asia, Scandinavian countries, the United States, Canada and the Gulf countries.'

The document talks of needing helicopters and luxury coaches to ferry tourists across the 'undulating landscape of Kerala', and calls for the establishment of an annual 'heritage fair'. But it ends with a poignant vow: 'Attempts will be made to set right the impression that tourism development only leads to environmental degradation and social decay... Unbridled tourism development without a clear understanding of the undesirable side-effects is certainly not to be encouraged. Appropriate controls and legal protections are indispensable for the healthy development of tourism. All tendencies that destroy our environment and our social and cultural values will be discouraged.'

The WTTC applauded Kerala in its 2003 report for achieving such rapid growth and for developing such a unique and sought-after 'product'. But it also offered a word of warning: 'Kerala has some of the finest beaches in India. However, unplanned construction, over-population and overcrowding can considerably diminish their appeal. One example is Kovalam beach which, due to its proximity to Thiruvananthapuram, was one of the first tourist attractions in the state. Kerala should ensure that newly developed beaches do not suffer the same fate.'

It's a fair point. Kovalam beach is the state's busiest resort and has expanded tremendously over the past decade, becoming a byword within tourism for how somewhere can be ruined by the rapid and unchecked introduction of mass tourism. But the WTTC's suggested solution speaks volumes about what the big beasts within the industry – of course, those with most to gain – often view as the most positive route forward: 'In order to tap the full potential of the beaches and backwaters for tourism, it is essential to have luxury boats, cruise boats, houseboats and yachts. These will help Kerala attract high-yield foreign and domestic visitors . . . the WTTC has noted that facilities for watersports are relatively undeveloped in Kerala. In order for the state to attract high-yield tourists to its beaches and backwaters, private investment in watersports facilities should be increased. What is needed is the full complement of facilities for every type of watersports – water-skiing, water scooters, para-sailing, airborne sailing, marine fishing and scuba diving . . . There is an urgent requirement for different kinds of tourism transport – luxury coaches, air-conditioned cars, luxury boats, yachts and speedboats. A drastic lowering of import duty and other incentives would help to divert money to the development of these productive tourism assets.'

It also called for the building of international-standard toll roads between tourist destinations, and for better rail and air links. And then, almost as an afterthought, it said at the end: 'Kerala has a fragile ecosystem and its backwaters and coastal lagoons are susceptible to pollution and overcrowding. In order to preserve its precious tourist attractions, and ensure sustainable development in the future, the Kerala government should conduct carrying capacity studies.'

Do speedboats, water scooters and luxury boats really help with this preservation process, you might wonder. This report highlights the dilemma facing the tourism industry around the world – how to grow and keep 'em coming, without trashing the very assets it relies on to draw tourists in the first place.

Sumesh Mangalassery waves his hand above his head to identify himself to me amid the sea of heads leaving Thiruvananthapuram railway station. Surrounded by *chai wallahs*, businessmen, beggars and schoolchildren, we shake hands and edge our way through the mass to the taxi rank outside. The inviting smell of *poori*, the popular

Indian snack being fried at food stalls outside the station, is over-whelming.

It's a twenty-minute ride in one of India's signature Ambassador taxis to Kovalam beach along the recently resurfaced highway from Kerala's capital (which many still call by its old colonial name of Trivandrum, if for no other reason than that it's far easier to say than Thiruvananthapuram). As we travel we pass many of the icons of roadside India: the lackadaisical cow munching alongside piles of rubbish, women on mopeds tightly gathering up their saris in the wind; heavily decorated and laden Tata trucks announcing their pres-ence by the constant sounding of their horns.

Sumesh, who is in his early thirties, has kindly travelled overnight all the way from his home in the far north of Kerala, tearing himself away from his newborn daughter, to meet me and explain why he is so passionately opposed to the way tourism is being developed here. He represents a new generation of Keralites that is angry with the state government for failing to meet its earlier policy promises of putting the welfare of the environment and local communities before that of devel-opers and tour operators.

Until three years ago, Sumesh worked for Equations in Bangalore, which describes itself as 'a non-profit organization that works towards transforming the inherently exploitative nature of mass commercial tourism and questions the real benefits of tourism to the host communities as well as its socio-cultural and economic impacts'. 'But I quit my job there,' he says, 'and decided to come back to Kerala to help set up Kabani Tours with some friends. For the past ten to fifteen years there's been a lot of talk about tourism in Kerala and its impact, but we now need solutions. Kabani is a non-profit group that does research, training and campaigning, as well as organizing alter-native tours. Our motto is "Minimize the impact, maximize the benefit".'

Sumesh has already made an impact: in early 2006 he caused quite a stir in Kerala and further afield when he wrote a strongly worded email to the WTTC, copying it to seventeen thousand other interested parties. At the time, Kerala was being considered by WTTC judges for the 'Destination Stewardship' category in its annual Tourism for Tomorrow Awards, which celebrate 'best practice' in tourism development. He wrote in a letter to the judges:

> We understand that the [Kerala] Tourism Department has painted a one-sided and biased picture of Kerala tourism. If the WTTC panel shows the determination to talk to a more representative cross section of stakeholders, they will be able to understand that Kerala tourism is not a sustainable tourism development model by any international standards . . . Recently introduced tourism legislations are undermining the legitimate powers of local democratic institutions, thus negating people's participation in tourism . . . stifling the local economies and depriving local communities of their livelihood systems. Kerala tourism has a strong record of proving that planning, policies and regulations to date have not effectively addressed major problems caused by tourism. These include the unsustainable extraction of ground water in tourism spots such as Kovalam, which is causing a serious lack of drinking water for local communities. Problems also include the pollution of the backwaters by the tourism industry, especially the increasing number of houseboats . . . Coastal Regulation Zone violations by hotels and resorts are a serious concern in the state . . . Prostitution, including the commercial sexual exploitation of children in Kovalam and Varkala, is rampant. Sustainable waste-management systems are completely lacking in the state.

The WTTC placed Kerala on a shortlist of three for the award, but in the end handed it to the Sierra Gorda bio-reserve in Mexico. Kerala's tourism officials blamed the failure to win on Kabani's 'malicious' campaign. Kabani's email came at a sensitive time for them as they had only recently condemned a report by the Institute of Social Sciences in New Delhi, funded by the United States Agency for International Development, that said India was becoming a centre for child-sex tourism. Kerala's tourism minister K.C. Venugopal had reacted angrily to this, saying that it would 'blemish the state's chances to grow as a tourist destination' and asking how such accusations could be made of a state where the standards of literacy and 'moral policing' were so high.

The descent from the main road into Kovalam is steep and the buildings and trees that line the street shield any good view of the sea below. It is only when we emerge into a ramshackle, muddy car park behind Ashok beach (Kovalam beach is actually four separate beaches divided by rocks and headlands) that I can see, rather than just hear, the breakers, swollen by the early arrival of the monsoon, hitting the sand. A large holidaying Indian family – children, parents, grandparents, aunts and uncles – play chase with the waves as they wash up the beach towards them. A group of fishermen heave their boat up out of the water. On the edge of the sand, by a pile of scattered rags and empty plastic bottles that have encroached on to the beach from the car park, three elderly women sit on their haunches cutting slices of mango for sale.

Sumesh and I begin walking slowly around the headland, which is home to the imposing sprawl of the five-star Leela hotel, towards the concrete promenade that extends over a mile along the built-up neighbouring Hawah and Lighthouse beaches. In the distance stands a red-and-white-striped lighthouse, positioned high on a hillside of coconut palms. As we walk, we pass small, haphazardly built souvenir shops and cafés, as well as larger Westernized hotels with clipped lawns, pools and balconies overlooking the sea. Sumesh shakes his head in disgust.

'I once counted 561 commercial operations on this beachfront.

Everything here is totally uncontrolled. Look at it. There is no basic infrastructure here such as water, sewage and waste management. Most of the owners are from Trivandrum or beyond, as opposed to locals, and they lease out the beachfront land every year, which just leads to a short-term mentality. It is technically illegal to build this close to the beach, but they all get away with it. In Kerala we have egotourism, not ecotourism.'

It is indeed an unsightly and disheartening view, especially for a place that once had such a positive international reputation for being a postcard-perfect tropical beach. Electricity pylons lean untidily over the promenade, the sand smells stale, and brown foam drifts beyond the surf, suggesting that raw sewage is being pumped out to sea close by.

'Water is probably the biggest issue here now,' says Sumesh. 'Most of the hotels rely on water being brought in by tank from nearby villages – except the Leela hotel, which used to be a government-owned property. Two years ago there were protests about the situation here, with villages complaining their water was being stolen. A handful of the villagers were selling access to their wells to the hotels, who were using them to fill giant ten-thousand-litre tanks on the back of trucks and transporting them down here. It still carries on because the law isn't very clear. For example, the Tourism Act 2005 doesn't talk about water, just planning issues. I once even got jaundice as a result of drinking the water here.'

It has taken just a decade for Kovalam to get into this state, says Sumesh. It ties in, he says, with the first charter flights starting to land at nearby Thiruvananthapuram airport in the late 1990s. Today charter flights fly direct from places ranging from Gatwick to St Petersburg, and Kovalam features in the brochures of major tour operators such as Thomas Cook and First Choice.

Kovalam is also a popular destination for domestic tourists – India has a so-called consumer class of approximately 300 million people, which is equal to the entire population of the US. The past few years have seen an explosion of travel from this group, both within India and abroad, as they rapidly acquire the taste for affordable holidays. According to Euromonitor, a market analyst, the number of outbound travellers from India grew by 15 per cent to 6.2 million in 2005 – almost double the number of tourists that visited the country. Indians have a particular taste for Singapore, Malaysia, Thailand, Sri Lanka and the Seychelles. At home, they are increasingly abandoning India's wonderful train network for burgeoning low-cost domestic airlines such as Spicejet and Air Deccan. Growth in India's low-cost domestic sector has been extraordinary, and is only surpassed by the growth witnessed in China. In 2004, for example, Air Deccan carried one million passengers, whereas in 2005 it carried 4.4 million. And at the Paris Air Show in 2005, IndiGo, a New Delhi-based budget airline, alone agreed to buy one hundred Airbus A320 planes at a cost of six billion dollars. Kingfisher, another new budget airline, ordered fifteen planes, including five Airbus A380 superjumbos.

We stop at a beach café for a couple of lime sodas and a brief respite from the heat and humidity, then get an autorickshaw back up the hill to the nearby village of Venganoor to meet Rufus Daniel, who was president of the village *panchayat* – a local council of elected members – from 2000 to 2005. Since then he has campaigned to enter state politics, after his village gained a reputation as far away as Pakistan for developing innovative ways to improve health and education among villagers without relying on state-level help. It is from this area that water is being extracted from wells and taken down to Kovalam.

'Twenty years ago this was a very beautiful place,' he tells me from his desk, which takes up almost half of his sitting room. 'There was lots of natural beauty here, but now there are concrete buildings everywhere. It is easy to get permission here and there are also lots of illegally built hotels. We did prosecute a lot of cases early on, but now many of the politicians also own the hotels, so there are no more prosecutions. We even got some hotels to be pulled down, but again, no more. In 2000, there were 721 CR2 violations [building within five hundred metres of a beach without permission] alone across Kerala. Sometimes it's corruption, sometimes powerful hoteliers, sometimes simply a lack of willingness from local authorities.'

I ask him about the water shortages and how they are affecting the villagers here.

'About 20 per cent of the water comes from the mains, the rest is taken from lakes, ponds and illegal sources. The high court recently ordered this to stop, but of course it continues. Sometimes I count forty trucks a day coming up from Kovalam to take water. The hotels pay just 650 rupees (£7.60) for one truck's worth of water. They are taking it all from seventeen or eighteen local wells that are owned privately. Other villagers complain as it obviously lowers the water table, and in the summer there are even fights among the villagers.'

Water shortage is not the only ill brought about by tourism. According to Daniel, 'Western influences are not liked here by my villagers. Twenty per cent of the tourists here indulge in drugs, violence or immoral activities. Some people who work in Kovalam get commission to push these things. Every year it is increasing. They are enjoying our natural resources, but introducing these problems. The people who want natural beauty now go to Papanasam. Some domestic tourists are now renting houses here instead of staying in hotels. This has pushed the cost of renting a house up to 5,000 rupees (£58) a month per 1,500 square feet.'

Just a couple of hundred metres down the road from Rufus Daniel's home is one of the area's few good-news stories. The Zero Waste Kovalam Project is an initiative run by C. Jayakumar, who is the coordinator of a local NGO called the Thanal Conservation Action and Information Network, which in turn works with Kerala's state tourism officials and Greenpeace. The project aims to manage the tonnes of rubbish being produced in Kovalam every day, much of it by tourists, by crafting as much of it as possible into various souvenirs and trinkets for sale back to tourists.

As I dip my head to enter the doorway to the workshop, a group of women sitting round a long table having their lunch turn around to greet me. C. Jayakumar stands up from his desk by the door and invites me over to a long stand that displays all the items the women have been making: letter racks, necklaces, candlesticks and handbags, all made from rags, newspaper, coconut shells and glass.

'We employ twenty-two women here,' he says. 'And 120 people benefit indirectly from our project. Plastic waste from Kovalam is sent all the way to Coimbatore, a few hundred kilometres away in Tamil Nadu, and hoteliers pay 100–150 rupees a day for their waste to be sent to the dump at Thiruvananthapuram, so it helps to reuse as much of it as possible here. Also, some of our waste is still thrown into the sea at night here. We teach schoolchildren to produce less waste and to make toys out of coconuts and other discarded materials. And the ladies here go out to villages to teach them about compost and bio-gas. Some hotels now even send their tourists here to learn about us and to buy our gifts. We find that our tailoring and coconut products are the most popular. I'm so proud, as this project now pays for itself.'

The project, he tells me, has created full-time employment for women who would normally struggle to find work outside the high-season months of November through to March. He was thrilled when the project was presented with an environmental gold medal by the Pacific Asia Travel Association at a ceremony in Thailand in 2006. As part of its presentation to the awards committee, the project displayed a large patchwork quilt made by the women, showing their view of Kovalam. It was hardly a vision of paradise. As well as the lighthouse and deep-blue surf, the quilt also depicted Western women in bikinis surrounded by Indian hawkers on the beach, AIDS ribbons to represent the spread of STDs through sex tourism, aeroplanes overhead, scattered rubbish, heavy traffic and shops with dollar signs displayed outside.

After we leave the workshop, Sumesh takes me to a busy restaurant by the junction leading into Kovalam to tell me about Kabani – which means 'other direction' – and his own vision for tourism in Kerala. We order vegetable *thalis* – large round metal trays with compartments for rice, curry, dhal, yoghurt and chapatti. The waiter fills our metal beakers with water and retreats to his station by a large pot of rice to await our signal, should we need topping up with more food or water. Without any cutlery on offer, I make a rather embarrassing attempt to eat with my fingers, like everyone else in the restaurant.

'We have very good health and education systems in Kerala, but very little income,' he says. 'We don't really produce anything, all our main income comes from workers in the Gulf region. The government here doesn't want big factories – instead it wants service sectors such as tourism and IT. Most of the tourism operators here to date have been small to medium scale, but the government now wants the big players, so we have Taj and Leela here now. We even have Best Western, and Marriott are coming. The government here thinks this is a good way of getting subsidies, but the money just goes to the big players.'

Sumesh believes this is wrong and has established Kabani to try to place the power back in the hands of the people. He says this is the true Keralite way.

'I come from a small village in Wayanad, which is a rural area in the north-east hills of Kerala. It is home to many *adivasis* [indigenous people]. We are now training farmers to offer homestay facilities to tourists as a source of supplementary income. We tell them not to rely on tourism, though, as it is even more fickle than growing crops. We also advise them to cultivate small kitchen gardens and to keep goats and cows for butter and milk. This way they don't need to buy food for tourists and also can feed themselves. We have to train them about hygiene, languages and etiquette. Most tourists want meals at exact times and don't like to get up early in the morning. We also want to educate tourists about such things as not bringing plastics with them, and dressing respectfully.'

Wayanad is now being promoted as a 'future destination' by the tourism department in Kerala due to its thus-far-unspoilt beauty and proximity to affluent cities such as Bangalore, a place full of people with money to spend on weekend breaks to the country. But it is not a place without controversy. In 2003, just a few weeks before India launched a tourism initiative promoting its religious and spiritual heritage, over a thousand *adivasis* were driven from their ancestral lands in the Muthanga wildlife sanctuary in Wayanad, home to a number of rare species including the tiger, as the area was set to become an 'ecotourism' destination. The government admitted that five people were shot dead, but eyewitnesses said the figure was as high as twenty. A number of prominent academics, politicians and journalists in India signed a letter condemning the action, which it pointed out had been done 'in the name of "development" and "wildlife protection"': 'The state's ... recourse to violent action to crush the *adivasi* movement in Muthanga raises several doubts about its promises of rehabilitation and justice to Kerala's *adivasis*, 90 per cent of whom are landless.'

The pressure to remove people from areas destined to become wildlife reserves open to affluent ecotourists is not confined to Muthanga. The Indian government, under huge international pressure to protect the near-extinct tiger from poachers, has set up a Tiger Task Force to protect its wildlife sanctuaries. It has also realized that tourism can be a useful tool in encouraging local people away from the tempting prices offered for tiger skins, bones and penises by illegal traders in the Far East and into catering for tourists instead. But its heavy-handed, sometimes deadly approach to clearing people from such areas has angered many, too.

Dr Ullas Karanth, the technical director of the Wildlife Conservation Society's tiger programme, says the impression among many local communities remains that national parks and sanctuaries are little more than 'gardens for rich people'. 'Even the largest so-called "ecotourist" operators have not put an effort into ensuring that the benefits reach the local people,' he told the *Independent* in 2006.

It's a difficult balancing act, says Sumesh. Ecotourism can offer many benefits, but only if the local community is fully engaged and sympathetic to the aims. He says that this is at the forefront of his thoughts now because many farmers in Wayanad have started to approach him and his friends to ask about homestays, as their plight has become so desperate.

'There have been around a thousand farmer suicides in recent years,' he says. 'The problem is that many of them invested in growing vanilla when prices were high, but the global price has plummeted. It's the same for coffee and pepper, too. Some of them hang them-selves, but most eat pesticides as they're a poison that is easily available. They take out big loans to buy pesticides, thinking these will help their crops grow, and then can't afford to pay back the debts as the interest increases. There have been severe droughts and crop fail-ures, too. Farmers are desperate. This is why we have to be careful about presenting tourism as an alternative. Tourism can leave them even more vulnerable. Banks have approached some of these farmers to lend them money to start homestays, but we warn them to be careful.'

Sumesh has spent a lot of time designing a 'product' to offer tourists, as well as training local communities to cope with visitors. 'We want it to be flexible: people can do birdwatching, help to harvest spices such as cardamom, go camping, learn about our Jain temple ruins, visit schools, or try the bow and arrows used locally. But all the money stays with the people.'

*

It's a vision shared by Gopinath Parayil, the chief executive of the Blue Yonder travel company, who at thirty-three is another young-blood responsible-tourism pioneer from Kerala, who also takes tourists to Wayanad and its surrounding area. He is much more the savvy businessman than Sumesh, though. Gopinath used to work as a software engineer ('building mainframe systems for Tesco from Chennai'), then completed an MSc at Cranfield University in the UK and an MBA at the Ecole Nationale des Ponts et Chaussées in France. But it was during a visit to Kerala following the death of his father that he felt, like Sumesh, a calling to return to the state. As he performed the death rituals for his father in the River Nila (also known as the Bharathapuzha), he became particularly incensed by the river's plight, which he says is 'dying before our eyes' due to damming, mining and water extraction. In three years, he has taken three thousand tourists around the area, with 20 per cent of the profits going to the Nila Foundation, which aims to battle the exploitation of the river. He tries to employ the 'sand miners and sand smugglers' who are otherwise helping to kill the river by illegally taking its sand and silt for the construction industry; he recruits them as guides or boatmen to tempt them away from their damaging practices, at all times following the guiding principles of the so-called '2002 Cape Town Declaration' on responsible tourism, which focuses on 'minimizing the negative economic, environmental and social impacts of tourism'.

'If we don't step in, our lands will be left to the hooligans,' he says. 'We've had tourists from the UK, France, Germany and the US come here with our company. We've even had one Frenchwoman come seven times in three years. But we attract domestic tourists as well. We want more of the young "neo-rich" from Bangalore to come here. Many of them now go to Thailand for the weekend to get drunk. We want to try and get as many of them as we can to come here and learn about the plight of the countryside around them.'

But Gopinath is highly critical of Sumesh and his campaigning ways. He says the email Sumesh sent to the WTTC judges was 'highly irresponsible' and has damaged Kerala's reputation. 'I don't know if there is any child-sex tourism happening in Kerala. Accusations are not based on any research, but on anecdotes from one or two individuals. But I accept that child-sex tourism is found in many places, even cities in Europe. Sex tourism is something that follows tourism all over the world.' Unlike Sumesh, he prefers to engage with the tourism officials in the state, even though they 'have no clue about development'.

There are just as many factions and opinions within the responsible-tourism sector, it seems, as there are in the wider industry.

Few tourists come to Kerala without taking a slow boat trip on the backwaters – a vast network of inland canals and waterways that sit just in from the coast, where up to fifty thousand people eke out a rather precarious existence in houses a metre or so above the water-line, largely by fishing and growing rice. It is billed as one of the quintessential tourist experiences of all India, up there with the Taj Mahal, the desert forts of Rajasthan, the Raj-era hill stations such as Shimla, and Varanasi, the Hindu holy city on the banks of the Ganges.

I am to board my *kettuvallam* – the Malayalam name for a houseboat roofed with palm leaves over bamboo poles – at Alappuzha, the main tourist entrance-point for the backwaters, as well as one of the world's main coir-carpet producers. Every August it is the site of the Vallam Kali, a festival of boat races that sees the area swell greatly with tourists. The monsoon rain showers down heavily on my back as I walk along a muddy path where dozens of houseboats are moored. It has taken me four hours by train and taxi, travelling due north, to reach here from Kovalam. I am soon greeted by Surdesh, the captain, and Pradeep, the cook, who both jump on to the path to take my bags aboard. After a few checks, the outboard motor splutters into life and we gracefully pull away from the bank and enter a large channel ahead.

The leaden clouds force out one last extra-strength torrent before finally giving way to the sun. The glistening water is neatly framed by thin, palm-lined strips of land; it is easy to see why the backwaters were described as the Venice of the East by Lord Curzon, the Viceroy of India from 1899–1905. Life seems sweet, as Pradeep prepares a lunch of fried fish, rice, cabbage salad, chillied beetroot, coconut stew and papadums.

Due to the early onset of the monsoon this season, the backwaters are relatively empty of tourists, but we do pass other houseboats every ten minutes or so. Most of the larger ones – some sleep up to a dozen people – seem occupied by Indian tourists, many of them groups of men enjoying music and beer. We pass through villages that each cluster tightly around a Catholic church, town hall and school. Women line stretches of the bank, washing clothes by slapping them hard on stones from high above their heads. Soap suds bleed down into the water.

Once lunch is over, I chat to Pradeep over a cup of milky sweet *chai*. He tells me that most tourists spend a couple of nights aboard the houseboats, touring the backwaters around Alappuzha. There is little to do other than just sit back and watch life pass by, he says. But he is quick to admit that even though this is 'paradise', it can be difficult to reconcile tourists with such a sensitive environment, even if the government here claims that touring the backwaters is an 'ecotourism activity'.

Somewhat nervously, he asks me how much I've paid for one night on board. It cost me about fifty pounds, which widens his eyes in shock. He explains that he gets paid about three pounds out of that, plus tips. Surdesh gets marginally more. The rest goes to the local company that owns the boat and the local agent with whom I booked the trip. There is obviously going to be little opportunity for me to spend any money elsewhere on the trip, so the main beneficiaries of my visit will clearly be the boat's owner and the agent.

The extent to which these houseboats affect the local community has been of growing concern in recent years, ever since villagers started to report increased pollution from the engines and onboard toilets that flush straight out into the water. A report published in 2005 by Tourism Watch, a German NGO that 'questions the assumption that tourism equals development', examined this very issue.

'The houseboats are a big menace now,' R. Visakhan, president of the *panchayat* at a backwater village called Kainakarit, told Tourism Watch. 'They are discharging human excreta, condoms and other wastes into the lake. The bottom of the lake is full of plastic carrier bags and bottles. The industry doesn't have any social commitment. We have to really look into the statistics – the foreign exchange rate, local people employed in tourism, subsidies given by government. We can see that this tourism is not profitable and does not help people. Here tourism destroys the traditional employment like fishing and agriculture by polluting the water.'

Tourism Watch also spoke to K. Raju, a fisherman from the same village. 'Husbands have blamed their wives for the kerosene taste of the food. They might have spoiled the food while cooking. Now we know that the kerosene taste is from the fish itself. We are not able to sell fish because of this kerosene. The houseboats are threatening our livelihood. The fish stock is also reducing.'

In response to community concerns – and those of an increasing number of tourists, it seems – some houseboats now have solar panels to help power the air-conditioning units, fans and water pumps on board. In 2006, the Kerala government, stung by reports about the 'alarming rise' in pollution from the houseboats, ordered all owners to change their engines from four-stroke to less polluting two-stroke ones. It also announced that two waste facilities were to be established at the main tourist centres of Alappuzha and Kumarakom to treat oil residues, sewage and kitchen waste from the houseboats.

Our boat enters a much wider expanse of water, which Pradeep tells me is a 'main road', despite there being hardly any roadways within the backwaters. Children run along the bank to a footbridge and wait for us to pass underneath. As we do, they shout, 'Hello, one pen. Hello, one pen.' It's an awkward moment. What do you do in such a situation? Should you encourage begging by giving them something? The Indian tourism department's website offers its own rather blunt and unforgiving view on what to do 'if pestered by beggars and street urchins': 'Well, you can start by ignoring them completely and if they get too persistent give them a stern look. If you must give them something, let it not be more than one to two rupees only.' I shrug my apologies a little shamefully and the boat pushes on. Near by a boatman cups his hand over his mouth and makes a call like an owl as he patrols the waters touting for water-taxi business.

Three hours later, the sun has set and the paraffin lamps are alight. After another voluminous meal I retreat to my small, airless bedroom and lie under the nylon netting to escape a swarm of mosquitoes that have gathered like bullies around the boat. Surdesh and Pradeep nonchalantly bed down for the night on the roof, completely unprotected. A motley chorus of frogs, crickets and jumping fish lulls us to sleep.

Before I leave Kerala, Sumesh has recommended that I spend a night at a homestay. Homestays are being touted as a win-win solution in Kerala as they provide an alternative income for communities, as well as helping to ease what state tourism officials say is a general shortage of hotel beds, due to the fast-rising number of arrivals. Homestays also claim to provide an opportunity to experience the way of life of Keralites at first hand.

About half an hour's drive from the historic fortified sea-port city of Kochi, on the edge of the backwaters, sits a small islet connected to the mainland by a short bridge. The islet is called Kallancherry and is home to around five hundred people, most of whom fish for prawns or work in the local coconut industry. Kumbalanghi, the large village near by, is described as the 'first model-tourism village in the country' by the state government, who say that the 'coastal hamlet without doubt provides a fascinating glimpse of the simple and prosperous livelihood of the villagers, and also unravels the age-old, magnificent culture and heritage of the place'. The scheme is supported with marketing and training by the national government and the United Nations Development Programme; Kumbalanghi is the first of thirty-one pilot villages across India experimenting with homestays.

George, a confident, handsome twenty-one-year-old, rushes out of his uncle's house – the Kallancherry Retreat, as it is listed for tourists – with an umbrella to shield me from yet another monsoon downpour. After showing me to my en-suite room, which is in an extension built on to the side of the home, we take a seat in the sitting room. There's cricket showing on a satellite channel on the large television and George leans over me to reach a socket to charge his mobile phone. I'm not sure what I had been expecting, but this homestay seems not dissimilar to staying in my own home. This view is compounded when cups of *chai* soon arrive.

'My uncle Lawrence started the homestay three years ago, after guests at his son's wedding here in the garden said how lovely it was and that it should be open to guests,' explains George. 'Tourism is half the income for the family now. In season, we have at least one Westerner staying here in one of our two rooms. And we host large lunches for family groups visiting from Kochi. We earn the rest of our money from farming crabs, catching prawns and fish, and processing coconuts into oil and coir. Lawrence's son now works as a chef in a restaurant in Welling Garden City in England. I'm helping out here while I wait to get into university...' He is interrupted by the Bollywood polyphonic ringtone from his mobile phone and spends the next few minutes making arrangements for a friend's party at the weekend.

After finishing our drinks and waiting for the rain to pass, we walk out into the garden; at the water's edge lie the large Chinese fishing nets that this stretch of coastline is so famous for. No Kerala tourism brochure is complete without a photograph of these large nets connected to a bamboo boom that can be lowered in and out of the water to catch 'small fry', as George calls it, such as mullet and prawns. George lowers a net, and within five minutes he raises it to reveal enough fish to make a modest meal for two. He throws them back into the water and we walk over to one of the tennis-court-sized ponds beyond the formal garden. The water seems to ripple with menace.

'This is where we farm crabs,' says George, lifting up a large net baited with fish and dragging it through the water. He then lets it rest on the bottom of the pond. Within a few seconds the handle jerks and he pulls out a huge crab. 'These get sent to Singapore when they weigh more than 2.5kg. We pack them live on to a train to Chennai and they go by boat from there. They can survive for seven days out of water without food.'

George walks me over to a nearby hut with mounds of coconut shells inside. 'Coconut is an important crop for us. We sun-dry the flesh, then extract the oil. We use the shells as fuel for fires, or to make curiosities such as hookahs for Arabian pipe smoking. The tuft is used to make coir carpet.'

It strikes me that George's family are not exactly on the breadline. They have a beautiful home and garden, and fingers in many pies, it seems. While it is undoubtedly a wonderful place to stay – my most enjoyable night in Kerala and a bargain at fifteen pounds for half board – it seems this might only really be an option for local families with enough money to offer a home that might attract tourists used to international hotel standards. Are these comparatively well-off families going to be the only ones in these communities to benefit from homestays? Does money always beget money? Even if that is the case, a homestay must still be a far superior option, both environmentally and socially, than building a hotel in the area to cater for tourists.

Later on, over an outstanding dinner of mullet curry, rice, dried prawns, onion curry and *appam* (fermented rice pancakes eaten across Kerala), made by George's aunt, Lawrence returns home. He greets me and asks how my time in Kerala has been.

'You follow in good company here,' he says. He reaches for the visitors' book on the sideboard and shows me the signature of V. P. Singh, the former prime minister of India, and on another page that of a daughter-in-law of Indira Gandhi. News of a good homestay travels just as fast as that of a good hotel, it seems.

4

A Pitching Wedge Away from the Sand Trap

Benidorm, Spain

No one forgets to pack their preconceptions when heading for Benidorm. This seaside town on Spain's Costa Blanca has featured in travel agents' brochures for half a century and has become synonymous with the 'sun, sand and sea' package-holiday formula enjoyed by many millions of tourists over this period. But since the 1980s, Benidorm has also come to symbolize the dog end of mass tourism: ill-conceived concrete façades; burger bars; kiss-me-quick souvenir stalls; crowded beaches; tattoos and beer bellies parading on the promenade.

As I approach Benidorm via the toll road from Alicante, a shimmer of skyscrapers slowly rises from the horizon in the desiccating heat. The town – the largest resort anywhere in the Mediterranean – tightly hugs two long beaches and contains some of Europe's tallest buildings. At fifty-two floors and fourteen years in the making, the Gran Hotel Bali is the tallest hotel in Europe and the tallest building in Spain. It stands in the south of the town, but as I continue along the five-kilometre length of Poniente and Levante beaches, dozens of other high-rise towers push into the sky along a grid of streets no deeper than a few hundred metres. There are said to be more hotel beds available in Benidorm than in any other place in Europe, except London and Paris.

I make my way through the traffic behind Levante beach – the focal point for British visitors – and park in the basement of Hotel Don Pancho, one of Benidorm's first high-rise hotels, with every one of its 252 rooms boasting a sea view. Built in 1972 during the town's earliest burst of skyscraper construction, the hotel sits on Avenida del Mediterraneo, the area's main thoroughfare, one block back from the beach. Inside, the hotel's décor still firmly embraces its 1970s roots, with brown and yellow featuring throughout.

In the lobby I am met by Francisco Selles, the hotel's director. He has worked at the Don Pancho since the very first day it opened and has watched Benidorm rise up around him. He clearly misses those early days of his career.

'Julio Iglesias once stayed here in our presidential suite,' he says with half a smile. 'But today it is reserved for our most important guests – the contract managers of the tour operators.'

Francisco's shoulders sink as he laments the changes that have occurred over the years. 'It is very different here now from when we first opened. Until 1976, we used to ask guests to wear a jacket and tie for dinner. Now we have difficulty getting men even to wear trousers to dinner. We have to have signs saying "Please do not wear shorts in the dining room". Everything changed in the 1980s. Television has changed people, I suppose, and we have had to change with them. Fifteen years ago we stopped having menus in the dining room and started doing all-you-can-eat buffets. That's what our guests want now.'

And yet, despite the hotel's efforts to meet the shifting demands of its clientele, business in Benidorm really started to drop away in the 1990s, Francisco tells me. 'The British-based tour operators – Thomson, First Choice, Airtours, etc. – have always been important to us. In the summer, 40 per cent of our guests are British. In the winter, this goes up to 80 per cent. We are very reliant on them. If we lose them, we will be finished. But now people have many choices.

The internet companies are a real threat to us. We used to get Americans staying here, but no more. The Italians and Germans don't come here any more, either. They say they don't like the buildings here being so high. We are now going to Russia, looking to get new guests. We didn't use to have any golf courses in Benidorm, but now we have built two as we are trying to get the Americans to return. We have built water parks and theme parks, too. People want more things to do than they did before.'

But, he says, Benidorm's increasingly desperate scramble for visitors is weakening the hoteliers' bargaining power with the tour operators. They are right to be fearful: in 2004 First Choice announced that it was axing the Costa Brava, the coastline north of Barcelona, from its brochures because of 'destination fatigue' and a lack of adequate hotels. In the same year, Club 18–30 dropped Benidorm as a destination.

'They always want lower prices from us,' says Selles. 'They never give us guarantees now about the number of visitors they are sending. They used to give us two to three weeks' "release time" on the rooms they booked, but now it is much less, which makes it hard for us to sell them if they cancel. The most important thing they ever write into a contract now is the price they will give for the room.'

Selles is perplexed by some of the other changes made by the tour operators. For example, he doesn't understand why they now send tourists from the airports without reps to accompany them. This used to be one of the ways in which the tour operators would earn extra income, by selling excursions to their captive audience in the transfer bus. However, the modern new world of 'dynamic packaging' – the latest buzzword among tour operators – whereby customers are encouraged to build their own holiday itinerary from a wide range of choices instead of selecting the pre-determined packages of old – doesn't seem to have reached the Hotel Don Pancho.

But not everyone in Benidorm mourns the changing habits of the world around them. Many within the town say most people have got Benidorm all wrong and any outdated misconceptions should be jettisoned. Matías Pérez Such, a former Benidorm councillor and now the tourism secretary of the Valencia region that includes the Costa Blanca, opposes those who sneer at the facilities Benidorm provides for its broadly working-class clientele. He describes the town as a 'living example of the democratization of tourism' that has occurred since the end of the Second World War. You can't knock a place that attracts over four million visitors a year, he says. Just because Benidorm is the 'best example of the society of social welfare and the society of the masses' does not mean 'that it is a mediocre place for mediocre people. The secret of Benidorm, and its success, lie in the fact that in its streets, hotels and establishments, miners, lawyers and aristocrats coexist with nobody bothering about the other's profession or the state of his or her bank account, or any other such prejudices. In short, it is neither exclusive nor excluding . . . Holidays are nowadays a right for everyone.'

I take a stroll along the promenade of Levante beach. It is clear that there are more labourers than lawyers or lords amid the ambling crowds, but the mix of nationalities is harder to pinpoint. The clientele certainly seems predominantly British; however, there are also Poles, Germans, Dutch, French and many Spaniards among the flow of people walking past me. The beach itself is clearly keenly managed at some expense, with clean, brushed sand sloping neatly down to the still sea fifty metres away. It has long held Blue Flag status from the EU. Men on the beach below the promenade earn tips from passersby with their epic sand sculptures depicting The Simpsons, Leonardo Da Vinci's *Last Supper* and a pair of braying stallions. A group of twenty or so pensioners swing their arms from side to side in an exercise class alongside a section of beach covered with umbrellas and neatly spaced sun loungers.

Just behind the now utterly dwarfed old streets of Benidorm's original village, which sits on a rock dividing the town's two beaches, I climb the steps to the new town hall. The building's sleek glass walls and crisp lines signal to all visitors that this is a town still extremely proud of its future-gazing heritage. While I wait in an antechamber to meet the town's new mayor, I am plied with pamphlets full of statistics about the town – 128 hotels, 38,000 beds, 343 restaurants, 247 cafés, 574 bars, 176 'disco-pubs', twenty-five discothèques, four bingo halls, six mini-golf courses, three theme parks and one water park. 'Big is best' has long been Benidorm's mantra.

I am shown into the wide, airy office of Manuel Pérez Fenoll. He stands up to greet me from behind his desk.

'It is hard to change the image people have in their heads of Benidorm,' he says, stroking his smart suit. 'But we really want to boast to everyone about all the changes we have invested in. Yesterday, I was in Hanover talking to Dr Michael Frenzel, the CEO of TUI.' TUI is Europe's largest tourism company: it owns 3,300 travel agencies, 100 aircraft and 300 hotels with 165,000 beds in 30 countries, and employs 60,000 people; in the UK, its best-known asset is Thomson, and in March 2007 it announced its intention to merge with First Choice. 'We only get 30,000 "TUI nights" from Germany,' he continues, meaning the total number of nights spent in Benidorm in a year by TUI customers. 'TUI wanted us to change our image, but we said no. We are going to show people in Germany new photographs of what we've done – the five-star hotels, the golf courses, the water park. But we need Italians and Scandinavians, too – we can't focus on just one market. I have many challenges as the mayor, but this is a very important one, of course.'

So other than attracting more visitors, I ask, what are his other challenges? Unemployment? Crime? Water supplies?

His face tightens at the mention of water. 'Spain has problems with water, of course. But I'm not worried about water here at the moment. We have a good system. We recycle our waste water here for the town's gardens. The Israelis have even come here to look and to learn about our system.'

There is a popular local theory that the skyscrapers of Benidorm actually provide a much more environmentally sustainable model for tourism in this arid area of the Mediterranean basin than the kilometre after kilometre of low-level developments that stretch along the length of Spain's costas, with their repeat motif of villa, pool, golf course, villa, pool, golf course. Better, so the theory goes, to have four million visitors contained in just a few square kilometres than spread out along many hundreds of kilometres of environmentally sensitive coastline that suffers from a dwindling natural supply of fresh water. As any gardener knows, it is more efficient to direct the flow of water neatly with a watering can than to cast it widely using a sprinkler.

Water has been a major political issue within Spain for many years. The country's key economic drivers – agriculture and tourism – are both highly thirsty beasts, drawing huge volumes of water each year from the country's rivers and aquifers. Inevitably, desalination plants have now begun to be built along the coastline; about 5 per cent of drinking water is already supplied this way. In 1975, the countries bordering the Mediterranean signed a convention and action plan, under the aegis of the United Nations Environment Programme, called the Plan Bleu, to help protect their common sea and its resources, including the sources of fresh water that run into it. Since then, scientists have monitored the impact of tourism in the region's main destinations, stretching from Spain, France and Italy, through Greece and Turkey, round to Israel, Egypt, Tunisia and Morocco. In 1984, these combined coastlines were visited by 96 million tourists. In 1990, this figure reached 132 million and by 2000 it stood at 176 million. By 2025, the prediction is that 312 million tourists will visit the region's coastlines. The Mediterranean coastline, 46,000 kilometres in length, is already 30 per cent urbanized; around popular tourist areas such as Málaga urbanization is higher than 50 per cent. If this predicted growth occurs, a further 5,000 kilometres of Mediterranean coastline will need to be developed to accommodate the tourists.

This is something that Spain, for one, can ill afford. Plan Bleu hydrologists estimate that the country is already over-exploiting its renewable water resources by 0.7 cubic kilometres a year, with an overall annual demand of 18.2 cubic kilometres. Sixty-one 'hydro-geological units' in Spain are now legally classified as 'over-exploited', as determined by a water law passed in 1985. For example, the Sierra de Crevillente aquifer near Alicante was first tapped in 1962; forty years later its water levels had sunk by 430 metres. Aquifers, as much of the world is now realizing, are not a limitless source of fresh water – their natural recharging process can take millennia.

Spain's efforts to work out a solution have been slow and riddled with political interference. The River Ebro in the north-east of the country, one of the Mediterranean basin's largest sources of fresh water, was long held to be the perfect answer. It was proposed that pipes would draw up to 3.35 cubic kilometres of water each year from the river and carry it down from its source in the Cantabrian mountains to supply hundreds of kilometres of parched coastline to the south. The plan, which also included the construction of 119 new dams, was finally ratified after decades of wrangling in 2002, but was then rejected again in 2004 upon the election of José Luis Rodríguez Zapatero's socialist government. An alternative plan was suggested: building twenty desalination plants at a cost of €3.7 billion. The new government claimed that these plants would be faster and cheaper to implement than the Ebro plan, but added that tourism facilities such as golf courses would be charged up to ten times as much for the water as farmers. Environmentalists were initially relieved that the Ebro wouldn't now risk being run dry through extraction, which would have threatened the protected wetlands of the Ebro delta. But desalination would require huge amounts of energy and would therefore present its own climate-change pressures. (A report published by Spain's Environment Ministry in 2006 said that sea-level rises caused by climate change would shrink Spain's Mediterranean beaches – many of which already have to truck or dredge in new sand before each season – by an average of ten metres over the next four decades.) Furthermore, the proposed solution only addressed the issue of supply, not the spiralling demand that was the root of the problem.

'It is a sickness of this area that we still don't have water,' says Pedro Zaragoza Orts, slapping the table with irritation. 'It has always been a problem. A big problem.'

Zaragoza, now in his mid-eighties, was the mayor of Benidorm from 1950 to 1967 and masterminded the plan to develop the then fishing village into a tourism jewel for Spain. He and his wife of fifty-six years still live in the same whitewashed villa a few kilometres back – and a world away – from Benidorm's hotel zone, set amid a peaceful garden of mature olive and pomegranate trees. It is humming with the sound of crickets on the evening I arrive to meet him. We sit together with his grandson, who has come to help translate, at the garden table, with a glass of Levantine wine to hand and the moon rising.

'We helped devise the plan to get water from the Ebro back in 1973, but today it is still associated by socialists with the Franco era, I'm afraid. They cancelled it.'

Like the Ebro plan, Zaragoza also still suffers from association with the period between 1939 and 1975 when Spain was under the dictatorship of General Francisco Franco.

'We took water from a nearby mountain at first, then built a reservoir between two mountains. Then we had to ask Madrid for funds. Now Benidorm takes its water from an aquifer near Alicante and from the same rain-water reservoir. But water is not the number-one problem here any more. No, the biggest problem is that the people are greedy. They love money and gold.'

Zaragoza's contempt for the current administrators of 'his' town is clear – in 2006 he publicly snubbed them by announcing that his personal archive would be bequeathed to the University of Alicante and not an institution in his home town. 'The marketing of Benidorm is now non-existent,' he says. 'You have to have the brain of a businessman to sell something, not that of a politician.' Zaragoza doesn't need much coaxing to tell me how he used his own skills to sell Benidorm to the world half a century ago. Even though he must have spoken of those days thousands of times before, he still has the enthusiasm of a schoolchild to recount it once more for me.

'I may be criticized now for being the mayor during the time of Franco, but I've always believed in the working people and in making peace. I invited Churchill here. I even had President Perón of Argentina stay here at my house for a month. I've hosted the Austrian royal family here. When I bought this house in the early 1950s we used to call Benidorm "paradise on earth". I had an idea to develop it for tourism.'

In 1953 he presented his *Plan General de Ordenación Urbana* to the local community, then just a couple of thousand strong. Their initial reaction must have been one of utter shock and bewilderment. A map he drafted of the fishing village and the surrounding farmland showed how a US-style grid of wide avenues would be created on fields which at that time were filled with little more than wandering goats and almond trees. As Zaragoza lays a copy of that same plan out on the table for me to study, it is striking how his vision is almost a carbon copy of the street layout today. He also shows me a map of the wider area, with the proposed plan to build a fifteen-kilometre canal to carry water from the Algar river, which runs through a small gorge towards the coastal town of Altea, just to the north of Benidorm. Again, it was carried out to the letter. It's tempting to think that things always tend to get done if it is the will of a dictator, but Zaragoza's ability to cajole, persuade and enthuse is still legendary today in Benidorm, despite his association with a time few seem keen to talk about.

'I took the grid model from how London and Berlin were rebuilding after the war. I had also travelled the world by boat as a boy aged twelve and had seen Sydney, London and Singapore. I thought this could be done in Benidorm. People in Madrid liked the idea.' By which he means Franco, of course. 'Back then it was easier than it could ever be now, because land was so cheap. We made some friends and we made some enemies, too. Most farmers said the land was too difficult to farm and welcomed the plans. But when we built Avenida del Mediterraneo in 1956 we had to move some farms to do so. It was tough at first. We only had the equivalent of a €400 budget today to clean the beach. We had actually already had a few tourists visiting Benidorm before the plan – Germans came here before the war because their doctors said the climate would be good for their health – but we didn't promote it. I had to come up with some ideas.'

He leans forward towards me out of his chair, as if to share a secret.

'I decided to grow orange trees for all my favourites – Queen Elizabeth II, Charles de Gaulle, etc. – and then I sent them the harvest each year as a gift. I had to travel to Helsinki to see a specialist about my psoriasis and I saw people castrating reindeer with their teeth! These were the indigenous Sami people from Lapland, who were being treated like Gypsies there at the time. I invited a couple of them to Benidorm and they arrived with dried reindeer in their suitcase as they didn't know what food to expect. But Franco himself received them personally when they arrived, and when they went into the sea for the first time they took all their clothes off except their socks. It created a huge media story. I also came up with the idea of sending the blossom of our almond trees to the citizens of Stockholm at Christmas time to remind them of the sun. Everyone got to know Benidorm's name. The price was also cheap – that's why the British came here on holiday. All northern Europeans were important to us, because they lacked sun.'

Zaragoza continues to reminisce about his glory days, to both our amusement. There was the time he brought the first British couple to Benidorm and they remained in their full complement of clothing throughout their entire stay. And there was the time he sent empty bottles labelled 'Benidorm Sunshine' to Buckingham Palace. And once he was almost excommunicated from the Catholic Church.

Zaragoza seems coy about telling the full story, probably because it is still seen today as a key turning point in the Church's centuries-old tradition of placing a firm, guiding hand on the policies of the state.

Tensions rose when Zaragoza signed an order authorizing the wearing of bikinis in Benidorm. 'The wearing of bikinis was a hot subject at the time,' he says. 'The minister of tourism had to go to the Church to get permission for people to wear them on the beaches.' The local archbishop was horrified and began the process of having him excommunicated, a fate worse than imprisonment in those days as he would have become a pariah in his own community. The Civil Guard began ordering female tourists to cover up, which upset their free-spirited northern European sensibilities and their desire to follow the fashion of the day.

'I decided to go and see Franco and sort it out,' Zaragoza says. 'I stuffed newspaper under my clothes to keep me warm and drove my Vespa through the night to Madrid.'

Within a few days, Franco had sent his wife, Carmen Polo, to Benidorm along with one of his ministers to show support for Zaragoza and soon the furore died down. The showdown is now seen as one of the first times that the state stood up to the Church and won. Quite why Franco risked picking a fight with the Church over such a seem-ingly trivial matter – especially when he was renowned for his moral austerity – becomes clear when you learn just how highly he valued tourism as a tool to legitimize his regime internationally.

Until the early 1950s, Spain was the focus of international sanctions following Franco's seizure of power during the 1936–9 Civil War. Despite being 'neutral' during much of the Second World War, Spain was viewed by the Allies as having barely camouflaged leanings towards the Axis powers, which meant that it had few international friends in the immediate postwar years.

However, as early as 1948, Franco had been using the slogan 'Spain is different' to try to promote the country as a tourist destination. He was wise enough to see that tourism would earn the country much-needed foreign currency and help broadcast Spain abroad – if not to the leaders of other countries, then at least to their citizens. A range of state-run apparatus for mass tourism was established – an airline, hotels, tourism offices, marketing associations – both to sell Spain abroad and to bring tourists, literally, to its shores. His efforts coincided with fledgling attempts elsewhere in Europe to begin cheap 'package tours' for tourists using charter flights.

In 1949, Vladimir Raitz, a twenty-seven-year-old Russian-born graduate of the London School of Economics, was on holiday in Corsica when he struck on the idea of chartering a plane and bringing tourists to the island, putting them in tents and feeding them local food and wine, all at an affordable price. Flying civilians around in anything other than a scheduled airliner was not looked on kindly by Britain's Ministry of Civil Aviation in the postwar period, but in early 1950 it agreed to the proposal, as long as it was for 'students and teachers' only. Confident of his idea, Raitz had already formed the Horizons Holiday Group, and in May 1950 a converted wartime Dakota took off from Gatwick airport heading for Calvi on Corsica, carrying the first-ever package tourists to travel by air – eleven teachers and twenty-one student friends of Raitz, each of whom paid £32.10s. Over the next decade, the destinations expanded to include, in turn, Majorca, Lourdes, Costa Brava, Sardinia, Minorca, Porto,

Costa Blanca and Costa del Sol. Spain became a much more attractive destination for companies such as Horizons from June 1954 onwards when, amid the thawing of international attitudes towards Spain, the Convention on International Civil Aviation was amended to ease the passage of charter flights into Spanish airspace.

By 1958, 300,000 Britons were holidaying in Spain annually. In 1960, with the aid of the recent devaluation of the peseta as part of a series of economic reforms, Spain overtook France in terms of the number of international visitors, and in 1964 it overtook Italy, too, to become the most-tourist-visited country in the world. Manuel Fraga Iribarne, who was Spain's minister for information and tourism from 1962–9 (that these two roles were shared says much), described tourism as 'our Marshall Plan': 'the great endorsement that the Spanish economy received from the developed countries and . . . the clearest cause of development for the Spanish economy'.

Iribarne helped to craft and sell an image of Spain abroad – flamenco, religious processions, olive oil, bull-running, locals on donkeys – that was largely reflective of Andalusia rather than Spain as a whole. It was a bit like saying to the world that haggis is the national dish of Great Britain. But as Zaragoza knew all too well, marketing Spain as 'different' to the sun-starved masses of the north was everything, and up until 1973, when the oil crisis temporarily dented the global tourism trade, Franco's plan to lure tourists to Spain worked – bar the odd hiccup over the wearing of bikinis – almost entirely to plan.

To see how dramatically tourism has changed Spain's Mediterranean coastline, you need only drive the length of the Autovía del Mediterráneo (listed on road maps as the A-7 and AP-7). This motorway, tolled much of the way, runs from La Jonquera on the border with France and sweeps down the coast, past Barcelona, Valencia, Benidorm, Alicante, Murcia, Almería, Málaga and Marbella, finally ending at

Algeciras next to Gibraltar. Along the way it ticks off all the Mediterranean-facing costas – Costa Brava, Costa Daurada, Costa del Azahar, Costa Blanca, Costa Cálida, Costa de Almería and, finally, Costa del Sol.

I pick it up as it passes Benidorm and travel two hours' south, skirting around Alicante and Murcia before turning off to join the road to San Javier, which sits at the northern end of the Mar Menor, the largest coastal saltwater lagoon in Europe and the location of La Manga, the giant sports resort made famous by the holidaying antics of various professional footballers.

The area is at the heart of a building boom that for the past decade has been raising large gated communities of holiday homes out of the dust-and-brushwood landscape typical of this corner of Spain. Just a couple of hours further south, near Almería, is a headland called Cabo de Gata, which is said to be the driest place in Europe. But in bold defiance of nature's will, these communities are verdant oases for their residents. It is rare for a villa not to have an inviting cerulean-blue swimming pool and be more than a pitching wedge away from a golf course. The stretch of coast from Murcia to Almería has been nicknamed the Costa del Golf by some, due to the number of courses being built: estimates vary, but in 2005 Spain's *El Pais* newspaper said that 130 golf courses were in development within the Valencia and Murcia regions alone, adding to the dozens there already. Many nationalities, including a large number of Spaniards, are drawn here to buy holiday homes, but the British are thought to lead the way, aided by the scores of flights arriving at the region's many airports from the UK each day. In 2003, 1.7 million Spanish homes were owned by foreigners, 400,000 of them by Britons. The Spanish Agency for Holiday Homes estimates that 50,000 houses a year are being bought by Britons. A significant number choose to move to Spain permanently, adding to the large ex-pat community, but many only visit their homes a handful of times a year. This has created a patchwork feel among communities, with a large number of homes empty at any given time. As thousands of villas continue to be sold to investors and second-homers from abroad, there has been growing resentment within Spain towards these developments. A select few – landowners and construction firms – have got very rich from the boom, but other Spaniards see it as fool's gold, a short-term rush for riches that is destroying the landscape and splintering any sense of community. Hand in hand with the industrial-scale agriculture that this land also has to sustain, the gated villages are adding to the strain on an area already gasping for fresh water.

In late 2006, a group who called themselves the 'Neighbours of Parcent' travelled to Brussels to hand in a petition complaining about the 'disastrous' development plans for Parcent, a village near Alicante with a population of one thousand, facing a tenfold increase in size due to a holiday-home construction project. In Alhama de Murcia, a town of 17,000 people just to the south of Murcia, the vote of one rebel politician in early 2006 temporarily halted Polaris World, one of the area's largest holiday-home developers, from starting a €4-billion 'Florida-style' project involving six linked resorts, eight Jack Nicklaus-designed golf courses, and three Intercontinental Hotels. Polaris World said it was the victim of a 'political and incorrect decision', which it said it would fight.

This discontent among the local communities taps into a growing sense of anger across Europe among residents of areas with a high concentration of holiday homes. In August 2006, Corsican separatists even went so far as to bomb holiday homes on the island, claiming that they were owned by foreign 'colonists' who were inflating property prices, making it impossible for Corsicans to buy properties in their own villages, thereby driving locals off the island and helping to erode the island's culture, economy and heritage. Similar sentiments have been aired from Cornwall all the way to Croatia.

The severe drought in Spain in 2005 – the worst in sixty years –

turned many Spaniards against the development companies and the swelling number of holiday homes. The Spanish government published findings that showed how much of the country's Mediterranean coast was being threatened with desertification – almost all the coastline around Alicante and Murcia was said to be under threat. It was not good news for a country so reliant on tourism: UNESCO, for example, estimates that tourists visiting Grenada in Spain use seven times more water than locals, with daily usage as high as 440 litres.

The government announced it was to begin a scheme to buy up ecologically sensitive areas of coastline threatened by development. The scheme included the enforced buy-back of some inappropriate building projects. Then in 2006 a special prosecutor announced that homes and hotels built without planning permission, or that failed to meet building regulations, would be demolished, whether or not the owners had been aware of this before they bought their property. Up to 100,000 buildings were estimated to be under threat, including one in Marbella owned by the former prime minister José María Aznar. In part, it was an admission that many buildings in the past had been thrown up behind a screen of corruption and kick-backs. It also reflected the views of tourists: visitor surveys showed repeatedly that tourists were not happy about the environmental degradation being caused by the building boom; this coincided with a slight drop in the number of visitors to Spain between 2002 and 2004, as well as a slowing down in house-price inflation. In 2005, Cristina Narbona, Spain's environment minister, issued a warning to the developers: 'In the short term, the construction boom can bring economic benefits with it; in the long run, it will most likely reduce the quality of tourism in the region.'

Also in 2006, a WWF report confirmed one of Spain's open secrets – that the country's already scarce water supply was being further exploited by more than 500,000 illegal boreholes. Water was being sold on the black market to farmers and developers operating in the country's arid regions. This followed an earlier WWF report, published in 2004, that studied the impact of tourism on the Mediterranean's fresh-water supplies. It said:

An area where tourism is having a great impact on freshwater ecosystems is the south-east region of Spain (Alicante, Almería and Murcia provinces), where the tourist sector has grown 50 per cent in the last five years and a further strong growth of the tourist market is foreseen. Murcia plans to double its tourist potential in the next ten years, to reach nearly one million hotel places and 100,000 new residences. This increase puts pressure on freshwater resources, especially during summer when the population in the south-east region is four times as big as during winter. With a corresponding quadrupling of water demand in the summer, water-supply systems are forced to base their dimensions on this period. Second-house tourism has the greatest growth potential in the tourist industry of the Spanish south-east: of every hundred houses built in Alicante, sixty are for the second-house market. Foreign tourists (80 per cent from Germany and UK) own 240,000 houses in the province of Alicante, which is the province in Spain with the highest number of residents coming from other EU countries. This residential tourism, normally characterized by high acquisition power, brings about water-supply problems. Indeed, residential complexes with gardens and swimming pools need significantly more water than flats with terraces (according to a study by the public-owned water company, in Madrid the difference in water use between these types of dwellings can be up to 100 per cent). Moreover, residential areas are often associated with the creation of high-water-consuming leisure activities like golf courses. Indeed, it is expected that the number of golf courses in the Valencia province will multiply by three in the next ten to fifty years and that Murcia province will host thirty-nine golf courses in the next ten years.

The report added that golf courses in the area need between 10,000 and 15,000 cubic metres of water per hectare a year – as much as a rice paddy. This means the annual water consumption of a whole course could reach one million cubic metres – the same as a town with a population of 12,000 inhabitants.

Golf courses have long been the focus of environmentalists, as well as groups concerned about 'land-use ethics', particularly in developing countries. In 1993 the Global Anti-Golf Movement was formed in Asia to protest at the spread of courses beyond Japan and across South-East Asia. The group's launch happened to coincide with the building of the world's largest golf resort – the 180-hole Mission Hills resort in Hong Kong. Chee Yoke Ling, who headed the movement in Malaysia, wrote in 1995 that 'besides displacing people, the golf business dramatically widens the gap between the rich and the poor. Contrary to the principle of sustainable development, the game, through alliances between politicians and developers, contributes to the conversion of livelihood-sustaining resources of the poor to opulence-sustaining resources for those who are already materially endowed.'

The movement seems to have largely failed in its objectives, as today there are about 31,500 courses around the world, up from 25,000 in the mid-1990s, which at the time would have covered an area the size of Belgium.

The group's manifesto stated that 'we reject the myth of "pesticide-free", "environmentally friendly" or "sensitive" golf courses'. Courses are built across a wide range of terrains from Thailand and Florida to Spain and Ireland, but just how much pesticide is typically sprayed on to these season-defying, emerald-green, weed-free stretches of clipped grass, and what impact does this have on wildlife?

Surprisingly little research has been completed on the subject, but there have been studies in the UK, which some claim to be the birthplace of golf. The UK has one of the highest golf-course densities in the world – about 0.6 per cent of the land is covered by 2,600 courses:

a 40 per cent increase in the past thirty years. Each course, at fifty to sixty hectares, is the size of a medium farm. However, in certain parts of golf courses, such as on the greens, the use of pesticides, herbicides and fungicides is higher than on farms. The pesticide-usage survey team of the Central Science Laboratory (an agency of Defra) found in the mid-1990s that on average 0.5 kilograms per hectare of 'active substances' were used each year on golf courses to defeat various 'problems', such as worm casts, moles, weeds, leather-jackets (daddy-long-legs larvae) and fungal diseases. The rate of application on greens was about fifteen kilograms per hectare, compared to 11.7 kilograms per hectare on potato fields.

Dr Alan Gange, a reader in microbial ecology at Royal Holloway, University of London, has examined whether courses act as 'habitat corridors' (sanctuaries for wildlife forced out of surrounding farmland and suburban sprawl), or as 'sinks' (initially attracting wildlife but then proving fatal to it due to the use of pesticides). Gange has found no evidence that they act as sinks, adding that some older courses (more than seventy years old) still contain much of the natural habitat from which they were originally constructed, thereby providing homes to rare species including natterjack toads, endangered orchids, red kites and sand lizards. The courses he cites as having a notably positive environmental impact include Royal St George in Kent (which hosts up to 90 per cent of the UK's tallest native orchid, the lizard orchid), Ipswich golf club (the only course to have twice won the British & International Golf Greenkeepers' Association's environment award) and Askernish on the Hebridean island of South Uist (the nearest the UK has to an 'organic' course, because the island's abundant seaweed is used for fertilizer, and the weather is so 'fresh' that many pests and fungi can't survive). These are the exceptions, though. Gange says that the average pay-and-play public course is 'environmentally quite poor', as are the top-end, exclusive clubs because of their above-average use of pesticides.

The challenges of maintaining courses in the temperate climate of northern Europe are quite different, though, from those of sun-blessed yet water-poor Spain.

My car pulls up at the entrance to the Mosa Trajectum Golf Resort, which is halfway between Murcia and San Javier. Two security guards armed with clipboards step out of their small office and approach me. I am directed to a large car park on the far side of the 360-hectare complex, next to the resort's social club. As I make my way along the main thoroughfare, I pass dozens of villas, most of which appear to be unoccupied. No one is walking along the pavements. There are no cars parked in the driveways. Few windows have curtains. Cranes stand over half-finished buildings. It has the air of an epic film set.

Mosa Trajectum is part of Key Resorts, a Dutch-owned group that has plans to build eight such complexes across Spain. This is the first in its plan, and when completed will offer 1,500 villas and apartments spread across a plot of land that contains three golf courses offering twenty-seven holes, plus a nine-hole pitch-and-put course. Such a lifestyle choice isn't cheap. The prices are as socially excluding as the high walls that ring the site: €200,000–600,000 for an apartment, or up to two million euros for a villa with a thousand-square-metre garden.

I'm met by Robert and Donald Voogd, two young Dutch brothers who have been responsible for building and maintaining the resort's golf courses since work started in 2000. They claim to have come up with a way to allow golf courses to exist in arid conditions without presenting a threat to water supplies. It seems like a boast only the most foolhardy would wish to make, but they are confident that their system could revolutionize not only the golfing world, but also the way that farmers maintain their crops in similar conditions.

'We hold the licence for Spain and Portugal to use a foam technology called Fytofoam, which was developed by a company called Verheijen Resins in Holland,' says Robert.

He explains that tiny foam balls are mixed with sand and gravel, which is then sown with Bermuda grass seed. The foam acts as a sponge, so that moisture is retained beneath the grass instead of draining away or evaporating. The urea-based resin used to make the foam is 'basically nitrogen' and will last in the ground for fifteen to twenty years.

'The Dutch owner was looking to save water here as he was concerned about the ecology of the area,' says Robert. 'Working with the Alterra Research Institute at the Wageningen University in Holland, we built two test greens here to show him how it worked. A typical US Golf Association regulation green needs about 1,800 millimetres of rain per square metre a year in this climate. But with the foam we got this down to a thousand millimetres. Our two sites – we now have one in Portugal, too – are the only golf courses in the world to use it, although I've heard that one in Australia is now experimenting with it. The Middle East would be the obvious place to take it next.'

We walk past their two test greens – one patchy and the other a more uniform green – to the tee of the tenth hole, which skirts a large artificial lake used to water the course and the surrounding landscaped gardens. The water level is extremely low, exposing the lake's white lining.

On the foothills in the distance, the plastic sheeting of the region's large farms glistens in the sun. Under it grow tomatoes, melons, cucumbers, and much of the other fresh produce that graces our supermarket shelves. Uniform rows of mandarin and lemon trees stand alongside.

I ask Robert what impact this foam might have on the soil.

'To treat a thirty-five-hectare course – tees, greens and fairways – you would need about 400,000 litres of resin. But this is biodegradable. It's a secret recipe, but it is basically methanol and urea. As it biodegrades it releases nitrogen into the soil which acts as a fertilizer. We also use controlled-release fertilizers here, using monitors linked to a computer. This means the courses need less maintenance and fewer pesticides. The foam means there's about 85 per cent less run-off compared to agricultural fertilizer.'

He says his dream is to convince farmers in the area to try using the foam.

'Farming here has changed a lot just in the last three or four years. There was a lot of potato disease. The farmers were using a lot of methyl bromide on the soil and now they have started building these plastic greenhouses you see everywhere. But the foam would drastically cut back their need for water. They currently have to pay to use water from the *trasvase* – canals used to move water around the area.'

Before this can happen, though, the brothers must prove themselves by using the foam successfully on their golf courses. But Robert seems bullish about his chances.

'Water is obviously a huge issue here. We get about six hundred millimetres of rainfall per square metre here a year. A normal golf course would use about three times this amount. But look how empty the lake is here. If there is less rain than average, as has been the case this summer, it is a big problem. We are all waiting for the *gota fria* – the annual "cold drop" of rain that we get each September to October. We have to cut down the trees now to save the greens and the tees. The law here says that you can't use well water or tap water for irrigation. But many courses do use well water – they have to, just to survive. Everyone talks about it, but no one acts. You're meant to be self-sufficient. Our plan is to use treated waste-water from the houses on the course. We will be able to sell any spare water to other developments near by, such as Polaris World, which has five thousand houses. This foam costs about €2.50 per square metre, so to treat a thirty-five-hectare, eighteen-hole course would cost about a million euros, but this would be paid back in water savings in two to three years. Some developments now just make the golf courses look green when they are trying to sell their villas; once they're all sold they stop main-taining the course because it's not cost-effective. Before working here on this course, I had a company exporting fruit from Spain up to Russia by truck, before the market collapsed in the late 1990s. Back then, I was exporting water from this country in the form of fruit. Now I like to think that I'm saving water for Spain.'

The Voogd brothers' enthusiasm seems genuine, but I can't help wondering whether this is yet another example of desperately trying to extinguish the fire, rather than taking preventative measures to stop it igniting in the first place. If it takes 400,000 litres of resin to prepare just one course with this foam, think of the volumes required to feed Spain's ballooning number of golf courses, let alone the many thousands of others in equally arid climates around the world. And even with the foam installed, according to the brothers' sums, a golf course in this area would still demand 66 per cent more water than naturally falls from the skies. Is our whimsy for hitting a small ball towards a hole in the ground with a metal stick really worth scarring these already water-imperilled landscapes to the extent that we do?

5

A Massage for Mr Average

Bangkok and Pattaya, Thailand

Som's night shift always starts with a takeaway. She pulls a range of steaming food containers from a plastic bag and lays them out between her five girlfriends, who are sitting cross-legged in a circle on the floor. The feast includes beef salad, fermented fish, sticky rice and Som's childhood favourite – a fiercely hot green papaya salad.

But the most important ingredient is still to come. Her friend Bom, the eldest of the group at thirty-three, is given the crucial task of pouring the drinks – a cocktail of Mekong rice whiskey and 'M-150', a super-strength high-energy caffeine drink. All six women stub out their cigarettes and start to eat. They need as much sustenance and vim as they can get: within an hour they will begin a ten-hour shift, competing with each other and sixty-five other women in a go-go bar in Bangkok's world-famous red-light district Patpong, trying to attract the eye – and cash – of a *farang*, the Thai term for a Westerner.

The women's daily ritual sees them find a quiet corner to eat and drink before putting on their make-up and red bikinis ready to start work. Tonight they have gathered on the third-floor stairwell landing of a run-down, dimly lit building. There is a pervasive sweet smell from the hair salon downstairs run by a Thai sex-worker charity called the Empower Foundation, which says it takes a non-judgemental stance on prostitution and offers free education, counselling and skills training. It was the hunch of Supreeya, my 'fixer' (the term foreign correspondents use for local translators who also help to arrange hard-to-secure interviews), that this would be a good place to come to chat to some sex workers – the women themselves hate the term 'prostitute' – about their lives. Without someone such as Supreeya, an ethnic Chinese Thai woman in her fifties who works as a fixer for the BBC, the *Washington Post* and various other major news organizations, there is no way that I, a male *farang*, could ever hope to get these women to talk to me openly.

At twenty-three, Som is the youngest of the women and the most eager to talk. The others all call her 'Superstar', as she regularly attracts two men a night to pay to have sex with her. Her earning power gives her a status and confidence among her friends that belies her youthfulness. Supreeya tells me that Som and the other women are not from Bangkok, but from Isan, the north-eastern region of Thailand. It is the poorest part of the country and by far the largest source of labour for Thailand's huge sex industry. Supreeya can tell where the women are from not only by their dialect and looks – having a darker skin tone and softer bridge to the nose than most other Thais – but by what dishes they're eating. Som finishes her green papaya salad, swigs some whiskey, and, with occasional pauses for nervous laughter or emotional reflection, tells us what led her to the neon-bright, bawdy streets of Patpong.

'My family are fishermen in Ubon Ratchathani [Isan's most easterly province that borders Laos]. My father doesn't know what I do. I'm a bad girl, I know, but I feed twelve people in my family by working here. I am very sad. The guys I sleep with are all bad men. They just want to fuck, fuck, fuck for two hours. Then they push me away and make me leave in five minutes. We all have to buy our own condoms.'

Som explains that she used to be a housemaid earning 4,500 baht (£65) a month, but got introduced to Patpong's earning potential a few years ago by a friend who knew the local value of her looks. She and her family have now become utterly reliant on this income. Som's friends say they earn a minimum of 10,000 baht (£140) a month, including tips, being 'go-go girls', but Som can earn 4,000 baht on a 'good night' which will involve two separate two-hour sessions with *farang*. She says with evident relief that due to her 'superstar' status, unlike her friends she doesn't need to have sex with Thai men, who pay much less.

All the women work for one of Patpong's biggest go-go clubs. As with most clubs and bars in Thailand, they earn a basic monthly wage – in their case around 5,500 baht – from selling drinks for a 40-baht commission and keeping a small cut of the 500-baht 'bar fine' that any customer needs to pay to allow a girl to leave the bar for an hour or two to have sex with them. If they don't earn this monthly minimum they are quickly fired. Some clubs have 'short-time' rooms which can be rented for an extra cost (the women keep 100 baht from this exchange), or customers can take the women back to their hotel for 'long-time', typically the whole night. Occasionally, they will be paid 'long-haul', meaning that a tourist will pay a lump sum for a woman to be with him for the length of his holiday.

'If we are late for our shift the owners deduct three baht for every minute we're late,' says Som. 'We are allowed two days off a month and we get fined 600 baht if we don't work on a Friday or Saturday night. Plus, 300 baht is deducted every three months for our blood test. I want to stand up to them and form a union, but the other girls are too scared about losing their job. The big boss never hears our cries.'

Som says that she meets many nationalities of men in Patpong. This prompts her friends to start grading them according to how much they pay. 'Americans, northern Europeans and Japanese give the most,' says Bom. 'Italians give no tips and Russians are bad, too. But what we always want are older men, over thirty. They always pay more and are usually not so violent.'

Bom says that she, like most of the other women, manages to send her relatives in Isan about 30–40 per cent of her monthly earnings. 'My family see me as an ATM. They don't realize that Bangkok is expensive. I sometimes spend up to 500 baht a day on taxis, food, hairdressing, clothes and make-up. The club doesn't pay for any of this, even though it is all for work. I often have to borrow money from the Indian loan sharks. They charge 20 per cent interest a week.'

It is no surprise that Bom appears utterly exhausted by her life: she has worked in Patpong since the age of seventeen. 'I have a fifteen-year-old son, who doesn't know what I do. I only see him for an hour in the afternoon before I leave for work at five p.m. He thinks I work in a factory. I have two younger children, too, but they are with my family in Isan. I see my four-year-old girl once a year when I return. My husband makes me be a prostitute as it pays well. He was in prison but is out now. He is out of work, though. He beats me if I don't bring home enough money, and says I must sleep with *farang* as they pay more.'

Tears start to roll down Bom's face, and she clutches Supreeya's hand tightly for comfort. Some of the other women are now sobbing, too. Both Supreeya and I gesture to her that we can stop and leave, but Bom insists that we stay. 'No, I want you to hear my life.' She lights a cigarette.

'We are all risking disease. We may have smiling faces, but we are very sad inside. It is very hard to tell if customers are good or bad, or have diseases. We have to have an internal check-up once a week by the company doctors. Luckily, I don't take drugs, but many girls here in Patpong are addicted to something. Most take *yaba* [tablets that contain a mixture of methamphetamine and caffeine; they are also commonly taken by long-distance bus drivers in Thailand]. All of us have to drink to get the courage to work.'

Bom stands up and announces to the other women that she wants Supreeya and me to see them 'at work' inside the go-go club. Half an hour later, Supreeya and I form a no-doubt-unlikely sight by entering the club together. At first, it seems a relief to get away from the bustle of the street, with men insistently hawking 'Bangkok's famous ping-pong show' at every turn and the dense throng of foreign tourists and ex-pats, many of whom are clearly here just to witness Patpong's notoriety first hand as sightseers. But there is certainly no comfort to be found inside.

The club is smaller than I had expected, considering how many women are said to work here. The ceiling is low and the mirrored walls and dim lighting around the edges of the room compound the sense of disorientation I feel as I enter. A rush of chilled air hits us as we are met by the *mamasan* (a Japanese term used widely in east Asia for an older woman who acts as cashier, supervisor and security officer in such clubs). She takes us to stools directly beneath the raised, thin stage, surrounded by a bar and further banquette seating behind. Around the room sit half a dozen *farang*, well apart from one another, each with two or three dancers sitting beside them holding drinks. No one is talking.

On the stage ten poles are fixed from floor to ceiling, around which ten women in identical bikinis gyrate slowly and somewhat unsteadily in high heels, each with a number pinned to their sides. Their expressions are vacant as the thud, thud, thud of the dance music pounds deafeningly. The *mamasan* shows me her laser pen and beams a red dot on a dancer to indicate how I should choose one to have a drink with me. She hands me a drinks menu and returns to her counter by the door.

As a new track starts to play, the dancers all leave the stage and are replaced by others, including Bom and Som. Upon seeing Supreeya and me, they nudge each other, force a small smile at us, and nervously join their colleagues at the poles. It is a deeply depressing and uncomfortable sight to see these two women, with whom we have just spoken at length, withstanding such obvious humiliation. What they must contend with beyond this stage, with customers such as those sitting around me, I fight not to consider.

We quickly order them drinks and they step down from the stage to join us. But with the music so loud it is hard to talk any further, so we sip our drinks and look awkwardly into space. Within ten minutes they gesture that they fear what the *mamasan* might be thinking, as I'm not motioning to her that I intend to pay a bar fine, so they stand up to return to the stage. As they leave, I notice that they both reluctantly peel their hands from Supreeya's motherly grasp under the bar. We motion our thanks and get up to leave. Their ten-hour shift still has over nine hours to go.

Sex tourism is defined by the UNWTO as 'trips organized from within the tourism sector, or from outside this sector but using its structures and networks, with the primary purpose of effecting a commercial sexual relationship by the tourist with residents at the destination'.

Of course, prostitution is available to tourists in some form or other in virtually every tourist destination in the world, but some countries and cities stand out – whether the reputation is justified or not – as magnets for sex tourists, such as Amsterdam, Prague, Las Vegas, Moscow and Rio de Janeiro. Thailand's reputation as Asia's major sex-tourism destination is probably only rivalled by the Philippines, although Cambodia and Vietnam are catching up fast. Travellers from the region have been paying for sex in Thailand for centuries, but the area was popularized in the minds of Westerners by the 'R&R' (Rest and Recreation) antics of American servicemen during the Vietnam war. Ever since, international tourists have been buying cheap sex in Patpong and Bangkok's other red-light areas, such as Soi Cowboy and Nana Plaza, which remain ever popular with *farang*. Further afield, popular Thai resort areas such as Pattaya and Phuket also have strong reputations as major sex-tourism destinations.

In 1998, the United Nation's International Labour Office published a study examining the social and economic forces driving the growth of the sex industry in Indonesia, Malaysia, the Philippines and Thailand. It estimated that between 0.25 and 1.5 per cent of the total female population in each country were engaged in prostitution, supplying both domestic and foreign markets. With Thailand's population now standing at around 65 million, this would, theoretically at least, put the number of sex workers in Thailand anywhere between 160,000 and a million women. Of course, many thousands of boys, men and *katoeys* (transsexuals, more commonly called 'ladyboys') are sex workers, too. The study added that because the sex industry had assumed the dimensions of a full-blown commercial sector within these countries, it was likely to provide direct and indirect employment to millions of workers and contribute substantially to each country's national income.

Interestingly, the report argued that in Thailand the growth of prostitution was probably driven not only by economic factors but also by the government's promotion of tourism as an important earner of foreign currency for the country. The Tourism Authority of Thailand (TAT) says it has worked hard to rid the country of its sex-tourism tag by heavily promoting it as a family destination, shopper's paradise and 'health-tourism destination' (health tourism is a booming industry that sees tourists visiting a country both for a holiday and to benefit from cheaper medical treatments or operations than they can get at home), but despite their efforts, Thailand is still perceived by many as very much a 'male' destination. It doesn't help that TAT's own message can, despite its promises, seem a little opaque at times. For example, in its *Travel Trade Guide 2006*, which it sent to UK travel agents to suggest how they should promote Thailand to customers, under the heading 'How To Sell' it recommended selling the country to 'singles': 'It's hard to imagine a better destination for single travellers ... Bangkok and Pattaya are especially single-friendly.' Anyone who knows Pattaya, in particular, would know what to read between the lines.

In 2004, Thailand received 11.65 million international tourists, according to TAT. It is impossible to know what percentage of these visitors were sex tourists – defined as someone who pays for sex abroad, whether or not this was their intention before setting out – but judging by the wide variety of tourists that can be seen with Thai 'girlfriends' on their arms, it is certainly not restricted to the cliché of the lonely, middle-aged man. Backpackers to businessmen travel to Thailand and buy sex.

According to Julia O'Connell Davidson, a professor of sociology at Nottingham University, who has been studying sex tourism around the world since the early 1990s, there are three broad categories of male sex tourist. They were laid out in a chapter called 'British Sex Tourists in Thailand' which she contributed for a book published in 1995 entitled *(Hetero)sexual Politics*.

'Macho Lad' describes 'skilled and unskilled manual workers in their early twenties, many with the tattoos and semi-shaven heads that are associated with the far-right in Britain'. According to O'Connell Davidson, these men 'were aware that rural poverty leaves most sex workers few alternatives. They conclude from this that sex tourism is a highly positive phenomenon, almost a form of welfare that the West can give a "backward" nation. One Macho Lad, with a paternalistic air, said, "If these men stopped coming here, I'd hate to think what would happen to these girls."'

Next is 'Mr Average'. Such men are 'usually older, widowed or divorced ... in Thailand for their second or third time. All had first come on package tours, some specifically for "single men". Mr Average may be a skilled manual worker, self-employed or in a junior or middle-management position . . . They claim never to visit prostitutes at home and the fact that in Thailand "you don't feel as if you're going with a prostitute" is of central importance. Mr Average spends a great deal of time telling himself and others about how "different" Thai women are: that they think differently, are more innocent and loyal than Western women, and find white skin attractive. He explains the women's involvement without referring to the commercial transaction that is taking place. Some are aware that poverty forces the sex workers into the industry. This is clearly a source of anxiety for Mr Average. They cannot fully convince themselves that they are truly desired or that a fair exchange is taking place. They then strive to "treat the girls well", by which they mean giving tips and gifts, which are hardly generous by British standards. A number of these men expressed great ambivalence towards the sex workers, moving from paternalistic sympathy ("They do it for their families") to hostility ("They're hard bitches, really") in the space of a few minutes' conversation.'

Lastly, there's 'Cosmopolitan Man'. He is more bourgeois, often well educated and well travelled. 'They are keen to differentiate themselves from their compatriots: "I am not a sex tourist", "I am not a package tourist", "I am here on business." Several said they would never visit a prostitute anywhere else in the world. Thailand is different, first because "it's very easy and convenient" to buy sexual services here, and second because Thai women are so "natural" and "innocent" that the transaction does not feel purely commercial.'

Dr Jacqueline Sánchez Taylor, a lecturer at the School of Sociology and Social Policy at the University of Leeds, has studied female sex tourism around the world, including at the popular Jamaican resort of Negril. Whilst researching a paper published in the journal

Sociology in 2001, she found almost a third of the 240 women she interviewed (which included other women in two similar resorts in the Dominican Republic) had paid for sex with local men, some in search of what was referred to as 'big bamboo'. Nearly two-thirds of the women who used prostitutes admitted to there being an 'economic element' to their liaisons with the men, but most did not see the men as prostitutes, believing they were helping the men by giving them money and gifts.

Sánchez Taylor said that many of the female sex tourists were able to delude themselves into believing that they were not users of prostitutes: 'Racist ideas about black men being hypersexual and unable to control their sexuality enable them to explain to themselves why such young and desirable men would be eager for sex with older and/or overweight women, without having to think that their partners are interested in them only for economic reasons.'

Delusion and denial of the sex worker's motives are clearly important parts of the equation for any sex tourist. An equally convenient forgetfulness about the health risks that both they and the prostitute face seems to help them justify their desires, too. STDs and the threat of HIV/AIDS remain huge concerns among sex workers in Thailand, even though the use of condoms is now thought to be near 100 per cent among those serving tourists, following a government-led campaign in the early 1990s. The rate of use is sadly lower for those serving the domestic market, where condom use is still frowned upon by some.

There are those that would argue that no matter how seedy or morally inappropriate the liaison between a tourist and a prostitute may be, it is still an encounter between two consenting adults. Furthermore, it is often a legal encounter. For example, in Thailand the legal status of prostitution is conveniently blurred. Brothels are illegal, but the rendering of 'special services', say at massage parlours or bars, is tolerated because such transactions are legally arranged between the client and the sex worker and don't, in theory, involve the venue. In Thailand, though, as in many other destinations, this argument is greatly undermined by the fact that many of the sex workers are under eighteen, even though the client may claim ignorance of this fact. Although the age of consent in Thailand is sixteen, it has been illegal to pay for prostitutes under the age of eighteen since 1996. Far worse, of course, is the active searching by a small minority of sex tourists for children with whom to have sex.

In 2001, UNICEF, the United Nations Children's Fund which 'works for children's rights, their survival, development and protection, guided by the Convention on the Rights of the Child', published research into the number of child prostitutes working around the world. It listed Thailand in third place behind India and the US as the country with the greatest number of child prostitutes. According to UNICEF's findings, about 200,000 'women and children' were being sexually exploited in Thailand, with a third of this figure estimated to be under eighteen. The report also said that prostitution accounted for 10–14 per cent of the country's gross domestic product from 1993–95. In comparison, Thailand's Ministry of Labour and Social Welfare estimated in 2001 that the number of children under the age of eighteen working in prostitution was between 22,000 and 40,000.

None of this is news to ECPAT (the acronym stands for 'End Child Prostitution, Child Pornography and Trafficking of Children for Sexual Purposes'), a network of organizations and individuals working across seventy countries 'to eliminate the commercial sexual exploitation of children'. The organization has been instrumental in persuading over two hundred tourism companies around the world, such as Kuoni, TUI and Virgin, to sign up to 'The Code', an educational, training and awareness campaign aimed at preventing child-sex tourism.

'When it began in 1989, ECPAT started off focusing on tourism,' says Luc Ferran, who works at the office of ECPAT's International Secretariat in central Bangkok as the programme officer for combating trafficking and child-sex tourism. 'Most of the hardcore sex tourists today would never touch children, but I think there are a lot of sixteen to seventeen-year-olds working as prostitutes. We operate under the international convention that anyone under the age of eighteen is a child.

'Many of the children, like most prostitutes here, come from northern Thailand and Isan. We ran a research project in the Chang Rai province and it was poverty, pure and simple, that was driving prostitution. They say they are supporting a family member. Many are from the ethnic-minority hill tribes up there, such as the Karen [who face widespread institutional discrimination and persecution in both Burma, where they originate, and Thailand]. I was interviewing some girls in a bus station, from where they were offering sex in a shabby place right next door. These tribes don't have citizenship status in Thailand and need a special blue ID card to travel outside their area. But the police will be bribed to get the children down to Bangkok and beyond. I met a tour operator up there who said he knew foreigners living in the area who had organized trips to Burma to have sex with children. He also said he had had some tourists asking for the same thing. This sort of thing is more common across the Cambodian border, though.'

Children are also trafficked, as are many women, across the border to work in the Thai sex industry. Most commonly they come from Burma, Cambodia, China and Laos. Boys and girls from neighbouring Burma and Cambodia are typically used as prostitutes or made to work in begging gangs. Most of the women who are trafficked are prevented from returning by being kept in 'debt bondage', whereby the criminal gang that orchestrates the trafficking pays the woman's family a large sum in lieu of future earnings. It then becomes impossible for the woman – or sometimes the child – ever to pay back the initial debt once it starts to accrue interest, and they become trapped.

The issue of child-sex tourism has received increased international attention in recent years, largely due to the case of the former pop star Gary Glitter, who in 2006 was jailed for three years by a Vietnamese court after it found him guilty of molesting two girls, aged eleven and ten, at his home in the resort of Vung Tau in southern Vietnam. He had earlier been permanently expelled from Cambodia and had also spent time in Cuba, both well-known child-sex-tourism destinations. He had also spent time in prison in the UK for possessing images of child pornography on a home computer.

Ferran says he is pleased that justice was served on Glitter, although he still has concerns. 'There is sometimes a danger that a case such as Gary Glitter's, or even an awareness campaign such as the one now being screened on Air France flights, can actually raise the profile of an area for paedophiles. But with the Glitter case he was sentenced by the Vietnamese authorities and that does send a strong signal.'

Ferran says that over the past decade the fight against child-sex tourism has resulted in a number of victories, but the issue remains a grave concern, especially as there's evidence that the problem can simply get displaced elsewhere. 'I think there is a general recognition that it has reduced here in Thailand, especially with regard to pre-pubescent children. It is still happening in Pattaya, but in my personal opinion it is moving away from here. There isn't much of a brothel child-sex industry here, whereas in Cambodia there most certainly is. Phnom Penh, the Cambodian capital, was a big destination maybe two or three years ago, but now it is the resort of Sihanoukville in southern Cambodia. We predict that it will improve in Cambodia, but this could mean the problem is displaced once again – say, to Laos, especially as there is a major road being built between Cambodia, Laos and China at the moment with money from the Asian

Development Bank. Manila in the Philippines is a big destination, too. More widely, India has the largest industry in the world, and Sri Lanka and Brazil are also very active. There are even reports of tours of the Amazon for child-sex tourists. Northern Russia is becoming a new destination. For example, Finns go to St Petersburg, plus the Baltic States are emerging, too.'

A number of African countries cause concern as well. For example, in December 2006, a UNICEF report stated that up to fifteen thousand girls aged between twelve and eighteen were selling 'casual sex for cash and goods' in the main tourist destinations on the Kenyan coast. A further two to three thousand girls and boys worked as full-time prostitutes. It said that Kenyan men were the largest single group of clients, comprising 38 per cent of the total, but that Italian, German and Swiss male tourists accounted for 18, 14 and 12 per cent respectively. The report stated: 'Child-sex workers are often compelled to deliver sexual services to Kenyans – beach boys, bar staff, waiters and others – in order to access tourists. During the low tourist season, the local market for child-sex workers keeps the system going.'

There has been some success in tackling child prostitution, due to the fact that a number of Western countries from which child-sex tourists travel have now passed laws allowing their own authorities to prosecute, even though the crime has taken place in another country. Ferran cites the case of Amnon Chemouil as perhaps the most high-profile instance to date.

In 2000, Chemouil, a forty-seven-year-old French public-transport worker, was sentenced to seven years in prison in France for raping a girl whilst on holiday in Pattaya in 1994. He was tracked down by the French police after a video of him molesting the girl was discovered by Swiss police during the arrest of two Swiss men Chemouil had met in Thailand. The video, shot by one of the other men, showed Chemouil forcing the girl to perform oral sex on him in a hotel room for the equivalent of £2. This was the first case in which the French authorities were allowed to use such evidence. It also saw the extraordinarily brave girl, aged seventeen by the time of the trial, travelling to France to testify against Chemouil.

The UK passed similar acts in 1997 and 2003, enabling British courts to prosecute against crimes committed abroad such as this. But to date only a handful of cases have been heard; the process is not helped by loopholes which allow known paedophiles making trips abroad that last three days or less not to register these with the police, and which only allow prosecution to be carried out if sex with an under-aged child is an offence in the destination country. In Australia, by contrast, over thirty people have been prosecuted under such laws. While other innovations now exist, such as an international register of paedophiles, which contains details of thousands of offenders and is widely shared among police forces, Ferran says that not all child-sex tourists are what could be described as archetypal paedophiles.

'There are two types of child-sex tourists – preferential and situational. The latter will only begin to experiment with having sex with children once on holiday and presented with the option.'

He also says that cultural demands can shatter the presumed profile of these offenders. For example, there is a practice among some African and Asian men of 'virgin seeking', which sees men pay a high price for sex with virgins. This inevitably leads many men into having sex with minors, even though this may not have been their initial intention. But sex with children is still sex with children, says Ferran. There should never be excuses. The motives make no difference to the children – or to the methods of finding them.

'In Pattaya there are some bars where there will be ten-to-eleven-year-old boys sitting out front. It is clear as day in some cases. At the ages of fourteen to sixteen it becomes more open. At seventeen, there are no bones about it at all. From what I have seen, there are areas where tourists know or have heard that sooner or later children will show up. Speaking to some of the Western police officers who have come here, they have followed child-sex offenders to areas that are known for having children around, either begging or for prostitution. Some have approached children who, say, are selling flowers at traffic lights and lured them this way. This is the classic 'raincoat' approach. Or a tourist will tend to get to know the child first – grooming them – by perhaps spending three or four days with them. In Pattaya you will find children in the eight-nine-ten age range. Many of them will be orphans or will have run away from home. Worryingly, it's plain as day in Pattaya that people are buying apartments there to be sex tourists. Most of the real estate offered is geared up to foreigners.'

Another obstacle is police corruption. Despite there being a mandatory sentence of seven to ten years in Thailand for sexual offences against children, Ferran says many men who get caught with children simply pay 'bail' and end up walking free, and then quickly flee the country.

Police corruption is a popular topic of discussion among Thais. Perhaps the most high-profile example involves Chuwit Kamolvisit. In 2004, Kamolvisit, Thailand's largest massage parlour and go-go club owner, formed a political party and ran for the office of Bangkok governor on a ticket against police corruption. He himself had been arrested in 2003, accused of trying to raze slums to build more clubs in Bangkok, and admitted he had made many bribe payments to hundreds of police officers over a ten-year period. In 2005, he was elected to the Thai House of Representatives, although the country's political crisis in 2006 saw him removed from parliament. In 2006, after a three-year trial, he was acquitted in the slum-clearing case and subsequently turned the area into a public park. He was also earlier acquitted of charges that three girls aged between fifteen and seventeen had been found in one of his parlours, after it was decided he could not have known they were using fake ID. His public stand against police corruption saw him jointly named 'Person of the Year' by the Thai paper *The Nation* in 2003.

'I have heard that people just say, "Here, I'm leaving this money on the table, can I leave the police station now?"' says Ferran. 'Anecdotally, we hear that some of the police have vested interests. You can't touch them, it seems.'

It is hard to believe, on the bus journey from Bangkok to Pattaya, that you are travelling from one of the most traffic-congested cities on the planet to the kind of coastal idyll that Thailand is so good at promoting. The three-hour, stop-start trip, much of it on a raised motorway, takes you past a long stream of grey factories and sprawling industrial parks. This, Supreeya points out, is the heartland of Thailand's vast chicken-exporting industry, where millions of battery chickens are killed, plucked, boned and filleted every day, before being packed off around the globe to sate our desire for cheap meat. If the smell of road fumes wasn't so overpowering, I'm assured that I would be able to smell death in the air.

I don't even notice our entrance into Pattaya, as its outskirts just seem to be a continuation of what's gone before. I am relieved when Supreeya finally points to our hotel on the horizon, beside the now-visible sea. Out of curiosity, I've decided we should stay at the Ambassador City Jomtien, a hotel far from convenient for accessing downtown Pattaya, but a draw simply because it claims to be the 'world's largest resort complex'. It boasts over five thousand rooms spread across forty acres of 'prime beachfront'.

As we pull off the main road and head down the drive the focus sharpens and the reality hits you. This is tourism on a truly Soviet scale – a series of drab, tired concrete monoliths built in the 1970s, set back from a far-from-prime private beach, centred around the forty-two-storey Garden Wing that shadows the 'largest and deepest pool in Asia'. Worse, we realize upon arrival that we're checking-in to the 'sensational' Inn Wing, a building that makes the Outlook Hotel from *The Shining* appear as intimate as a boutique hotel. The long, imposing corridors overlook a central four-storey atrium and our rooms are damp with the smell of old air-conditioning units.

The only other guests we see are a group of American students on a break from their studies in Bangkok, and a two-hundred-strong tour group of Koreans who appear to be having the time of their lives playing a tournament of beach volleyball. We learn that it is mainly conference guests from Thailand and other east Asian nations that tend to stay here now – it's been a while since *farang* were regularly in residence.

But it has been worth making the trip, if only because the epic scale of the place allows us to chat to some of the staff about their working conditions without the looming presence of line managers. Some of the staff probably don't even see a colleague for hours at a time, such is the cavernous nature of the hotel.

We find Atchara pushing her cleaning trolley on the second floor of the Inn Wing. She tells us that she's fifteen and from the Udon Thani province in Isan. This is her third month away from her family working at the hotel.

'I work three days a week, from eight a.m. to four thirty p.m. I got my job through my teacher. I did a one-month unpaid trial at first because my boss wanted to "test my patience" to see if I was a good worker.' That would have tested my patience, too.

Atchara explains that she is part of a three-strong cleaning team based in the Inn Wing, headed by her eighteen-year-old supervisor; together they must clean twenty-five rooms per shift. She earns just 700 baht (£10) a month (the same as our low-season rooms cost per night, although they rise to 1,400 baht at peak times), even though the official minimum wage in Thailand is 184 baht a day, and never mind the fact that she is too young to be legally in work. Tips, she says, are everything to her.

'We might be left tips on the pillow by guests, but this gets shared amongst the team,' she says. 'A 20-baht (30p) tip is usual, but the Chinese and Japanese don't tip. Some weeks we might only earn 100 baht a week extra in tips each. The locals always get the best jobs here. The waiters and cleaners all seem to come from Isan.'

Atchara seems positive about her future prospects, though. She is studying two days a week at a hospital and says she dreams of becoming a hotel receptionist. To help her achieve her ambition, she has just started to learn English. She says her ambition is to become a permanent member of staff as they earn upwards of 4,000 baht (£57) a month, even though they have to pay 500 baht for the privilege of sleeping on a mattress on the floor, five to a room, within the resort complex.

It's a short walk to the altogether plusher – all things being relative – Ocean Wing, where the better restaurants and rooms can be found. Past the Jomtien Garden restaurant, which serves both braised-shark-fin soup and goose-foot soup for the many Chinese guests, and beyond the Atrium café, where eligibility for the children's menu is determined by whether a child can fit under an eighty-centimetre gauge, we meet Metha, who works in the main reception area. It soon becomes evident why Atchara aspires to fill his shoes one day.

'I've been working on the front desk for five years,' he explains. 'I get 10,000 baht (£143) a month and now only get 400 baht a month deducted for my room, which I share with one other man. I also get three free meals a day.' But he's not entirely happy with his terms. 'Guests must pay a 10 per cent service charge on their bill. But the hotel doesn't give this to the staff, whereas I know other hotels do.'

I later ask to speak to the hotel's management to get a response from them to what Atchara and Metha have told me, but they decline to be interviewed.

We catch a *sawngthaew* into the centre of Pattaya. These are privately operated, hail-and-ride pick-ups converted to carry passengers on two benches in the back, and are common on local routes all over Thailand. As we approach the two main streets that run parallel to Hat Pattaya, the five-kilometre crescent-shaped sandy beach that is the city's focal point, we pass a huge Tesco supermarket (called Tesco Lotus throughout Thailand). In the car park we see *farang* with Thai wives, some with children, loading shopping into their cars. Squint and this could be Peterborough, not Pattaya.

We make a brief diversion to stop by the city hall that sits opposite Tesco Lotus to speak to Wannaporn Jamjumrus, director of public health and environment for Pattaya. The city has been experiencing some dire water-supply and water-quality problems in recent years, which the tourism burghers have been anxious to play down. There have been reports of rubbish from hotels being dumped at sea then washing back up on to beaches, and some areas have experienced severe water shortages, some claim because of the excessive demands of the tourism industry.

'Trash is our number-one problem caused by tourists,' she admits. 'There are 200 tonnes of waste created every day in Pattaya, 350 tonnes in high season. We did a study recently and found that one kilogram per day was being generated per tourist, whereas for local citizens the figure was 0.8 kilograms per day. Once a day dustcarts visit the hotels. About 70 per cent of the waste is sent to landfill, the rest is recycled. None of it is incinerated. And there is now a 500,000-baht fine for anyone caught dumping in the sea. Yes, restaurant owners used to hire boatmen to take away their rubbish and dump it at sea. But this has stopped now.'

She is less forthcoming, though, when it comes to the issue of water, other than to reassure me that there is enough to go round. It's left to Montri Chalittaporu, her chief of water-quality management, to tell me about Pattaya's thirst for water.

'One million cubic metres of water are used in the greater Pattaya region every day, but the golf courses have their own reservoirs. There is currently no law requiring the reuse of swimming-pool water on gardens, but it is now forbidden to pump waste water out to sea. On average, citizens here use 200–300 litres of water a day, whereas tourists use 500–600 litres a day if you include the demands of golf courses, pools, showers and the like.' He, too, is non-committal about whether this obvious extra demand causes major supply-side problems.

But a casual glance through any of the local papers will reveal pages of letters from angry readers expressing their frustration at the city's water problems – a black market for clean drinking water even operates now in some parts. Local MPs have started to warn that this could have 'dire consequences' for the region's tourism industry. In August 2005, the *Bangkok Post* reported that the 180-room Green Park Resort Pattaya Hotel was being forced to use underground water and to buy water from tankers after its water bill had risen tenfold to 200,000 baht (£2,800) a month. The report added that the city's hotels together were drawing 60,000 cubic metres of water a day, at a daily cost of about six million baht (£85,000).

One person who isn't surprised to hear any of this is Barry Kenyon, the UK's honorary consul in Pattaya. He has lived in the area since 1992, after coming here initially to teach English, but he first visited Pattaya in 1975, 'when there were just a few hamburger stands on the beach'. These were presumably there to sate the needs – as, of course, did the then-emerging red-light district – of the last US servicemen based at the nearby U-Tapao airbase (now Pattaya's civil airport), from which B-52s took off for Vietnam, before they were all forced to withdraw in 1976.

We meet in a coffee shop in Pattaya's main shopping mall, the Royal Garden Plaza, which sits on South Beach Road facing the sea that is thick with swimmers, jet skiers and parasailers. It is a common meeting point for *farang*, due, no doubt, to its air conditioning and the familiar presence of McDonald's and Burger King.

'Water is the single biggest problem for Pattaya. Last year even the police station was without water for six weeks. Five hundred thousand people live here in the city itself, but the wider catchment area is much larger. Some hotels now have their own springs. Capacity is being increased. They're starting to build a pipe to connect us to a nearby river. There is still a problem with waste, though. We're just being swamped by growth. This is a town in revolution. There's talk of a ring road and rail line to Bangkok within ten years. The first road from Bangkok to Pattaya was only built in 1968. Before then you had to cross a river to get here. It's going to get bigger and busier, warts and all. It's going to become a mini-Bangkok. But the debate really is whether resources will ever catch up with demand. For example, tourism has caused a rise in crime and traffic pollution. This is discussed in the English-language media here, but not the Thai papers. There is just no culture of pressure groups here.'

Kenyon was asked to become the British honorary consul in the region after he had helped the embassy in Bangkok deal with the death of a friend in 1996. He now has four volunteers helping him with his daily tasks and is soon to get an office, after years of asking. 'I'm here to represent the embassy in Bangkok, really. I deal with what we call "DBNs" – Distressed British Nationals. There are seven thousand DBNs in Thailand a year and I handle 25–30 per cent of them. I deal with roughly one death a week here, but in ten years I've only dealt with the deaths of three women.'

It's one clue as to the profile of the typical British visitor to Pattaya: namely, single men broadly akin to Mr Average.

'Most of the deaths are from natural causes,' he says. 'There's an increasing number of older men. People come here thinking it's the Wild West. They have sex every night, and that's why so many die here as their hearts can't cope.' (In the 1990s, there were numerous reports of *farang* in Pattaya dying after prostitutes drugged them by rubbing tranquillizers on their own nipples before sex.) 'The accidental deaths are mostly traffic deaths, or people falling off balconies when drunk. I've only dealt with a handful of murders. Most of the people who die are Britons in residence here. Only 10 per cent of the bodies go back to Britain, as it costs £3,000 to get a body back there. They just get cremated here.'

In his time in Pattaya, Kenyon has seen the number of British visitors swell. In 1996, he says, around 150,000 came to the city, whereas a decade later at least 300,000 of the 700,000 Britons who come to Thailand annually visit Pattaya. He says around 20,000 of them spend at least six months of the year here.

'Why not?' he says. 'Air fares can be as cheap as going to Spain and the pound is strong here. You can get a two-bed apartment for £50,000. But I think the stereotype of the single man is now being diluted. There have always been the backpackers, for example, but there are more families now. The package tours have dropped off and there's a lot more affluence now. There are twenty golf clubs within an hour of here. And medical tourism is big here, but so far it's mainly visitors from the Middle East, Japan and India using the hospitals.'

The diversity of the people milling around us in the mall certainly implies that these two contrasting visitor categories – families and single men – can co-exist in harmony. The size of Pattaya, with its three main beaches, also allows each group – or nationality – their own space. There are distinct German and British areas in the city, as is evident from the restaurant signage and menu offerings.

Pattaya's shifting visitor profile fascinates Kenyon. 'We are really in the foothills of demographic change here, with Russian, Indian and Chinese tourists, especially families, now arriving in numbers,' he says. 'The Chinese are suddenly the number-one visitors here. We get about a million a year now, but this is predicted to rise to three million by 2009. There are also lots of Russians – there are three flights a day from Moscow to Bangkok now. The Tourism Authority of Thailand is really going after these markets. The legalization of casinos will be the next phase – very important for the Chinese. The mayor of Pattaya is really keen on this. And he wants theme parks, too. It will be very different here in thirty years.'

But Kenyon will always have his bread-and-butter work to do – assisting DBNs. 'We get one or two Brits a week presented to court here. The biggest reason – 60–70 per cent – is visa overstay. Their money has run out and they're sleeping on a beach somewhere. They will be sent to the immigration detention centre in Bangkok until they can raise money for a ticket home. Working without a visa is the next category. Two a month get locked up for crimes such as assault, violence against a Thai woman, drugs, credit-card fraud, etc. And there's drunk and disorderly, of course.'

Overall, there are around 120 Britons in prison in Thailand at any one time, according to Kenyon. 'There are up to eight Britons in prison here in the Pattaya area most times. I will try to visit them all once a month, and I visit the police station and the hospitals once a day to see what's happened. One in two travellers here don't have any travel insurance. But a bed in an intensive-care unit here costs $1,000 a day at the best hospitals. And if you get in trouble with the police here, you might wait two years as there's such a backlog. That's why many simply pay "police bail", as it is the softer option. We point out that they could get out if they just pay it. I suppose I'm part of the demystifying process for tourists. I couldn't order a cheese sandwich in Thai, but I know how to say "deportation order".'

It's hard to sum up Pattaya neatly as the contradictions hit you thick and fast: smiling families on holiday strolling past transvestite beggars; men hawking flick-knives and hardcore-porn DVDs on the street alongside fake Bart Simpson T-shirts and seashell souvenirs; a hotel named 'Shagwell Mansions' with its 'Long Horn' restaurant – the somewhat unlikely venue for 'Writer's Corner', a monthly meeting of ex-pats 'interested in writing'.

But when the sun goes down, it becomes obvious why so many of Pattaya's thousands of visitors each year make the journey. The website of Juthamas Siriwan, the governor of the Tourism Authority of Thailand, says 'any fantasy can be fulfilled, especially after sunset', whereas *Time* magazine is altogether less ambiguous: 'This is Sin City, Sodom-on-Sea, the Gomorrah of Tomorroh.'

Supreeya and I join the throng of people heading to 'Walking Street', a strip of South Beach Road a few hundred metres long that is pedestrianized at night. There are the restaurants and shops, of course, but the main draw are the dozens of beer bars and go-go clubs that line the street, as well as all the less brightly lit and far seedier *sois* (side streets) that run off it. Before we reach Walking Street we pass the tatty, palm-lined beach promenade, where after dark dozens of 'freelancers', often off-duty 'beer girls', call out to tourists in the hope of some extra work. All but the most single of men seem to be avoiding this side of the street.

Under the arch marking the start of Walking Street stands a parked police van with a trestle table at the back. Manning the table are a few tourist police and *farang* volunteers, who try to warn visitors about bag-snatchers, drink spiking and all the other dangers that could befall them as they seek to fulfil their fantasies. Wuttichart Luaensucant, the superintendent of Pattaya's tourism police, seems confident that he is largely in control of what happens on his patch.

'Some of the tourists get drunk and fight among themselves,' he says. 'We get between ten and twenty tourists a day coming into the station. We work from eight p.m. till two a.m. on Walking Street with a high-profile presence. There are around ten to twenty officers and volunteers in total. We give people brochures and tell them to be careful with alcohol and their bags. We try to mediate between the prostitutes and the men when there's a dispute. We only have a few spiked drinks a year. They use sleeping pills. We get big tour groups of Chinese, Koreans, Taiwanese and Russians now on Walking Street. Germans are the biggest tourists here, but the number-one problem country is England.'

A flick through *Pattaya Today*, one of the city's English-language papers, gives a good, if lurid, sense of what tends to fill up the police log book. These are just a handful of the stories published while I'm in Pattaya:

UZBEKISTAN PROSTITUTES ARE BACK IN TOWN

After a lull lasting several months, groups of Uzbeki tarts (who have entered the country as tourists) have been selling their intimate wares to Europeans in the Walking Street area . . . The women admitted that they used local hotels to rent rooms and slept in relays to save money. They denied actively soliciting in the streets, but said they did not turn down offers if Europeans were insistent on a short time.

PAKISTANI NOTICES A BEAUTIFUL GIRL APPROACHING — THEN REALIZES HIS MOST AWFUL BOOB

A Pakistani national was idly strolling down Beach Road at around 11 p.m. when he noticed a very sexy lady coming towards him in the distance. However, when the figure embraced him without further ado, he realized he was in the clutches of a ladyboy with evil intent. As he fought to ward off unwanted kisses, the thief in the night succeeded in stealing 3,000 baht from his pocket and making good an escape on a handy motorbike.

EARLY MORNING BRIT TAKEN TO HOSPITAL

A drunken British guy wandered into a bar in Soi Yamoto and demanded a drink at six o'clock in the morning. The bar girl tried to say that she was about to shut up shop, but the Englishman insisted she remain open for a while to imbibe the orange nectar before breakfast. But he became abusive and a passing Thai cracked him over the head with a beer bottle as a salutary reminder not to swear in public.

We decide to follow a large group of Korean tourists into the 'I'm Easy Too' beer-bar complex. Inside are a dozen separate bars centred around a boxing ring. Each bar is staffed by half a dozen women who, as we enter, erupt into a screeching cacophony of 'Hello, welcome. Hello, welcome' in an attempt to get us to drink with them. Thankfully, their attention is quickly diverted by two American men entering behind us.

We each take a seat at a bar close to the ring and are handed a drinks menu by the *mamasan*. Next to us, two Chinese men are in discussion with one of the women behind the bar. After a minute or so, all three of them leave together through a door at the back.

Just as in Patpong, the menu lists separate prices for 'ladies' drinks'. For example, a Heineken beer costs 85 baht for men and 110 baht for women. As we order drinks, two boxers enter the ring and begin their bout. It is billed as traditional *Muay Thai*, or Thai boxing, but seems to have as much commitment and theatrics from the fighters as a US-style wrestling bout. After three rounds, the puffing men climb out of the ring and go round collecting tips.

Ka, the *mamasan*, tells us that each boxer earns about 300 baht a fight. 'The boxers are our security, but we rarely get trouble here. We have hidden security, too.' Sitting on a low chair so as not to prevent potential customers from seeing the younger women behind the bar, Ka proceeds to explain how things work at beer bars such as this one, which, she says, is owned by a British man who pays 50,000 baht (£715) a month to rent the site.

'There's a 300-baht bar fine here, of which the girls keep 50 baht if they use a room upstairs.' She nods when we ask if that's where the two Chinese men have just gone. 'The bar girls earn a minimum of 3,000 baht a month from the bar, and 1,000 baht an hour for sex. I look after the girls. If new girls come here looking for work, I say we have two rules: "Not fat, and not younger than twenty".' We get many girls approaching us in high season. Police come by from Bangkok occasionally and check papers and ID.'

Another group of Korean tourists comes in, triggering another frenzied round of cries from the bar staff. The group consists of three men and ten women, all in their twenties, along with a young girl of around ten years of age and a tour rep. They all sit down, like us, near the boxing ring. Once drinks have been ordered, the women behind the bar somewhat incongruously produce sets of Connect 4 and Jenga.

Ka smiles at my reaction. 'We use the games to break the tension. The Korean tourists love playing them, but they are also good when men have nothing to say to the women and they feel awkward.'

So before plucking up the courage to ask how much it costs to have sex with a woman behind the bar, it helps to get to know her first over a nice game of Jenga?

'Not always. We have mostly Brits here, and they never want to play games. They just drink.'

Ka says the Asian tourist groups always have a guide with them and are usually back at their hotels by eleven p.m. 'The programme is strict as they will visit the islands off Pattaya the next day. We like them because the Japanese, Koreans and Chinese never look at the bar bills, so the girls can overcharge them. We say no to Arabs at this bar, though, as four of them tried to rape one of my girls once.'

I ask Ka how she ended up working in Pattaya.

'I'm forty-two now and I'm separated from my Thai husband. I first came here ten years ago looking for an English husband instead. I keep coming back as I'm still searching. It is my destiny to meet an Englishman. I have a fifteen-year-old boy, but I haven't seen him since he was seven. He's somewhere in Bangkok. His father took him from school one day. I keep looking for him. But I'm so tired now. I was looking after my dying mum until two months ago, but before that I was looking after an American kid for a family in Bangkok.'

It isn't long before the two Chinese men reappear with the woman. They quickly depart and the woman, who can be no more than twenty-one, returns to the bar. She is visibly upset and starts talking to Ka in Thai. Supreeya tells me later that she could overhear her saying, '"They made me have sex with them both together. I hate Chinese guys."'

A ten-minute stroll away from the entrance to Walking Street lie the more notorious areas of Pattaya. As you start drifting off the main drag and down the various *sois* that head away from the beach, the signage becomes much more sexually explicit and the street hawkers much more crude when describing what's on offer behind the doors to 'their' establishments. We stroll through 'Boyztown', one of the largest gay red-light districts in Asia, where Supreeya informs me that sex with 'men', many of whom look very close indeed to the legal age of eighteen, is said to be half the price of sex with the city's female prostitutes. This means, she says, that many of the men loitering by the doors to the bars, most of whom are dressed in skimpy white tennis shorts and vest tops, are forced to have much more paid-for sex in order to earn a living wage than the women. Some earn as little as 1,600 baht (£22) a month, in a city were a basic room can cost 2,800 baht a month to rent.

Further on is Sunee Plaza, an area that forms an enclosed 'U' shape by doubling back on itself. This is said to be the principal area where child-sex tourists congregate to pursue sex with children. It sets itself apart, if only because the street lighting is so much dimmer than anywhere else. As we pass down the street, I notice that it is lined not with bars but with cafés. Through the gloom, it is still possible to see men sitting around tables with boys who look as young as ten. Some are even sitting together on sofas. It seems gut-wrenchingly obvious what must be going on, but Supreeya explains that even though the police know what is happening, they must catch the men in the act of paying for or actually having sex with a child to be able to prosecute. There are occasional crackdowns, but the cafés, most of which are owned by Europeans, just get fined.

The local modus operandi for these paedophiles, it seems, is that they groom a boy – or less often a girl – in one of these cafés, then 'order them up', as Supreeya describes it, by telephone and have them delivered on the back of a moped to their room. This is child abuse made as easy as ordering a pizza.

Some of these men do receive justice of sorts, though – even if it is very much Pattaya style. During our time there, news breaks of the suicide of a British man accused of child abuse. His story, as reported in *Pattaya Today*, is not an uncommon one in the city; his method of suicide is said by police to be 'a favourite among paedophiles'.

BAILED BRIT COMMITS SUICIDE AT HOME

Nicholas John Rabet, a British expat aged fifty-seven, was found by a neighbour suffocated to death by a plastic bag covering his face. He had been arrested last year on suspicion of having sexually abused around twenty young teenage boys whom he had befriended by opening up his rented home near Carrefour store as an Aladdin's cave of computer games and thrills. He had obtained bail on security of one million baht, but had told friends he would not try and flee as his whole life was in Pattaya.

Police Lieutenant Colonel Aomsin Sukkarnkha said he was satisfied that this was a case of suicide. There were signs Mr Rabet had consumed a large amount of whisky and sleeping tablets before affixing the plastic bag and snapping into place a pair of handcuffs which made immobile his hands and feet as he lay on his bed. Additionally, the dead Brit had left a suicide note exclaiming his despair about his future and, according to neighbours, had unsuccessfully attempted to take his own life a few days previously.

The British embassy representative on the scene, Barry Kenyon, said that an autopsy would take place in Bangkok to confirm the cause of death and that the deceased's next of kin in the UK had been traced through the database on his mobile phone.

Neighbours said that Mr Rabet had few friends and kept himself to himself: 'He often talked about suicide,' said one, 'and how he had no future outside of Pattaya.' If found guilty, Mr Rabet would have faced at least fifteen years in prison as the boys involved were as young as twelve.

6

The Trail on Trial

Bangkok and Ko Phi Phi, Thailand

Set up in Bali, Ko Pha-Ngan, Ko Tao, Borocay, and the hordes are bound to follow. There's no way you can keep it out of *Lonely Planet*, and once that happens it's countdown to doomsday.

The Beach, Alex Garland

KHAO SAN ROAD IN BANGKOK has been described as a 'decompression chamber' for backpackers entering or leaving South-East Asia. A place where two worlds – the West and the Orient – fuse, even if the coupling is at times somewhat uneasy. Ever since the 1960s, backpackers have used the area of Banglamphu, which has this now-famous road at its heart, to book plane, train and bus tickets, write or phone home, reunite with friends, or just shop and flop. Within walking distance of the stunning Grand Palace and the wide, muddy Chao Phraya river that cuts through the city, Khao San road is one of the world's major backpacker hubs, attracting hundreds of thousands of travellers a year. The vast majority of backpackers passing through Thailand will at some point spend a few days here, among the street hawkers selling bootleg CDs, tie-dyed T-shirts and chicken satay. *Lonely Planet*, the backpackers' bible and one of the principle reasons why so many flock here, calls it 'a kind of backpacker cabaret in which you are both a spectator and a participant'.

It is on the steps in front of the tourist police station on the corner of Khao San road and Chakraphong road that I start chatting to Sara and Matt, a Canadian couple who have been travelling through Asia for the past few months. Bangkok, they tell me, has become a second home to them since they first met here during a water fight at the Songkran Thai New Year festival a few years ago. They now both spend periods working intensively at home to help fund their next round of travelling, with Sara using Bangkok as a base from which to export clothes for sale back in Canada. As is the ritual for backpackers, talk quickly moves on to where they have just come from.

'We're just back from China and Tibet,' says Sara, who is thirty. 'And before that we were in Ko Pha-Ngan for a month.' Like Khao San road, in the past couple of decades the small island of Ko Pha-Ngan in the Gulf of Thailand has become a Mecca, as backpackers say, for the more hedonistic, party-seeking traveller, a place sold very much as an alternative to the mass-tourism haunts of southern Thailand such as Phuket and Koh Samui.

'I first went there about ten years ago. But there are ATMs and 7–11s there now. Plus, there are more parties. It used just to be the Full Moon Party on Hat Rin beach, but now there are Black Moon parties and even Half-Moon parties. There's a party every week, basically. Even the party drugs have changed. In 1998, diet pills, which are a bit like speed, were the drug of choice. Now everyone drinks Sangsom whiskey mixed with Red Bull from a straw out of a bucket. The party used to be just on the beach, but now there are jungle parties with dance floors actually built within the jungle. But I always stay with "my family" when I'm there. They're a local family that I spent months with when I first visited.'

Matt, twenty-seven, says change is happening everywhere they've been. 'Ko Chang [a large island that sits within a national marine park east of Pattaya near the Cambodian border] is going, too. I went there first in 1999 and stayed on "Lonely Beach". We had to climb over the hills to reach it, but now there are bungalows, resorts and roads there. Apparently, the authorities don't want cheap backpackers, they just want rich tourists.'

Their faces light up, though, when I ask them about Tibet.

'Yeah, it's still the Holy Grail for backpackers,' says Matt. 'It took us three weeks to get in. We met amazing travellers there – the best. We met someone who'd been there ten years earlier and said it was exactly the same. There were a surprising number of backpackers there. But they were older backpackers, less into their partying. Also, lots of Chinese tourists.'

Matt says they were both deeply affected by what they saw in Tibet. 'It was depressing to see the contrast between the Tibetans and Chinese. We tried never to buy anything from the Chinese. The Tibetans tell you privately they don't want the Chinese there, but run away if you mention the Dalai Lama. The Chinese tell you that you have to stay in official hostels that charge four dollars a night in a dorm and the guides try to feed you misinformation. The Ganden Monastery in Lhasa was closed when we were there due to a riot by the monks in which they raised the Tibetan flag. Six were killed and thousands jailed, apparently. But they never mentioned this.'

I ask them what the 'route' is now in South-East Asia: the places that most backpackers tend to visit when travelling around.

'Everyone is doing the Thailand–Cambodia–Vietnam–Laos circuit now,' says Sara. 'No one is doing the overland route from Bali to Bangkok, through Indonesia, Singapore and Malaysia, any more because of the Bali bombings. Laos is like Thailand ten years ago. It's the best. There's a weird place called Vang Vien which is on the Mekong river. Backpackers sit in rubber inner tubes drinking *bhang lassi* [a cannabis-laced yoghurt drink that originates in India] and float down the river to bars along the banks where there are TV screens showing *The Simpsons* and *Friends*. It's like being the Swiss Family Robinson, but with beer.'

Sara and Matt invite me to join them for dinner with two friends they originally met in China but have now reunited with in Bangkok after keeping in touch via email. Sara takes us all to a small street market away from Khao San road, where she knows a place that serves 'the best seafood at local prices'.

On our way to the market, we walk along Khao San road. This is a place where you can get your iPod illegally filled up with tracks for the equivalent of just a few dollars; where a one-hour Thai massage with oil costs 100 baht; where fake designer clothes and software CDs are being flogged outside a Boots chemist; and where the tuk-tuk drivers whisper, 'Hey, you need a massage with Mona Lisa' as you walk past. In the cafés and restaurants that line the road, backpackers watch pirate copies of the latest Hollywood offerings, sip beer over a game of pool, or choose large bowls of noodles from menus that also list home comforts ranging from 'Apple Pie' to 'American Breakfast'. Of course, everywhere boasts that worldwide backpacker staple: the banana pancake. We walk for ten minutes before the backpackers finally begin to dilute, and soon they are just a minority among Bangkok citizens once more.

Eirin, twenty-four, and Siri, twenty-six, are university friends from Norway. They left home three months ago and began their trip in India. 'We just wanted to live in a hut and try to get the snow out of our minds,' says Siri, who has let her hair dreadlock during her travels. 'We wanted to go to Latin America, but Asia was cheaper, and Tibet has always been on our list. We weren't interested in the rest of China.'

Siri seems jaded by her travels, though, particularly by some of the other travellers she has met along the way. 'In Vietnam there were people boasting about how little they had paid for everything. The hardcore backpackers also go overland rather than fly and show off their visa stickers in their passports. There seems to be a hierarchy among backpackers now, with more people just joining the backpacker trail for a couple of weeks as a short holiday.'

Matt nods. 'Yeah, I used to try and go everywhere as cheaply as possible, but I'm more secure now about how much I spend. It isn't an issue.' He tells me that it is possible to travel round Thailand on a budget of about £15 a day, but he's left those days behind him. 'Why pay 200 baht in Khao San road for a box room, when you can get a double with air con for 360 baht if you ask around? Hell, a beer is more expensive here than a room sometimes.'

Siri says that the locals sometimes don't do themselves any favours, either. 'I didn't like Vietnam that much. You get scammed a lot. They don't think that we've worked hard to be able to come to their country. You're moved around like cattle. The system they operate for the buses means that you only ever travel with tourists.'

Sara says that from what she's seen – this is her eighth trip to Thailand – the relationship between backpackers and host communities is getting more and more fraught. There is simply an ever-growing number of backpackers, plus a more diverse range of nationalities, now 'on the road'. She says she's met Mexican, Indian, Brazilian and Argentinian backpackers for the first time on this trip.

'The locals just seem more tired and cynical these days, especially here in Thailand. They're smiling through their teeth now. I get embarrassed by backpackers yelling at people and speaking down to them. In India and Vietnam travellers always feel they're being ripped off. We are really blessed to be able to come travelling. But many people don't think like this any more. I think it's because it's so easy and cheap to travel now.'

She tells us about an assault she witnessed in 2000 when travelling through Thailand, which still haunts her. 'I was on a night bus down to Ko Pha-Ngan from Bangkok for Millennium New Year's Eve. It had been voted the best place in the world to spend the night by a British magazine. There were these eight guys from Liverpool drinking heavily on the bus. They were saying that they were basically there to "fuck the girls". This other English guy leant over and said to them "Enough." They ignored him and started to flick food around the bus. When we got off the next morning they all got this guy and started to really beat him up.

'The trouble is this attitude has a real ripple effect and is sometimes reciprocated by the locals if it is aimed at them. You can see it in their faces. They are not happy. You can't blame them: who would put up with that much shit at home?'

Tourists have always sneered at other tourists, particularly those who travel to a place after them and, ergo, help to 'ruin' it. It has been a familiar cry since the days when English gentlemen took in the sights of Western Europe on the Grand Tour.

In 1844, the poet William Wordsworth wrote a letter to the editor of the *Morning Post*, in which he protested at the proposed building of new railway lines in his beloved Lake District, one hugging the coast and the other from Lancaster to Carlisle. To make the point about how these new routes might blight the area for ever, Wordsworth compared a journey he had twice made, thirty years apart, along the Simplon pass in the Lepontine Alps between Switzerland and Italy, the first time 'before the new military road had taken place of the old muleteer track with its primitive simplicities':

> It was impossible to suppress regret for what had vanished for ever . . .
> Instead of travellers proceeding, with leisure to observe and feel . . .
> pilgrims of fashion hurried along in their carriages, [many] of
> them . . . discussing the merits of 'the last new novel,' or poring over
> their guide-books, or fast asleep. Similar remarks might be applied to
> the mountainous country of Wales.

John Ruskin, the Victorian cultural and social critic, also bemoaned the 'stupid herds of modern tourists' in his autobiography, *Praeterita*:

> The poor modern slaves and simpletons who let themselves be dragged like cattle, through the countries . . . they imagine themselves visiting can have no conception whatever of the complex joys and ingenuous hopes, connected with the choice and arrangement of the travelling carriage in old times.

The mourning of a paradise lost, combined with a belief that they alone have experienced the true essence of a destination, is still a common motif among tourists today, but particularly among backpackers. These predominantly young travellers, often armed with little more than flip-flops and rolling tobacco, are in many ways modern-day Grand Tourists, a privileged generation undergoing a rite of passage between the irresponsibilities of childhood and all the leaden accruements of adulthood – jobs, mortgages and kids. Time away from the suppressive shackles of the West can enable them to muse on their future life through the prism of other cultures; to 'find themselves' and broaden their minds. Their meditative quest is helped if they experience hardship and edgy adventure – relative to their home lives, of course – such as epic bus journeys, bouts of tropical illness, and near misses with danger or crime.

This is the script, anyway. But is their pursuit of the real, the authentic and the otherly really an existential excursion into the heart of darkness, from which they will emerge enlightened and worldwise, or is it just a journey through a series of guidebook-determined places that have been shaped and developed to reflect their own desires, and now offer little more than convenient cover for one long party under the sun where the natives provide the beer, the cheap beds and, most importantly, the excuse?

The Bali bombings in 2002 and 2005, in which tourists were killed by Islamist terrorists in the Indonesian backpacker haven of Kuta and nearby Jimbaran, fuelled this debate. Some commentators pointed out that the targeting of a nightclub packed with backpackers raised serious questions about just how appropriate it was for these tourists to be so disengaged with the cultures they found themselves in. Writing in the *New Statesman*, David Nicholson-Lord, an environmentalist who has long questioned the true value of tourism to developing nations, said the actions of the majority of backpackers in Bali smelled of 'moral casuistry, of self-indulgence, even of that much-debated commodity, decadence'. He went on: 'Given that there's good reason to regard tourists as the shock troops of development and post-colonialism, it's really not surprising, however awful the consequences, that they find themselves targeted by anti-Western militants.'

Again, this is not a new accusation thrown at tourists. Thomas Cook, the nineteenth-century travel agent whose first organized trip took place in 1841 from Leicester to Loughborough before he went on to offer somewhat more exotic destinations, was blamed for this, too. Critics used the charge of imperialism against him in relation to his tours of Egypt, saying he was the 'Napoleon of excursions' because he was gaining financially from a system that further exploited and oppressed the local people, who were already under British command. The tourists he catered for were also mocked for slavishly following their own bibles, the tell-tale red-covered guides published by John Murray and Karl Baedeker which would rank sights and hotels, and suggest itineraries.

Others, though, staunchly defended backpackers after the Bali bombings, suggesting that their journeyings could sow the seeds of future global harmony and tolerance. 'If we ever manage to build a world based on mutual respect and understanding between peoples, tourism will deserve much of the credit. That's particularly true for one class of traveller: backpackers,' wrote Michael Elliott in *Time* magazine in the days following the 2002 bombing. 'Few modern social developments are more significant and less appreciated than the rise of backpacker travel. The tens of thousands of young Australians, Germans, Britons, Americans and others who wander the globe, flitting from Goa to Costa Rica, from Thailand to Tasmania, are building what may be the only example of a truly global community.'

Elliott went on to cite another defence of backpacking: research by Dr Mark Hampton, who is now director of studies for the tourism-management degree at the University of Kent, that estimated that 70 per cent of the money spent by backpackers in Indonesia ended up with local small businesses, compared to just 30 per cent of the money spent by 'mass' tourists.

Few disagree, though, that backpackers act as 'wedges' for tourism to develop in a location. Once backpackers have 'found' a place, there is little turning back. This directly correlates with 'Plog's Model', a seminal theory of tourism development that has been taught to tourism students for the past three decades, which was originally formulated in a paper by Dr Stanley C. Plog called 'Why Destination Areas Rise and Fall in Popularity', published in the *Cornell Hotel and Restaurant Administration Quarterly* in 1974.

The theory centres on so-called 'psychographic personality types of tourists'. At one end are the 'Venturers' and at the other the 'Dependables'. The Venturers are the 'intellectually curious', who make decisions quickly, spend discretionary income more readily, and who 'look to their own judgement, rather than authority figures, for guidance and direction'. They typically are the first tourists to 'discover' a destination and are the category that many 'hardcore' backpackers would fall into. At the other end, the Dependables are 'somewhat intellectually restricted', are cautious and conservative in their daily lives, prefer popular, well-known brands of consumer products, and 'like structure and routine in their relatively non-varying lifestyles'. They will typically travel in highly organized tours with reps and stay in places such as all-inclusive resorts.

So far, so obvious. Plog devised a sliding scale between these polarities, consisting of Venturers, Near-Venturers, Centric-Venturers, Centric-Dependables, Near-Dependables and, finally, Dependables. Many destinations will, as they develop, see these groups pass through in that order: as the next group arrives, the one in residence before tends to move elsewhere. Plog claims this forms a very predictable transition that, if understood, can help a destination grow without suffering the decline in numbers that usually follows the arrival of the Centric-Dependables. (Plog also acts as a consultant to destinations that fear they're sliding towards the Dependable end of the market when visitor numbers start falling away. For example, he was asked by the tourism director of Tahiti to help re-brand the French Polynesian island as a getaway for 'stressed-out Venturers', free from constant interruptions by modern communications, instead of a once-popular destination with sun-seeking Dependables from the US. Tourism revenue grew 18 per cent or more per year for a period after the island's image makeover.) Plog says in an updated version of his original paper, published in 2001:

Having been discovered, the destination soon confronts the pressures arising from rapid growth and development. Not only has the press started to put out the good message, but near-Venturers also talk about their exciting vacations with their mid-Centric friends who have Venturer leanings. These people want to visit, too, especially because the destination now has developed a reasonable infrastructure. Growth rates can be high during this period, since there are far more Centrics with Venturer leanings than there are Near-Venturers. Up to this point, everyone seems happy at the destination. Tourism growth continues unabated, property values rise as hotels continue to pop up, more local residents have jobs, tax receipts have increased, some rundown areas have been cleaned up, and most residents believe that they have discovered the perfect industry. No ugly, smoke-belching factories need to be built; unskilled workers find good-paying jobs that require little training in the new hotels and restaurants; and developers are not asking for tax concessions, unlike the situation for manufacturing industries. Local politicians and tourism officials congratulate themselves because they think they are pretty smart to have attracted or created what appears to be a never-ending, expanding business.

Then comes the tipping point, when the Centric-Dependables become the dominant force and the downward curve becomes steeper.

During this time, development continues almost unabated. Elected officials, who recognize the contributions of tourists to their area and their constituencies, happily proclaim their support of tourism and all of its benefits for their community. So they approve plans for more hotels that will add to the tax base, the larger number of which fall in the mid-price range and a few in the luxury category . . . Tourist shops, some representing large chains, sprout up around town. Fast-food chains make their appearance and help to make the place seem more like the hometown that the visitors just left . . . To deal with the what-to-do issue for those who need activities beyond enjoying the destination itself, video arcades, movie theaters and other entertainment facilities arise. Gradually the place takes on a more touristy look. Construction has either sprawled or high-rise hotels begin to dominate the original architecture . . . Local planning to control the spread of tourist sprawl has been woefully inadequate because elected officials have seen no need to regulate a business that they believe is a great benefit to their community. Then, when the realization finally dawns that regulation is necessary, the officials have no experience with such land-use planning. They allow small businesses of all types to spring up around town in an uncontrolled manner (e.g., T-shirt shops, beach or ski shops, pseudo-native stores, bars). The place begins to look like many other overdeveloped destinations, losing its distinctive character along the way.

The destination is now arguably in its death throes: once the Dependables take hold the end is nigh, according to Plog.

The destination can draw only from shrinking segments of the population after its psychographic positioning passes the magical mid-point on the chart . . . The base of potential tourists is diminishing, as those with Venturer leanings desert this now-tawdry destination for the next new, unspoiled place. All of this compounds the misery now felt at the destination. Nothing has changed, the locals believe, so they can't understand why fewer visitors come each year and spend less while they're in town.

Plog's Model illustrates just how significant Venturers, such as backpackers, can be to the development of a destination. They represent the first plots on a bell curve of development that is notoriously difficult to influence in a truly positive manner once underway.

It's a responsibility accepted by Tony Wheeler, co-founder of the Lonely Planet guides and a legendary figure among backpackers, so influential are his guides. The *New York Times* has described him as 'the most influential man in travel'. His publishing empire now boasts over 650 titles, covering 'every corner of the planet', but began in 1973 with *Across Asia on the Cheap*, known popularly among travellers as the Yellow Book, which was born out of his trip with his wife Maureen on the then-classic overland 'Hippie Trail' from his native England to Australia, where they have now settled, via countries such as Iran, Afghanistan, India, Burma and Indonesia.

'Yes, backpackers are the forerunners of things to come,' says Wheeler. 'They're the ones who go to places first and open doors. They're the indicators of what's going to happen in the future. But I think the idea that tourists just go in and wreck a place just isn't really true. Overall, I believe tourism is a positive force on the world, but, of course, it will always present problems. Greedy development and poor planning are often to blame, though. I've seen that in so many places – the first backpackers turn up and before you know it the first hotels and restaurants are there and the tourism office is already planning a five-star place without any regulations, such as not building on the beach, or proper sewage. They're just letting this stuff happen.

'But I think in the developing world you can't blame people for being short-sighted – they need the money, they want to put their kids into school, they need a bicycle or motorbike. And yet they are killing nearby reefs in the sea to use as building material and the next thing they know the beach has washed away. I've seen this so many times that it drives me bloody crazy. I've seen it in Bali, especially at Candidasa. They grind the coral down and use it as a constituent in concrete. Other places where beaches have been totally overdeveloped that were once beautiful include Kuta, again in Bali, and Kovalam beach in Kerala. The whole coastline of Spain, practically.'

But does he himself feel a sense of responsibility, because a recommendation in one of his guides can lead to a place being overrun by backpackers?

'In some places a mention in Lonely Planet is useful, no more. Rome, London, etc. But for some places it is clearly very important. Yes, it is a real concern to us, because you can make or break a place. The one thing we never try to do is rave about a place. We've introduced this feature in our guides called the "Writers' Choice" and there is a danger, I guess, that this is where everyone will head to. We're cautious about doing too much of that. Plus, in places where there's a lot of choice about where to stay or eat, we try to recycle recommendations in each new edition by pulling a few out and replacing them with others. We do know it is a huge responsibility, but you cannot cover everything that's out there. And sadly some people do follow the guides a little bit too religiously. But backpacking puts money into the hands of the locals, not some international company.'

Wheeler says he can think of quite a few places where tourism, but particularly backpacking, has been a largely positive force, both environmentally and socially.

'I think tourism in Nepal has been a positive force in so many ways. Just what employment was there out in the country in Nepal before tourists arrived? You had farmers scratching a living out of the ground, burning all the trees to cook on, with their kids going off to India to find work. Trekkers took employment straight out into the country by employing locals as porters and guides in guesthouses up in the hills. We hear all this stuff about the trashing of Mount Everest, but on the tourist trails you just do not see rubbish in general. You see places advertising that they use solar panels for their showers and that actually attracts trekkers because firewood is not being burned. It's a virtuous circle. I do think that tourism has been generally positive there. We've been watching this happen for twenty years or so now. But on the other hand it's all relative: more people enter Yosemite national park in California in one weekend than trek the Annapurna circuit in Nepal in a whole year.'

When asked for similar examples in a coastal setting, Wheeler appears to struggle. 'One place that interests me is the Yasawa islands in Fiji, where there is one very expensive resort called Turtle Island. Recently a string of little backpacker-level places have been developed near by and the story there is that Turtle Island has encouraged these places to develop because they're quite happy to have backpacker places near them, but they don't want any other luxury hotels popping up. I've heard that it is all very environmentally sensitive, and it is sufficiently remote that you are not going to get people turning up easily.'

He says the point about access is important as, of course, it will always determine how overrun any place might become. 'If you added up every single hotel room in French Polynesia – in Bora Bora, Tahiti, etc. – there is still just one hotel on Waikiki beach in Hawaii that has more rooms than all of them put together.'

But relying on exclusivity or inaccessibility alone hardly seems a practical or convenient way of protecting beach areas facing over-development, as southern Thailand knows only too well.

The route from Bangkok to Ko Phi Phi, the isolated islands where *The Beach* was filmed and that still remain a backpacker magnet today, takes me through Phuket. This large island – the country's biggest, in fact – lies in the Andaman Sea off the eastern coast of southern Thailand, but is attached to the mainland by a road bridge. It represents what many regard as a crystal-ball view of what Ko Phi Phi will become in a few years' time: a place where once-pristine beach areas have been allowed to develop unchecked. Both Ko Phi Phi and Phuket are united, though, by being part of the much wider area that was so gravely damaged by the 2004 Boxing Day tsunami.

Directly under the flight path of Phuket International Airport, at a none the less pretty beach called Nai Yang, I meet Songpol Tippayawong, the head of the marine and coastal resources unit at WWF Thailand. As we pull up our chairs to a table at a beach café under the palms, he watches me looking out to sea then up at the trees around us. He knows immediately what I'm thinking.

'Two metres,' he says. 'Here, exactly where we are sitting, the water from the waves was two metres deep. Taller than you.' He points at some dead trees a few hundred metres inland. 'They were killed by the salt water. This café used to be one hundred metres nearer the beach before, but they are not allowed to build that close any more.'

I've made the diversion to visit Songpol as I want to learn more about the impact of tourism on Thailand's much-visited tropical coastline. He has lived in the area all his life, and until seven months ago worked for the local water authority. Songpol has first-hand experience of the various demands and stresses caused by tourism.

'The tsunami was nothing compared to the impact of tourism,' he says. 'It is a much larger, long-term problem.'

This is quite some statement, considering that, according to the UN, 8,212 people were killed by the tsunami in Thailand, including many hundreds of foreign tourists.

'I was born in 1972 and when I was eight or nine it was still largely virgin rainforest here on the island. By the late 1980s, though, it was mostly developed. We have now lost so much biodiversity and primary forest and the soil is destabilizing in many places. The construction of hotels upstream is creating a lot of sediment in the water and this causes damage to the coral reefs when it washes out to sea. It also affects the mangroves on our east coast. A lot of our waste water – about 40 per cent – is still being pumped into the sea on the west coast where all the resort areas are.'

But these are far from the only problems Songpol has witnessed. 'Land is now so expensive here due to tourism; the cost of living is even higher than in Bangkok – it has meant that many local people have been forced to sell off their ancestral land and have now lost their only real asset. There is even competition for schools here for the first time. And there is a lot of overfishing here; this is for export rather than for the tourists per se, but lobsters are now being brought over from Burma to meet the tourists' appetite for these vulnerable creatures.

'The corals are also damaged by tourism. Snorkellers actually cause more damage than divers because they touch the coral more often. There is also a trend for "seawalking", in which people literally walk into the sea off the beach wearing a helmet fed with air. The tourists then pick up giant clams and feed fish underwater. Some operators even catch the fish for them and hand them to the seawalkers later in a plastic bag.'

Songpol believes that it is too late for Phuket to 'be saved' from tourism. Nothing, he says, is sustainably managed here. Of the hundred tonnes of waste created each day on the island, the local incinerator can only process 60 per cent. The rest is either illegally fly-tipped, often at sea, or used to 'reclaim' some land from the sea in a former mangrove area off the east coast of the island. Car pollution and traffic are also major concerns. If anything, he says, the tsunami has only exacerbated the damage caused by tourism development, as so many areas have needed to be rebuilt. Worse, many of the original problems have simply been repeated.

'Patong beach is the worst example of over-development on the island, but was the first and fastest to be rebuilt. Our government is just too weak in the face of pressure from the tourism developers. For example, the waste-water costs here for hotels is just 50 baht a month per room. It's nothing. They have caused far more damage than this represents.'

There aren't many good-news stories, he says when probed. The only one he can actually think of is when the nearby J W Marriott resort became involved in a leatherback turtle conservation project here at Nai Yang beach, which lies within a national marine park, but that was only after there was a local protest when the hotel chain first bought the land.

It is interesting for me to compare the views of Songpol – someone very much 'on the ground' – with those of his colleague John Parr, the director of conservation at WWF Thailand, whom I had met earlier in Bangkok. He had appeared altogether more cautious about blaming tourism for some of the environmental pressures facing the country. 'Tourism is very visible in Thailand, but has quite a minor impact, I believe,' he said. 'Even if we put Bangkok's

Oriental Hotel in the jungle, the impact would be small, even minor. Hunting for trade, food and sport is more of a problem. Forest fires are also a major threat. Tourism in national parks actually helps to preserve habitats and the education given about wildlife is important, too. Sambar deer here in Thailand, for example, are benefiting from tourism as lots of people come here to see nature. This is probably one of the most environmentally aware countries in South-East Asia. It has 102 national parks, 55 wildlife sanctuaries and 23 marine parks.'

Parr said that tourism does present other conservation problems, though. The sale of seashells and turtle parts as tourist trinkets concerns him, as does the open sale of ivory to tourists at Bangkok's vast Chatuchak weekend market and at some of the major hotels in the city. He said a loophole is used whereby African ivory is imported via Kuwait to avoid the ban on Asian ivory.

'Broadly speaking, the terrestrial impacts of tourism are positive, but within marine areas it is negative. I was in Ko Phi Phi in 1987 and stayed in a bamboo hut, but now there are mini hotels. You need zonal development systems and more local ownership in places like that. The guys at the top of the pyramid like things to be very vague when it comes to regulations. There should also be a cap every year on the number of entrants to any given park or reserve. But in a wider context, climate change is actually a far greater threat to the corals, for example, than tourism.'

It's a forty-minute taxi ride to Phuket city, the administrative heart of the island but not a place frequented by tourists, other than those on their way through to catch the ferry to Ko Phi Phi. On the way you pass many snake farms, crocodile shows and other visitor attractions. Thailand, like so many countries, has a somewhat dubious reputation for parading animals before tourists. Perhaps the most extreme example is the Night Safari in Chiang Mai in the far north of the country, the home town of the former prime minister, Thaksin Shinawatra, who is said to have come up with the idea. When it opened in late 2005 (a few months before Thaksin was ousted in a coup), it caused an international outcry after the project's director was quoted in the Thai media as saying the zoo would offer 'visitors the chance to experience exotic foods such as imported horse, kangaroo, giraffe, snake, elephant, tiger and lion meat. We will also provide domestic crocodile and dog meat'. According to the Born Free Foundation, a deal was struck between the Kenyan and Thai governments to capture 175 wild animals in Kenya for export to the 'safari', principally for display. But following the controversy the director backtracked and announced that the menu would only offer 'crocodile and ostrich'. Unbelievably, the Thai 'natural resources and environment' minister described it as 'a magnet for foreign tourists, making the area the new ecotourism site of the Asia-Pacific region', showing just how abused the term 'ecotourism' can be.

Before heading to the city's harbour to catch a morning ferry, I make one final diversion to Phuket Provincial Hall, a Sino-Portuguese-style building from the early twentieth century that doubled up as the French embassy in Phnom Penh for the 1984 movie *The Killing Fields*. Today it houses the office of Udomsak Uswarangkura, the governor of Phuket province.

Sitting under the national flag and a near-lifesize photograph of the Thai king, Uswarangkura invites me to take a seat in front of his expansive, highly polished desk. My first questions naturally centre on how the island is coping, over a year on from the tsunami. Uswarangkura was the highest-ranking politician in the area when the waves struck and is credited as being a figurehead in the local response to the emergency. He seems bullish.

'Thaksin ordered me to finish rebuilding the beach areas within three to six months of the tsunami because tourism is so important to us. Both Patong and Kamala beaches were finished on time and it is really only Ko Lak, where there was the most damage, that is still being rebuilt now. Ko Phi Phi is functional, but will be back to normal next year. Patong was finished first as it is our most famous beach. We spent 200 million baht (£2.9 million) there alone.'

Uswarangkura explains that the reconstruction has been financed through a mixture of state and federal money, NGO donations, insurance claims and a soft-loans programme for hotels. 'We have also given a gift of 20,000 baht (£290) to each of the street hawkers and vendors who lost their businesses, to help them restart their livelihoods.'

He describes just how reliant the island is now on tourism. 'Our economy used to be tin mines, but they've now closed and tourism represents almost half of our income, with fishing at around 10 per cent. The rich people here who owned the tin mines now own the land the hotels are built on. We offer fifty-year leases to hotels for them to use government land. Yes, there are problems with land use and we want the big hotels to use their land properly, but we need more tourists. First it was the backpackers who came in 1980. Then the first hotel was built in the south of the island where they stayed. But now it is high-class tourists who come here and they need yachting, diving, swimming pools and golf. We will soon have a helicopter service taking tourists from the airport to their hotels.' I can't help wondering what Dr Plog would think upon hearing this.

Uswarangkura reaches into a drawer in his desk and begins thumbing through a set of papers. 'Ah, here we are,' he says. 'Here's our latest visitor figures. We have about four million people visiting our island a year. The Brits used to be the number-one nation, but now it is the Koreans. The Tourism Authority of Thailand has tried advertising on the ITV channel in Britain to encourage more visitors from Britain to come to Thailand, and this month my staff are in Korea and China to drum up business. The Japanese are the most profitable nation for us, although the Chinese are spending more and more as they come in groups of one hundred now.'

He flicks to another page: 'Each tourist here spends, on average,

4,000 baht (£57) a day and 70 per cent of this money stays here on the island. We have five hundred hotels here and only ten chain hotels. But if more want to come, of course we will invite them. The Four Seasons are coming. Peninsula [a Hong-Kong-based hotel group] are coming, too, and Intercontinental are looking for land now, but are having some problems. Yes, the cost of living here is high, but people are earning lots from tourism. People come here looking for work – we have 150,000 unregistered workers on the island among a local population of 280,000. They come from all over Thailand to look for work. We have hill tribes from the north coming here now because they can speak Chinese. This is what makes the house prices so high.'

What effect, I ask, is this tourism gold-rush having on the island's environment? Is this growth sustainable?

'Water is an issue, but reverse-osmosis desalination plants are being built to feed the hotels with water. We have one reservoir near Patong, but we are planning another two. Nineteen old tin mines have been flooded, as well, and they help serve the island with water. Of course, hotels use a lot of water. Tourists want a shower after being on the beach each day. We also need another incinerator. But tourism is the golden egg for the government. They want 10 per cent growth for the industry every year over the next five years, but this is difficult for us as we always depend on the airlines and tour operators. We used to have direct flights to Phuket from Hong Kong, Melbourne and Japan, but now they go via Bangkok. We want more direct flights to our airport. We have the capacity for more visitors.'

Bring it on, seems to be the message from Uswarangkura. But some campaigners have expressed deep concern about how the tsunami has been used in some of the tourist-rich countries struck – Sri Lanka and Thailand, in particular – to secure prime beachfront real estate for future projects. In October 2005, Tourism Concern, a UK-based group that campaigns to 'ensure tourism always benefits local communities', published a report called 'Post-Tsunami

Reconstruction and Tourism: A Second Disaster?' It detailed how vulnerable people, still recovering from the disaster, were being pushed aside to make way for large-scale tourism-related projects.

'Post-tsunami reconstruction in Thailand appears on the surface to have been conducted overall in a speedy and seemingly efficient, if at times over-zealous and authoritarian, manner,' said the report. 'However, the private sector, criticizing the government for inaction, has started to re-build tourism amenities. Much of the re-building (for example, on Ko Phi Phi) is theoretically illegal because laws on buffer zones [that set limits on building too close to beaches] and building regulations have been ignored, just as they were before the tsunami.'

The report pointed out that this seems to fly in the face of the so-called 'Phuket Action Plan', which was formulated at a meeting organized by the UNWTO in February 2005 in an attempt to help the tsunami-struck countries rebuild their tourism industries. 'The plan was hailed as an ideal opportunity to foster cooperation and coordination among all the affected countries, to share knowledge and ideas, to develop joined-up regional tourism clusters and to "correct the mistakes of the past" by "making the re-emerging destinations among the best in the world in terms of more environmental conservation and community involvement in the planning process". In other words, at least some positives could emerge from the disaster.

But there seems to be little evidence of this actually happening. 'Many survivors were ordered by the government to live away from the sea and were provided with housing that was too small, hot and inappropriate. The government is attempting to evict people from land they have traditionally occupied for decades or centuries. Many individuals and communities complain that they "fell through the net" and have received no assistance at all. This especially affects owners of unregistered businesses, such as small traders in the informal tourism sector and owners of small guesthouses made from natural materials and not permanent concrete ... The land rights issue in Thailand is extremely complicated and has been a major issue for decades. The tsunami has not caused land disputes but has exacerbated them by displacing and devastating the communities involved. Nearly all the land in question is prime land for tourism development. Some of the coastal communities do not have the relevant title documents to prove ownership of their land. They always thought that as long as they had occupied and cultivated the land for at least ten years, their tenure was secure. Increasingly, they are threatened with eviction and intimidation from private investors and public authorities, who may or may not have had the legal rights to their land. The tsunami took away their homes, livelihoods, families and friends. When they were still looking for lost relatives and recovering in temporary shelters, companies and/or government agencies moved in, claiming the land as theirs.' (A three-hour BBC drama aired in November 2006 called *Tsunami, the Aftermath*, which centred on Phuket in the days just after the disaster, helped to bring this issue to popular attention in the UK.)

The ferry from Phuket to the remote cluster of islands known as Ko Phi Phi takes nearly two hours. My boat joins five others to form a stretched-out flotilla across the warm Andaman Sea. As we pass the iconic giant limestone karsts that pepper these waters, reaching a hundred metres or more into the air, I sit on the bow counting jellyfish and plastic water bottles bobbing together on the sea's surface. Around me a hundred or so other tourists, a mixture of backpackers and a large Chinese group, top up their tans.

I've purchased a ticket to the main island of Ko Phi Phi Don, which includes in the price an excursion to its neighbouring smaller sister, Ko Phi Phi Le, the place where *The Beach* was controversially filmed in 1998. All visitors to the island want to see Maya Bay, a truly picture-perfect cove where Leonardo DiCaprio and others were filmed acting out the story of a backpacker community that sought an untouched, off-the-map tropical island all to themselves.

But when the boat finally pulls round the high cliff shielding the tight entrance to the cove, it is a huge disappointment to see it congested with other boats. I count twenty-seven in total – some speed boats, some large passenger boats such as mine – although one of the crew tells me there can be twice this number in high season. The water glistens with a diesel sheen as the crew throw down the anchor.

Everyone is offered a snorkel and we are told we have half an hour to spend swimming in the cove before the boat will leave for the main pier at Ko Phi Phi Don. Most of the Chinese women stay on board in the air-conditioned cabin and toss bread out of the windows for the waiting fish, but everyone else takes the opportunity to cool off. Before we dive in, however, we are warned that we must not swim to the main beach a hundred metres away, as there is a 200-baht charge for doing so, enforced by the marine park authorities. It isn't that appealing a prospect anyway, as there are already dozens of people on the beach from the other boats.

Once I am in the water, it is evident just how lifeless the coral beneath the waves is – surely a result of so much visitor traffic in the bay. I watch someone from our boat swim over to a tiny, empty cove to the left of the main beach, even though we've been told not to by one of the crew shouting from the boat. The man steps up on to the beach out of the wash, walks over to a large rock, and leaves his mark by urinating against it.

The use of the bay as the location for *The Beach* caused huge press attention at the time because the crew was given permission, despite the area being within Ang Thong national marine park, to alter the beach to suit their aesthetic needs. There are differing views as to whether the film crew actually caused any lasting damage – some palm tress were planted and dunes moved to give the beach a 'better' look, after which it was returned to its natural state, according to the park authorities – but what is certain is that Ko Phi Phi became a much more popular destination with tourists as a result of the film's high profile. It now seems ironic that, at the time, the film's director Danny Boyle said, 'We got a chance to speak for Thailand, to tell these Westerners to go home and stop treating it like a playground.'

As we climb back on board, we are each handed a slice of watermelon. Water bottles are banned on the boat to 'protect the environment', according to a sign, but there are plastic cups on hand to fill from a water cooler. I watch on as discarded watermelon skins, plastic cups and cigarette butts all make their way into the sea, either by intention or accident, as passengers dry themselves off.

It's a short ride around the island, past the tall sea-caves where men climb long ladders to harvest birds' nests for the famous Chinese soup, to the approach into Ko Phi Phi Don. As we travel towards the pier, there is little sign of the damage caused by the tsunami that cruelly swept twice over the island's double-crescent beach, which sits shaped like an apple core on a kilometre-long isthmus, killing over seven hundred people. Across the water, I can hear a fusion of hammering from building sites and Bob Marley from beach cafés. The pier itself is busy with boats being unloaded. The main cargo, judging by the writing on the boxes, is beer and bottled water.

Once we are off the boat, it becomes evident how much reconstruction is going on, with bamboo scaffolding poles standing against many of the taller buildings. A long stretch of beachfront buildings that lines the right-hand side of the beach seems to be the heart of the action, where all the backpackers from my boat are now flocking.

As I walk down the main drag towards my accommodation on the other side of the beach, it is clear how much the tsunami has come to dominate island life – understandably so. Warning signs along the beach, sponsored by Coca-Cola and the UN, instruct people to 'go to higher ground inland in case of earthquake'. Huge piles of flotsam from smashed buildings still line some backstreets. There is also much that is of questionable taste – before-and-after tsunami postcards and 'Still Alive' tsunami T-shirts on sale in shops, and even Discovery Channel tsunami documentaries being shown in some cafés – in sober recognition of the fact that the islands now have a name for themselves among tourists beyond just being the location of *The Beach*.

Amid the bars, restaurants and shops serving the large throng of backpackers – most of whom are walking around in bikinis or swimming shorts, seemingly oblivious to the fact that the islanders are predominantly Muslim – I meet up with Andrew Hewett, a Briton who runs the Adventure Club dive shop, and who has lived permanently on the island since 1994 with his Thai wife and their two children. He orchestrated a huge effort by hundreds of volunteer divers to clean the islands' waters of the many tonnes of rubbish that were washed out to sea during the tsunami. He is also one of the most vocal critics of how environmentally damaging the tourism industry has become on these sensitive islands.

'Sure, when I first arrived here it was already developing. The large concrete Phi Phi hotel by the pier was already built, but it was mostly just sand streets and wooden buildings then. The boats that arrive here now are much bigger than before. *The Beach* made a difference, but it took a while for visitor figures to rise.'

Hewett has been offering diving and snorkelling trips for years and knows the various reefs around the islands intimately. 'The tsunami didn't actually do that much lasting damage to the reef. It's the tourists who do the real damage. Eighty per cent of divers contact the reef three to five times per dive. Some reefs I knew six years ago have been totally destroyed by people standing on them. We're really trying to educate divers about all this now. For example, divers should be in the perfect position to learn about climate change as it is causing such obvious coral bleaching.'

But he says that he is largely alone on the island in implementing high standards and generating awareness among divers. Most of his competitors just train people too quickly, he says. 'People are being taught to dive in the minimum allowed period of two to three days, plus undertrained people are doing the teaching. Certificates are far too easy to obtain. We only take divers out who have dived at least twenty times before. The marine park rangers here are more forest rangers by trade. No one knows where the 200 baht they collect at Maya Bay goes. The term "marine park" is virtually meaningless here. No-go zones for diving for even just a year would make a huge difference, but nobody uses their initiative here. They see the views of the *farang* like me towards the environment as condescending and lecturing.'

He says his approach is actually starting to damage his own business, as he finds it hard to compete with rival dive companies.

'It's just not a topic that is attractive to 90 per cent of people visiting here. They are always looking for the best price. Everyone is told to haggle here in Thailand, so I now have backpackers trying to beat down my prices by comparing me to other companies. I just stick to a fixed price, though. It makes me laugh that beer always seems to be recession proof.'

Hewett is proud, however, of the response by many backpackers to the tsunami. Hundreds of volunteers flocked to the islands to offer assistance in the clean-up; many had stayed here before and said they felt an affinity to the place when they watched the images of destruction on the television. Hewett himself had been in his dive shop the moment the waves struck. He says that he thought initially it was 'another Bali-style bomb or someone with a gun' as people ran screaming past his shop. He survived by wading through waist-high water, past bodies, up to the popular Reggae Bar that sits on higher ground, where he was reunited with his family. He says the smell of bodies lingered on the island for five months.

'I organized the Phi Phi Dive Camp afterwards to help clean the coral reefs. For six months we had sixty people diving every day, and in total four thousand volunteers helped to remove three hundred tonnes of debris. They worked for free and the islanders covered their accommodation and food. Heavy debris from the island – fridges, air-con units, etc. – was cast about eight hundred metres offshore. Soft coral, such as fans, was all snapped and hard stuff, such as table corals, was lifted and dumped on others. The water also moved tonnes of sand and dumped it on to corals. I have recently started experimenting with transplanting healthy coral from one area to another, using marine cement to secure it. We've set up a coral nursery and I've had good results. There's some new growth on some of the corals. We're not technically allowed to do it, but the marine authorities know what we are doing.'

But he feels this effort is overshadowed by the impact of tourism, even though he readily admits his role in oiling the cogs of change. In 2000, he started offering 'shark watch' day trips; soon all the other operators copied him and now the island is awash with signs offering similar trips. It has quickly become a 'must-do' among the backpackers. Once the market was ripped away from him – he says he refuses to use agents to sell tickets as others do – he came up with the idea of cliff-jumping and mountain-trekking trips, which again were soon copied.

'I have to be careful what I offer now, as sometimes I have thirty people in boats following me to see where we've gone and what we're doing. I'm trying to set up a sustainable tourism campaign on the island, but it is very difficult. We are simply going to run out of resources. The electricity here is privately owned and costs a fortune. Water does too, with it mostly being shipped in in tanks. There's only one well on the island and they're building a water-purification plant and a reservoir now. The garbage boat arrives three or four times a week to take the rubbish to an incinerator on the mainland. And the sewage is basically a deep hole in the ground. There's a theory here that the government wants us to suffer so they can turn the island into a luxury resort.'

*

It takes about half an hour to walk away from the town on the beach and up through the jungle to a look-out point on the highest point of the island. It offers a tremendous view over the two bays that back so dramatically and perfectly on to each other. Down below, dozens of boats rock gently in the harbour, their engines still audible from such a distance. Most of the old, flimsy wooden beach huts are gone, of course, but from here I have a clear view of the new replacement buildings that are being thrown up – many illegally, according to Hewett – with concrete foundations and supports, which the government now says are obligatory.

It is impossible not to imagine what the tsunami must have looked like from up here as it washed over the ten-thousand-strong community of locals and tourists below. Perched on such a thin bar of sand, their vulnerability is starkly apparent. It is perhaps inappropriate to refer to the 'tsunami of tourism' that has also swept over these islands, but there is obviously a capacity issue for a place such as this. Just how many visitors can it truly sustain before it starts to degrade so much that visitors begin to reject it, as the Plog Model predicts? Perhaps reducing numbers by increasing prices is the right thing to do? But what is a 'fair' price for the privilege of being able to stay here – the few dollars backpackers pay, or the hundreds of dollars luxury resorts would charge?

If that isn't a fair way to restrict access, then what is the alternative? In 2006, the Centre for Future Studies, a British thinktank, put forward an interesting idea. It said that some of the most vulnerable tourist destinations on earth, such as the Great Barrier Reef in Australia, Athens, Italy's Amalfi coast, Croatia's Dalmatian coast, Kathmandu and Florida's Everglades, should be restricted to visitors who have won entrance tickets in an annual worldwide lottery. It would both raise money and limit visitors. Furthermore, it would be equitable and would presumably attract the most passionate of visitors. Australian tour operators were appalled at the idea, saying that they relied on the Great Barrier Reef's health to maintain the 1.8 million people that visit the reef each year and therefore work hard to protect the local environment. But in much smaller, super-sensitive destinations such as Ko Phi Phi, perhaps this would be a sensible option to explore? It is certainly questionable just how long it will otherwise last before it starts to plummet down the wrong side of Plog's bell curve.

7

The Dragon and the Mouse

Sanya and Hong Kong, China

IN TERMS OF ENLIGHTENING WISDOM, it's not exactly Confucian, but there is a saying being uttered throughout the global tourism industry: 'If you seek riches, look to the East.'

China is, simply, an obsession for the industry, as it has become for so many others, too. A tourism conference isn't complete nowadays without a debate about the impact this 'Rising Dragon' will have on the number of tourists travelling around the world in coming years. The frenzy of speculation was fuelled greatly in 2003 when the UNWTO made some striking forecasts. It predicted that China would produce 100 million outbound tourists annually by 2020, making it the fourth-largest source of tourists in the world behind, in order, Germany, Japan and the US (with the UK fifth). This compares to just 20 million outbound tourists in 2003, itself a fifty-fold increase in twenty years. This is a remarkable turnaround within a generation, considering that before the death of Mao Zedong in 1976 going abroad was considered wasteful and bourgeois, even unpatriotic. But even if a significant percentage of the predicted total consists of people crossing over the 'border' into Hong Kong or Macau – they currently account for about two-thirds of all outbound tourists from

China – it's a trend that is still demanding attention. (The UNWTO also predicted that China would become the world's most-visited destination – ahead of even France and the US – by 2020.)

This new passion to travel among an albeit still small portion of Chinese society has even started to be reflected in everyday culture. The Beijing-based newspaper *China Daily* noted in 2006: 'For decades, Chinese greeted each other by asking: "Have you eaten?", a custom rooted in the country's time-honoured food culture. In recent years, those getting richer started to ask: "Have you bought a new home (or a car)?" Today, a more common daily greeting has come into vogue: "Have you been playing abroad?"'

How to tap into this potentially enormous market has become a much-asked question within the travel and tourism industry. But as China's increasingly affluent and aspirational population seeks to mirror consumers in the West by adding foreign travel to its list of conspicuous spending, important questions are raised. What effect is this considerable extra load going to have on tourism infrastructure around the world? Where will the Chinese wish to go? How will they get to their destinations? What will they want to do once there? And what impact will this onslaught of new visitors have on environments and host communities already under severe pressure from present-day tourism demands? Ultimately, is this growth sustainable?

Many consultants are making handsome sums attempting to answer just these questions for the airlines, travel agents, hotel groups and tour operators hoping to attract China's tourists, or indeed send tourists in the other direction. But tantalizing clues are already emerging as to the opportunities – and problems – this vast movement of people is likely to bring.

In July 2005, just two weeks after suicide bombers attacked London's underground network, causing a significant if short-lived depression in visitor numbers, the city received its first ever Chinese citizens travelling on tourist visas. The group of eighty tourists from Beijing and Shanghai were welcomed like – and by – royalty, with the Duke of York hosting a gala dinner for them at the Tower of London. Their week-long visit began in the capital, much like that of any other tourists, with trips to Madame Tussauds, the London Eye, the Victoria and Albert Museum and the British Museum, before moving on to other UK destinations they had requested to see: Shakespeare's Stratford-upon-Avon, Manchester United's Old Trafford stadium and J. K. Rowling's Edinburgh. In total they each paid £1,200 – the equivalent to the annual salary of an average Chinese worker.

Some of the party told the *Guardian* during their trip that Londoners were 'very clean' – no doubt, they felt, because of 'Britain's famous gentleman culture – James Bond and Hugh Grant'. The advice they offered London's tourist operators was always to serve Chinese-style food and to provide more guides fluent in Mandarin. According to Calum MacLeod, director of the Great Britain–China Centre, many Chinese people have a particular, if outdated, view of the UK: '*Oliver Twist* is a very popular book in China and the title of the Chinese version translates as *Foggy City Orphan*. When I tell Chinese people I live in London, they often ask me how bad the fog is.'

This first wave of tourists from China was just a small indication of how removed expectations can be from reality. But visitor and host are likely to become much better acquainted with each other's foibles in coming years: VisitBritain, the UK's tourism promotion body, estimates that about 400,000 Chinese tourists could be visiting London by 2020, about as many as are likely to come from Japan or the US.

A similar familiarization process is now happening in many of the world's leading destinations as they ready themselves for greatly increased numbers of Chinese tourists. The trigger for this rush, in addition to China's growing prosperity, has been whether the destination country has received its Approved Destination Status (ADS) from the Chinese government. Since the early 1990s, an increasing number of countries has been approved by the Chinese authorities to receive Chinese tourists. Before then, foreign travel was tightly restricted to people either on business, visiting family or going to study. At first, only a handful of countries were granted the honour, most of them countries close to home such as Thailand, Singapore and Malaysia. In 1999, Australia and New Zealand were added, and in 2005 the UK joined a wave of countries finally receiving ADS clearance from China. Over one hundred countries have now received ADS, although the US and Canada remain notable exceptions, despite repeated promises from all parties to resolve the issue, which is largely due to a wrangle about how to control the potential rise in illegal immigration from China. In the meantime some touristic US states, such as Nevada and Hawaii, have struck up their own ADS arrangements with China, evidently more concerned about losing potential income than immigration issues.

Tourists from China still face restrictions, though. For example, they must travel in groups with a minimum of five members, organized and escorted by Chinese-approved companies. But compared to just a generation ago, this new freedom to travel represents significant liberation, for those who can afford it. As was shown by the first Chinese tourists to come to London, these new travellers inevitably bring with them their own traits and demands. Wolfgang Georg Arlt, a professor of international tourism management at the West Coast University of Applied Sciences in Heide/Holstein, Germany, and author of *China's Outbound Tourism*, has lectured widely on the subject and speaks of a current 'cultural distance' between Chinese tourists and their destinations. Even when visiting China's own Special Administrative Regions (SARs) of Hong Kong and Macau, mainland Chinese tourists have a very particular agenda, as Professor Arlt explained in a paper presented at the Tourism in Asia conference held at Leeds University in 2006:

'For Chinese visitors it is, for obvious reasons, not the "Suzie

Wong" oriental flavour in a former British colony which is exotic, but the visitation of the remains of Western domination of the SARs now back in Chinese hands, as well as the surviving "Western" elements of these places' (for instance the pub scene of Lan Kwai Fong, a destination in Hong Kong popular with hard-drinking ex-pats). '"Being photographed by Mainland Chinese tourists" is indeed already mentioned in the Lonely Planet guide to Hong Kong as a "must-do" for backpackers. Such Mainland Chinese tourists' behaviour is informed in the SARs by a "secure" way of gazing at non-Chinese cultural elements, combined with pride that symbols of colonialism like the Governors' houses are now back in Chinese hands. Still many Mainland visitors, especially Non-Cantonese, complain about being mistreated and looked upon as easy exploitable "country cousins" by Hong Kong tour operators and shop-owners.'

This 'cultural distance' is frequently noted in the South-East Asian countries that Chinese tourists have now been visiting for over a decade. Problems include a perception among Chinese tourists that they face racial discrimination. In contrast, some destinations accuse the Chinese of arrogant behaviour. In 2005, a group of three hundred Chinese tourists took offence at the image of pig faces on their tickets to a casino in Malaysia, a predominantly Muslim country. The casino said it was intended as a way for their staff to distinguish their Chinese guests from Muslim guests, who cannot eat pork (or, in theory, gamble), but the tourists staged a sit-in and sang their national anthem in protest. In the end, police with dogs were forced to clear them from the lobby.

Another point of conflict has been the widespread use of 'zero-dollar tours', whereby Chinese tourists are offered 'free' trips – often including flights and accommodation – so long as they pass through certain shopping centres, restaurants and souvenir stands during their holiday. The Chinese have a reputation for shopping a lot when abroad, and the tour guides, of course, take a hefty commission from any sales, thereby offsetting the subsidised parts of the package. But the practice has now been largely banned in Thailand because it was damaging the perception of Thailand within China; many tourists felt they were being exploited by ultimately paying more than if they had just gone on a conventional tour.

Other tensions arise from some of the reported habits and demands of Chinese visitors: smoking in no-smoking areas, taking pillows from hotels as souvenirs, stubbing cigarettes out on hotel carpets, and persistent haggling, even in fixed-price countries. *The Economist* has noted that Chinese tourists will put up with 'hard beds and cold noodles' and stay thirty kilometres away from a city centre, just to save money, because they are 'champion shoppers' who prefer to spend their money on luxury branded goods and visits to casinos (which are banned in China, despite the country's famous passion for gambling).

'Compared with the Japanese, Chinese mainland tourists coming to Europe for the first time are ruder, louder and more demanding,' says Professor Arlt. He isn't intending to be critical per se – even though it may come across like this – stressing that the 'cultural distance' needs to be bridged quickly as visitor numbers escalate. As Arlt says, Western tourists have many preconceptions in their heads about holidaying which are largely based around individual values. In other words, in general we don't tend to like doing things with other tourists in large groups; instead we try to seek our own little private corner of paradise in our time and under our own steam. Arlt's thesis is that those trying to engage with the emergence of China's tourists on to the global market will have to put aside many of their assumptions about tourists' behaviour. 'Ruder, louder and more demanding' is just part of Chinese culture – albeit measured against the bar of the Japanese. If we don't learn to work with it, they may become the new Ugly Americans – a highly lucrative but little liked breed of tourist.

But shouldn't one of the goals of tourism be a meeting of peoples on equal terms, where both tourist and host respect each other? If there's going to be any bias in the relationship at all, surely the tourist – who is effectively a guest in someone else's home – should be the one trying to create the fewest ripples of discontent by adhering to the 'When in Rome' mantra whenever possible?

'Please don't climb over that wall into the naval base during your stay.'

I assure Zhang – or 'Frank' as he prefers to be called by the growing number of Western tourists that use him as a translator and guide when visiting Sanya – that I have no desire whatsoever to scale the three-metre-high fence surrounding the large barracks that house hundreds of Chinese military personnel. It seems wise, given his anxieties, not to tell him that my fourth-floor hotel window happens to overlook the whole compound and gives me clear sight of the many naval warships docked at the nearby harbour. Or that I've just been sitting at an internet terminal in the lobby, testing which websites are censored in China. (BBC News is blocked, but strangely not CNN or the *Guardian*.)

Frank has come to meet me at the less-than-inspiringly-named Sanya Water Industry Sea-View Hotel, a modern, four-star beach resort that is, according to the pamphlet in my room, 'nestled away' in Sanya's Dadong Bay to the far south of tropical Hainan Island, which itself is the most southerly point of China. The truth is that the hotel fronts on to a busy road and is a good twenty-minute stroll, past the entrance to the military base guarded by four rock-still soldiers, to the beach.

Even though he appears a little edgy upon first meeting me, Frank tells me that he always likes to explain the dos and don'ts to new visitors, and has years of experience showing tourists around the sights of Sanya, the second-largest city on Hainan Island and a leading holiday destination for domestic tourists. He boasts that he has recently acted as a personal guide for Julia Morley, chairperson of the Miss World competition which was held in Sanya for three consecutive years from 2003–5.

'This really made Sanya famous around the world,' says Frank proudly, which is exactly what the city's tourism chiefs were hoping for when they brought the outdated beauty pageant to a corner of China that few Western tourists are familiar with. Sanya now follows a long line of destinations – including South Africa's Sun City, the Maldives and the Seychelles in recent years – trying to place their name on the map by hosting the annual event. And when Miss World departed Sanya for Warsaw in 2006, the invitation simply went out to the World's Strongest Man competition instead.

This raising of Sanya's profile might just have worked, as Frank is getting ever busier. In 2007 the first charter flights from the UK started landing at Sanya's Phoenix airport. MyTravel's Airtours is the first major tour operator from the UK to offer two-week packages to China that include ten days on the beaches of Sanya and three days touring the sites of Beijing, such as the Forbidden City and Tiananmen Square. The company is gambling on the fact that some people will be willing to fly fifteen hours each way, via Bahrain, largely to just sit on a beach. The *Daily Mail* greeted the landmark moment with the headline 'Sun, Sea and Soy Sauce', proving that the 'cultural distance' Professor Arlt refers to has some way still to go before it is bridged. 'This is for the more adventurous holidaymaker who wants a bit of hand-holding because they've got a few concerns about China,' Airtours managing director Steve Barass told the *Guardian* upon announcing the package. 'As for showing Chelsea on a big screen and eating roast beef on a Sunday, I don't know if it will appeal to that market.' Airtours is obviously confident that a broad-enough section of the UK market is now ready to step into China under the aegis of the conventional package holiday, whereas to date the country has been much more of a destination for the adventurous end of the market. It's another sign that China looks set to make a big impact on the global tourism market.

Hainan Island has been receiving visitors from mainland China for many centuries, but most have been criminals on the run or political exiles. It achieved additional notoriety for being the winter-holiday destination of Mao's fourth wife Jiang Qing, or 'Madame Mao' as she was known, a key player in the Cultural Revolution. Its isolated location has always given the island an identity distinct from the mainland, which was reinforced in the 1980s when it was granted 'Special Economic Zone' status, allowing a rush of investment in the province. Despite some economic hiccups in the early 1990s which left a number of new buildings half-built, Hainan has since become a playground for China's rich élite, with luxury hotels and golf courses being built along the island's southern coastline that centres on Sanya. It is only in the past few years that foreigners have started to travel to the area that is now widely referred to as 'China's Hawaii', given its tropical climate and palm-fringed, fine-sand beaches. Some also come to Sanya as 'health tourists', to make the most of both the restorative climate and the medical facilities. (China was internationally criticized in 2006 when it finally admitted that organs of executed prisoners were being sold to foreigners visiting the country on tourist visas. The health ministry said it would be banning the sale of organs to 'transplant tourists'.)

'The Finns and Russians are our most frequent long-haul visitors at the moment,' Frank tells me as we step into his car for a tour of the area. As we pass a parade of shops close to the hotel, he points to the sign above a seafood restaurant.

'Look, even the signs are written in Russian. They have been coming since 2003, after SARs finished. There's an Aeroflot flight direct to Sanya from Moscow every ten days now. But the Russians are low educated. They start drinking in the morning and they don't play golf. Do you play golf? We have twenty-seven courses in Hainan now and three more are being built. The Japanese and Chinese love golf. We have many foreigners now buying villas here for the beaches and the golf. A big luxury villa here only costs 3 million yuan (£200,000). Many are bought by Brits and Italians who rent them out, or turn them into small hotels.'

Before leaving Sanya, we stop off briefly at a supermarket for some water. Inside, amid aisles filled with toothpaste, laundry powder and packets of noodles, something stops me in my tracks: a vacuum-packed bag of three dried seahorses. The label prices them at 32 yuan (£2). Above them, fixed to the wall, is what looks like a commemorative frame containing two large seahorses, all for the equivalent of £40. It is well documented that the demand for seahorses in China – for traditional medicine as well as for decorative souvenirs – is placing these creatures under extreme threat, but seeing them makes me wonder what cultural demands the Chinese will bring with them as they begin to travel more and more. For example, Sanya seems awash with seafood restaurants, which typically have entire walls lined with tanks full of live fish, crabs, shrimps, eels, sea cucumbers and anything else that is liable to move under the waves. Will they expect live seafood to be on sale wherever they travel around the world, just as many Western tourists expect, say, a hamburger, fries and Coke, or wall-to-wall air conditioning? Is always giving tourists what they want – in this instance, live seafood, framed seahorses and the large conches sold by the city's many beach vendors – what is meant by bridging the 'cultural distance', even if in this case it can threaten the depletion of marine resources?

It takes about an hour to drive out of modern, Westernized downtown Sanya, past the airport, along the new expressway running parallel with Sanya Bay, towards one of the island's premier tourist attractions, the Nanshan Buddhist Cultural Park. In 2002 the Chinese National Tourism Administration made it a 'national priority tourist-development project' to build the world's tallest maritime Buddhist sculpture within the park. In just two years, a 108-metre-high sculpture of Guan Yin, the 'Bodhisattva of infinite compassion and mercy', was erected on an artificial island just off the coast facing Nanshan Mountain. The opening ceremony in 2005 was said to be the largest religious activity held in China since the founding of the People's Republic of China.

The large car park is packed with coaches when we arrive. The midday heat is so intense that Frank thoughtfully arranges for an umbrella to be fetched to shield me from the sun. We bypass the large groups of Chinese tourists queuing for tickets, as Frank is already clutching a pre-paid pair for us, and jump aboard the electric tram to the Nanshan Temple, which sits on the verdant hillside overlooking the giant sculpture of a three-headed, bright white female figure.

As we enter the cool interior of the temple, Frank tuts when we pass a group of Japanese men browsing through souvenirs. I look at him quizzically.

'I don't like the shops here. It is too commercial and busy here with people. This is meant to be a temple. And look how many of these Japanese men are single. Where are their wives? The Japanese men come here to Sanya for our nightclubs and prostitutes.'

Frank's forthright views about the manners of foreigners don't seem to need much coaxing.

On a nearby balcony that offers a panoramic view of the statue and surrounding coastline, a family asks me to take a picture of them. Afterwards, the father beckons his teenage son towards me and gesticulates in my direction. Frank tells me that the boy's father is ordering him to speak to me in English as he is learning it at school. He nervously comes towards me, smiles, and in a questioning tone asks, 'Westlife?'

My confused expression deflates the boy, so I respond with 'Hello, my name is Leo.' This just causes more confusion. Frank puts us all out of our misery by asking the boy in Mandarin what he was saying. He chuckles to himself. 'He was asking if you like the music stars Westlife.'

I nod at the boy, if only to put him at ease. He fires back more names. 'Backstreet Boys. Mariah Carey. Celine Dion. Very much I like.' As we run through more pop acts, Frank and the father break into conversation.

'This man says his family are from Shanxi province,' Frank tells me. 'It's in the north, near Inner Mongolia. He has brought the family here on holiday for a week as a reward because his son has passed some exams. He is studying to get into a technical college in Hong Kong. The father came here on business a few years ago and promised to bring the rest of the family. They're staying at the four-star Phoenix Hotel. It's very nice.'

I ask Frank to enquire where else they've been on holiday. 'Everywhere,' comes the reply. 'Malaysia, Thailand, Singapore, Hong Kong, Macau. Europe next time.'

On our return to Sanya, we stop off briefly at the 'End of the Earth'. This is the most southerly point of China (bar some internationally disputed islets in the South China Sea) and is famous across the country because a painting of the large rocks on the beach inscribed with the Chinese words *Tianya* (edge of the sky) and *Haijiao* (end of the sea) feature on the two-yuan banknote. Hordes of Chinese tourists visit the site every day to be photographed in front of the rocks.

The visit to the rocks seems routine until we are stopped by the police for speeding upon rejoining the expressway. Having already been a little spooked by Frank's warning about the naval base, I am fearful of the consequences. But Frank simply calls a number on his mobile phone, hands it over to the policeman, and we are quickly waved on. I ask Frank who was on the phone. 'Oh, it was my friend at the police station. We mustn't interrupt our tourist visitors.'

Before re-entering downtown Sanya, we pass a long strip of hotels facing the sea close to the airport. Frank tells me that this is known as the Haipo Resort District and is home to a number of big hotels, including the Holiday Inn. (The InterContinental Hotel Group, which owns the Holiday Inn and Crowne Plaza chains, plans to have about 125 hotels in China by 2008.) A large red banner hangs from a fence, which Frank explains is the local government's boast that these new hotels will improve the environment and create jobs.

'This is where Kempinski, a big German hotel company, are building their hotel,' he says. 'The other big tourist zone here is Yalong Bay, just the other side of Sanya. That is where most of the luxury five-star hotels are, such as Hilton, Marriott, Sheraton and Crowne Plaza. Further along the coast is Haitang Bay, which is just now being developed. The land there is being bought by a consortium of developers from Hong Kong, Singapore, China and the US. Between 5 per cent and 10 per cent of the tourist dollar goes to the government here. That's why they push it so hard.'

It is true that many of the major international hotel chains have now invested in Sanya. One such chain is Mandarin Oriental, the luxury-hotel group that owns or operates thirty hotels across the world and is itself part of the Jardine Matheson Group, a vast Bermuda-listed multinational corporation that is the biggest employer, apart from the government, in Hong Kong. The 297-room Mandarin Oriental 'hideaway' resort, which includes 'thirty-eight private infinity-edge pools', opens in Dadong Bay in 2008. Edouard Ettedgui, the French chief executive of the hotel group, sees Sanya as a strategic gateway into China's luxury-tourism market.

'There are ten to fifteen brand-defining cities in the world and everyone knows them: London, New York, Paris, Tokyo, Hong Kong, Los Angeles, etc.,' he tells me. 'It's the same for all luxury brands, not just hotels. There are no such cities in the Middle East, Africa, South America – not yet at least. At the moment they happen to be in the so-called developed world, which is where the culture, money, history and so on is. This is not a judgement, just a simple statement of fact. At the beginning of the century, I wouldn't have put Beijing or Shanghai in there among them, whereas they most certainly are there today. And I foresee a time soon when Mumbai and Delhi will be included, too. Between India, China and Russia, which is where the big trends in tourism are happening, we will probably soon have 200–300 million travellers, simply because of the creation of wealth.'

The problem, he says, is that Mandarin Oriental won't, for a number of reasons, be opening its hotels in Beijing or Shanghai until at least 2009, and he views Sanya as being a 'loud-hailer' for his company's brand before this time. 'Sanya, they say, is the Hawaii of China. The rich people from Shanghai and Beijing go there. It is also only one hour's flight from Hong Kong, where there are, of course, many rich people. There are only twenty million people in China at the moment with a passport. But there are a large number of rich people there who don't have a passport yet, so the Sanya Mandarin Oriental will serve them.

'The other point – and this is not to be underestimated – is that many Chinese don't speak another language and they are therefore ashamed to go abroad. This makes Hainan an easy place for us to invest. It is simply an attempt to have our brand operating in the Chinese market before we are ready to open in Beijing and Shanghai.'

Ettedgui also says that the huge investment in infrastructure on Hainan Island – roads and airports are being upgraded, and a new railway will soon open, cutting the journey from Sanya to the bridge over to the mainland from three hours to seventy minutes – is highly attractive to hotel groups such as his.

'Without mass-market tourism, you don't have a luxury market,' he says. 'We have to have the infrastructure that the mass market necessitates. I don't believe in travelling through hell before reaching paradise. Some places take twenty-four hours just to reach. The reason Phuket in Thailand is a success as a luxury destination is that there is mass-market infrastructure. You can always choose some land that is secluded, but you still need the airport. That's why Latin America, Africa and India, which have a wealth of possibility for tourism, have not yet been able to develop. That's why our industry is always lobbying governments for infrastructure. We have to tell these governments to look beyond the individual hotels, restaurants, etc., and see the whole picture and the job-creation opportunities. Without roads, airports and an open-skies policy there is nothing. This is the problem with India. It has three million foreign visitors a year – Hong Kong has twenty-five million. Why? Because of its closed-skies policy.'

But upmarket hotels are not the only ones eyeing up potential business possibilities in China. The arrival of Chinese tourists across the world will be felt right across the industry, according to Tony Wheeler, co-founder of the Lonely Planet guidebooks.

'Chinese tourism really is taking off like a rocket ship, just as all the predictions have been saying. From my point of view, you will definitely get Chinese backpackers – and Indian ones, too. We are already translating and adapting our guides for these markets – destinations such as Australia, Germany and Malaysia have already been done. I just don't think the Chinese are always going to be like the Japanese, travelling en masse. They're much more independently minded.'

On his own travels through China, Wheeler has found evidence of an already blossoming market for home-grown tourist guidebooks. 'I picked one up there recently and took it back home for someone to translate. The cover said, "For young people who want to travel to Tibet in a culturally sensitive manner." It shows that they are setting off to travel around their own country more and more, and then internationally. I recently noticed that some of the guesthouses in

Kathmandu, Nepal, have now switched over entirely to cater for Chinese guests. China is, of course, changing at breakneck speed internally, too. They have built their motorways, for example, in just five years, whereas it took the US and Europe decades to build a similar network. However, I don't think we could translate our English-language China guide into Chinese, as we wouldn't be allowed to mention Tibet, the Cultural Revolution or what happened at Tiananmen Square. I wouldn't be prepared to compromise on this.'

This raises one of the most fundamental questions facing tourists travelling to China, or any country run by an oppressive, undemocratic government with a notorious human-rights record. By doing so, are you supporting their actions? After all, if the government collects a tourist tax, as most countries do in some way, you could be said to be directly contributing to their coffers. Or can you visit such a country on holiday and somehow not be complicit?

This is a dilemma that Tony Wheeler has first-hand experience of, having seen his company become the focus of a boycott call by pro-democracy campaigners desperate to see the military junta controlling Burma expelled. In 1995, the National League for Democracy, the party led by Aung San Suu Kyi that was democratically elected to power in 1990 but prevented from taking office by the dictatorship, called for tourists and the tourism industry to stay away from Burma in protest. 'Burma will be here for many years, so tell your friends to visit us later. Visiting now is tantamount to condoning the regime,' said Aung San Suu Kyi, the Nobel Peace laureate who has largely remained under house arrest within Burma since 1990. The Burma Campaign UK, joined by a number of other campaign groups such as Tourism Concern, have pressed for a tourism boycott of the country ever since. Lonely Planet has been criticized because it continues to publish a guide to the country.

'Tourism to Burma helps sustain one of the most brutal and destructive regimes in the world,' says the Burma Campaign UK. 'A regime that was weak and bankrupt in 1988 has used foreign invest-ment and hard foreign currency to double the size of its military and strengthen its grip on power . . . More than one million people have been forced out of their homes in order to "beautify" cities, suppress dissent, and make way for tourism developments, such as hotels, airports and golf courses . . . There is simply no way to operate in Burma or visit the country without providing funds to the dictatorship.'

Lonely Planet joins other guidebook publishers such as Fodor's and Insight Guides on Burma Campaign UK's so-called 'Dirty List' of companies 'supporting the regime in Burma' through tourism. In contrast, Rough Guides have made a stand by not publishing a Burma guidebook.

'Burma has caused me more headaches than any other place,' admits Wheeler. 'Yes, Rough Guides, on principle, do not publish a Burma guide. We had a guide for fifteen years before anyone thought to go to Burma. If Rough Guides had had a guide and withdrawn it, I might feel differently, but to say they don't have one is a different question, I think. Quite frankly, Burma is a place with a terrible government, but there are lots of other places with terrible govern-ments, like China, which we don't seem to treat with the same attitude. Burma gets about 100,000–200,000 visitors a year, mostly Italians and French, but Cambodia gets one million and Thailand gets eight million. But Burma has fantastic tourism potential. It's got just as much going for it as Thailand, Vietnam, Laos and Cambodia, but gets far fewer tourists than those places. It's got wonderful people. I hadn't been to Burma for quite a while and after all this boycott stuff started I began going back, because I was being accused of so many things that I wanted to see it with my own eyes again. As a result I made a lot of friends there. We now have a Lonely Planet Foundation that puts money into things there. The people involved in tourism in Burma definitely want it. I know one person who was imprisoned there and knows Aung San Suu Kyi personally and who wants tourists to come and stay in his hotel. It's a curiously British thing to say that if only tourists stayed away everyone in Burma would be very happy and the government might fall.'

But Lonely Planet isn't criticized by all Burma campaign groups. Voice for Burma, for example, believes, like Wheeler, that the issues are far from black and white.

'In 1999, Suu Kyi again reiterated that tourists should not come to Burma,' says Voice for Burma. 'However, she did also concede that in terms of "alternative tourism", "visitors to the country can be useful, depending on what they do, or how they go about it" . . . All tourists, particularly those visiting developing countries, should be aware that their presence can lead to cultural erosion, environmental devastation and the exploitation of local workers. Burma is no exception, and we urge visitors to do all they can to minimize their contribution to these effects . . . Overall, we feel that a blanket boycott on tourism does more harm than good. While widespread, mainstream tourism may shore up the government and provide no insight for tourists into Burma's unique situation, we feel that ethical tourism can, for the most part, avoid these negative effects. Instead, it can provide much-needed income for the small percentage of ordinary Burmese working in the industry. A blanket boycott would deny these people an income.'

Tourism Concern, however, feels this view is naive. 'The concept of encouraging responsible travel in Burma is an attractive one, with tourists only travelling through small privately run businesses and buying goods from locals. Unfortunately this is a very simplistic and idealistic view of international tourism. It is obvious from witnessing trends in neighbouring Thailand that this is not how the majority of tourists operate. It is not possible to encourage one type of tourist to travel to Burma but ban another inevitable set of travellers.'

China has also been the focus of tourism boycott calls, though more for its actions in Tibet than for what Amnesty International describes as 'serious and widespread human-rights violations perpetrated across the country'. The very act of visiting Tibet as a tourist has been controversial ever since the People's Liberation Army first entered Tibet in 1950, and a year later China formally annexed the territory. In 1959, 87,000 Tibetans were killed in the capital Lhasa, according to the UN, when Chinese troops violently put down an uprising. The massacre forced the Tibetan spiritual and political leader, the fourteenth Dalai Lama, to flee to India with 80,000 other Tibetans.

Travelling to Tibet has since been seen by some as supporting China's actions. In July 2006, for example, the Free Tibet Campaign called for a tourist boycott of the newly built Golmud–Lhasa railway in Tibet. The 'celestial railway', as it has been dubbed in China, now makes it possible to travel by train all the way from Beijing to the Tibetan capital in around forty-eight hours. It is the realization of a fifty-year ambition by the Chinese authorities to build a rail link across the inhospitable permafrost of the Tibetan plateau. Having posed extraordinary engineering challenges, the route is a trainspotter's marvel: it is now the highest passenger railway in the world, with some stretches above five thousand metres. Some carriages even have oxygen available for passengers should they suffer altitude sickness.

But it is also the world's most controversial railway, having become the most high-profile symbol of China's determination to push forward with its 'go-west programme' to increase transport, cultural and economic links with the underdeveloped western regions of the country. The Office of Tibet, the 'official agency of HH Dalai Lama and the Tibetan government in exile', condemned its inauguration: 'The US$3 billion, 2,000-kilometre railroad could become an effective weapon for Beijing's alleged plan to "Sinicize" the restive region through the introduction of tens of thousands of tourists and private entrepreneurs into the inhospitable highlands every year,' it said. It added that the railway would greatly increase China's military hand in this strategically important area and allow exploitation of its rich mineral resources.

But in recent years, and in contrast to Aung San Suu Kyi's position on Burma, the exiled Tibetan government has seemingly endorsed trips to Tibet, as long as great efforts are made by tourists to use the services of Tibetan businesses instead of those run by the Han Chinese who have been encouraged to settle there.

The Free Tibet Campaign has urged tourists not to use the services of three UK travel agencies, including G W Travel, which now operates tours on the Golmud–Lhasa railway. G W Travel replied that it had briefed the Office of Tibet, and responded as follows: 'They have asked us that . . . we employ Tibetan people on the train and we will explore this . . . The fact of the matter is that the railway line has been built, individual travellers will use it and if we did not provide an extension to our tours then somebody else would. By providing these tours we believe that we are assisting the situation for the Tibetan people.' It was hardly the stand the Free Tibet Campaign was seeking.

Until 1998, the descent into Hong Kong by air used to be one of the most spectacular landing experiences in the world. Passengers would talk of being able to look directly out of the plane into the windows of the high-rise apartment buildings in Kowloon that lined the approach into Kai Tak airport.

But as aircraft traffic, noise pollution and capacity concerns increased, the Hong Kong government decided in the 1980s to look for an alternative airport site, away from the built-up Victoria Harbour area of downtown Hong Kong. The ambition was to turn the new airport into a 'superhub' for east Asia, building an airport terminal that was nine times larger than Kai Tak and served by two

3.8-kilometre runways, allowing the handling of 750 aircraft movements a day and 45 million passengers a year. It was to be the region's gateway to China. The project took eight years to complete and cost $20 billion; it also involved the construction of new roads, railways, bridges and even a new town alongside it. But with land at such a premium in Hong Kong, the decision was also taken to reclaim land from the sea – as has historically happened in a number of places across the territory – in this case off the northern side of Lantau Island, Hong Kong's largest island that juts into the delta of the Pearl River. In total, 1,248 hectares of new land was created by dredging the seabed near by, adding 1 per cent to Hong Kong's land mass. (The old runway at Kai Tak is now being turned into a large cruise-ship terminal, as the new generation of cruise ships that are increasingly visiting Hong Kong can't fit into the present berths at Tsim Sha Tsui.)

As my China Southern Airlines flight from Sanya banks left over Victoria Harbour and aligns itself for the approach into Hong Kong International Airport, I can just make out my intended destination in the distance – Hong Kong Disneyland. Like the airport, the latest theme park to join the global Disney family is also built on reclaimed land, but this time on the other side of Lantau Island. What was once a shallow inlet called Penny's Bay has been filled to form a flat platform that stretches out into the Pearl River delta. In the middle of this artificial land mass sits the 126-hectare theme park that opened in late 2005. Behind it I can see the cable-car network that forms the Ngong Ping Skyrail, which carries tourists up over the barren undulating hillsides to the giant 250-tonne bronze Tian Tan Buddha sitting high on a promontory on the western side of the island.

Once I am out of the airport, it is only a ten-minute taxi ride to the entrance of Hong Kong Disneyland. It is hard to imagine that this was once the site of a decrepit shipyard on the edge of a bay. The only sign of the expanse of water that once existed here is the twelve-hectare 'Inspiration Lake' and its recreation centre, the only part of the theme park that is free to enter. The taxi sweeps around the outskirts of the theme park, past the 600-room 'Disney-Deco'-style Hollywood Hotel, before dropping me off in front of the only other accommodation at the park, the 400-room Disneyland Hong Kong Hotel. In contrast to the Hollywood Hotel, this building is designed in a 'Micktorian' style that, according to my pamphlet, 'recalls the romance and luxury of grand, Victorian-era hotels made famous in England, France and America'. I'm about to be as immersed in Disney culture as it is possible to be. I take a deep breath.

Some might call it 'taking the Mickey', perhaps: the hotel interior is a visual assault of Disney motifs set against cream wall finishings, chandeliers, glass lifts and headache-inducing carpets. Every now and again you come across 'Hidden Mickeys': the familiar two-eared silhouette pops up everywhere from the wallpaper to the tomato ketchup on a plate of French fries. For Disney fans, this must be heaven. It's fitting, I feel, that Disney hosts weddings here.

It's a short ride in the complimentary coach from the hotel to the entrance of the theme park itself. At the ticket booths, I meet Man Lee, my tour host. She is one of the 5,500 'cast members' (they're never referred to as staff) that work at the park. Her sheer enthusiasm and bouncy, bright zeal help explain why there are so many wide-eyed children around us clearly beside themselves with joy. She, and the other staff around her, are certainly a crucial component in the creation of that famous 'magic' that Disney tries to instil in visitors. To me, though, this utter belief in the Disney Way seems almost cultish. In children it is understandable, perhaps, but to see an adult so devoted to what is admittedly an intoxicating, yet suffocating, brand is a little unsettling.

Man Lee and I spend the next couple of hours jumping on rides, being photographed next to Goofy, watching the parade, and wandering up and down one of the quintessential Disney theme-park experiences – Main Street USA, a place that harks back to the family-orientated, unthreatening time of turn-of-the-century Marceline, Missouri, the hometown of Walt Disney. I find it interesting to note all the subtle attempts at assimilating the often blunt Americanized Disney branding into its locale. Disney has obviously taken heed after it was criticized for being culturally insensitive when it opened its theme park in Paris in 1992; it famously didn't offer wine to guests at first, which didn't exactly enamour it to French visitors. Here, there is little use of the number four (no fourth floors in the hotels) and plenty of number eights, reflecting Chinese superstitions. The date of the park's opening was also selected because it was 'lucky', and incense burns at the entrance to many buildings.

When we finally get to sit down at a café for a rest, Man Lee continues to enthuse about the Disney experience, which she says is now being enjoyed by the Hong Kong population and visitors from across Asia. 'This is East meets West here,' she says. 'We have a target of 5.5 million visitors for the first twelve months since opening. We are a little below this target, but we are aiming to do some big promotions soon. The whole theme park has been designed to incorporate Feng Shui principles. There's a bend in the walkway at the park's entrance to stop the *chi* flowing into the sea. The Chinese visitors here love Disney characters. The local favourites are Mickey [pronounced 'My-Kay' in Cantonese], Winnie the Pooh and Buzz Lightyear.'

It's easy to succumb to the Disney charm, but Man Lee's comments disguise a controversial gestation for this theme park that even the Feng Shui consultants were unable to divert.

The logic seemed impeccable. Disney sought an entrance into the emerging Chinese market, one that already had a huge appetite for theme parks. Hong Kong wished to cement its position as one of the most popular destinations in Asia. And with major transport links already in place on Lantau Island to feed the new airport, it seemed natural to position a theme park close by. A deal was struck: in

December 1999 an official agreement was signed between the Hong Kong government and the Walt Disney Company.

The terms of the agreement have been interpreted by some commentators within Hong Kong to have been in Disney's favour. After all, Disney had to be initially wooed by the Hong Kong government. However, both Disney and the government have said the deal was, and still is, mutually beneficial for both parties. Disney invested $320 million for a 43 per cent stake in the business (it also receives management and franchise fees), and the government paid $418 million for its 57 per cent stake. But it also agreed to spend $1.8 billion on infrastructure costs, such as land reclamation, sewage and power services and a new railway station. Of course, it immediately placed a huge expectancy for the success of the park on Hong Kong's seven million taxpayers.

The first negative reports about the park began during the land-reclamation phase. Local environmentalists reported that fishermen in the area were claiming that farmed fish worth $3.5 million had been killed by silt, which was being disturbed by the dredging and was drifting into the waters of fish farms ten kilometres away, an allegation supported by a study by the City University of Hong Kong. Disneyland responded that the government was responsible for the reclamation, but that it had been reassured by the government that there was no link between the reclamation and the fish deaths. The government added that the fish most likely died from a bacterial infection.

Then Friends of the Earth Hong Kong learned that the site's Environmental Impact Assessment had uncovered the presence of '30,000 cubic metres' of mud containing dioxin, a carcinogenic contaminant, around the area of the old shipyard. The campaign group discovered that this was to be trucked to a temporary site near by on Lantau Island for processing, before being incinerated on another island. 'Who has sold our soul and made a mouse of our investment?' it asked in an angry statement aimed at the government. A Disney executive said at the time that Disney would monitor the situation and make sure the park was safe for visitors, and that the mud was the government's responsibility: 'That is their responsibility. We're making sure we monitor that very carefully. We're not sharing the cost.' The on-site treatment of the contaminated mud was safely completed in May 2003, fully meeting the conditions required by the site's environmental permit, according to government records. The park finally opened, on schedule, in September 2005.

But even once the park was completed, the problems continued. First, local residents in nearby Discovery Bay complained about the noisy daily firework shows that are a key feature of all the Disney theme parks around the world. Disney responded by introducing fireworks propelled by compressed air rather than explosives. Much worse, the park was the subject of negative headlines around the world when it was revealed that it planned to serve shark-fin soup, a traditional delicacy at Chinese wedding banquets, alongside abalone and suckling pig, for wedding guests. A boycott on all Disney products and services was called for by environmentalists, appalled by the way in which demand for shark fin was killing so many sharks around the world. The pressure on the company was intense and it finally offered a compromise.

'We have heard many opinions and have given the matter careful consideration,' said Irene Chan, spokeswoman for Hong Kong Disneyland. 'But most importantly, [the dish] is an integral part of Chinese banquets in Hong Kong culture, and we strongly believe we should give choice to our guests.' The soup was taken off the wedding-banquet menu and made available only on request. The company said it would hand out a leaflet explaining the environmental impact of shark fishing to any customer seeking this option.

There were unseemly scenes on the first Chinese New Year after the park opened, when angry tourists from the mainland clutching valid tickets were turned away. The park had failed to predict demand at a time of year when people in China are granted an enforced seven-day holiday known as the Spring Festival Golden Week. (Two other Golden Weeks are also granted by the authorities, one around May Day and the other around National Day on 1 October. These holidays traditionally lead to a huge surge in domestic – and now international – tourism.) Local TV news crews filmed children being passed over barriers by parents desperate to gain entry. Hong Kong's finance secretary expressed his fear that these images would damage Hong Kong's tourism industry. The park responded by saying it wouldn't make the same mistake twice.

Then a few months later a workers' union representing cast members within the park publicly complained that there was a 22 per cent pay discrepancy between workers taking part in stage shows and those walking around the park dressed in Disney character costumes. The company responded by raising the pay by 11 per cent for the latter and arranging that break times would increase from thirty to forty minutes to help combat the physical problems some workers said were being caused by wearing the heavy costumes in the heat.

The issue of worker pay and conditions is a sensitive one for Disney. In 2005, the Hong Kong-based group Students and Scholars Against Corporate Misbehaviour released videotaped interviews with four factory workers making Disney merchandise in Guangdong Province, explaining how they worked for as little as 33 cents per hour. Disney responded by saying it was not aware of the abuses and launched an independent auditor to investigate and redress any possible violations.

Then to cap an eventful first year, the park missed its visitor target by around half a million. Jay Rasulo, the global chairman of Walt Disney Parks and Resorts, admits that Disneyland Hong Kong has made mistakes and suffered 'teething problems'. But he is still confident that there is huge demand for the Disney experience in China, and around the world. You might expect, perhaps, such belief from one of world tourism's most powerful players, someone who is in charge of an organization that generates $10 billion revenue annually.

'We aggressively continue to look for expansion possibilities elsewhere around the world,' he tells me. 'We are in a dialogue with the Chinese central government about expanding our presence in China, and that could some day take the form of a second Disney destination in China. This is one of many focuses we have. We opportunistically think about a couple of things. First, we pretty much know from research that most people in the world would welcome a Disney entertainment venue of any sort. There's lots of interest from private investors. I get calls all the time. Company X says they have land and will do whatever we want. Secondly, Disney destinations are big economic drivers in terms of employment and ever-sought-after foreign expenditure. They have served in Paris and Hong Kong, for example, as the catalyst for incredible tourism infrastructure development. Countries see the Olympics or World Expos, and do them for pride, but also as a catalyst for infrastructure development. Our destinations have fundamentally the same effect, but the difference is that it is really for the long haul.

'Having said all that, there are a great series of components that have to come together for the successful development of a Disney destination. Just as an example, look at India. It has an incredible population, great interest in Disney, very willing capital market, stable government, relatively stable economy, etc., but there's one big piece missing. There's no tourism infrastructure. We can't imagine people from different parts of India converging in one place: it's too difficult. No roads from the airports. Will we be ready some time? Probably. Is that time now? No. Same with South America. Lots of interest. Young population. Growing economy. However, it's unstable. Wild fluctuations in the economy and a big fixed-asset business are not a happy marriage.'

But doesn't Disney suffer from the anti-Americanism that is expressed throughout so many parts of the world, or, worse, stand accused of cultural imperialism?

'Anti-Americanism really doesn't affect our business in Hong Kong,' says Rasulo resolutely. 'It was the same when I was CEO of Disneyland Paris. First of all, Walt Disney brought his work to Europe very early on. Many Europeans grew up with Disney. Topolino in Italy, for example. As a child, of course, it's not very evident that this is an American thing. At an intellectual level, Disneyland Paris is a company with American roots. There's even an Americana aspect of our Main Street product offering, but I think when we are in France people think of Disneyland Paris as a European version of something American.

'In Hong Kong, people clearly know that the Hong Kong government has partnered with this American entity called Disney to present a form of entertainment with American roots that's very culturally adapted, as Disneyland Paris is. I think they think of it as *their* Disney park. "Oh great, it's our Disney park." Subsequently, they embrace it as a local form of entertainment. There is some hypothesis rather than fact to that, but our experience in Tokyo and Paris tells me those parks get locally embraced and people don't think, "Oh, I don't like what America is doing, so I'm not going to go."'

So does that mean, I ask, that Disney is set to keep expanding and building more resorts and theme parks – eleven theme parks across five sites, to date – across the world?

'Many countries are waking up to the fact that tourism is a significant way to jump-start fledgling economies. People see that sixteen million people are employed in tourism in the US – more than in the entire manufacturing sector. Tourism accounts for about 13 per cent of the US gross national product. We're very interested in bringing our form of immersive entertainment aggressively to as many people as we can around the world, and when we have seen the opportunity to do so we have leapt. The interesting thing about, say, Asia is that you have very fragmented markets with a high Disney affinity, a rapidly rising middle class and pretty good economic stability, so what we are doing quite aggressively is looking at products and experiences that might have a quite different footprint from a traditional destination.

'A traditional Disney destination requires between ten and fifteen million people to converge on a single location annually to holiday. When you start thinking what's another logical place after Hong Kong and central China where that many people could converge, you might think perhaps of the Middle East, but our answer is "No" and that might be the case for a long time to come. So rather than sit on our hands, we have started to examine other ways to present our immersive form of entertainment. Disney cruise lines is a perfect example of that.' (The company has two cruise ships operating out of Fort Lauderdale, Florida.) 'But you could also imagine smaller land-based concepts that give people a Disney immersive-entertainment experience but don't have the requirements of infrastructure and population.'

Does that, I ask, mean 'mini-parks'?

'We have to be very cautious about, say, a mini-park. When people hear the words "Disney" and "Park" they are not going to think "mini" so their expectation will not be well met. On our cruise ships, there's great hospitality, immersive Disney theming, access to the characters, live entertainment, programming based around all kinds of things for kids and adults. You come to the realization that people can experience something very Disney in their minds, without getting on an attraction. Previously, everything has been based around theme-park concepts and everything grows out of that – themed hotels, themed dining, golf courses, convention centres. The cruise line really demonstrated to us that attractions and adventures may not be what are essential to have in people's minds for the Disney experience.

'What I worry about as a creator and provider of entertainment is staying relevant to a much more rapidly changing entertainment environment than we've seen in a long time. As a consumer experience, we do everything: you show up, sit in the conveyance and everything happens around you and is controlled by us. That form of entertainment is becoming more and more interactive. What Walt was all about was taking a two-dimensional film and walking through the screen into a three-dimensional version. People want to become players now in the story, just like they do in multi-player games online.'

It is clearly crucial for any theme park not to become stale and to continue to evolve; otherwise they risk becoming hugely expensive white elephants. This is a particular danger for China, it seems, where a staggering 2,500 theme parks have been built in just twenty years. In 2005, Sui Fabo, the director of the China National Ride Inspection Group, stressed just this point in a speech to the International Association of Amusement Parks and Attractions:

'More than 150 billion yuan (£10 billion) has been invested in about 2,500 theme parks in China: 70 per cent of them are in debt, 20 per cent in balance and only 10 per cent in profit,' he said. 'Based on the changing market competition and consumer demand for freshness, curiosity and strangeness, only with scientific research, planning and detailed augmentation, will it be possible for theme parks to renovate and replace their facilities, improve their service and enhance their image?' Only then, he said, could they 'stay young and reach a new climax'.

In the Main Street Corner Café, I watch Filipino waiters, wearing Great Gatsby-style 'Newsboy' caps, serve mainland Chinese visitors to the sound of ragtime jazz. On the menu are congee (Asian rice porridge) and Mickey Mouse-shaped waffles. The confusion of ethnicities, cultures and histories seems overwhelming.

The street outside is starting to swell with people waiting for the evening's climactic firework display over the Sleeping Beauty castle. I finish my drink and walk over to one of the busy shops selling Disney merchandise. All the favourites are there – Mickey, Minnie, Donald Duck, etc. – but many are wearing Chinese-style costumes or bearing Chinese good-luck messages. In the Victorian-style Plaza Inn next door, large groups cram around tables eating Cantonese food. It is billed as the ideal place to enjoy *yam chah*, a traditional Cantonese breakfast of tea and dim sum.

A 'cultural distance' is certainly being bridged here at Hong Kong Disneyland, but quite where this bridge leads isn't clear. Is this a vision of a future where the world's richly varied identities and cultures – arguably one of the key driving forces that compel us to travel abroad – continue to be boiled down together into a bland, homogenized glop found anywhere, anytime on the planet? As more and more of us begin to travel internationally, will the tourism 'products' we consume inevitably have to be tailored to suit all comers and all tastes? In places such as Hong Kong Disneyland, it is easy to believe the cry that tourism is one of globalization's most strident attack dogs.

8

All at Sea

Miami, Florida

SUNDAY IS FAR FROM BEING A DAY of rest at the Port of Miami. This is the location of perhaps the largest mass check-in of tourists anywhere on the planet, with the exception of the world's leading airports. There's certainly no single hotel that sees anything like it. Over ten thousand passengers, crew and ground staff – slightly fewer on the other days of the week – convene to embark on the cruise ships that dock briefly at this southern Florida port to disgorge themselves of last week's guests and devour another load, before setting sail once more on their ceaseless loop of the Caribbean.

In 2005, 1.7 million passengers departed from here, according to the Cruise Lines International Association (CLIA), the industry voice for this market. The two next-busiest ports of departure for cruisers are also both in Florida – Port Everglades and Port Canaveral. These three ports account for almost half of all US cruise embarkations between them. This isn't surprising when you consider that one in every ten of the world's cruise-going tourists lives in Florida. The Sunshine State is also the geographic gateway to the Caribbean, where almost half of all the world's cruises are now based.

As the thousands of passengers, who have travelled here from all over the world, pass through security and step on to the escalators up to the ships – gangplanks are from a long-gone era – hundreds of crew dart about like krill on the harbour side, loading trolleys of luggage and provisions into the depths of these vast caverns of steel. Just a few hours earlier, this whole process was operating in reverse as last week's passengers disembarked and headed home. Their esprit and joviality belies the effort such an impressive display of logistics must require from the crew.

I play safe and arrive three hours before my ship is due to set sail. Everyone knows that these ships must depart on time – no ifs or buts. It takes over an hour to clear the formalities of passport control and the X-ray scanners, before I finally step aboard my passage to the Caribbean, the *Freedom of the Seas*. At 339 metres long, 39 metres wide and boasting a gross tonnage (the ship's volume, not weight) of 160,000 tonnes, she is the largest cruise ship ever built. To put that into perspective, the *Titanic* was 269 metres long and 28 metres wide. Or to use an even more familiar unit of measure, she is just a fraction longer than the Eiffel Tower.

But beyond the engineering marvels lie the real reasons why the 4,375 passengers that this ship can carry would want to come aboard. She is described by her owners, Royal Caribbean, as a floating resort. If any passenger attempted to use all the facilities on board, there would be a danger that they might even not notice the Caribbean destinations passing them by each day. For many, the ship itself is the real destination.

Here are just a few of the offerings listed on my itinerary sheet, which I find on the desk in my stateroom (the term 'cabin' is frowned on by Royal Caribbean): ten restaurants, sixteen bars, an ice rink, a rock-climbing wall, three pools, a children's water park, a boxing ring, a crazy-golf course, a shopping arcade, a basketball court, a surf machine, a karaoke club, a casino, an art gallery, nightclubs, a fitness centre and spa, and a 1,350-seat theatre. (I can't find quoits listed anywhere, though.) This is literally like taking one of the giant casino hotels of Las Vegas and floating it out to sea.

There is a compulsory mustering at four forty-five p.m., when we all gather at our muster stations wearing lifejackets to go over a safety briefing and await the all-clear from the captain over the tannoy. And then, dead on five o'clock, the ship slips from her mooring and glides gracefully out to sea, leaving the Miami skyline shrinking in the distance. As she does so, she follows in the wake of *Carnival Valour* and her three thousand passengers. Even once we are past the break-waters, the only sense that the ship is moving is a slight vibration underfoot. The ship's vast stabilizers, tipping back and forth under the waterline to counter any roll from the waves, prevent any notice-able rocking sensation.

Cruising is one of the major boom areas of modern tourism. People are drawn to these huge ships for many reasons, but principle among them is the fact that they offer an all-inclusive, sanitized world where many of the perceived kinks of modern travel are ironed out. The food and entertainment keep coming, a new destination appears each morning outside your window and all the comforts of home are never far away. There's also an important psychological sense that you're among your own: they are, in effect, gated communities on the high seas.

It's a winning formula, particularly in the North American market where about 80 per cent of the world's cruise-goers originate. CLIA estimates that in 1970, 500,000 people from North America took cruises. By 2005, this figure had risen to 11.2 million. Cruise analyst Tony Peisley estimates that 14.4 million cruises were booked worldwide in 2005. And all the signs are that this trend is to continue. Most of the major cruise companies have more ships on order and, significantly, these ships are much bigger than their predecessors. Royal Caribbean (which also owns Celebrity Cruises), for example, announced in 2006 that it had ordered the first of its 'Genesis Class' of ship, to be delivered in 2009, which will carry 5,400 passengers and is expected to be in service for thirty years. If no more orders are announced for the rest of the decade, which is unlikely, between 2000 and 2010 ninety-six new ships will have been added to the global fleet of cruise ships. The Carnival Corporation (which owns Cunard, Princess Cruises, P&O Cruises, Swan Hellenic and Costa Cruises, among others), by far the largest cruise company in the world, will have almost one hundred cruise ships operating by 2010, pushing the global fleet towards three hundred. This will allow the total number of cruise berths to grow from 350,000 in 2006 to 588,000 in 2015, meaning that the number of people cruising in 2015 is predicted to reach 25 million. Cruising is now very much a mass-market sector of tourism, having long ago shed its somewhat élitist image – where once families and retirees made up a significant proportion of cruisers, now cruise companies also lay on singles-only and gay cruises (which have caused great controversy in some of the more conservative Caribbean islands such as the Cayman Islands). Since 2005, the no-frills business model of the low-cost airlines has been applied to the cruise sector through the introduction of thirty-pound-a-night easyCruise ships in the Mediterranean, the Caribbean and through Holland and Belgium.

Freedom of the Seas departs Miami every Sunday, heading out on a seven-day circuit that circumnavigates Cuba and takes her, in order, to Cozumel, Mexico; George Town, Grand Cayman; Montego Bay, Jamaica; and Royal Caribbean's own private port of Labadee in Haiti, before returning to Miami.

I have joined her for two nights to travel to Cozumel, an island off the Yucatan Peninsula close to Cancún. It is the world's most popular cruise port of call, with nearly three million visitors a year. I am therefore passing through the busiest cruise-filled waters on the planet.

My first few hours on board are taken up exploring this vast ship. My stateroom is located on Deck Eight (out of fourteen) and has a small shower room, sofa, desk, flatscreen TV and double bed. I also have a small balcony with a view out to sea. My room is located on a long corridor that runs almost the length of the ship. It is busy with stateroom attendants, as they are known on board, delivering barcoded luggage to guests. Before I leave my room, I spot on my desk a prominently positioned sheet of paper entitled 'Gratuities'. It lists the 'customary gratuity amounts' for different crew members to be left on the final day by guests: $3.50 a day per guest for stateroom attendants and dining-room waiters; $2 a day per guest for assistant waiters; and $0.75 a day per guest for the head waiter.

The centre of the ship, beneath the exterior decks, is dominated by the Royal Promenade, a three-storey shopping arcade longer than a football pitch and home to various bars and restaurants (including the Bull and Bear pub and a Ben & Jerry's), as well as shops selling anything from suntan lotion to diamond necklaces. On the deck beneath is a casino, already busy with people pumping bucketfuls of quarters into the dozens of slot machines that fan out from the poker, craps and roulette tables in the middle of the room.

Up on deck, in the bleaching sunshine, are the various pool areas and zones offering outdoor activities. Naturally, there's a much higher density of children up here. I make my way to the stern, where around a hundred people are watching children line up to have a go on the Flowrider, a wave machine that is forceful enough to allow surfing on boards. I start chatting to Sandy, a grandmother from Lewes, Delaware, who is watching her teenage grandson earn a round of applause for staying upright on a board for more than ten seconds.

'I've brought him and his sister here on the cruise as his graduation present,' she tells me. 'I don't know where she is now, though. Wherever.' She shrugs her shoulders.

Sandy explains that she's paid $6,200 for the three of them, which includes return flights to Miami, a shared stateroom and food at most of the restaurants. Most drinks are charged as an extra, which is one of the things that Sandy has already found fault with.

'I once went on the *Crown Princess* [part of Carnival Corporation's fleet] for a seventeen-day cruise of the UK, Denmark, Iceland and Greenland. I preferred the range of eating on that ship. I resent having to pay extra here for some of the restaurants, such as the Johnny Rockets burger bar. I don't think the glasses are clean enough in the main dining room either. I'm going to tell my waiter tonight.'

But she's only been on board for a few hours, I say to her. 'I know,' she replies. 'But I've paid a lot of money for this trip and I want everything perfect. I don't bite my tongue.'

An hour later, I've changed for dinner – it's 'casual attire' tonight – and made my way down to the two-storey main dining room that handles hundreds of diners over two separate sittings throughout the evening. I already have a pre-assigned table number and find myself sharing a table with a honeymooning couple, Bill and Melanie from Montreal. Neither they nor I are particularly comfortable with this arrangement, especially as it's their first night together since the wedding. I am surplus to requirements. I race through my courses and make my excuses so as to leave them in peace, but before doing so we all chat to our waiter, Valentiano, from Goa in India. He says that he has been working on the ship ever since she left the yard in Finland where she was built.

'I'm working six months on, two months off at the moment. My baby girl was born five months ago so I can't wait till I get home.'

After leaving the dining room I head upstairs to the Olive & Twist bar up at the highest vantage point on Deck Fourteen, where the Australian Jazz Quartet are playing Miles Davis on the stage. I sit at the bar talking to Ban, the 'Bombay barman', as he describes himself.

'I've worked for Royal Caribbean for eight years now,' he says. 'I enjoy it. It's very social on board. There are 1,400 crew on this ship and two hundred of them are Indian. The Filipinos are the biggest group, though, but they tend to work out of sight of the passengers in the kitchen and engine room because their English isn't so good.'

Looking out of the bar's panoramic window at the setting sun to starboard and a moody storm brewing to port, I ask him about his typical day.

'We work ten-hour shifts every day. It's very tiring, but you get used to it. I swap bars every two weeks so I don't get bored. This kind of life helps me save money, though, as I can't really spend it on the ship. I have my food and accommodation paid for, too.'

I notice a logo on his name badge that says 'Save the Waves'. I've seen other staff wearing it, too. Ban tells me that everyone is trained about environmental awareness on board. Neither crew nor passengers are allowed to throw anything overboard – it's a sackable offence for any crew member. Cigarette butts are particularly frowned on, he says, as they can cause fires if blown back on board.

Back in my stateroom I notice Save the Waves stickers on the sliding doors out to the balcony, requesting to keep them closed to save energy – the whole interior of the ship is air-conditioned – and in the shower room, saying not to flush anything down the loo other than toilet paper. There's also the near-ubiquitous note found in hotels around the world about not putting your towel out for washing unless absolutely necessary.

The environment has become a major concern for the cruise industry over the past decade. It is also one of the easiest sticks with which to hit it. The main reason why I have chosen to come aboard *Freedom of the Seas* – other than to see what the largest cruise ship in the world looks like – is to find out what impact this most technologically advanced ship, fresh out of the shipyard, has on the seas it will now sail upon for decades to come.

The issue of ship pollution has been in the public consciousness ever since the *Torrey Canyon* oil tanker spill off the Cornish coast in

1967, which led to 120,000 tonnes of crude oil pouring into the Atlantic. The disaster directly led to the drafting of the first international convention for minimizing the environmental impact of all maritime vessels. Known commonly as MARPOL, the convention, which is administered by a UN specialized agency known as the International Maritime Organization (IMO), did not actually come into force for a further sixteen years. At first it principally dealt with the issue of oil spillages – just one pint of oil can cause a surface sheen across an acre of water – but it has been amended since to set standards for the disposal of sewage, bilge water, waste and other toxic substances by ships at sea. Before MARPOL, ships largely treated the sea as a dustbin.

It also deals with the considerable air pollution that can be attributed to ships. The maritime heavy oil used to power most ships has an extremely high sulphur content compared to diesel road fuel – as much as seventy times more, in some cases. According to the European Commission, 'unless action is taken, emissions of sulphur dioxide and nitrogen oxide from ships in EU seas are projected to be greater than all land-based emissions in 2020.' Just one typical cruise ship produces the same amount of emissions as about twelve thousand cars, according to Professor Ross Klein of the Memorial University of Newfoundland in Canada, who is the author of *Ship Squeeze: The New Pirates of the Seven Seas*, and who maintains the website www.cruisejunkie.com.

Broadly speaking, all ships are prevented under MARPOL from dumping anything within three nautical miles of a coastline. 'Comminuted [broken-up] and disinfected sewage' can be discharged from three to twelve nautical miles away, and beyond this boundary, which officially marks the limit of a country's territorial waters, 'it is generally considered that on the high seas, the oceans are capable of assimilating and dealing with raw sewage through natural bacterial action'. (This is also the limit for discharging oil at a concentration in water of no greater than fifteen parts per million.) Since 2005, any new ship carrying more than fifteen people must be fitted with 'either a sewage treatment plant or a sewage comminuting and disinfecting system or a sewage holding tank'. Existing ships have until 2010 to retrofit these systems.

The dumping of any plastic overboard has been banned since 1988, as the IMO estimates that it can take a plastic bottle 450 years to biodegrade in the sea, compared to a 'paper bus ticket' which it says can take two to four weeks, or painted wood which can take thirteen years. MARPOL also 'severely restricts discharges of other garbage from ships into coastal waters and "special areas"', which include many of the most popular waters frequented by cruise ships, such as the Mediterranean Sea, the Baltic Sea, the North Sea, the Caribbean and Antarctica. In these areas, no rubbish can be thrown overboard less than twelve nautical miles from shore. In any other area, this falls to three nautical miles if the rubbish has been shredded to particles no wider than 25 millimetres. A 25-nautical-mile limit applies everywhere for 'dunnage' (materials such as wooden supports and sheeting, used to protect cargo in the hold and keep it dry), and 'lining and packaging materials which will float'. MARPOL does not specify a limit, however, for the amount thrown overboard, other than what is 'operationally' generated. For a cruise ship carrying thousands of passengers this could, in theory, be several tonnes of waste every day.

The MARPOL convention has been criticized by many environmentalists over the years for not being anywhere near tough enough. It is notoriously hard to police, too, because there are few witnesses at sea to report any offending ship to the authorities, which tend to be the closest national coastguard authority to the offence. (Officially, a ship is answerable to the 'flag state' where it is registered, but more on this later.) And with ports charging high fees for handling waste, there has traditionally been a temptation to save money by throwing waste overboard.

For a long time many ships got away with such actions, but throughout the 1990s a number of countries started to crack down on offenders. The US, in particular, gained a reputation for handing out considerable fines to ships that fouled its territorial waters. (In addition to MARPOL, there are some tougher national and state laws governing ships in its waters.) With so many cruise ships passing through these waters, some particularly big fish have been caught.

According to a US Government Accountability Office (GOA) report published in 2000, there were eighty-seven confirmed illegal-discharge cases in US waters involving cruise ships from 1993 to 1998. All but six of these involved the illegal discharge of oil or oil-based products; the rest involved discharges of rubbish or plastic.

'The volume of discharged material associated with these cases varied widely, from hundreds of gallons of oil to drops of oil-based paint that spilled into the water during painting of a ship's hull,' said the report. 'The volume of garbage discharged also varied. In one case, investigators determined that a cruise ship had illegally discharged garbage after more than thirty plastic bags of garbage were found floating offshore and investigators were able to link the garbage to a particular ship. In another case, a few bottles containing plastic pieces washed up on shore with information that linked them to a cruise ship that had recently passed through the area. In contrast to these accidental cases, we judged eleven cases to be intentional (i.e., a ship's crew was actively discharging illegal quantities or types of oil or garbage).'

A range of cruise companies were prosecuted, but one was punished particularly severely with the broader intention of shocking the industry into a culture change with regard to marine pollution. In 1998 and 1999, Royal Caribbean was fined $8 million and $18 million respectively by the US Department of Justice. In the first incident, staff on *Sovereign of the Seas* were identified discharging oily bilge water, falsifying oil record books, and making false statements to coastguard officials. In the second incident, the company 'pled guilty to charges of fleet-wide practices of discharging oil-contaminated bilge waste, regularly and routinely discharging without a permit waste water contaminated by pollutants through its ships' grey-water systems, and making false material statements to the coastguard', according to the GOA report. The report also singled out 'repeated oil discharges from the *Nordic Prince* into the waters of Alaska's Inside Passage during 1994'. In addition to paying the fines, the company was required to hire a senior vice president to oversee an 'environmental compliance plan', hire an outside independent environmental consultant to conduct audits that would then be filed with various federal agencies, and, finally, appoint a committee from the board of directors to monitor the company's environmental policies. The company was also placed on probation for five years. It all amounted to a very public and humiliating dressing down and helped to bring the issue of cruise-ship pollution to international attention.

But Royal Caribbean is not the only large cruise company that has received such large fines. In 2002, Carnival Corporation was fined $9 million, with a further $9 million court-ordered community service to fund environmental projects in south Florida for similar offences, namely deliberately falsifying oil record books related to bilge discharges between 1996 and 2001. It, too, was placed on probation for five years.

Together, they were landmark rulings as between them these two companies control around 80 per cent of the global cruise industry. Even though the sums involved sound huge, it was always going to be the negative publicity that would have the more lasting effect. These firms could more than afford such fines, after all. For example, in 2006 Carnival had revenues of $11.84 billion and generated $2.28 billion in profits. In the same year, Royal Caribbean had revenues of $5.2 billion and generated $634 million in profits.

The US GOA report in 2000 concluded by warning against

complacency, signalling that, although cruise companies were making progress, the task of cleaning up the cruise industry was far from over:

'Cruise-ship companies must demonstrate a sustained commitment to eliminate illegal discharges at sea. One area that Department of Justice officials believe should receive increased scrutiny by the coastguard and other cognizant agencies in future cruise-ship-pollution cases is the discharge of "grey water", which is untreated water from showers, sinks, kitchen and laundry drains, dishwashers, and other areas of a ship. Each year, cruise ships legally discharge millions of gallons of grey water into both US and international waters. The Department of Justice recently prosecuted a large cruise-ship company that was found to be improperly disposing of printing-shop, dry-cleaning and photo-lab wastes into its grey-water system. These wastes, which included potentially harmful chemicals and toxic silver, were discharged into the sea along with the grey water.'

It also highlighted how difficult it was to prosecute when so many companies could, in effect, hide their ships behind their flag state – or 'flags of convenience' as they are more commonly known – with many registered not in the ports they most frequently visit, but ones that conveniently lie beyond the reach of the US authorities. 'The process for referring to [flag states for] alleged discharge incidents occurring outside US jurisdiction does not appear to be working either within the coastguard or internationally . . . The coastguard appears to have given up efforts to develop these cases, perhaps because the response rate from flag states has been so poor.'

Since these high-profile prosecutions, the cruise industry has begun to engage with some of the environmental groups that have been critical about its practices. Conservation International, for example, now works with the International Council of Cruise Lines (ICCL) in attempting to promote far better environmental stewardship by the cruise companies. Some groups, however, remain fiercely critical. The Bluewater Network and Oceana, for example, have been trying to get the US Congress to pass the Clean Cruise Ship Act. The aim is to ban any discharges in US territorial waters, require onboard monitoring, and give the US Coast Guard authority to regulate effluent standards between twelve and two hundred nautical miles from shore. Two Democrats – Senator Dick Durbin and Congressman Sam Farr – have tried to steer the act through Congress.

This combination of pressure has had results – of sorts. In 2006, the industry pledged via the ICCL to begin adopting a series of measures recommended by a panel of scientists convened by Conservation International, which go beyond MARPOL standards. These include not discharging treated waste-water unless at least four nautical miles from the 'twenty-metre depth contour' and travelling at a speed of no less than six knots. It also recommended improving this 'voluntary prohibition' to twelve nautical miles over time. In addition, the industry said it would commission a 'global mapping project to identify and integrate into navigational charts the sensitive marine areas where discharge should be avoided'. That this doesn't already exist is perhaps an indication of how complacent this industry has been in the past.

Some US states, though, have taken matters into their own hands rather than wait for tighter international, or even national, regulations. Alaska, for example, receives what some say is an unsustainably high number of cruise ships into its environmentally sensitive coastal waters. It has also been the location of a number of cruise-ship pollution spillages over the years, dividing a community that on the one hand welcomes the business the cruise ships bring, but on the other resents their environmental impact. In 2006, Alaska's voters narrowly approved a series of measures aimed at making the cruise ships pay a more just price for entering their waters. The measures included a fifty-dollar tax per passenger, a 33 per cent tax on gross income from the ships' casinos when they sit just outside the coastal waters to avoid Alaska's ban on casinos, and the levying of state corporate income tax on all cruise ships.

The issue of – albeit legal – tax avoidance is one that hangs heavily over the cruise industry. Royal Caribbean, for example, has its global headquarters in a smart building on the harbourside at the Port of Miami. However, the parent company has been incorporated in Liberia since 1985. And despite running out of Miami every Sunday, *Freedom of the Seas* is actually registered in Nassau, the Bahamian capital. Likewise, Carnival is incorporated in Panama. This allows both companies largely to escape the clutches of the US taxman, and also means that, in theory, they are not answerable to the US authorities – both in terms of environmental, safety and labour laws – when operating outside its territorial waters. Why would these giant international corporations bother to do this if it wasn't to their advantage? They are called 'flags of convenience' with good reason, it seems.

After an American breakfast buffet at the Windjammers Café, which has a view over the ship's long wake of white froth receding into the horizon, I make my way to the bridge to meet Erik Tengelsen, the ship's captain. It is located on the deck, beneath a long row of exercise bikes facing out to sea in the fitness centre, and is almost a five-minute walk from the café at the stern.

Captain Tengelsen is holding a mug of coffee, looking out across the bow when I enter the bridge. It is a wide, if surprisingly empty room with floor-to-ceiling windows. The only equipment of note is a panel of controls wrapped around two raised armchairs in the middle of the room. It looks uncannily like the bridge on the Starship Enterprise. This, I am informed, is the 'wheel house'.

In one of the seats sits an officer, who, Captain Tengelsen assures me, is currently driving the ship. I find the lack of anyone gripping a large wheel a little disconcerting. The ship is actually being steered, I am shown, by a dial no larger than a beer mat.

'I'm one of two captains on this ship,' says Tengelsen, a grey-bearded Norwegian who joined Royal Caribbean in 1999 after almost three decades working as a merchant seaman, which included a spell captaining a ferry between Morocco and Spain. 'We each spend fourteen weeks on, fourteen weeks off. It's the same pattern for all our marine officers.'

We sit down on a sofa beneath a wall of certificates and commemorative plaques marking each port the ship has so far visited.

'Safety and guest satisfaction are my priorities. The ship is the hardware, but the real "wow" for guests comes from the crew. On this particular cruise we have 1,393 crew members and 4,169 guests aboard, 2,846 of whom are Americans. About 1,000 of the guests are children and about 1,000 are repeat guests. Crew welfare is obviously important to me. Crew all have to keep daily time sheets of their working patterns. They each must have ten hours rest a day, with six of those continuous. But they can only work a maximum of fourteen hours a day for three days in a row.'

I ask him to give me a sense of the true scale of this ship. He calls over to one of the four officers standing at the wheel house, and some print-outs are brought over.

'About 22,000 meals a day are served on board this ship, although serving an ice cream is classed as a meal,' he says, glancing through the papers. 'This is a major logistical operation. All the food is loaded at Miami. This food obviously creates waste, as do all the bathrooms. But we add another nautical mile to the MARPOL limit and only discharge grey water thirteen nautical miles from the shore when we are travelling at six knots or more. We have an Advanced Water Plant on board for "black water", such as sewage. Any hard matter left over we incinerate. The US Coast Guard will come aboard our ships about twice a year to inspect our certificates, have a look around, and then issue reports.'

Looking out across the bridge, I ask him how far it is to the horizon.

'From this height, about seventeen miles. We have wonderful

visibility. We have radar, of course, but someone is always standing here looking out to sea for potential hazards. If we spotted a floating tree I wouldn't worry too much, but a container that's fallen off a ship can be a real hazard to us. But there aren't too many ships bigger than us. The actual weight of this ship is 71,000 tonnes.' (I later calculate that this is equivalent to 400 empty Boeing 747-400s.) 'Her propellers can generate 18,000 horse power and a maximum speed of $22\frac{1}{2}$ knots [26 mph].'

Tengelsen is called away to go over some navigational details, so I leave the bridge and take a lift down to Deck One. The only passengers who would come down here would be those wishing to see one of the ship's medical team or to leave the ship via the tenders that take people ashore when there is no access to a pier or harbour. Otherwise, this is exclusively crew territory, as signalled by the absence of the lavish interior decoration that graces every other deck.

Unlike the rest of the ship, Deck One has a long, unbroken central corridor that runs the entire length of the ship. The crew have nicknamed it 'I95', after the interstate that runs along the entire eastern seaboard of the US from the Canadian border at Maine down to Miami. It takes me a few minutes to find the office of the ship's forty-year-old chief engineer, Baard Westlund.

'Sorry, I'm just finishing off an email,' he says in a thick Norwegian accent, as I enter. 'I won't be a minute. Please take a seat.' His small windowless office is decorated with technical drawings pinned to the walls. 'I'm just putting in an order for some fuel at Montego Bay. We buy it there rather than at Miami because it is better quality.'

I ask him how much it takes to fill up the tank of the world's largest cruise ship. He smiles, then grabs his calculator and starts tapping in some figures.

'Well, this ship needs 238,000 gallons of fuel for the week. That's 900 metric tonnes of what we call heavy fuel. At today's prices, that means our fuel bill is $40,000 a day. We could travel at twenty-two knots, but that would just cost too much, so we tend to travel at around sixteen knots.'

He tells me that he is in charge of all the ship's technical equipment and oversees a team of fifty people. 'I work fourteen weeks on, and tend to do twelve-hour days. Up at seven a.m. and then I'm usually done by seven thirty p.m. In our control room down here on Deck One there are about 16,000 alarms that can go off. There's usually a few alarms sounding at any time, but it could be for trivial things such as a blown fuse. But 80 per cent of my time is spent doing admin such as this email. I now split my time between being on the ship and living in Koh Samui in Thailand, where I have a property business.'

He begins to explain to me some of the key technical systems on board.

'Most of the fuel we burn is used to generate electricity – 98 per cent, in fact. The other 2 per cent is used to generate steam which is used to produce hot water for the ship. A ship this size also cannot carry all its own water from port to port. We have to make our own as we go. At Miami, for example, we only take on about 10–15 per cent of what we need. The rest we make via an 'economizer' in the ship's funnel, using seawater. It can make about 1,200 cubic metres of fresh water a day via reverse-osmosis desalination.

'The maximum electricity-generating capacity of this ship is 75 megawatts. About 42 megawatts is needed to propel the ship through the water and 13 megawatts is used up by what we call the "hotel" above our heads. The remaining 20 megawatts of capacity we don't generally need, so are just happy to have it as back-up.'

I'm keen to know about the ship's waste treatment system, given that it should, in theory, be among the most advanced on the sea. 'Our Advanced Water Plant, or AWP as we call it, cost us about €2.5 million to install.' (The ship is estimated to have cost almost one billion dollars to build.) 'It's still being tested now by its manufacturers.'

He pauses to point out Asgeir Wien, the Norwegian chief technical officer of Scanship, the firm that has fitted the AWP, who is sitting at a desk outside Baard's office. I ask Baard why the ship is staffed by so many Norwegians. He says that Royal Caribbean was a Norwegian company when it was founded in 1968, and there is still a tradition of Norwegians working as officers.

'Our AWP is very new and it isn't quite working properly yet. That's why Asgeir is doing tests. But all water is cleaned before being released into the sea. The AWP has a capacity of 2,160 cubic metres of water a day. About 75–80 cubic metres of this can be black water, the rest grey water. Each guest uses roughly 240 litres of water a day. At the moment, though, we are generating about 1,500 cubic metres of waste water, with around 40 cubic metres of black water. By the time we have de-watered the black water, it leaves around ten cubic metres of sludge which we incinerate. The plan is that the water quality will be so good that it could be pumped into the waters off Alaska, but I don't believe we will go for this as we can just wait until we are further offshore. We also have a plan to incinerate all our organic waste, but some is still ground up in a macerator and placed overboard. We land a lot of the waste that we can't incinerate at Montego Bay.'

On my way back up to find some clean, fresh sea air after being cooped up in the deepest part of the ship – quite how the staff put up with this for the vast majority of their days on board, I don't know – I stumble across the ship's ice rink, where over two hundred people have gathered for a 'Discover Shopping' session. I had noticed it being heavily advertised on the TV in my room earlier. On a stage, a smartly dressed woman with a microphone attached to the side of her head is whipping up the crowd.

'Does anyone want a free sapphire!' she screams. The crowd whoop with excitement. It doesn't take long for me to work out that she is telling people where the best shopping is to be found on each of the ship's ports of call. 'Don't forget that at Montego Bay for twelve dollars you can buy a wristband that will get you on to the air-conditioned bus that will take you straight to the craft market in the city centre. It will also get you into Jimmy Buffett's Margaritaville, which is the best place for a cocktail. And don't forget Casa de Oro for your duty-free jewellery. Ask for Daniel and Arun, and the price will be as good as paying cash. And, ladies, they even have Tiffany and Co!'

Another scream erupts from the crowd.

'But remember, people, Jamaica is a "No, thank you" island. If someone offers you some "Jamaican oregano", what do you say?' In unison, the crowd shout back, 'No, thank you!' There's nothing like a bit of racial stereotyping to whip up a crowd.

I look at the flyer being handed out among the audience. It lists dozens of 'recommended shopping' outlets and 'must see' places. Nearly every entry is accompanied by 'Ask your Discover Shopping guide how to get your free diamond bracelet here,' or something similar. But in the smallprint on the back is a sentence that sums it all up for me: 'Participating merchants have paid an advertising fee for inclusion in this programme.'

The relationship cruise ships have with their destinations and the communities that live in them is another area for which the cruise industry is often criticized. Just how much does a port of call gain from a cruise ship docking and disgorging thousands of tourists for just a few hours before pulling up its anchor and departing? If these tourists are sleeping and eating on board, what economic benefits will their visitation bring, other than a possible splurge on souvenirs or an organized shore excursion?

In 2001, the Florida-Caribbean Cruise Association (FCCA) published research conducted by PricewaterhouseCoopers that found that during the 1999–2000 season, a typical cruise ship carrying two thousand passengers and nine hundred crew generated on average almost $259,000 in expenditure at each Caribbean port of call. This worked out as an average spend at each port of call of \$103.83 per passenger. This generated a total of \$1.4 billion of direct spending by passengers in the Caribbean ports of call during this period, as well as generating 60,136 jobs and \$285 million in wage income.

The FCCA was evidently very pleased with these findings. 'Dear tourism partners,' began the report, largely directed at the Caribbean ports of call, 'see for yourself how the cruise industry is positively impacting the economy of your country.'

Not everyone sees it this way, though. For a start, if the Discover Shopping event is anything to go by, most passengers are guided like precision missiles towards the few shops that have enough financial clout to pay for this privilege. It is also fair to assume that the cruise companies can earn extra commission through any sales they help to generate – Professor Ross Klein says this can be as high as 40 per cent. This inevitably means that the big players at each port of call are the most likely to gain from visiting cruise ships. And by bussing passengers direct to these shops, there is little economic leakage likely to trickle down to taxi drivers or the small-scale stallholders that might line the streets leading to the big, air-conditioned duty-free shops.

Sir Arthur Foulkes, a former newspaper editor and cabinet minister in the Bahamas who now writes a weekly column in the *Nassau Tribune*, criticized the spreading reach of cruise-ship tourists across the Bahamian islands – ironically, where many cruise ships, including the *Freedom of the Seas*, are registered – in an article in 2006:

'A cruise is the ultimate all-inclusive vacation as the whole idea is to cater to the passengers on board, not encourage them to spend money at the destination. The cruise operators even begrudge the destination a decent passenger-landing tax and have forced tax competition between Caribbean countries . . . Cruise-ship operators do not have the same loyalty and commitment to the destination as those developers who build hotels and resorts and who over many years have, along with the government, committed considerable resources to the promotion of the Bahamas internationally. When there are problems to be addressed, resort developers will be reliable partners because their money is in the ground. The floating resorts can pull up anchor and go somewhere else . . . The government has been talking a lot about giving downtown Nassau a makeover, and that is surely needed. But care should be taken not to turn the waterfront into a cheap attraction for cruise passengers, most of whom are not big spenders.'

In 2004, the Travel Foundation, a UK-travel-industry-funded charity that 'cares for places we love to visit', commissioned a report examining the impact that all-inclusive tourism, including cruise ships, was having on the Caribbean island of Tobago. It concluded: 'Cruise tourism has not made any significant impact on the local economy of Tobago. At US$5 per passenger "head tax" plus a surcharge of US$0.30 per passenger on an organized tour, the Port Authority of Trinidad and Tobago (PATT) reports that each year it collects less than £50,000. Historical records show that on average only 30 per cent of passengers purchase organized tours, with a further 20 per cent hiring taxis. Tour prices range between US$20 and US$50, averaging £19. This means that, with an average annual volume of 14,924 passengers and after deducting the PATT levy, only £118,000 is spent by cruise passengers on organized tours and taxis, bringing very little benefit to the local economy. Craft sellers, local entertainers and restaurants receive little or no benefit, unless the tours are specifically structured to include them.

'Any intervention [by the tourism industry to tackle this situation] must take account of the reality that the principal stakeholders are large American companies that own, market and operate these cruises, and whose interests are often vertically integrated with supplier companies in the metropolis. Previous attempts at the regional level to negotiate terms and conditions with the Florida-Caribbean Cruise Association have achieved little or no success.'

*

Adam Goldstein is resolute in defending the cruise industry from all charges placed at its door. As well he might be, as the president of Royal Caribbean International. Speaking from his home near Miami, he tells me what takes up most of his working day:

'I'm surprised since I became president just how much time I spend on the following things: safety, environment, security and public health, particularly food safety.' (The industry has been dogged over the years by outbreaks of food poisoning, which the enclosed confines of cruise ships encourage. Just a few months after my time aboard *Freedom of the Seas* it was twice struck by outbreaks of noroviruses, which led to hundreds of passengers falling ill.) 'Our ships need to be self-sufficient and able to take a lot of stress,' he continues. 'The environment is particularly associated with the cruise industry, in part because in the 1990s we had some environmental challenges. I believe we have responded to those challenges by completely revolutionizing who we are; for example, we now run auditing and evaluating programmes. There's also the capital investment in things such as the Advanced Water Plants we're installing on all our ships by the end of 2008. These are extraordinarily sophisticated and are a remarkable improvement in a ten-year period. We believe our environmental leadership is as good as, or better than, any other maritime entity. There's no pure, clean utopia out there, but what I do think is that we leave a very minor, superficial environmental footprint in comparison to the number of people that we carry from point A to point B.'

He is equally forceful when it comes to explaining the relationship the cruise industry has with its destinations. He doesn't accept the criticism that cruise ships tend to take a lot and give little to each port of call. But why, I ask, does *Freedom of the Seas* load up all its supplies at Miami, for example? Couldn't it buy supplies at the ports it visits, thereby boosting these local economies?

'In the Caribbean we have struggled to identify and maintain suppliers who meet our specifications for quality, volume and price. Often it's simply the volume. There aren't that many small communities that can meet our requirements. There have been some success stories, but they have been relatively few and far between. It's much more efficient for us, in general, to run things from places such as Miami. Shore excursions, though, are nearly always run by a local company. We have two destinations that we own, but other than that we use local companies.'

Why, I ask, does Royal Caribbean – along with other companies, such as Carnival – feel the need to own its own private destinations? What message is sent out by Labadee, Royal Caribbean's private port in Haiti, having a high fence around it to stop locals entering?

'We like to have private destinations as it's easier to control the environment compared to an open-to-all-comers place. Our guests like the ambience of Labadee. It meets their expectations of what a Caribbean island should be like. Guest satisfaction is key. Going on a cruise is a very significant purchase and is a discretionary purchase, too. Nobody has to take a cruise, after all.'

Does Royal Caribbean, I wonder, ever stop visiting a port if it doesn't meet its requirements? If so, I point out, it shows what incredible power and leverage the cruise companies can wield over a destination.

'There are three reasons why we might stop going to a place,' he says. 'First, if our guests didn't like it. That would be by far the dominant reason why we wouldn't go any more. We also might stop going somewhere if it was getting too busy and was causing guests hassle. Or we might have concerns about safety. But after Hurricane Wilma devastated Cozumel in 2005, it didn't cross our minds to leave. Cozumel is strategically very important to the cruise industry. The relationship between the industry and the community there is extremely good. We have played a leading role in the recovery – both physical and economic – after the hurricane. We bent over backwards to help out there. Within two to three days we had people on the ground there surveying the damage. We have also set up charities around the Caribbean that operate in the communities we visit by donating to hospitals, schools and orphanages.'

One final issue I'm very keen to hear Goldstein's views on is that of labour conditions aboard cruise ships. War on Want, a campaign group that 'fights poverty in developing countries in partnership and solidarity with people affected by globalization', has called these vessels 'sweatships' due to the fact that 'long hours and low pay are the norm for workers'. In 2002, it published a report in conjunction with the International Transport Workers' Federation (ITWF) called 'Sweatships – what it's really like to work on board cruise ships'. The report contained a quote from Professor Tony Lane, the then director of the Seafarers' International Research Centre at Cardiff University, in which he remarked: 'Without doubt, the "hotel" employees on cruise ships, those in the galley, laundry, etc., suffer the highest levels of exploitation in the whole maritime industry.'

The report, which included first-person testimony from a number of crew members, detailed the reality of life on board for the crew on some cruise ships: 'It is thought that there are about 114,500 seafarers, both marine and hotel/catering staff, working on board the world's cruise ships. They are also deeply hierarchical and even segregated workplaces. Jobs are allocated downwards through the decks according to gender and nationality/skin colour. Developing-world workers -- particularly from Asia, the Caribbean and Latin America as well as Central/Eastern Europe – are the ones doing the menial jobs in the restaurants, bars and cabins, and in the engine-room and galleys below. Virtually the only Westerners below decks are in supervisory positions.'

Central to the report's claims is that this segregation often leads to a vast gulf between the working experiences and conditions of the various sub-sets of crew. An upstairs-downstairs culture pervades, whereby the Western crew members – typically physically higher up the ship than the crew members from developing countries, and often working on board for lifestyle reasons as opposed to bare economic necessity – enjoy higher pay, better hours and other more favourable terms of employment, such as less-restrictive contracts and employment-agency fees comparative to their income.

For example, crew from developing countries typically sign contracts without knowing the precise role they will be undertaking. The report claims that the fees they are charged by the crewing agents 'reduce them to virtual bonded labour whilst on board the ship'. This is because new recruits are often charged up front for their air fare, visa, medical examination, seafarer's book and an administrative fee, which can bring the total sign-up fee to as much as $2,000. For workers from countries such as the Philippines, Indonesia and India, this huge sum means that most inevitably turn to local moneylenders charging high interest rates. It can take many months for this debt to be paid off.

'It is only for perhaps the last few months of contract that they are able to save or send money home,' says the report. 'Typically, the total sum sent home is about US$300 a month for three to four months. This adds up to around US$1,000 for seven months' work plus two to three months' lay-off. Even at Third World living costs, US$100 a month is barely a "living wage",' Compounding the problem is the fact that many workers rely on voluntary tips from guests to top up their income – and are therefore vulnerable to the vagaries and whimsical nature of their generosity. Plus there is little realistic opportunity for promotion up and away from these conditions.

The chance to enjoy any meaningful time off appears limited, too. The report cites an ITWF survey of nearly four hundred cruise-ship employees which showed that over 95 per cent were working seven days a week. 'The only time off is when the vessel is in port for turn-around or, for favoured crew members, if they are allowed ashore during the passengers' sightseeing trips. It used to be common for ships to spend the night in port during turnaround. But in the highly competitive market of the 1990s, this time was compressed. These days, the next set of passengers embarks within hours of the last leaving. This gives the crew members only a few hours onshore to call home, shop and rest, before the next cruise starts. Recreation such as sport seems pretty much out of the question.'

In contrast, Goldstein says Royal Caribbean's staffing policy is underpinned by the credo 'Anchored in Excellence'. All staff are versed in it, he says. He reads it out to me:

'We always provide service with a friendly greeting and a smile; we anticipate the needs of our customers; we make all effort to exceed our customers' expectations; we take ownership of any problem that is brought to our attention; we engage in conduct that enhances our corporate reputation and employee morale; we are committed to act in the highest ethical manner and respect the rights and dignity of others; we are loyal to Royal Caribbean, and strive for continuous improvement in everything we do.'

The company employs 30,000 people from 107 countries, he adds. 'Our people work really hard. Depending on who they are, they work four, six or eight months on. We don't do contracts longer than eight months any more. The vast majority of our staff have a very strong bond with the company. Most of them are earning far in excess of the median income of the countries they come from.'

We have an early start the next morning: before I have even woken, the ship has already anchored just off the Mexican island of Cozumel. As I open the curtains, the sun floods my room. On the horizon I can make out the Mexican mainland about twenty kilometres away.

I have booked myself on to a shore excursion, before leaving the ship for good at Mexico. And so at seven a.m. I join around one hundred people on Deck One to jump aboard a tender, which takes us to the hurricane-damaged pier where before Hurricane Wilma all the ships used to dock. On the quayside we are met by a cluster of men holding up signs with the names of each of the shore excursions on offer. There's plenty to choose from and they range in price from $50–$100, all of which has already been settled on board: diving, snorkelling, golf, jungle hikes, deep-sea fishing, horseriding, 'Mexican folkloric show and shopping', parasailing and 'tequila tasting seminars'. The longest queue, though, is for the 'dolphin swim adventure'.

I am booked on to the 'island jeep off-road snorkel experience'. Eduardo, our young guide who is wearing a safari suit and hat, greets the dozen or so people who have gathered under his sign with a firm handshake and broad smile. He walks us past a parade of duty-free shops over to a dusty car park where we are shown to our jeeps. It's only a ten-minute drive through downtown San Miguel, the capital of this forty-kilometre-long island, to our first stop – a snorkelling beach facing out towards the *Freedom of the Seas*, which is a few hundred metres offshore.

After he has run through a safety briefing in the grounds of a private house overlooking the beach, I ask Eduardo what business has been like for him since Wilma swept through and severely damaged or destroyed the cruise-ship piers.

'We used to have thirty-seven cruise ships docking here every week, but they all stopped for a few weeks after Wilma. Things are slowly getting back to normal now. The piers for Disney Cruises and Norwegian Cruises are nearly rebuilt, which will help business.'

Time is tight, he says, so he leads us all across a busy main road and down to the thin, coarse beach. We are directed across a series of sandbags that have been laid on the rocks to protect our feet. Eduardo says they're there in case any Americans sue him should they twist their ankle. None of the Americans in the group laugh.

Once in the water, we notice another couple of groups being directed our way. By the time we actually put our masks over our faces, as many as fifty people are in the water around us. A jet ski speeds around the group, corralling us. The driver blows a whistle whenever anyone strays beyond the grouping.

The seabed under the water is utterly lifeless, bar the odd grouper. On the coarse sand lie dozens of pieces of smashed coral. Eduardo tells us that Wilma snapped off all the fan corals. I can't help but wonder what our group, and the thousands of others that come to play on the Great Maya Reef – the second-largest coral reef in the world – must be doing to its health, too.

It seems pertinent that of the top thirty cruise destinations in the world, twenty are located in the Caribbean and Mediterranean, two of the world's most important biodiversity hotspots, according to Conservation International. And of these twenty, the ten most popular ports of call are all found in the Caribbean basin. In 1997, the cruise ship *Leeward*, owned by Norway Cruise Line, actually ran aground on the reef further up the Yucatan peninsula, near Cancún at the Isla Mujeres marine park. Oceanographer Roman Bravo Prieto told television reporters at the time that it would take five hundred years or more for the reef to recover. 'The damage is worse than if a full-force hurricane had run ashore,' he said. According to Conservation International, a single cruise ship's anchor and chain can weigh as much as 4.5 tonnes and can damage up to 195 square metres of ocean floor at a single anchorage site on a calm day with no swell or current.

Sadly, more and more cruise ships are now also heading to destinations that are arguably even more ecologically sensitive than the reefs of the Caribbean. The Galápagos Islands, which lie almost a thousand kilometres to the west of Ecuador and are famed for their endemic species studied by Charles Darwin, have witnessed a rise in the number of cruise-ship visits in recent years. In 2006, the Galápagos Conservation Trust launched a campaign to raise awareness about the impact these ships are starting to have by offloading sometimes hundreds of tourists at a time. It said that the rapid increase in visitors caused by the arrival of the ships could risk the introduction of non-indigenous species that could then threaten the islands' delicate ecological balance. Similar concerns have been aired about the swelling number of cruise passengers visiting Antarctica – between 1994 and 2004, the number rose from 8,000 to 28,000 a year, according to the International Association of Antarctica Tour Operators. Attempts have been made to amend the Antarctic Treaty to better protect the continent from cruise ships, and in particular to restrict the number of passengers that go ashore – they now outnumber resident scientists – but the legal and diplomatic uncertainties that have plagued the treaty since it was first signed in 1959 by the twelve countries 'active' in the region (nine with territorial claims) have hampered these efforts.

It takes my tour group twenty minutes to drive across the island to the other side of Cozumel. On the way we stop at a 'pee-pee station', which just happens to have a gift shop alongside selling ceramic dolls, toy donkeys, sombreros, chess sets and all manner of T-shirts.

It's a relief to get to the eastern coast, which is much more rugged and exposed to the elements than the western side, where *Freedom of the Seas* is anchored. It is also devoid of any real development, which is surprising given how many tourists visit the island.

Eduardo directs us to park our convoy of jeeps beside a beach café, where a buffet of bland chicken fajitas and nachos has already been laid out for us under some palm-leaf umbrellas by two men wearing plastic gloves. Ice boxes full of Coca-Colas stand near by. After lunch, while most of the group play volleyball, I chat to Eduardo some more. I ask him what benefits all these cruise-ship tourists bring to Cozumel. He raises his eyes and smirks.

'My house is expensive now. This is good for me, yes. But everything here is expensive now. For example, all the gas stations are owned by one man here. It's the same price for gas for locals and tourists. Many things are a monopoly here. Even the ferries going over to Playa del Carmen on the mainland, where I buy my supermarket shopping, are expensive. It would be better, yes, if they slept in the hotels we have built for them and not on the ships. It's difficult to make friends with them when they are here for just six hours.'

9

Turtles and Towers
Cancún, Mexico

'IT WAS ALL MANGROVE AND DUNE habitats here before. The concept for introducing tourism wasn't actually that bad in the beginning. The buildings were two to three storeys high to start with. Now they're twenty storeys or more and there are so many buildings that you can't even see the beach from some hotels.'

Araceli Dominguez sighs, then folds away a tourist map of Cancún and places it back in the revolving stand by the reception desk of her hotel. Hotel El Rey del Caribe is not a place where too many of the 3.5 million people that visit Cancún each year tend to stay. Adjacent to a busy crossroads in the centre of downtown Cancún, its twenty-five rooms face on to a tranquil courtyard thick with palms. It is fifteen minutes by car – and a world away – from the strip of 190 hotels that line Cancún's 22-kilometre-long, 400-metre-wide *zona hotelera*.

Araceli and her husband built the hotel themselves in the 1980s and have seen Cancún rise up around them to become one of the most visited beach destinations in the world. El Rey del Caribe, though, is situated out of sight of the *zona hotelera*, in the sprawling, chaotic, low-level metropolis that has sprung up to provide the pool of labour needed to serve the area's tourism industry. The hotel offers a rare commodity for the area – a setting charged with deep environmental empathy. The hotel's hot water is heated by solar power, rainwater is collected for laundry, and all kitchen waste is composted for the lush tropical garden.

Araceli, who also heads a local environmental group called Grupo Ecologista del Mayab, has started to acquire a reputation in recent years for speaking out about the impact of tourism, not just in Cancún but along the entire coastline of Quintana Roo state on the Yucatán peninsula. In April 2005, she was held in police cells for five days for protesting against the importation of twenty-eight dolphins from the Solomon Islands for a local water park and dolphinarium. She was freed without charge following an international campaign; protesters included travel agents concerned about the negative impact of such publicity on Cancún's reputation.

'I'm still protesting,' she says defiantly, 'but the dolphins have nearly all died now.' She says the incident is symptomatic of a general attitude that tourists should just be given what they want – or what is thought to be what they want – without thinking through the consequences. She also says there is deepening resentment among locals that many are being treated like second-class citizens compared to the tourists.

'The hotels now have sewage-treatment plants,' she says. 'They have trees planted along the *zona hotelera*. But this town of 750,000 people has only 40 per cent sewerage. Some sewage is even now thrown down wells. There's no recycling and people have been jailed for protesting about being moved from their homes to make way for landfill sites to bury the rubbish produced by tourists. This town was built so quickly and with so little planning that there is not even any culture here. There's no theatre, sports centres, recreational parks. Nothing. There are even houses made with oiled paper for roofing – 100,000 people live here in these conditions. The people can only work; some even do two shifts a day with their children left home alone. This is a society with many insecurities, but there's no time to even worry about it as people have to work so hard to earn a living wage.'

The whole of the Cancún area is in fact an artificial creation, she says. Nothing is really what it seems. In the early 1960s no one lived on the island of Cancún except a few fishermen and their families and some coconut farmers. But then the Mexican government pinpointed the island as being a prime place to build a strip of hotels, serviced by a nearby airport that would ferry in tourists from cities in the US and further afield. This was seen as a way of earning foreign currency for the economy that might even rival the remittances from Mexicans working in the US. As the tourism infrastructure increased throughout the 1970s, so a migrant workforce from across Mexico began to arrive in Quintana Roo. In those goldrush days, little attention was paid to the town planning of downtown Cancún, which has resulted in the problems today, according to Araceli.

'The government wanted to create a "bankers' dream". Everything was perfect here. Land was incredibly cheap and it had all the right conditions to lure tourists – beautiful beaches, blue seas, Mayan ruins, the limestone sinkholes we call *cenotes*. The plan was to build thirty thousand rooms in thirty years on the island of Cancún. But then they started to dredge the lagoons and destroy the vegetation.' There has been a combination of environmental decline, blind greed and incompetence ever since, she says.

'There are hotels trying to build in protected areas now as there just isn't enough prime land left any more. Two hours down the coast from here there are the Mayan ruins of Tulum, which since 1980 have been within a 664-hectare national park. The National Anthropology Institute of Mexico recently wrote a letter to the governor of Playa del Carmen, asking him not to allow any building there as there are so many archaeological sites that have yet to be fully studied. But just before Hurricane Wilma in 2005, a delegation including President Fox went to Spain to sign a contract to sell some nearby land to hotel groups. Tulum is in big danger now because of this type of planning-permission abuse. The politicians just don't see that ecotourism projects could bring in more money in the long run than the chain hotels.'

Araceli leans towards me across the table as if she is about to let me in on a secret.

'The whole of the Caribbean has this problem,' she whispers. 'I now have a network of friends all over the region sharing information about these developments. And it always seems to be the same hotel groups – usually Spanish, I have to say. We just have so many Spanish chains here now. They tend to be all-inclusive, which means everything is organized and paid for already – the airport bus, the food, everything. This means the chains keep all the money. I've heard that some of them pay staff as little as 49 pesos (£2.20) a day as a basic wage, and expect them to make up the shortfall with tips.' (The minimum daily wage in Mexico at the time of this interview ranged from 45.81 to 48.67 pesos, depending on the region.) 'But because it's all-inclusive, no one really tips. Plus, staff rarely live at the hotel and have to travel in each day. The rooms only cost around $160 a day, all-inclusive. All-inclusive packages are very cheap to buy now, especially in Europe, so the hotels cut their costs by paying low wages. No money really reaches the community. The government never really thought much about the people when they brought tourism here – they just wanted the foreign currency to enter the economy.'

On 5 August 1971, some bankers gathered in Washington DC to authorize loan application 'ME0016' to the tune of $21.5 million – a sum equivalent to about $240 million today. The deal was quickly done, but their decision to approve the loan proved to be a landmark moment that shaped the tourism industry in Mexico. It also caused a ripple of copycat loan applications across the world.

The successful applicant was the Mexican government, and many other governments soon followed in its path. It had approached the Inter-American Development Bank (IDB) – a multilateral development institution set up in 1959 to provide 'financing for economic, social and institutional development in Latin America and the Caribbean' – for funds to help kick-start the tourist industry to boost the economy. Just four years earlier, the government had used a computer to help identify suitable locations in Mexico to build 'mega-resorts' in the mould of places such as Miami. The computer came up with three stretches of near-perfect coastline that would, the government believed, attract the dollar-wielding American tourists lying just over the border: Cancún on the Yucatán coast; Ixtapa on the Pacific coast a few hours north-west from Acapulco; and Los Cabos on the southern tip of Baja California Sur.

It was the first time the IDB had lent money to a major tourism project, but other loans quickly followed. Before then it had tended to back more traditional infrastructure projects, such as schools, agriculture, waterworks and hospitals. But between 1971 and 1993, seven loans were agreed for Mexican tourism projects, totalling $457.5 million. Other countries in the region, particularly Panama, Peru and the Dominican Republic, and later Brazil, Bolivia, Venezuela, Ecuador and Trinidad and Tobago, also approached the bank for tourism-related loans, once they saw tourists starting to be drawn to Mexico's popular new tourism developments, especially Cancún, throughout the 1970s.

Many governments also drew inspiration from how the Mexican government had gone about realizing its vision, namely, by passing new acts of parliament, creating new unified government departments and setting ambitious targets. Once the first loan was received, the Mexican government brought together its previously fragmented strategies for nurturing tourism, creating one central agency called the National Trust Fund for Tourism Development (FONATUR) in 1973. Its task was to oversee the development of large-scale tourism projects across the country and, crucially, aggressively seek foreign and domestic investors, as well as secure further development

loans from international institutions such as the IDB and the World
Bank.

It's a strategy that has changed little in thirty years. What has
changed in this time, though, are the terms of lending. The interest
rates and repayment periods may have remained broadly the same,
but ever since the early 1990s, following the concerns debated at the
Earth Summit in Rio in 1992, projects seeking development loans
have needed to prove that they meet social, economic and environmental criteria – the so-called 'triple bottom line'. Bank officials are
now expected to interrogate loan applications with this in mind, and
to continue to inspect loan projects as they progress. But these three
balls are notoriously hard to juggle. Also, multi-million-dollar development loans fed through government hands typically tend to benefit
the big players in the tourism industry, rather than, to use banking
lingo, the SMMEs – Small, Medium and Micro Enterprises – that the
development banks now say they like to help out. It pays to look at
just a couple of recent examples of loans handed to tourism projects –
one in Cancún and one in its regional rival, Jamaica – to see who these
loans tend to aid.

In 2003, the International Finance Corporation (IFC), the
private-sector lending arm of the World Bank, authorized an $80-
million loan to four hotels in the Cancún area owned by Occidental
Hotels. That's an awful lot of money to help out an SMME, you
might think. Occidental is, by the IFC's own definition, 'the third
largest Spanish hotel chain worldwide, operating eighty-five hotels
with an aggregate of 20,400 rooms in Europe, Latin America, the
US and Africa'. The World Bank says it acts as a 'vital source of
financial and technical assistance to developing countries around
the world', but should Occidental's Spanish shareholders, venture
capitalists and institutional backers really gain by accessing this
vital source, too?

This is how the money was to be used by Occidental, according to the IFC: 'The project is aimed at restructuring and refurbishing four hotel properties owned by Occidental in Mexico. The project is part of Occidental's expansion strategy in Central America and the Caribbean. It will allow Occidental to continue its growth while recovering from the impact of the events of September 11th and an economic downturn . . . The project will strengthen environmental affairs and quality management, life- and fire-safety programs in the four hotels and at the corporate level.' In other words, the loan helps the self-proclaimed 'worldwide leader in all-inclusive resorts' to strengthen its position in the marketplace. It also helps the hotel chain strengthen its 'life-safety' programmes, but should a global company the size of Occidental really be tapping the World Bank for $80 million to fund such requirements?

And it shouldn't be a surprise to see FONATUR's name all over the loan application: it says that FONATUR will 'consider becoming a minority shareholder in the company through the contribution of hotel assets or plot of land suitable for hotel development'. Today, FONATUR is seen as both an inspiration and a menace across Mexico. On the one hand, it has helped to turn Mexico into the eighth-most-tourist-visited country in the world, according to the UNWTO. But on the other hand, developments such as Cancún are seen by many as being among the very worst examples of what can happen when tourism is allowed to develop largely unchecked, oiled by development loans, across such an environmental, geological and cultural treasure trove. FONATUR is far from finished, either. Having added the Bays of Huatulco and Loreto Bay to its original three tourism mega-projects, it announced plans in 2001 to develop Escalera Nautica (now renamed the Sea of Cortez Project), a network of marinas and villa/hotel/golf complexes running down the Cortez coast. The local governor, rather ironically, called it a 'detonation of economic and social development' for the area, whereas environmentalists feared it would blight a region which boasts a natural World Heritage site and three biosphere reserves, as well as turtle habitats and whale nurseries.

But it's not just the World Bank that lends millions of dollars to large hotels and tourism projects. In 2003, the Inter-American Investment Corporation (IIC), the private-sector lending arm of the IDB, approved a $10-million loan to Sunset Beach Resort and Spa Hotel Ltd in Jamaica for the 'expansion and upgrade' of two hotels, one in Montego Bay, the other in Negril. (The Montego Bay hotel is an eleven-storey, 430-room all-inclusive hotel with its own water park, 'English Pub' and private nudist beach.) Again, the bank's own words say much about the true reasoning behind these large loans:

'The project will allow the company to: strengthen its market position in the all-inclusive market as the largest independently owned hotel in Jamaica; meet currently unmet demand; expand hotel operations to one of the most sought-after tourist destinations in Jamaica and in the Caribbean region (Negril); increase profitability by gaining significant economies of scale by leveraging existing management and marketing infrastructure; and benefit from an overall favourable investment climate.'

At least, unlike the Occidental loan deal, this time the company is 'locally owned', according to the IIC. But how much did triple-bottom-line concerns influence the deal? Here's what the application's 'Review of Environmental and Labour Issues' said:

'Specific impacts may result which can be avoided or mitigated by adhering to generally recognized performance standards, guidelines and design criteria. The principal environmental and labour issues related to this project include liquid effluent treatment, solid waste disposal, water use, fire safety, and worker health and safety.'

It's reassuring that these issues have been noted, but there's little scope for public scrutiny of how the loan money is being spent and whether the various criteria will be met once these loans have been approved, be they from the IIC, IFC or one of the other development banks around the world that lend to tourism projects, such as the Asian Development Bank and the European Bank for Reconstruction and Redevelopment. Should this really be the case when the World Bank is technically part of the United Nations and is owned by the bank's 184 member countries? For example, a document produced by the IFC in 1992 entitled 'An Evaluation of IFC's Experience in the Tourism Sector' would presumably make interesting reading for anyone wishing to see what lessons have been learned by banks supporting tourism projects, but it isn't available to the public. Also, the various development-bank websites offer little opportunity, if any, to follow the progress of any loan project.

In 2005 the World Bank announced a $200-million 'sustainable development' loan to Mexico, which would help fund projects across five broad areas: energy, forest, water, environmental management and tourism. The intentions for tourism sound exemplary on paper: 'Establish new tourism destinations and promote sustainable-tourism action plans in selected tourist destinations. Improve environmental conditions – especially waste-water and solid-waste disposal – at existing tourist sites, and decrease over-exploitation of natural tourism resources.' But there's no way of knowing where this money has been spent, or even how much of the total loan has been spent on tourism initiatives. This is all the more worrying because, as the World Bank admitted itself in a 2006 report into its tourism-related activities in Africa, 'there is very little expertise within the institution' about tourism, even though it has a current active port-folio of tourism-related lending of $3 billion across 114 projects around the world, and makes grand claims about how tourism 'creates opportunities for biodiversity conservation, urban growth and regeneration, private sector and SMME development, infra-structure overhaul and planning, rural development, environmental restoration and safeguarding, coastal protection and cultural-heritage preservation'.

It's no wonder, really, that the international development banks, especially the World Bank, have been accused so often in the past of being little more than neo-liberal, neo-colonial instruments of the developed nations, tending to lend money to projects that reflect their own ideas about what is the best way forward – in these examples, the apparatus for high-volume, all-inclusive mass tourism.

Just three years after the Jamaican loan was agreed, the government there commissioned the Planning Institute of Jamaica to carry out a study on the sustainability of the country's entire 'Tourism Expansion Programme'. According to a 2006 report in the *Jamaican Gleaner*, 'the findings of the study were grim. The research team found that Jamaica was at risk of endangering its natural resources, the very essence of its tourism product, for a few Cancún-style developments on its shorelines . . . According to the study, Jamaica stands to lose significantly if it apes the typical designs of Spanish resorts in the Dominican Republic and Mexico, where the same developers applied conventional building designs and development ideas to environmentally sensitive areas.'

The paper was furious with the government for not heeding the study's warnings: 'The government must have known there would be implications for such fast-paced development. And the sores have already begun to fester. Current Cancún-style hotel developments on pristine protected land and overdevelopment of our resort towns are putting endemic wildlife and flora at risk and putting pressure on community infrastructure. The Glistening Waters Lagoon in Oyster Bay is already losing its luminescence because of development there, while in Pear Tree Bottom, St Ann, mangroves have been destroyed to facilitate the development of the Bahía Príncipe. Ocho Rios, Negril and Montego Bay are already bursting at the seams because of excessive development. Schools, housing, roads, water and sewerage and power supply are under strain. It is not clear where the government wants to lead the country, but creating 12,000 rooms by 2010 in sensitive zones is not sustainable, according to its own research . . . Too often, foreign investors have breached environmental guidelines without consequence.'

Financial assistance from the development banks for the tourism industry keeps coming, though. For example, in 2006 the IDB agreed a $1.6-million grant to a tourism project in the Mexican state of Jalisco to build a 'Tequila Trail' that 'will highlight the natural and cultural attractions of this region known not only for the world-famous Mexican liquor but also for its traditional horsemen, the *charros*, as well as for its *mariachi* music'. And who might be supporting a project that celebrates tequila and, therefore, arguably has most to gain? The major tequila distillers, of course, who include Jose Cuervo, part of Diageo, the world's largest drinks company, which in 2005 had a turnover of £9 billion with an operating profit of £1.9 billion.

'Nature is going to stop them here in Cancún,' says Araceli mournfully. This realization came to her when she turned her hotel into a refuge for ten days for some of the thirty thousand tourists who fled the beachside hotels during the twenty-four hours that Wilma, a rare category-five hurricane, enveloped Cancún in late October 2005. Only three months earlier, Hurricane Emily had struck the southern section of the Riviera Maya, as the coastline from Cancún to Tulum is known. The total clean-up operation took months and is estimated to have cost around $8 billion. It was the worst natural disaster to hit the area since Hurricane Gilbert in 1988.

'Many people have left Cancún because they fear more big hurricanes as they're coming more frequently now. Our weather is changing so much. Last week we had a tornado near Mexico City and for the first time there was hail there, too. Cancún, though, is just so vulnerable because it is completely reliant on tourism. I recently saw some plans to build hotels further inland, which shows at least someone is starting to think sensibly. The big chains, though, didn't learn from Wilma as they all just claimed on their insurance. Some are even using Wilma as an opportunity to build bigger hotels out of the wreckage. The lessons were all there for them to learn from: the buildings that survived the best during Wilma were the ones close to mangroves. But they keep chopping them down to build more marinas and hotels, which just makes everyone more vulnerable. Protecting the remaining mangroves has become one of my biggest passions.'

Araceli is keen for me to see the 'different' Cancún, as she calls it, so has arranged for a taxi-driver friend to pick me up and drive me around. His battered white taxi draws up outside the hotel and I hurry into the back to escape the fierce sun outside the hotel's temperate courtyard. He has brought along his niece Marcela to help as a translator.

The road out to the decrepit suburbs of Cancún where the bulk of its citizens live takes us past some familiar signs of a modern, globalized Mexico that feels the heavy influence of its neighbour to the north – Wal-Mart, Costco, Sam's Club, McDonald's. But the giant superstores soon begin to melt away and are replaced by row after row of low-level housing set against cracked and dusty potholed roads. Some roads are filled with long terraces of two-up, two-down brick houses, but just as many are decorated with what Marcela calls *palapas* – open-sided, flimsy structures made out of scraps of wood, bitumen sheeting, palm fronds and corrugated iron. Uncollected rubbish is strewn along many of the streets.

Marcela points to a tangle of wires cascading down from a pylon. 'Look, the residents here are stealing electricity. It is very dangerous; they do it themselves. Some steal water, too, and build pipes to feed into their homes. They are desperate. There are no hospitals here. The people have to go to either the Red Cross or state-run hospitals on the road out to Merida [Yucatan's largest city]. And housing is expensive.

The brick houses here cost about $16,000. With the minimum wage at 40 pesos (£1.85) a day, it can take people living in the *palapas* about five years to save enough for a deposit. This community is unique in Mexico because it is totally made up of people who have migrated. There are no local traditions. No one is very religious. And there are many gangs and drug traffickers operating here.

'Drugs are a real problem. People sell cocaine and ecstasy in the hotel discos to fund their own habits. And they drink, of course. Many men get drunk in the *cantinas* here after work. Look how every street we pass has a "Super-Mini" shop on the corner. This is where people buy cheap alcohol. Why do you think there are also so many pawnbrokers everywhere?'

Marcela is in her mid-twenties and used to work as a spa assistant at a major hotel chain. But she has returned to her studies following the slump in available work after Wilma. Most of the people she knows who still have jobs are working in Cancún's tourism industry.

'Work is tough here. Most hotels only hire people on twenty-eight-day contracts. This is bad for many reasons, but most of all it means people can never build up their social housing credits to qualify for a better home. We used to have worker rights in Mexico, but no more. There are two unions operating in the hotels, but in general they don't really help us much. Some hotels my friends work for made them sign resignation letters the day they joined. You don't get the job otherwise. This means the hotel can fire them at any time and just wave the resignation letter at the unions to stop any action. Everyone knows this happens.'

The taxi pulls into a ten-by-ten-block district known simply as 'One Hundred'. All of downtown Cancún is carved up into small numbered regions. Many side streets don't have official names and this is ingeniously used by locals to help with security. If a stranger approaches an area, they are asked by locals to name the street they are standing on. Often only the local residents will know its name.

Marcela says that in some neighbourhoods outsiders are routinely stabbed because there is such fear about gangs infiltrating an area.

We all step out of the car and take a seat at a food stall on a street corner. A middle-aged, portly couple wearing baseball caps and aprons are cutting onions and meat on wooden boards inside, in preparation for the evening rush. Marcela says both María and Silvestre used to work in hotel kitchens before Wilma, but now they've set up their own business closer to home. I ask them, through Marcela, what their work in the hotels was like.

'I spent sixteen years working from six a.m. to two p.m. in the staff restaurant,' says Silvestre without taking his eyes off the slicing blade. 'Two of those hours were considered "extra time" and I didn't get paid for them. I'm pleased Wilma came as I got fired and it made me set up my stall here. I now sell tacos and sodas. Our speciality is a local dish called *cochinita pibil* [pork marinated in orange juice and spices, then roasted in banana leaves]. There's no pressure now and fewer hours. We are really busy on Friday and Saturday nights here.'

Silvestre smiles at María with pride. He reaches into an icebox and offers us all sodas.

'Before Wilma I was earning 1,600 pesos (£74) every fifteen days. This was considered a professional wage. If we got sick for three days, we didn't get paid, but if you were sick for seven days you got half of your pay. About 80 per cent of the people here in Region One Hundred work inside the hotels. Most hotels share out tips among the staff. Kitchen staff like us would get a 10 per cent cut of all the tips collected in the hotel. The people from the unions collect the money and then distribute it once a week. Sometimes chefs are promised by the hotel chains that they will be taken to hotels in other countries to train, but this is just an incentive they use to make us work. It rarely happens.'

I ask María if some hotel groups have a good reputation among the workers. Or do they all get viewed in the same way?

'People talk about this a lot here when they're eating at our stall. There is a pecking order, yes. People always say that the Ritz Carlton pays the best. Also the Fiesta Americana Grand Coral Beach hotel and the various Palace Resorts, as they are owned by Mexicans. The Spanish chains have a bad reputation for pay. They think they are the second Conquistadors. After Wilma, many claimed they were bankrupt and didn't pay any salaries, even though they got insurance money to rebuild. A lot of the waiters, chefs and security guards even ended up working for the construction companies because they had no work.'

The roundabout that leads from downtown Cancún on to Boulevard Kukulkan presents the first evidence that this is a tourist destination, after all. The landscaping by the side of the road suddenly improves, with clipped lawns and neat rows of palms stretching into the distance. Boulevard Kukulkan runs the entire length of the *zona hotelera*, like a huge lasso around the Nichupté lagoon that lies between the mainland and Cancún island.

After around ten minutes of travelling nose-to-tail in dense traffic, the taxi reaches Punta Cancún, the bend on this '7'-shaped island and the heart of the *zona hotelera*. This is where the tallest hotels stand, as well as the convention centre, nightclubs and main shopping malls. It is the principal draw for the tens of thousands of American students – some estimates put the number as high as 200,000 – that flock to Cancún each March for the notorious Spring Break. Taking advantage of the fact that, in contrast to home, super-cheap alcohol is served to those aged eighteen and up, these students turn Cancún into a bacchanalian temple of excess. It is so popular that there is now a Summer Break, too.

Ever since the 1960s, there has been a tradition among North American students to take a trip during the Easter holiday whose sole focus is some hard partying in the sun. Over the years, places in

Florida such as Fort Lauderdale, Daytona Beach and Panama City Beach have proved highly popular, but when the city burghers started to clamp down, various Mexican resorts replaced them in popularity. Cancún is now very much the Spring Break capital: MTV broadcasts live from the resort each March, hosting guest celebrities such as Paris Hilton and 50 Cent, as well as some of the world's leading DJs; mariachi bands play along to wet T-shirt competitions, as students order pitchers of beer and await sundown so they can move on to the foam parties held each night at the many nightclubs.

Most of the major US distillers and beer companies swamp the area with advertising and promotions, realizing they can reach the under-twenty-one market they are not legally allowed to tempt in the US. Many of the bars and clubs now operate an 'all-you-can-drink' entrance fee – a night-long wristband can cost as little as $35. Some travel companies even offer week-long wristbands that cost $400 or more and include VIP nightclub entrance, unlimited alcohol, free meals at McDonald's, a free tank of petrol for the hire car, free jet-ski hire and a range of discounts at shops. Many of these all-inclusive deals are sold to students whilst they are still on campus. This is how Studentspringbreak.com, for example, sells its Cancún packages:

> Benefits of going to Cancún are many, yes, but most students just care about the abundance of alcohol, alcohol and wait, you guessed it, more alcohol. Your yearly intake of alcoholic consumption could happen in one small week in Cancún, Mexico, on Spring Break. Do I have to say more? For those of you worried about what your parents might say, tell them it's an 'educational trip'. You are working to graduate college with a minor in heavy drinking. And best of all, Mom, I don't have to worry about drinking the water and getting sick, because I will only be drinking beer.

It is impossible to park the taxi anywhere, so Marcela and I jump out and decide to take a stroll around the area. We pass a mass of nightclubs and restaurants tailored to Spring Breakers that wrap around the Cancún Convention and Visitors Bureau – Hooters, TGI Friday's, Hard Rock Café, Coco Bongo, Bulldog, Señor Frogs, and Fat Tuesdays – before reaching a strip of shops selling a range of frat-boy T-shirts printed with slogans such as 'FBI: Female Body Inspector', 'Sex Police: K9 Doggy-style Unit' and 'For my next trick I need a condom and a volunteer'.

A small gap between the high-rise hotels offers a chance to get down to the beach. The Cancún authorities spent $20 million hiring dredgers from Holland after Hurricane Wilma to come and restore the beaches in this area, after all the sand was blown away by a vortex caused by the winds buffering the high-rise buildings along the *zona hotelera*. Within a year, the sand had started to wash away again. Marcela says that although in theory all beaches are public, this is one of the few places in this whole area where locals can actually gain full access to the waterfront. Elsewhere, the wall of closely packed hotels forces them to walk through a hotel lobby to reach the beach, which most are prevented from doing by security guards.

On a strip of sand no more than a hundred metres long, dozens of Mexicans lie under umbrellas. Further down the beach I can see far less packed expanses of white sand where the foreign tourists are. A thick rope runs down the beach and into the sea, marking out the dividing line. We stop to chat to Carmen, a woman selling bags of coconut strips with chilli and lime juice for fifteen pesos to locals on the beach:

'I come from Merida and I've been in Cancún for fifteen years now. I've been selling fruit on the beach for six,' she says as she hands a bag to Marcela, who says they are her favourite snack. 'I make about 150 pesos (£7) a day. I start at ten a.m. and finish by eight p.m. On Sundays I bring my eleven-year-old daughter to help me as it's so busy. I'm meant to get permission from the government, but nobody does. The authorities let me sell here, but not to the tourists. There is no turf warfare here among the fruit-sellers on this stretch of beach, but it is tough where the tourists are as you can make more money there. It's usually men who sell fruit there, though, as they can carry more on their trays. They are not allowed to approach the sun loungers, or else the hotel security guards will run after them.'

Marcela's uncle's taxi can't wait any longer or it will get moved on by the police, so I thank her and she leaves for home. I make my way back to the road that runs parallel to the beach. I find myself being drawn to the wedding-cake architecture of the Riu Palace hotel and its neighbouring sister – the 569-room, sixteen-storey Riu Cancún hotel that dwarfs all around it. As I enter the lobby of the Riu Cancún, a security guard approaches me immediately.

'Hello, sir. Are you are guest with us?'

I shake my head.

'This is an all-inclusive hotel I'm afraid, sir. Only guests can pass this point.'

I mumble something about needing a brochure and wander over to the reception desk. Through a doorway out to the beach I can see the pool area – some people are drinking at the poolside bar and a large group is playing water polo. A steep wall down to the beach prevents anyone accidentally stumbling into the hotel that way; the steps are guarded by security. I see a large noticeboard listing all the activities and eating times for the day ahead. Behind the reception desk are lots of plaques, including one from Thomson Holidays awarding the hotel 'Best Faraway Shores Accommodation' status. There's also a note saying that all taxes and gratuities are included in the price. So with just one upfront payment, a guest at the hotel could, in theory, never need to open their wallet or purse during their entire stay. I pick up a brochure for Riu's hotels in the Caribbean region. In total, I count twenty-six all-inclusive hotels in its stable across Cuba, Mexico, Jamaica, the Bahamas, the Dominican

Republic and Florida. They include the monster-sized 846-room hotel at Ocho Rios in Jamaica.

All-inclusive, according to Riu, 'means enjoying your vacations without limits, without having to worry about anything, not even to pay during your stay. To choose freely and forget the money, to taste the finest cuisine, drinks, sports, shows and entertainment. The privilege of enjoying every place to the maximum, and at all times savouring intensely everything around you.'

Others beg to differ. Tricia Barnett, the director of Tourism Concern, has described all-inclusive holidays as the 'cutting edge of what is of concern ethically about tourism globally'. In a letter to *Geographical* magazine in 2004, she elaborated:

'Sure, they can offer brilliant beaches, wonderful food and drink and entertainment, but, please, think twice. All-inclusives are great for people who want to curl up and think about little else than which restaurant to try that evening or which watersport to indulge in. Such places can be alluring, but the economics of all-inclusive vacations are grim. Recently, I was in the Dominican Republic, which has more hotel beds than any other Caribbean island, most of which belong to big US and European chains. One of the biggest chains showed me the results of some research that demonstrated how little of tourists' money reaches the destination. Of the money that we pay for our holiday, 89 per cent stays here with the operator, the air carrier, insurance cover, commissions and the travel agency. Of the remaining 11 per cent, the hotel gets 3 per cent. You can imagine how much is left for the staff. We're delighted when we get a bargain and [we have become] increasingly aware of the environmental costs of these goodies. Hopefully we'll soon wake up to the social costs of our cheap holidays.'

In 1994, the Mighty Pep, a local singer, won the annual National Calypso Monarch crown in St Lucia for a calypso entitled 'Like An Alien In We Own Land'. In St Lucia, tourism accounts for 72 per cent of the country's goods and services industry; the calypso's lyrics show the strength of local feeling about the situation:

All-inclusive tax elusives
and truth is
they're sucking up we juices
buying up every strip of beach
every treasured spot we reach
for Lucians to enter
for lunch or dinner
we need reservations, passport and visa
and if you sell near the hotel
I wish you well
they will yell and kick you out to hell.

Derek Walcott, the Nobel laureate poet from St Lucia, has also voiced his views about his country's reliance on tourism. 'Our future is dependent on tourism and we are ruled from the outside, certainly in terms of economics,' he told the *Observer* in 1999. He went on to say that tourism 'needs some sense of self-respect and dignity. In the Caribbean context, that means not whoring out our beaches because there's a dollar to be made; respecting the cost of integrity. My rage continues because in these deals (the big beach-front developments) the public is never consulted. You may say, the public is never consulted anywhere; but when you are dealing with a very small beautiful space and a very valuable, limited amount of real estate, it is clear what will happen – a succession of mini-Miamis all down the [Caribbean] archipelago, devoted to exploiting our resources ... The real problem is an indifferent recklessness that happens in small Caribbean governments claiming they have no alternative ... The problem can only be defined in abstract terms – spiritual, sacred, a violation of some kind of spiritual wholeness. These islands are settled by people who have experienced slavery, and our philosophy of self-respect should have come from that experience. And we should be able to say "fuck off" to certain things, to say, "No, we have come from the lowest pitch of experience and you cannot degrade us further" . . . The politician never makes a sacrifice; he benefits. And you run all the risks of having a very disaffected society if you build exclusive hotels, if you build not a direct, but certainly a visible, segregation. There will be no beaches for St Lucians to swim on very soon. Oh, they can come, but there are beach guards and they won't feel welcome.'

One surprising consequence of all-inclusive and other large-scale hotels is that they help perpetuate a fear among tourists that eating local food will make them sick, by tending to offer only bland Westernized buffets. A paper published in the *Cornell Hotel and Restaurant Administration Quarterly* in 2004 showed that many hotel chefs were now forced to buy in frozen seafood and meat from outside the state to allay fears that local produce might make tourists sick, even though there was little evidence that this was the case. 'Quintana Roo growers supply only a small proportion of the food consumed by [Cancún's] hotels,' said the paper. 'For example, only 4.5 per cent of fruits and 3.4 per cent of vegetables were from Quintana Roo, even though there is considerable potential to produce these products for tourism locally.' It's yet more evidence of how these hotels often fail to benefit local economies.

Before getting a bus back to Hotel El Rey del Caribe, I take a quick detour to the Cancún Convention and Visitors Bureau, located in a large white windowless building in the centre of a traffic system in Punta Allen. Jorge Luis Tellez Vignet, the promotion director, travels the world trying to sell Cancún to tour operators at the many travel trade shows held each year in cities such as Berlin, London and

Miami. I'm interested to hear how he convinces companies to fly tourists sometimes thousands of miles to this corner of Mexico.

'This area wasn't even a state of Mexico thirty years ago,' he says. 'The Mexican government opened it up as a tourist destination so that they could claim the land. Today, the government has developed five different areas in Mexico for tourism, but Cancún is still the only one that is fully developed. This is to our advantage. In our research, we discovered that as many foreigners have heard of Cancún as they have Mexico. Also, security is excellent in Cancún due to its lagoon geography. There is next to no crime here, as all the people are employed in tourism and no one wants to scare away the tourists.'

Once people have heard of Cancún then you have to convince them to come, he explains. 'Take Japan, for example. It took us a lot of spit to get the Japanese to start coming to Cancún. But now Japan is one of our biggest customers. The secret to attracting them was good hotels. There are three categories to the Japanese market: the elders; the single office-worker ladies aged between twenty and thirty-five; and the families. These are the groups we chase. The biggest change came in 1988 when we convinced American Airlines to start flying charters to Cancún via Dallas from Japan. We started doing our own trade shows in Japan. We did some TV adverts. Then, luckily for us, the Japanese stopped going to Jamaica, our biggest rival, almost overnight because of two high-profile tourist murders on the island. In 1987, 2,500 Japanese visited Cancún. By 2000, it was 55,000.'

Jorge says that not every market requires the same approach. 'The British are only really interested in the beach product. Price is also an important factor for the British, but not as much as for the Germans. They want their holidays to be really cheap. I think the Europeans are too demanding, actually. Everything must be cheap for them. As a result, wages in Cancún haven't gone up in years. With our rivals, it's always a war of who can be the cheapest to attract the visitors.'

*

Highway 307 from Cancún down to Tulum is a near-seamless stretch of tourist offerings – golf courses, water parks, Mayan ruins, *cenotes* and theme parks. Every few minutes during the two-hour journey, the bus passes large ranch-style gated entrances to the many hidden hotel complexes that lie behind the few hundred metres of forest that shield the view to the coast. Every hotel chain you can think of is present, it seems, along this coastline – the official Riviera Maya website lists over two hundred – ranging from family resorts to an adults-only resort for swingers.

Just a few kilometres past the world-famous Tulum ruins, which look out so imposingly over the sea from a cliff top, stands the small, unremarkable town of Tulum itself. Manuel Quezada meets me at the bus station and we hop straight into his jeep and head south to the Sian Ka'an biosphere, Mexico's third-largest nature reserve and the only thing preventing the creep of hotels from Cancún spreading any further down the coastline.

Manuel is a twenty-six-year-old guide for Community Tours Sian Ka'an (CTSK), a local alliance of Mayan ecotourism cooperatives that was established in 2004 to help raise awareness among locals that tourism could be used both to earn money and to achieve environmental sustainability. The scheme has won international acclaim and now receives logistical support from the UN, the US conservation group RARE, Aveda and the Mexican government. It is also part of a new venture set up by the online travel company Expedia and the UN Foundation called the World Heritage Alliance, which aims to raise ring-fenced funds through tourism in order to help preserve the eight-hundred-plus world heritage sites – which include the Pyramids, the Great Barrier Reef, the Grand Canyon and the Galápagos Islands – and the communities that live within them or close by.

As we travel along the bumpy dirt track that leads into this 530,000-hectare world heritage site – home to 103 mammal species,

336 bird species and one of the Caribbean's most biodiverse stretches of coral reef – Manuel explains to me the pressures that forced the local communities in the area to unite and form CTSK.

'Places such as Sian Ka'an will disappear unless we control tourism. It gets more and more crowded around us and now the government wants to build a new airport at Tulum for tourists, which will only make things worse. But we are just the people who live here. If you imagine a pyramid, we are at the bottom and are never heard by those few at the top.'

Manuel explains that CTSK was set up to form a louder, bolder voice for local communities and to help redistribute the income from tourism more fairly, by allowing communities to deal directly with tourists instead of being at the mercy of middle men.

'Only 10–15 per cent of the hotels along the whole coast, up to and including Cancún, are owned by Mexican companies. The foreign-owned companies have the attitude that they can just take what they need from us. We have a phrase here that translates as "It is easier to ask for forgiveness than to ask for permission." Some hotels here violate planning permission then just pay the fine. They don't care as it's peanuts to them and they now have the big hotel they wanted all along.'

Should, I ask, tourists even be allowed into a protected and highly sensitive area such as Sian Ka'an?

'It's a difficult balance, using tourism to protect an area. If we can keep numbers down with small, exclusive groups then this is good. But tourists should pay much more for the privilege, I believe. The park entrance fee for tourists is just four dollars. It should be much higher to keep numbers down and still earn the same income. In 1986, just four hundred tourists – mostly backpackers – entered the reserve. Now about thirty thousand are entering a year. This difficult road used to be the main barrier that prevented more tourists from coming, but now it is being improved and people can just drive their hire cars in. There's a lot of corruption here, sadly. No one is meant to build in the reserve's buffer zone without permission, but houses have been going up along this road. Some international NGOs such as the Nature Conservancy have started to buy plots of land to protect it from development. The fact that this is a UNESCO world heritage site helps us greatly as it means central government listens. But UNESCO only has the power to shame our government, not to stop violations happening.'

After driving for around an hour and a half through low-level scrubland and pockets of jungle, the road finally starts to run adjacent to the coast. The sea is choppy from an offshore breeze, but still retains its striking turquoise hue. It's not long before we pull into Punta Allen, a small community of five hundred or so fishermen which sits on a jut of land facing out on to some of the best diving and snorkelling sites anywhere in the Caribbean.

'Lobster fishing is the main trade here,' says Manuel, 'but the season only runs from July to February, so they also use the boats to take tourists out on trips to the reefs. Before this arrangement started there were coconut plantations here, but the trees got destroyed by disease and hurricanes. Most of the community would hunt for crocodiles, manatees and turtles, too. Hopefully, this income from tourism can persuade the community not to hunt any more.'

Manuel points out, though, that the locals are finding it hard to juggle the new demands that come with the arrival of more and more tourists. One of the fishermen cooperatives has broken away from the local alliance and begun to undercut the prices other boatmen charge by 200 pesos per trip to get more business.

'This is making everyone angry,' says Manuel. 'We must stick together, I believe. Every Saturday we pay the restaurants and boat owners the money we have earned from the tours. We give the fishermen 1,200 pesos (£56) for every two-hour trip they have run that week. We pay this whether there was one or six tourists in the boat.

We charge the tourists about ninety dollars so, as you can see, most of the money goes to the community. In fact, about 90 per cent of the money collected is redistributed locally to the cooperative. The rest goes on administration such as our website – 25 per cent of business now comes this way. Hopefully, Expedia will now be sending us tourists, too, through the World Heritage Alliance scheme. We have tried to arrange tours, with the help of the World Heritage Alliance, which tourists want to do. As well as the day trip to Punta Allen, we also offer birdwatching, flyfishing and the "Muyil Float", where tourists float down a freshwater Mayan canal.'

After a lunch of fried fish and rice at a beach café, we change into our swimming shorts and climb into one of the small fishing boats tied up on the beach. It slaps through the surf at speed as we move around the headland and out into a wide lagoon surrounded by mangroves. The birdlife is spectacular – roseate spoonbills, ibises and huge herons cluster on the mangrove branches. Buoys in the water mark out their nesting sites to prevent boats from getting too close.

The boat then heads straight out to sea, towards the reefs which are visible from far off due to the white, fizzing surf breaking on the submerged coral. Manuel lays out some ground rules – don't touch anything, stay close to him, keep my lifejacket on – before we both drop overboard for a joyous half an hour's snorkelling. The water offers about thirty metres' visibility, but there's plenty to see at close hand. As Manuel leads he points out dozens of interesting sea creatures. We pass lobsters, cat sharks, eels and schools of groupers, all set against the background of giant fan corals swaying in the current.

Back in the boat on our way to another dive site, we pass a female dolphin with her calf close to her side, and a community of black starfish sitting beneath the waves on a sand bar. Then the boatman shouts and points into the distance. Manuel looks up excitedly and gets out of his seat. The boat races over to a dark shadow darting around under the water at speed.

'Turtle, turtle,' says the boatman excitedly.

As he does so, a leatherback turtle the size of a washing machine rushes to the surface before us, gulps a huge breath of air, then drops beneath the wave. It is there for just a couple of seconds, its dense shadow quickly melting away as it swims off. It's a magical and privileged moment for me, but when I sit back down in my seat I notice four other boats racing towards us.

'Their boatmen have seen us rush over here,' says Manuel. 'They know we have spotted something good and are bringing their tourists to see, too.' The snowball effect of tourism strikes me hard: tourists such as me – such as all of us – simply beget more tourists. Can any form of tourism really be a safe and trustworthy mechanism by which to secure the world's most prized natural assets, such as Sian Ka'an – a place so precious that its name translates from Mayan as 'Gift from the Sky'?

10

Green Gold

La Fortuna, Costa Rica

AGAINST THE ROAR OF THE seventy-metre-high waterfall, a menacing buzz akin to an angry horsefly is rapidly getting louder. A man attached to a harness suddenly bursts through the rainforest canopy on a long steel cable that stretches out over the deep ravine. He lets out a throaty, exhilarated yell as he descends.

'Whooooaaaaaa!!'

Carlos Espinoza turns to me with an exasperated expression on his face. 'All this noise disturbs the animals here. These zip-wires in the rainforest are not a good thing. It's just for fun, not for looking at the wildlife. It's better just to walk. At that speed how can you enjoy nature? Many tourists complain to me that we have these zip-wires in the rainforest. They just want to enjoy the beauty around them, not listen to this noise.'

Carlos and I are standing on a wooden viewing platform built by a local community group, Associación de Desarrollo La Fortuna, that overlooks La Fortuna waterfall in Costa Rica. Carlos, the group's executive secretary, has helped mobilize local farmers to begin to turn this fifteen-hectare plot of former state-owned land, which was too rough to farm, back to its original rainforest state. Since 1980, the money raised from the six-dollar fee charged to tourists to enter this 'transitional forest' has helped to build a road to the site, as well as a car park, toilet block, small café and souvenir shop.

'This site generates 150 million colones ($75,000) a year for this community,' says Carlos. 'Six people work here and many more are employed indirectly. We want to build better trails through the rainforest here, as tourists love to walk. But the waterfall is the big draw for them. We don't advertise as we don't want to be swamped with visitors – we get between two and three hundred a day.'

The town of La Fortuna lies ten minutes away by car and is one of the principal tourist hubs of Costa Rica, the small Central American country sandwiched between Panama and Nicaragua. Costa Rica is roughly the size of Croatia and has a population of only four million, but has gained a worldwide reputation among tourists for its stunning biodiversity – 5 per cent of the world's total within 0.1 per cent of its landmass – varied terrain and at least six distinct types of ecosystem. Around 1.5 million international tourists arrive each year – the government wants to double this by 2012 – and many of them pass through La Fortuna, which sits high on the country's volcanic spine, due to its convenience as a hopping-off point to many of northern Costa Rica's attractions.

A couple of hours west along a notoriously difficult road – the key to its survival, some say – lies Monteverde, a nature reserve established by American Quakers evading conscription for the Korean War in the early 1950s. This is now the most popular place in the country to experience a cloud-forest habitat, one of only twelve true primary rainforests in the world, where there are areas of forest that have never been cut down. It is also the location of the Children's Eternal Forest, a 22,000-hectare reserve saved from loggers in the late 1980s when thousands of schoolchildren across the world were moved to save their pocket money and raise funds to buy it collectively. Today it bars tourists, except along a solitary trail.

Just half an hour to the north of La Fortuna lies the active Arenal volcano, which draws the eye wherever you are in the town or surrounding countryside. Behind the perfect cone-shaped volcano spitting molten ash down its sides is a huge man-made lake – the largest in the country – which is said to offer some of the best wind-surfing in Central America, and good fishing, too. Just by the hydroelectric dam that formed the lake is a network of hanging bridges that allow tourists to walk through the rainforest canopy. And dotted around this geothermal land are a number of hot springs. Combined, these attractions are enough to draw nearly half of all the tourists visiting Costa Rica.

'I've spent twenty-two years here farming this land,' says Carlos, as we drive down the road to his farm. 'I kept some cattle, like everyone around here, and I grew macadamia nuts, but it wasn't good business and I knew I was damaging the environment by doing so. The soil is too soft here to farm commercially, really.'

The road is steep, potholed and muddy, with only the occasional patch of tarmac. Carlos says the road is only repaired if the Associación de Desarrollo La Fortuna earns enough money at the end of each year. Tourists on quad bikes speed past us in the opposite direction, over-taking other tourists on horseback as they go. The car pulls off the road and up a long drive lined with striking sunset-coloured heliconia, known locally as maracas or 'shampoo plants' due to the water that collects in the corrugated flowers, which becomes soapy over time.

'Two years ago I decided to build two ecolodges here. My farm is worth more and more each day now.'

We take a walk around his five-hectare farm. Carlos picks up a spade off the moist, dark soil in a field and digs up some cassava root to show me. 'We grow pumpkins here, too. And cashew trees. I just planted some teak trees. Farming is just a hobby now. I do it for the guests to see. I have built a freshwater pond for tilapia. This fish can then be sold or served to guests. We recycle all the water here and the ecolodges were built with timber from my land.'

I ask Carlos how he could afford to switch from farming to tourism.

'I took out a ten-year loan from the bank two years ago,' he explains, saying such a business strategy is becoming increasingly popular among his neighbours. 'This was half of what I needed; the rest was from hard work and savings from the farm. I can charge eighty dollars a night for our eight-person cabin.'

He fears, though, that his community might become complacent about the financial benefits tourism has brought. 'We want tourism here, especially if it respects nature. But we need to unite as a community to survive. The banks always want to lend us more to expand, but we have to be careful. We don't want bus loads of tourists coming up these roads.'

It's not a vision shared by all in La Fortuna. Just on the other side of the deep ravine cut out by La Fortuna waterfall is land owned by the company that built the zip-wire through the rainforest so resented by Carlos. Arenal Mundo Aventura is an 'ecological tropical park' that has been created by a local businessman who also owns Luigi's, the largest hotel in the centre of La Fortuna. As well as the four kilometres of zip-wires that cut through the rainforest, the park also offers a netted butterfly garden, horseriding, abseiling and a Maleku village, 'built by an indigenous tribe under the most authentic tradition'.

I join Julio Madriz Nunez, my guide throughout my stay in Costa Rica, in Arenal Mundo Aventura's car park. Julio was recommended to me by ACTUAR, a national association of community-based rural-tourism operators. He has spent over twenty years showing tourists around the country and his intimate knowledge of the country's flora and fauna has led to him being employed by the BBC's Natural History Unit when filming wildlife documentaries in Costa Rica, as well as by biologists at Harvard University. Like most 'Ticos', as his fellow countrymen call themselves, he has a dry sense of humour (known locally as *choteo*) and a mischievous sense of fun.

We mount a pair of rather emaciated horses and ride up a trail beside a swollen river to the Maleku village. We are joined by a couple on holiday from Mobile, Alabama, and two of the company's own guides. On the way up, we chat with these guides about the company's plans for this land, which it has only acquired within the last few years.

'This is a good business for the owner,' says one of the guides. 'About seventy tourists come here a day, mostly in groups. It costs $55 a person to go on the zip-wire, visit the Maleku village and ride on the horses. All the guides working here get paid $250 a month, which means the owner has cleared our salaries within about three days of the month. He bought another new tractor for $9,000 just two days ago to tow the tourists to the top of the hill. As I said, it's good business.' He adds that a spa, mountain resort and 'tropical golf course' will soon be added.

The horses amble into a large clearing, in the centre of which is a *palenque* – a rectangular building with bamboo walls and a thatch of long leaves, built on a packed-earth foundation. Around it stand some smaller round structures, from which Maleku men and children wearing only grass skirts and jewellery come out to meet us. They give a traditional greeting of 'Capi Capi', accompanied by a double thud on our chests with their fist.

The Maleku are indigenous to Costa Rica and, like so many similar communities around the world, have suffered a long history of persecution and suppression, particularly when they were forced into slavery by local rubber-plantation owners in the nineteenth century. Today, it is estimated that only about eight hundred Maleku remain in Costa Rica, mostly living in government-protected reserves around La Fortuna. Many of them have integrated into Tico life, but they proudly maintain their heritage, culture and language.

This 'village' has been purpose-built for tourists, as is immediately obvious from the number of trinkets hanging up for sale on the walls inside the *palenque*, marked with dollar price tags. We are each handed half a coconut shell filled with *chicha* – a sweet drink of fermented corn and pineapple juice that we are promised will 'make us happy'. The patriarch of the group then orders a welcome dance to be commenced and the group walk around in a tight circle, singing.

Such contrived interaction between tourists and indigenous groups always strikes me as being uncomfortable for both parties. But once these formalities are over, we spend half an hour chatting to the patriarch about his life. He tells us how the Maleku all take it in turns to leave their reserve fifty kilometres away and spend time here at the tourist village. The park owner doesn't pay them anything, he says, but they make money by selling their rain-makers and balsa-wood face masks to the tourists.

After our sixth cup of *chicha*, we get up to catch a ride to the car park on one of the tractor trailers bringing tourists back down the hill from the zip-wires. As we set off, I see some of the children changing back into their jeans and T-shirts, and the patriarch making a call outside the *palenque* on his mobile phone. Is it our desire as tourists to see the 'natives of the land' that leads the Maleku to dress up like this, thereby satisfying our pre-determined assumptions and stereotypes? Or is it their belief that this is what we want to see? Either way, this is as much of a theme park as anything in Orlando.

Julio and I spend the night at Arenal Oasis, an ecolodge just a few kilometres away. Like Carlos's lodges, it is set on land that was once farmed but has now been converted into accommodation for eco-tourists. The country has become a beacon around the world for ecotourism. About a quarter of the land in Costa Rica is now within national park boundaries. This compares to 7 per cent in Brazil and 3.6 per cent in the US. Since the mid-1980s, tourism has been aggressively pursued by government, meaning that within a few short years this new sector has overtaken agriculture as the most important economic driver for the country. This remained the case until 1996, when Intel invested in Costa Rica by building a vast $300-million semiconductor factory near the capital, San José. Other high-tech firms such as Microsoft and Siemens followed, keen to exploit Costa Rica's highly educated workforce. That such large multinationals have chosen to invest so heavily in this country is testament to its reputation as 'the Switzerland of Central America' – a country that has a stable economy and the second-highest GDP per capita in Latin America, constitutionally abolished its own army in 1949 following a civil war, and since then has played a central role in negotiating peace between its often warring regional neighbours.

The next morning, we walk down from our lodge through a beautiful tropical lush garden, wet with dew and loud with birdsong, to tuck into a breakfast of *gallo pinto*, a Costa Rican one-plate meal of rice, black beans, tortilla and fried plantain, spiced up with a ubiquitous bottle of chilli sauce called Lizano Salsa. The meal has been prepared for us by Rosa Vásquez, the owner of Arenal Oasis. We invite her to join us for a coffee.

'This rural life is in my blood,' she says, wiping her hands on her apron. 'My husband and I have been here on this land for twenty-three years. Before that we worked on a coffee plantation to the east on the Caribbean coast. We got together with forty-eight families and approached the government to buy some land here. We each bought five hectares with a bank loan and started to grow plantain, papaya, cassava, potatoes and corn, and reared cattle, too. Then in the late 1980s the government wanted us to grow ornamental plants such as hellebores for export abroad. Then they said cardamom, then they said cocoa, but they all got diseased. It cost us a lot of money to buy the seeds off the government, and the plants only gave a good harvest for three years. We had to keep applying pesticides because they made us use hybrids. Then there was a big corruption scandal with the agricultural ministry and we were desperate and wondering what to do.'

Rosa, a devout Catholic, says God then blessed her with good fortune. Conservation groups operating near by were keen to introduce buffer zones in the area between the national parks to create 'biological corridors' – areas where hunting was banned and certain farming methods restricted to allow wildlife to pass between the parks without danger. (There has long been an attempt to create a so-called MesoAmerican biological corridor, a contiguous chain of protected land the length of Central America. In theory, this might allow an animal such as a jaguar to walk from Colombia to Mexico without hindrance or threat.) Local farmers such as Rosa were approached by WWF, who offered financial help to introduce these buffers.

'We all went to the meetings to listen to their proposals. We formed a neighbourhood collective called "Z13"; this was what we all branded our cows with as it's the name of our shared road. It was the start of a new way of thinking for us. We started to ask why our soil was being ruined by pesticides and why the river kept flooding. We started to think about the air, and the flora and fauna. It was then that we started to think about tourism.'

Rosa says she opened her first lodgings to tourists in 1996, offering four beds and a small restaurant.

'Everyone was pessimistic about our position along this road and thought tourists would never find us. We made a brochure and handed it out at a tourism fair in San José. I then waited by the gate to see if anyone would come. It only took two days before the first people arrived – a couple from Germany. We had to use sign language as they didn't speak Spanish and we couldn't even speak English. They said they would recommend us to Lonely Planet and the next year we were included in their guidebook for Costa Rica. We've been busy ever since. It has only taken us eight years to pay back our original bank loan, which charged 21 per cent annual interest. Now our children are studying ecotourism and we have built three ecolodges costing us $6,000. It is still mainly word of mouth that brings people here, but we also work with six travel agents. Next we want to have solar panels and use biogas, but it is too expensive at the moment. People say they love the tranquillity of our land.'

As if on cue, a hummingbird appears at one of the many bird feeders piled high with cut oranges that Rosa has placed around the breakfast veranda. On the lawn below, a long column of leaf-cutter ants marches forth.

'Tourism has given us a chance to have dignity on our land again,' says Rosa. 'We now have the chance to trade directly with people without the middleman. Our children will not have to be farmers now. But this community doesn't want to invest completely in tourism, as it's too risky. We are looking into hydroponics as we want to try and grow tomatoes, peppers, lettuces and cucumbers in green-houses. We need to integrate tourism with agriculture. Every fortnight our community meets up to discuss all the local projects – the road, the school, the soccer field, the cultural programmes and recreation for the children. We want to form a tourism union to protect everyone here. We all now charge the same – $40 a night for lodges that sleep four people. We have to stick together.'

Rosa's enthusiasm is infectious, but some of her direct competitors in La Fortuna seem to have grown wary of the impact that tourism is having on the area, so much so that a number of former farmers who tried tourism have now switched back to farming.

Later in the day, back in the town itself, Julio and I meet Saray Quesada, the owner of a modest eighteen-room B&B called Hotel Macua.

'Yes, we all have a better life now than when we were farmers,' she says, sitting in an armchair on her veranda. 'But there are too many rooms now for this area. The tourism department gave us predictions about the number of visitors that were too optimistic and now we suffer from over-capacity here. Ninety per cent of people used to be dairy farmers, then everyone in La Fortuna was employed in tourism, but it is slipping back a bit now. Tourists have other places to go near here now. Some are going to Guatemala and Panama, instead. These countries saw Costa Rica as a school for how to develop tourism and they have copied us.'

In contrast to Rosa, Saray says that in the past year the local community has started to talk openly about tourism in negative terms.

'We now want to rescue our culture. Our traditional music is disappearing. It was a very connected, sharing community before, but some people are starting to become more individualistic and selfish as tourism money has increased.'

Isn't this, I ask, just the inevitable consequence of globalization? This, surely, is happening all over the world?

'We are really vulnerable to the changing winds. We need to find other activities to invest in. Some people are deciding to return to farming as a safety net. If the volcano goes dormant again we will have a huge problem as the tourists won't want to come here any more to see it. This eruption of tourism can't last for ever.'

It's a short drive in the shadow of the Arenal volcano to Puentes Colgantes del Arenal, the hanging bridges that allow tourists to walk through the rainforest canopy. On the way, Julio and I chat about his years as a tour guide to ecotourists.

'Some people make me really smile,' he says. 'In the twenty-seven years I've spent walking through my country's national parks I've seen a jaguar just five times. But some tourists think they have a right to see every animal because they have paid a lot of money to travel to Costa Rica. They've spent the money, so they expect a guarantee. Some even ask me in the morning how many birds they will see that day. How can I know? One even asked me once where the elephants were! I wonder why some want to come here sometimes when they have such little knowledge. But others are very emotional when they get here. I've seen birdwatchers cry when they see a bird that it's been their lifetime's ambition to view in the wild.'

Julio's main grumble, though, is with Costa Rica's Tourism Board (known locally as ICT). 'They demand licences for every tour guide, but they don't do any training. It means there are guides giving out the wrong information. It took me two years at university to get my qualifications. But when I applied for a licence, all they asked me was whether I could speak English. When I said yes, they issued the licence in two days. My qualifications didn't matter to them. The ICT spent millions of colones helping to put on a Pavarotti concert in San José, but they don't spend enough on conservation and park rangers. There are only eight rangers working in the Arenal Volcano national park, for example. And they support huge mega-projects for tourists like the one in the Gulf of Papagayo in the north-western Guanacaste region, where lots of international hotel groups such as Barcelo, Four Seasons and Occidental have been handed government land concessions to build all-inclusive or luxury resorts. It's right near Liberia international airport, so tourists go there without even visiting the rest of the country. This was not meant to be how tourism developed in Costa Rica.' (In 2007, First Choice became the first company to offer direct flights from the UK to Costa Rica, when it began a route from Gatwick to Liberia.) 'And they are letting the cruise ships come to Costa Rica more and more. I used to take groups from cruise ships, but I refuse now. It's just too many people to deal with and they only have a few hours here. What can they really see in this time?'

The car pulls off the main road by the hydroelectric dam at Lake Arenal and continues up a winding drive to the hanging bridges. Alexander Gonzalez, the site's general manager, meets us at the café, which has a fantastic view of the volcano now half shrouded in cloud. Julio unpacks a telescope from the boot of the car and fixes it to a tripod, so we can all take a closer look at the trail of smoke calmly rising from the caldera. Through the lens finder, I can make out smouldering boulders running down the side of the volcano; they have smashed into pieces by the time they are halfway down the slope.

A huge scar of deforestation wraps around half of the volcano's base, marking out the area that was burned to ash when the volcano dramatically blew back into life in 1968 after centuries of dormancy, killing seventy-eight people in the process. Julio points to a hotel complex on a ridge that looks far too close to the volcano for comfort.

'They are crazy to build there,' he says. 'No one should have allowed them to build so close. The guests are in the potential path of a pyroclastic flow. I wouldn't even go up to that hotel. Tourists [not from the hotel] have tried to climb the volcano and been killed.'

Alexander orders some coffees and we take a seat at a table outside the café. 'About five years ago, something really significant happened in this area,' he says as he sits down. 'For the first time a hectare of forest became more expensive to buy than a hectare of land for pasture. This changed a lot of farmers' minds about protecting the rainforests. Three years ago, this former farm owned by a local businessman was converted to a nature reserve in which tourists can walk through the canopy and see the wildlife. It's twenty dollars for tourists and six dollars for locals. We will get about 50,000 visitors here this year and we employ eighteen people full-time. It is easy to convince the people who live here that tourism is the best thing for us. The cattle farmers even sell their steaks to tourist restaurants. Everyone is happy this way. The ICT issues us with an annual permit to run the hanging gardens, but they don't do any checks for biodiversity here. We do it ourselves. Sometimes tourists throw plastic water bottles or chocolate wrappers off the bridges, but generally they are very good and respect nature. In places such as the Manuel Antonio national park on the Pacific coast it is much worse. People feed the white-faced monkeys there.'

As the sun sets, the volcano's hot ash glows red in the descending darkness. After a quick tour with Alexander of the largest hanging bridge in the fading light, we depart for an appointment at a thermal spa near by called Ecotermales Fortuna. It is owned by a family well known in the area for making a considerable fortune from their cattle ranching. Even so, they have still sought to join the local goldrush for the tourist dollar.

Herrold Vega Hidalgo, the twenty-nine-year-old manager of the spa and family heir, shows us around the site, which is full of tourists bathing in the steaming sulphur waters set against rainforest undergrowth dramatically lit with spotlights.

'We are lucky to have thirteen springs on our land along a one-mile stretch of river,' he says, pointing at a cascade of hot water coming down over rocks from higher up the hill. 'We only need to use three of these springs to fill our three pools here. The water in the top pool is 42C and it has cooled to 25C by the time it reaches the lowest pool. To be honest, we still make more money from the beef, but six years ago my grandma took this up as her pet project on her seventieth birthday and designed the whole spa on a piece of paper. It took two years to build with thirty-five people working here. About fifteen years ago the word got around the town that tourism was the way to make money, but my parents ignored it and carried on farming. Then we decided to give it a go on our terms. We didn't need a loan and it has paid itself back in just three years anyway. It's all word of mouth.'

We take a seat in the bar area, where a barman is serving bathers fruit cocktails on crushed ice as they cool themselves after leaving the waters.

'We have eighteen people working here full time. I work a twelve-to-fourteen-hour day here and make it my way of life. We have four other competitors in the area. Some of them have drilled into the ground to reach the springs, but we are completely sustainable. We are taking only water that comes to the surface naturally and don't use any chemicals. We've used pumice from the 1968 eruption to make our paths through the rainforest – the lava reached our farm, only two miles from here. Next year, we will start a waste-management system to compost all our organic trash from the bar area. We are a spa for real eco-tourists.'

*

Is there a term more used and abused in the tourism industry than 'ecotourism'? What does it even really mean? The prefix 'eco' implies that it is a form of tourism that both seeks and celebrates ecology – the planet's wildlife in all its natural habitats. It also carries with it an implicit suggestion that it is somehow 'environmentally friendly' – a form of tourism that allows us to view ecology in situ without harming the very habitats on which we tread. In fact, we might even act to preserve and protect these increasingly vulnerable habitats through our very arrival. But this is an idealistic view: upon closer inspection, the term throws up far more questions than answers. It is a term that is now at the heart of a fierce debate within the industry.

There have been various attempts to define and refine the term 'ecotourism' since the early 1980s, when a Mexican architect and conservationist called Héctor Ceballos-Lascuráin claims he coined the expression (although others have since disputed he was the first). It is interesting to see today what he originally intended the term to refer to, given how it can now be used: 'Ecotourism is tourism that involves travelling to relatively undisturbed natural areas with the specific object of studying, admiring and enjoying the scenery and its wild plants and animals, as well as any existing cultural aspects (both past and present) found in these areas,' he said in 1983. 'Ecotourism implies a scientific, aesthetic or philosophical approach, although the "ecotourist" is not required to be a professional scientist, artist or philosopher. The main point is that the person who practises ecotourism has the opportunity of immersing him or herself in nature in a way that most people cannot enjoy in their routine, urban existences. This person will eventually acquire an awareness and knowledge of the natural environment, together with its cultural aspects, that will convert him into somebody keenly involved in conservation issues.'

Of course, this form of tourism didn't start in 1983. Tourists have been travelling with the aim of immersing themselves in 'nature' for many decades. Yosemite Valley in California is often referred to as the world's first state park, established in 1864, when Abraham Lincoln declared it would 'be held for public use, resort, and recreation . . . inalienable for all time'. Yellowstone became the world's first national park in 1872. However, Fontainebleau forest near Paris was turned into the first nature reserve in 1853, after the Barbizon school of painters, which included Théodore Rousseau and Jean François Millet, lobbied for 'artistic reserves' to be created in which to study and paint nature. And before that, in 1826, some small woods in Sicily were also protected under royal order.

These early initiatives helped set a precedent of regional and national governments safeguarding tracts of land from development to help preserve natural habitats. The Kruger national park in north-eastern South Africa evolved out of the Sabie game reserve, which was formed during the Second Boer War at the turn of the twentieth century. In 1948, Kenya opened its first national parks – Amboseli, Tsavo East and Tsavo West. Neighbouring Tanzania opened the Serengeti national park in 1951 (it had been made a game reserve in 1921 by German colonialists), and it has since become part of the famous 'Northern Circuit' for tourists visiting Tanzania, which includes the Ngorongoro crater, Arusha and Mount Kilimanjaro.

But does this mean that anyone who peers at lions through binoculars from a convoy of jeeps on safari in Kenya is partaking in ecotourism, as Ceballos-Lascuráin's early definition might have us believe? What about those trekking in the Nepalese Himalaya? Or snorkelling on the Great Barrier Reef? Or paying $250 to see gorillas in Uganda? Are these tourists all 'keenly involved in conservation issues', or are they on a holiday where the natural environment around them is just part of the entertainment?

Noting this oversight, Ceballos-Lascuráin revised his definition in 1993: 'Ecotourism is environmentally responsible travel and visitation to relatively undisturbed natural areas, in order to enjoy, study and appreciate nature (and any accompanying cultural features – both past and present), that promotes conservation, has low negative visitor impact, and provides for beneficially active socio-economic involvement of local populations.' Three years later, this definition was adopted by the World Conservation Union (IUCN), a grand coalition of governments, NGOs and scientists concerned about conserving nature, founded in 1948.

Throughout the 1990s, the term 'ecotourism' gained much currency and rapidly entered mainstream consciousness among tourists. It was hailed as recognition of the fact that, yes, tourism can be environmentally damaging, particularly because tourists tend to prefer holidaying in sensitive habitats, such as coastlines, tropical islands and mountains, but that something can be done to mitigate their impact and allow tourism to continue in a sustainable manner.

This realization was timely. In 1998, the UNWTO published a report forecasting what tourists might be demanding in the years up to 2020. It said the 'trendiest' destinations would be the 'tops of the highest mountains, the depths of the oceans and the ends of the earth'. The spread and reach of tourists in search of the 'other' or the 'exclusive' would, in other words, push them into areas previously untouched by tourism. It was a canny prediction: tourists now make footfall in Antarctica in their tens of thousands each year via cruise ships, and the first tentative steps are even being taken by space tourists.

Broadly, 'ecotourism' has come to include not only the preservation of wildlife habitats visited by tourists, but also their human cohabitants. The International Ecotourism Society (TIES), a US-based institution founded in 1990 that 'provides guidelines and standards, training, technical assistance, research and publications to foster sound ecotourism development', defines ecotourism as 'responsible travel to natural areas that conserves the environment and sustains the wellbeing of local people'. It believes that these are not mutually exclusive ambitions, whereas some believe that you either protect the animals or you forgo them for the concerns of local communities. This division has helped ecotourism splinter into a number of confusing and sometimes contradictory sub-categories. For example, how many tourists can honestly tell the difference between these commonly used terms: geotourism; nature-based tourism; pro-poor tourism; responsible tourism; and sustainable tourism? Most of them have the same core intention – a more considerate, lighter-footed form of tourism – but are all subtly different.

There were hopes that some of these niggles might be ironed out in 2002, which the UN designated the 'International Year of Ecotourism' (IYE). Conferences were organized, reports commissioned and initiatives rolled out across the world. Ecotourism was billed by some as a superhero coming to save the day. The highlight of the year was the World Ecotourism Summit held in Québec, Canada, in May. Over a thousand delegates attended from 132 countries to thrash out a consensus on what ecotourism should mean and how it should be applied across the world. After three days of debate, the forty-nine-point 'Québec Declaration on Ecotourism' was agreed. As is the case with most international declarations of this sort, the wording was bland and riddled with compromise so as not to tread on sensitive toes. What was more telling was the passion felt by some of the stakeholders raising their voices at the fringes of the debate. That they felt they were at the fringes at all was, indeed, largely the problem.

'We are extremely concerned that this UN endorsement of ecotourism, in the light of all the fundamental problems related to the industry – in many cases another greenwash – will destroy more biodiversity and harm even more local communities,' said Chee Yoke Ling, a representative of the Malaysia-based Third World Network, an 'independent non-profit international network of organizations and individuals involved in issues relating to development, the Third World and North–South issues'.

'I really think this is going to be worse than the launch of package tours to the Third World,' said Nina Rao, a tourism academic from India, who acts as the 'southern co-chair' of the NGO Tourism Caucus to the UN Commission for Sustainable Development. But perhaps the most stinging attack came in the form of a letter signed by twenty NGOs, campaigners and academics from the North and South, including Rao, sent to Oliver Hillel, the United Nations Environment Programme (UNEP)'s tourism programme coordinator:

Too often, international agencies have used the South for misguided and outright destructive development experiments, and in the light of this conventional wisdom, we oppose the idea that the IYE serves as an instrument for ecotourism experiments in developing countries, which are likely to cause more harm than good. Ecotourism cannot thrive without the mass travel and tourism industry, nor the construction, real estate and other industries. So one can expect that those who will benefit most from the IYE will be large companies providing most of the physical infrastructure, facilities and services that make ecotourism possible, while once again local people will be put off with empty promises or chicken feed.

That ecotourism is a viable strategy to replace other more unsustainable development activities is another myth that needs to be exploded ... Ecotourism development has opened opportunities for a whole range of investors to gain access to remote rural, forest, coastal and marine areas. There is the observation that the more transportation systems are established into remote areas, the more encroachments, illegal logging, mining and plundering of biological resources occur, including biopiracy by unscrupulous individual and corporate collectors ... We fear that the IYE in combination with the globalization policies underway will make things worse.

As supranational institutions such as the World Bank, the International Monetary Fund and the World Trade Organization are pressuring developing countries towards trade and investment liberalization, national and local governments are increasingly disabled to plan and manage tourism – and ecotourism – on their own terms . . . As nature-based tourism is presently seen as one of the most lucrative niche markets, powerful transnational corporations are likely to exploit the IYE to dictate their own definitions and rules of ecotourism on society, while people-centred initiatives will be squeezed out and marginalized.

We demand a complete review of ecotourism issues that take into consideration the political, social, economic and developmental conditions and the serious issues of globalization. It is also necessary to examine why existing recipes to tackle ecotourism-related problems – planning and management tools, best practice initiatives, etc. – have not worked in practice and sometimes even create new risks.

A popular solution often put forward to prevent ecotourism being oversold and, worse, used by companies as a Trojan horse to gain entry to locations they would otherwise be denied, is a system of independent auditing and certification. Just as we might buy fair-trade coffee or organic milk, why not go on an eco-certified holiday? As tourists, we are already used to hotels and restaurants being inspected and graded by the likes of the AA, Les Routiers and Michelin, so why not use a similar mechanism?

But certification raises yet more thorny issues; principally, what are the criteria, who should pay for the auditing, and who should be the examiner? Repeated failure to achieve consensus on these issues has led to the inevitable – over four hundred certification labels around the world, few of which are globally recognized. More significantly, few, if any, are familiar to tourists.

Green Globe, one of the few worldwide certification schemes, was established in 1993 by the World Travel and Tourism Council (WTTC) in response to the concerns about environmental sustainability raised at the Rio Earth Summit. Any hotel, say, can apply to be affiliated to, benchmarked or certified by Green Globe. The only prerequisite for an affiliate is that they should pay $220 to be affiliated for the first year and be 'committed to being aligned with the Green Globe Vision to create a sustainable travel and tourism industry or just want to learn more about the program before undertaking benchmarking'. No inspectors, no self-declaration forms to fill. Nothing. Just a willingness to learn more about 'Green Globe's Vision'.

For those looking to place a benchmark sticker in their window, the annual fee jumps to $395 for hotels with no more than nine rooms or nine members of staff, and rises to $1,610 for hotels with fifty or more staff, or seventy or more rooms. For 'large operations such as airlines' (a green airline is an interesting concept, isn't it?), the fee is $7,500. The entire benchmark process is underpinned by forms filled out by the applicants themselves. The only time when an inspector must actually pass through the door of an establishment is during the certification stage. The cost of this isn't made public, though: applicants must 'contact Green Globe for more information'.

So who boasts such a prestigious award? Go to the Green Globe website and search for 'Accommodation' across the whole of Central America, and just four companies are presented as being certified – all of them large-scale hotel groups in Mexico that include the Viva Wyndham all-inclusive resorts, the Spanish chain Barceló, and a 992-room 'mega-resort' on the Riviera Maya. Is this really what is meant by ecotourism? Or is it just greenwash for the few companies – largely Western-owned – that can afford the indulgence? This is what Geoffrey Lipman, the then president of the WTTC and now assistant secretary-general at the UNWTO, 'responsible for promoting the fair and sustainable liberalization of tourism services', said upon the launch of the Green Globe scheme in 1993:

'The Green Globe symbol means that a company is committed to environmental improvement. It does not mean that a company has achieved it. I describe this as a diagnostic and self-fitness programme, not an accreditation programme. It offers business benefits, it offers cost saving and commercial positioning. I call this putting a green glove on [free marketeer] Adam Smith's hidden hand of the market place'. Well, at least he was honest.

Over the past few years, there has been a collective effort by a number of groups that include the UNWTO, UNEP, TIES and the Rainforest Alliance (a conservation NGO that receives project funding from the Inter-American Development Bank) to unite and produce once and for all an ecotourism certification scheme recognized both by tourists and the industry across the world. An eighteen-month feasibility study was published in early 2003 which concluded that an accreditation body called the Sustainable Tourism Stewardship Council (STSC) should be formed that could grant powers of certi-fication to a harmonized network of regional certifying organizations. To date, the only regional network up and running is the Sustainable Tourism Certification Network of the Americas, which launched in September 2003.

Achieving global uptake is clearly a slow process. Perhaps the costs are deterring others from joining in? After all, the feasibility studies estimated that the annual operational costs of an STSC network with '2.5–3.5 staff' would be $250,000–400,000. Once it reaches accredita-tion status, the annual costs would rise to $850,000, 'including housing expenses'. Any revenue – the report says 'donor funding to meet operational deficits' is projected to be $982,500 in the first year – would come from membership fees, conference fees, training fees and licensing fees. It isn't really that surprising that some within the industry see proposed certification schemes such as this as little more than jobs for the boys. The report admits that one of the scheme's weaknesses is that the costs could create 'barriers to entry for developing countries and small firms', making them dependent on 'government intervention and international aid'.

Critics of current certification efforts say that until there is real demand for certification from tourists (very few to date, when surveyed, express a desire for such schemes), tour operators and small businesses, then these efforts are likely to be doomed. 'Good intentions, no doubt, lie behind the creation of ecotourism certification schemes. But few of the schemes actually work,' says Ron Mader, founder of Planeta.com, a website dedicated to debating ecotourism issues, who has also been involved in a number of the preliminary discussions about establishing certification schemes. 'There are a number of serious problems, starting with the lack of consumer demand. Also, most stakeholders have been left out of the process, including community representatives as well as owners of leading ecotourism businesses. Many leading tour operators don't believe certification and accreditation schemes will work as envisioned in the short term. Their voices, however, are rarely heard in official meetings. The result is that institutional funders have no idea that certification is such a hornet's nest . . . If certification has value, it will be in certifying the accomplishments of consultants, NGOs and government leaders, in addition to local companies and hotels.'

But opposition to ecotourism runs far deeper than simply the vexed issue of certification. For some, it is a flawed and self-serving concept dreamed up and implemented by First World interests, often to the detriment of its Third World practitioners.

Wangari Maathai, the founder of Kenya's Green Belt environmental movement and 2004 Nobel peace laureate, has expressed harsh words about ecotourists visiting her country. 'They fly to Nairobi, then fly to the animal reserves without seeing or interacting with the people of the country to whom this rich and wonderful heritage should belong,' she said in an interview with *E/The Environmental Magazine*. 'The government gets the tourist's dollar and uses it to enrich itself. But if the people benefited from tourism, they would attach more value to the animals.'

For Dr Erlet Cater, a senior lecturer in geography at the University of Reading, ecotourism is an élitist construct that often patronizes host communities and largely fails as a tool for sustainable development. 'In the same way that anti-developmentalists romanticize the lifestyles of indigenous peoples, so, too, may Western-constructed ecotourism impose an artificial, "zooified" lifestyle on local populations, simultaneously assuming that the poor are happy as they are,' she wrote in a paper for the *Journal of Ecotourism* in 2006. 'This approach tends to ignore local peoples' aspirations for higher living standards founded on a clear understanding of the costs and benefits of development ... Wholesale, unconditional acceptance of ecotourism as a sole development strategy by local people is both unlikely and unrealistic. Poor households' income needs are not fixed and they are likely to aspire beyond just holding their own economically. Consequently, they may divert to, or supplement with, other, less sustainable activities, particularly when the dimension of seasonality of tourism visitation is added into the equation.'

Cater also says that many of the ecotourism awards given out each year are handed to hotels and tour operators that only the super-rich can afford, and are therefore hardly viable role models to be copied more widely. 'Cousine Island Resort in the Seychelles describes itself as "Seychelles' premier private island resort. This remote island can be reached only by private charter helicopter ... Resort occupancy is limited to ten guests." The peak-season rate for this exclusivity is US$1,280 per person per night. Tiger Mountain Lodge is situated a thousand feet above the Pokhara valley in Nepal. The nineteen-room lodge commands panoramic views of the

Himalaya. Tiger Mountain Lodge has won several awards, including the *Condé Nast Traveler* magazine Ecotourism Award 2000, and highly commended status for the Conservation International Ecotourism Excellence Awards 2000 . . . The exclusivity and exclusionary nature of both locations is evident when we find that Paul McCartney and Heather Mills spent their honeymoon at the former, while Princess Anne stayed at the latter in 2000.'

Tourists are always consumers in the first instance, not anthropologists, says Richard Sharpley, professor of tourism at the University of Lincoln, writing in the same edition of the *Journal of Ecotourism*. Tourism is primarily a form of entertainment, he says: 'It is highly unlikely that tourists will be motivated to "work" at tourism, to adopt responsible behaviour or to ensure that their tourist-consumer behaviour will be directed towards optimising the benefits of tourism to the destination. Not only are tourists generally unaware of tourism-related consequences and tensions in destination areas, but, as tourism is an essentially egocentric, escapist activity, tourists do not want to be burdened with the concerns of the normal world . . . Tourists pay significant sums of money in search of relaxation, fun and entertainment. They are, therefore, most likely to give priority to satisfying their personal needs rather than demonstrating and responding to a positive concern for the consequences of their actions.'

Dr Rosaleen Duffy, a senior lecturer at Manchester University's Centre for International Politics, is even more dismissive of the true motives of ecotourists, many of whom seem to enjoy the 'roughing it' that this form of tourism often involves: 'Their travel acts as a marker of social position, which separates them from conventional tourists,' she wrote in her 2002 critique of ecotourism, *A Trip Too Far: Ecotourism, Politics and Exploitation*. 'Their self-denial of the luxuries of conventional travel is motivated by a need to demonstrate to themselves that they can cope with the hardships that they do not have to face in their comfortable lives at home. They want to believe that their vacationing does not have the same impact as that of the mass tourists from whom they like to distinguish themselves.' Speaking of ecotourists diving in Belize, whom she interviewed for the book, she said that they did not 'reflect on the environmental impact of the construction of hotels, the use of airlines, the manufacture of diving equipment, the consumption of imported goods or even something as visible as taking a motorboat out to the reef, which polluted the water with petrol'. In essence, they were egotourists rather than ecotourists.

Wade Davis, a Harvard-trained ethnobotanist and anthropologist who also happens to have one of the world's most enviable job titles – *National Geographic* 'explorer-in-residence' – has witnessed examples of ecotourism all over the world and is more sympathetic: 'I think that in principle, the idea of ecotourism . . . is a wonderful idea, and the idea of seeking knowledge through travel can only be beneficial for the world,' he said in a 2005 interview with *Courier*, the magazine of the US National Travel Association. 'What I find is that there is a correlation between sensitivity and difficulty of access; the harder you have to work to get to a place, the more interesting the interaction or sensitive the encounter. But I've always found that "ecotourism" as a term is kind of a conceit, because it maintains the assumption that somehow if you travel with a backpack, polar fleece and a Nikon, as opposed to loud Bermuda shorts, a funny hat, sneakers and an old Kodak, you're somehow a different kind of tourist. I think that much of what ecotourism does is simply increase penetration of the hinterland, and I think ecotourism gets into serious problems in the realm of culture because it invariably then becomes a form of voyeurism. I've seen ecotourism operations that are set up in a competitive fashion with the goal of "contacting unknown peoples". I think it's extraordinarily problematic and exploitative in its essence. With that said, it's also important to note that tourism, when practised sensitively, can be an incredible source of empowerment for local people – and not just economically.'

But should tourists be allowed to access some of the most extreme and sensitive wildlife habitats on the planet? Wouldn't it be better if such places were restricted to all but a few scientists and indigenous communities in order to better protect them? There does seem to be growing evidence that some animals are adversely affected by ecotourism.

'The massive growth of the ecotourist industry has biologists worried,' said a report in *New Scientist* in 2004. 'Evidence is growing that many animals do not react well to tourists in their backyard. The immediate effects can be subtle – changes to an animal's heart rate, physiology, stress hormone levels and social behaviour, for example – but in the long term the impact tourists are having could endanger the survival of the very wildlife they want to see.'

The report was linked to a paper published in the journal *Biological Conservation*, which showed that schools of bottlenose dolphins in New Zealand become 'increasingly frenetic when tourist boats are present. They rest for as little as 0.5 per cent of the time when three or more boats are close, compared with 68 per cent of the time in the presence of a single research boat.'

Polar bears in Manitoba, Canada, were also being disturbed, said the paper, by the arrival of vehicles carrying tourists at 'a time when the animals should be resting and waiting for Hudson Bay to freeze over so they can start hunting seals. But often the bears are not resting as they should.'

In addition, yellow-eyed penguin chicks in areas visited by tourists on New Zealand's Otago peninsula were found to weigh 10 per cent less on average than chicks in areas not visited by tourists. This could be a result, said the paper, of parents delaying landing on the beaches to feed their chicks when tourists are clearly visible at their normal landing sites. The paper's authors said that heavy tourist traffic in the area could ultimately spark the failure of a colony.

While some species seem to adapt or become sensitized to the presence of tourists, subtle detrimental changes in their behaviour and wellbeing are hard to detect. For example, who's to say what effect whale-watching – one of the most popular forms of ecotourism in the world, which has grown to become a multi-billion-dollar industry – is having on these animals' migratory habits or long-term health? Do we really have the right to view species such as the blue whale in their natural environment just because we can under the guise of ecotourism? Or should this be allowed to continue because it might convert a tourist 'into somebody keenly involved in conservation issues', as Héctor Ceballos-Lascuráin originally envisioned?

'Our hotel is not an ecolodge,' says Alonso Bermúdez, general manager of Hotel Punta Islita, in a resolute tone. He shifts into a lower gear and tentatively drives his 4×4 across a wide, shallow river. 'We still offer air-con to guests and we have a big swimming pool. This is what most of our guests still demand.'

Alonso is transporting me along the track from the town of Sámara, the bus drop-off point on my six-hour journey from La Fortuna to Islita, a remote small village on the Nicoya Peninsula that juts into the Pacific Ocean. The village is dominated by the forty-six-room hotel built in 1994 that won the 2006 Tourism for Tomorrow 'Investor in People' Award at the World Travel and Tourism Council summit in Washington DC. The award threw the hotel – an exclusive luxury hotel popular with affluent honeymooning Americans – into the international spotlight and it has since been hailed as one of the best models for high-end sustainable tourism anywhere in the world. I'm curious to see how these two seemingly unlikely bedfellows – luxury and sustainability – can sit together.

The vehicle finally pulls up at the top of a headland. Before us lies a crescent-shaped cove, with a series of small buildings dotted across a large expanse of former pasture, which stretches from the coast up a hill towards a band of thick rainforest about a kilometre inland. One building stands out from the rest among the patchy tree cover – the hotel's restaurant, with its tall, spire-like roof. All the other buildings, either blocks of rooms or individual villas, blend more sensitively into the terrain.

We drop down off the headland on to a track to the beach. We pass a small beachside bar, where a smattering of tourists are lying on sun loungers on the dark sand, and then begin to climb again up to the reception area behind the restaurant. I'm quite shocked to see a modest nine-hole golf course behind a cluster of mango trees. Alonso seems to have been expecting my reaction. 'Our owner, a rich lawyer from San José, wanted a golf course, even though we said it would be too much maintenance. It is his hobby, and there was demand, too, from some of the rich foreigners who own their own private villas close by. We are currently experimenting with using certain grasses that can handle a mixture of seawater and fresh water. We are very remote here so there is no mains water. We are also looking to drill a seventy-metre-deep bore hole through the rock for our water.'

I'm somewhat deflated to hear that they have succumbed to building a golf course in such a location, but Alonso insists it's what a lot of guests, particularly Americans, who make up 80 per cent of the visitors, ask for when they enquire about a booking.

The 4×4 pulls into the car park and we begin a tour of the grounds. Alonso takes me first to the spa.

'This is a big hit with our guests. Nearly everyone wants to come here for a treatment.' It seems we are slowly ticking off boxes on the list of 'must-haves' expected at luxury hotels: golf courses, spas, air conditioning, swimming pools, etc.

Further down the hill, tucked away from the guests, is a building marked *centro de acopio* – the hotel's recycling centre. Alonso is very proud of it, and says it is the pinnacle of the hotel's environmental practices. Two staff members work in it full time, sorting the large volume of plastics, bottles and cans that this hotel, like all luxury hotels, generates. They then give it all to the local community to sell to scrap dealers, who travel the half a day's journey from San José to pick it all up. There is also an impressive compost heap, which in Costa Rica's tropical climate can turn kitchen waste into dry, rich humus in less than a fortnight.

Next Alonso shows me the hotel's large greenhouse, where they are experimenting with growing various fruit and vegetables to serve guests. 'Most of our food comes direct from San José, but we are looking for more local suppliers. We are finding that a lot of our European guests are really starting to ask these kinds of questions now. They really want to know the details of how we operate. Not so much our American guests.'

The village of Islita a few hundred metres away is an absolute delight. Around a neatly clipped football pitch stands a petite two-spire church, a nursery school, a *pulpería* (small convenience store), a community centre, an art gallery and a terrace of cottages. All the buildings – and even the tractor tyres half buried in the grass for football spectators to sit on – are brightly painted with mythical figurines, patterns and the faces of local characters. It's like the backdrop to a Gabriel García Márquez novel.

'We employ 150 people at our hotel and 80 per cent are from this local community,' says Alonso, who started working on the reception desk in 1999 and was rapidly promoted to general manager. 'Nearly everyone living here is connected to the hotel in some way. It is our relationship with this community that we are most proud of and why we won the award. Our philosophy is that we show the people how to fish, but we never give them the fish. What we mean by that is that we try to teach them to establish their own businesses and skills and become self-reliant. People here now supply us with fish for the restaurant, drive guests to our airstrip, make furniture for the hotel rooms, make souvenirs from driftwood for the guests. Many have gone on to expand their businesses and start to trade more widely than just here. This is what we believe is sustainable tourism that benefits the community.'

I later meet Eduardo Villafranca, the hotel's executive vice-president, who expands on the vision he and the owner have for Hotel Punta Islita: 'Ten or so years ago there was nothing really being said about social and environmental stewardship for hotels. This country was positioned as an ecotourism destination – seeing wildlife – but there was nothing about what we now call "responsible tourism". People sometimes confuse philanthropy with social responsibility. What we do at the hotel is operate under a free-enterprise model with the local community. It must be symbiotic. There is no charity. We try to make a good environment for micro businesses. Our fish supplier might have his own business problems but he has to sort them out. We must only be a client for him.'

But, I put to him, the hotel has such a dominant presence in the area that surely it casts a heavy monopolistic shadow over these businesses? The hotel holds all the cards.

'These businesses are learning and trading with us, but many have expanded. The guy who used to drive our guests to the airstrip to fly back to San José has now bought more vehicles and we are just a small part of his business now. Before our owner bought this site and had a vision for this hotel, this was slash-and-burn country for cattle farmers. The local community would dig up the turtle eggs on the beach and eat them. There was hunting in the rainforests. There was a lot of ignorance about the environment before this hotel was built. Now this has nearly all stopped. We are teaching our guests, too. We now have a scheme whereby guests get to plant a tree during their stay, so they leave something positive behind them when they depart. And we operate trips to the beach for our guests to watch the conservationists who now monitor the turtles coming ashore to lay their eggs. Nearly 10 per cent of our guests say they have come to stay with us because of our social-responsibility programme. After we won the award the local franchise holder from the J W Marriott hotel group rang us up to see how they could do the same things. But we don't have a template that will suit everyone. Everyone needs to design their own recipe.'

The relationship the hotel has with the community does, indeed, seem to be special, and not like anything I've seen elsewhere, but my stay at Hotel Punta Islita still leaves me uneasy about its environmental claims. The energy and water demands of this hotel seem just as high as most others offering similar luxury facilities – the sink in my room doesn't even have a plug – but the awareness among staff seems much higher than average, even if they do admit it is hard to square their guests' expectations with their instincts. But if other hotel groups are now approaching them to learn about their methods then it must ultimately be a huge positive force.

Before leaving Costa Rica, I make a diversion to San José's smart embassy district to visit Carlos Manuel Rodríguez, the country's former minister for environment and energy, and now director of Conservation International's Mexico and Central America programme. Popularly known in the country for his love of surfing, he has gained a reputation internationally for trying to establish a network of marine parks around the world and calling for a United Nations moratorium on high-seas bottom trawling by fishing fleets. From within the high walls of the Conservation International compound, he tells me how ecotourism in Costa Rica has developed.

'It was actually a book published in the late 1980s that was the trigger finally for the government to become aware of the potential for tourists to come to Costa Rica to see the wildlife,' he says. 'When *A Guide to the Birds of Costa Rica* by F. Gary Stiles and Alexander

Skutch was published, the government noticed that it was bringing birdwatchers here. From then on, a national tourism plan was developed. But in my time as environment minister it was always a battle with the tourism ministry. We are sending mixed signals now to the world about our tourism. We began well: while the rest of Central America was at war, we were developing our national parks. At first, it was only tourists interested in wildlife who came here, but this has changed.'

Rodríguez says that as a minister he always argued that the country should only ever market its ecotourism offerings. His frustration at losing his office following Costa Rica's presidential and legislative assembly elections of February 2006 is much in evidence. 'We don't have a clear picture of how we are different from other countries. We measure success on profitability per square metre and the number of beds per hotel. We need to stop promoting mass tourism and get fewer tourists who pay more. I would set rules about density and capacity. We see foreign operators and investors generating problems by causing real-estate prices to go up. Most Costa Ricans can't afford housing now. The Americans have a big hold over us. I was talking to the US ambassador recently and he said to me that there are more Americans in Costa Rica's prisons than there are Costa Ricans in US jails. This says it all to me. Costa Rica is sold as "sex in the tropics". We get sex tourists when we should be attracting families. Married men from America come here to go fishing, get drunk and find women. I go into fancy restaurants and always see rich Americans with whores on their arms. The casinos here have huge power and are mostly owned by Americans, too. I would ban them right now, but the tourism minister says it is impossible. I don't think the big hotel chains should be allowed here, either. We are like a beautiful lady. Everybody wants to talk to her, wants to dance with her, and then wants to fuck her. But we need to be choosy with whom we dance.'

Is, I ask, Costa Rica's reputation as one of the world's leading ecotourism destinations justified then?

Rodríguez looks to the ceiling to ponder. 'Yes and no. There are more positives than negatives. I've been to Botswana, Tanzania, Gabon, etc., and the locals there can't afford to enter the national parks, but here there is a law that says local residents living close to the park get in free. The benefits of the parks go well beyond their boundaries. We have a unique tax system starting here, where farmers are paid not to touch the rainforest areas on their land due to the benefits of their "environmental services" – carbon offsetting, water, biodiversity, etc. It's called the Environmental Services Payments Programme (ESPP). The national parks help to raise $1.6 billion a year from tourism because of the country's green image, but only 1 per cent of that money actually goes back into protecting the environment. Everyone is frustrated that more money isn't raised to protect our natural assets. ESPP should help do this.'

Earlier in the day, I had listened to Diego Bermudez, the president of Costa Rica's tour guides union and a professor of guiding techniques at the Costa Rica Learning Institute, express the same degree of exasperation. He told me that the national parks need at least three hundred extra rangers to protect them more effectively. 'Many parks now exceed the maximum amount of visitors that are allowed to enter each day,' he said. (In December 2006, the Inter-American Development Bank (IDB) announced it had agreed to a $20-million loan to 'support a program to promote sustainable tourism in protected wilderness areas in Costa Rica'. One of the loan's goals was to 'reduce the burden on the six areas that draw the vast majority of visitors'.) Bermudez continued: 'Ten years ago I would see five pairs of quetzal [one of the region's most treasured birds] a day in some parks, but now I have to walk for hours off the trails to find them. You never see mammals any more from the trails, either. It's poor handling of our natural resources that's to blame. Too many visitors and, despite our national parks, a deforestation rate that's among the fastest in the world at 4 per cent a year, according to the World Resources Institute. The tourists aren't to blame – they don't come across the sea just to destroy our habitats. We need to have an ethical code among the companies bringing people here to agree on visitor limits.'

I put this point to Rodríguez. He shrugs with resignation. 'What can I say? There is simply a basic lack of vision. 'I spent a lot of my time as environment minister and now in my role with Conservation International dealing with tourism-related matters, in particular impacts on coastlines. There are no guidelines, for example, about building higher than trees, or in areas where turtles nest. Everything in tourism should be environmentally certified, but at the moment the scheme in Costa Rica is voluntary. On these issues we always say that we are the champions of the second league, but we just can't get into the premier league.'

It's sad to hear such defeatism within a country that so many still hold up as a shining example of tourism best practice.

11

Party Politics

Ibiza, Spain

'YOU CAN'T FUCKING FAULT IT, CAN YOU?'

Steve lifts his bottle of San Miguel to the air and toasts the setting sun. As he closes his alcohol-glazed eyes and directs his face towards the warming rays oscillating across the sea, he takes a long, pleasurable swig of beer. One of the DJs leaning over a pair of decks on the terrace of beach cafés behind him raises the tempo from a lazy lilt to something with a more driving, euphoric beat. A man with a Bristol accent answers a mobile phone close by: 'Yeah, we're all at the Café del Mar in Ibiza. We're watching the sun go down, then we're off clubbing . . .'

'Have you ever seen so many beautiful people in one place?' slurs Steve. 'The women here are just stunning.'

Steve and I are sitting on a rock on San Antonio's sunset strip. Around us hundreds of people are packed tightly together on the beach, taking part in one of Ibiza's best-known rituals: applauding the sun as it melts away beneath the horizon and passes out of sight for another day. The moment acts as a traditional starting pistol for another long night of partying.

'I don't know where my three mates are,' says Steve, a twenty-one-year-old student from Leicester, offering me a beer from his carrier-bag full of chilled bottles. 'We all got here at the beginning of the week. We went straight to the beach and got wrecked. The next day we went clubbing till the next lunchtime. That's our plan. Get drunk one day, then go clubbing the next. But I lost them this morning. They must be here somewhere, though.'

Steve stands up unsteadily and starts turning like a lighthouse, scouring the myriad faces around us. A young Englishwoman walks past, whispering surreptitiously under her breath: 'Need any pills? Anyone need any pills?'

'I've been down here for the sunset pretty much every day,' says Steve, sitting back down. 'My mates are all complete mugs for the free shots those girls PR-ing for the bars around here hand out. They're probably pissed somewhere. If the shots weren't watered down, I'd drink them too. These girls come up to you and say, "Absinthe or Aftershock?" They line three up and you're meant to knock them back. We watched this one lad last night do the "Centurion" at one of the bars. They lined a hundred little 20ml shots of red wine up on a table and he downed them all. One of my mates did it last year and was sick out of his hotel window later. We stick to cider and beer now. You can get a whole jug of Magners or Strongbow for ten euros in the West End here, no problem.'

A respectful hush descends as the base of the sun finally kisses the horizon. In the diminishing light, half a dozen dreadlocked jugglers fan out across the beach and start lighting their paraffin-soaked torches. In the air above us all, a trapeze artist in a bikini glides past on a parasail advertising a nightclub. Other women in bikinis struggle across the beach in high heels, handing out flyers. Discarded pistachio shells crack underfoot.

The moment the sun disappears, a ripple of applause washes up the beach towards us. For most of the crowd it's the signal to get up to leave. The remaining few look out to sea or watch the jugglers throw their flaming torches high up into the darkening air.

Steve picks up his carrier bag. 'Right, I'm off. I'm going to find my mates, then I might see if they want to get the disco bus over to Space. Haven't tried there yet. We went to Eden the other night and there was a big fight. The bouncers here have such a fucking attitude. Everyone here takes the piss. A lad in our apartment block hired a moped yesterday and the bloke riding on the back fell off. He was grazed from his whole chest down to his feet. The hospital had the nerve to make him pay €850 just to discharge him, because he had no insurance. It's a scam. The people who hire them out don't tell you about this, do they? There were eleven of us in Malaga last year and it was the same there, too. We got done by the police on the bikes and had to pay €450 to get free. Wankers. We might all go to Bulgaria next year. We've heard it's good there . . .'

Something diverts Steve's attention. He waves goodbye with his bottle of beer, and disappears into the crowd.

San Antonio, or San An as some tourists call it, is the main draw for many of the young Britons visiting Ibiza (or *Eivissa*, as most of the Catalan-speaking locals say), the small Balearic island that lies in the Mediterranean eighty kilometres to the east of the Spanish mainland. The town stands on the west coast of the island and has a reputation for hosting a sometimes incompatible combination of clubbers, bar crawlers, football fans and families. Ten minutes' walk from the sunset strip, a small grid of streets on a slope in the town's centre is known to tourists as the West End. Hundreds flock to its neon-lit streets each night for its kebab shops, spit-and-sawdust nightclubs and English pubs showing Premiership football.

The sunset strip has largely emptied within twenty minutes of the sun going down. As I return to my hire car parked up the hill, I walk through a throng of PRs – people, usually Britons, living on Ibiza for the summer season, paid to tempt you to visit one of the hundreds of bars, restaurants or clubs on the island. Chrissie, a twenty-four-year-old from Nottingham, thrusts a flyer into my hand for a club just down the road.

'It's happy hour until eleven tonight,' she says with a forced smile. 'Just say I sent you at the door.' I thank her, then ask her how long she has been PR-ing.

'For the past three months. I work six or seven days a week, from about eight p.m. till midnight. It's a good life. Some PRs get paid a commission, but I get paid a flat fee of €190 a week and the club owner gets me on to the guestlists for most of the nightclubs here. There's a whole social life just for the PRs here; there's so many of us. I PR-ed in the West End for a bit, but it's too aggressive and no one looks at you. I'm a mental-health worker back home, but I'm spending the summer here deciding what I really want to do with my life. So far I've been too busy to make up my mind.'

The drive to Ibiza Town on the other side of the island takes about half an hour. The PM731 is nearly straight, yet in 1995 was named among the ten most dangerous roads in the world by the IDB. (For the record, Bolivia's La Paz–Coroico road was listed number one.) In the daytime it isn't immediately obvious why, but by night the obstacles become all too clear as thousands of clubbers – many of them lurching in their own pharmaceutical- and/or alcohol-induced fug – make their way in and out of the enormous nightclubs that line the sides of the road as it passes high over the spine of the island near the small town of San Rafael. Every year, a handful walk straight into the oncoming traffic. In 2003, the British consulate on the island estimated that at least thirty Britons had died on the road since the early 1980s. The morbid count occurred after an MP drew the road's woeful safety record to the attention of parliament following the death in 2002 of David Holloway, a seventeen-year-old tourist from Wrexham. By the early hours of the morning, the roadside is busying with clubbers looking to get home after leaving Amnesia and Privilege – the former famed for its foam parties, the latter officially the largest nightclub in the world, with a capacity of ten thousand, and the location every Friday night of Ibiza's most infamous club night, Manumission, which achieved tabloid notoriety for its live sex shows before they were toned down in the late 1990s.

As my car passes the extensive roadworks enveloping San Rafael and drops down over the brow of the hill towards the eastern side of the island, the glow of Ibiza Town begins to fill the night vista. It is the administrative and historic heart of the island and the spot where many clubbers base themselves, due to the location of some of the other superclubs Ibiza has to offer, such as Pacha, Space and Bora Bora. A two-kilometre beach just to the south of Ibiza Town and close to the airport, called Playa d'en Bossa, is one of the most popular resort areas on the island with young clubbers.

Just beneath the imposing fort and walled old town – now a world heritage site, but originally fortified by the Romans and greatly strengthened in the sixteenth century by Felipe II to stop raids by the French and Turks – I park my car in front of Pacha, the island's oldest nightclub. Built in 1973 by its Spanish founder Ricardo Urgell, who began his empire with a club in Sitges on the coast just south of Barcelona in 1967, Pacha (the name is derived from *pasha*, the Persian term for a king) is now an international nightclub franchise present in more than a dozen locations around the world, from Marrakech and New York to São Paulo and Munich. The brand – represented by a pair of red cherries – is now used to sell CDs and clothing, and is even being developed into a luxury hotel chain.

This former farmhouse once surrounded by fields has come a long way since the 1970s, when celebrities ranging from Freddie Mercury to James Brown came to party here. I arrive ahead of the main crowds that gather each night by the white picket gates and palms outside, as I want to talk to Danny Whittle, Pacha's brand director, about why clubbers still make the pilgrimage to Ibiza in their hundreds of thousands each year. A bouncer guides me through the doors, past the restaurant and shop, over the main dance floor, and up on to the roof terrace. Even though it's gone midnight, the paucity of clubbers suggests the night is still young.

Danny is a native of Stoke-on-Trent in his mid-forties, who was once a naval weapons technician. He meets me by the roof terrace's DJ booth, which sits behind a large rectangular bar. Around us a fashionable crowd mingle and chat: this is a long, long way from the streets of San Antonio's West End and is regarded as the epicentre of Ibiza's high-profile 'hip celebrity set'.

'My first visit to Ibiza was in 1979 as a kid on holiday,' he shouts over the loud bass line. 'But I started working as a club-night promoter in Ibiza in 1995 and I've been here at Pacha full time since 2000. We can get about two thousand people in here and every night during the summer season we are basically full. We are the only club in Ibiza that stays open through the winter, too, for Friday and Saturday nights. People come here to be entertained, not educated. Musically, it's not a trainspotter crowd here at all. Once a month we even do a seventies retro night. But in Ibiza you can find anything you want: clubbing here is what gambling is to Las Vegas.'

Danny breaks off to say hello to Trevor Nelson, the Radio 1 DJ and MTV presenter. The crowd is starting to thicken now and the music rises accordingly. I ask Danny how a club of this size operates.

'We have a night-time director who overseas five night managers, thirty-five security and eighty bar staff. It is collectively our job to watch for the signals. If four or five hands go up to the music on the dance floor we'll push the volume up. Our staff stay with us for three or so years and will come back each summer. They are mostly clubbers who came here and loved it. They work night shifts from eleven thirty p.m. to seven a.m. In terms of generating income, this club has probably peaked now. The average entrance cost is €40. A VIP table for four people will cost €1,000–1,500 and will include four bottles of spirits. Each night we turn over about €400,000, and €40,000 of that will be spent on the DJs and promotion.'

Danny says most of his time is now spent developing Pacha's image. 'Around the world, more people visit Pacha nightclubs in a year than go through the turnstiles at Barcelona and Manchester United combined. We're at about three million a year now. In five years' time, we will have nightclubs in Thailand and Shanghai. In places like New York it is easy to manage our brand as we have entrusted it to Erik Morillo [one of the world's highest-paid DJs and record producers], but in places such as Dubai and Sharm El Sheikh, where we have nightclubs now, you have to be much more careful.'

It must help the brand, I say, being forever in the newspapers for having celebrities turn up at Pacha – the week before I arrived, Prince William was reported to have spent a night here.

'We really do treat everyone the same. I can honestly say that. You will see Claudia Schiffer here dancing next to a lad from Manchester. Penelope Cruz will ring us a month in advance to get a table. When Puff Daddy turns up with an entourage of twenty-eight people, we will tell him if he's being out of order. It's good to say "No" now and again. We've now carved out a niche. We have a good-natured rivalry with the other clubs here in Ibiza. In the 1980s the relationships were a lot worse.'

It is impossible to come to a nightclub in Ibiza and not ask about the impact of drugs. In 2003, researchers from Liverpool John Moores University published a study in *Addiction Journal* examining the drug-taking habits of tourists visiting Ibiza. By comparing hundreds of interviews with clubbers leaving Ibiza airport in 1999 and 2002, it found that there had been a significant increase during this period in the number of clubbers using ecstasy, cocaine, GHB (also known as 'liquid ecstasy', although chemically it is very different from ecstasy) and ketamine. Clubbers taking ecstasy rose from 35 per cent of those interviewed in 1999 to 43 per cent in 2002. With cocaine, use had increased from 15 per cent to 25 per cent, and 18 per cent of those admitting to using ketamine said they had first tried it whilst in Ibiza. There was also a direct correlation between increased use and increased visits to the island – half of those on their fourth visit to the island said they used cocaine. Professor Mark Bellis, the report's author, said: 'Once abroad, the sense of freedom and atmosphere of excess and experimentation means that some individuals who have never used drugs experiment with ecstasy, cocaine and even new drugs, such as GHB and ketamine.'

The huge demand for drugs in Ibiza has seen English dealers – especially gangs from Liverpool – dominate the market for years, although territorial shoot-outs on the island between rival drug-dealers in 2006 led the police to believe that Eastern European drug gangs, especially from Romania and Russia, might be gaining influence. In 2005, after the death of an Irish tourist who had consumed GHB on a night when twenty-five people were admitted to hospital for consuming the same drug at clubs in the Playa d'en Bossa area, the Spanish government said it was going to adopt a 'zero-tolerance' approach to drugs on the island. This was after years of being criticized by many local residents for not tackling the problem effectively. 'Our nerve won't fail us when the time comes to close down night-clubs to fight the drug menace – however much that hurts the tourist sector,' said the government's chief representative for the Balearic Islands, Ramon Socias. 'More important than everything is the health of people and the image of Ibiza.' In the summer of 2007, the authorities finally took action by temporarily closing down DC10, Amnesia and Bora Bora for not doing enough to tackle the drug problem.

'To be absolutely honest, we have more trouble with alcohol at this club,' says Danny. 'But we have a low-key security presence always looking out for anyone taking or dealing drugs. With a dealer we would always contact the police, but we would rather send an eighteen-year-old kid off with a flea in his ear than dob him in to the police. Sometimes a shock like that is more of an education and will do him more good in the long run.'

The roof terrace is now tightly packed. I leave Danny and head back downstairs. A slope of private tables faces on to the main dance floor, which is dominated by two podiums on which the club's professional dancers act as a focal point for the sea of thrusting arms and nodding heads beneath them. The DJ, located up on a raised platform, occasionally drops the volume to shout to the crowd.

I retreat again into the cool air of the roof terrace, and edge through the crowds to another bar area surrounded by cushioned seating. In front of the bar, inside a cordoned-off VIP area, a topless dancer gyrates inside a six-foot-tall cocktail glass filled to her waist with water. At the bar, bottles of water cost €8 and cans of Red Bull €13. I don't even ask how much alcohol costs.

A group of six female friends from Wigan arrives at the bar beside me. Kathy, a twenty-two-year-old design student and the group's nominated spokeswoman, tells me what has brought them to Pacha. 'Basically, we want to dance and have a good time. You just know at a place like this you will enjoy yourself. We're all mates from back home and we go clubbing together every weekend. Some of us have been to Ibiza before, so know where to go. I hate the whole Club 18–30 thing over in San Antonio. It's just blokes fighting and being sick.'

As her friends suck on their cocktails through straws, Kathy tells me about their itinerary. 'We know all the right club nights to go to from being clubbers back home. So we knew we wanted to come to Pacha tonight for Defected in the House' (a 'twenty-first-century disco, hi-energy soul, classic uplifting house' club night that hosts events all over the world). 'We bought most of our club tickets in advance back home, but we have a spending-money budget for each night. Tonight we have €40, but we have an overall budget of €900 for our two weeks here. We got a package for £350 back in February with Thomson which covers our flights and a place on Bora Bora Beach, in the middle of Playa d'en Bossa and close to Space. They advertised it as the "Number One clubbing apartment". We spend the day on the beach, then start getting dressed up to go out at six o'clock each night and then drink on our terrace for about three hours before coming out. I've got £10,000 of student debts, but I've been working all summer in a bar back home to be able to afford to come out here. We just love it here.'

A track they all recognize starts up and they rush downstairs to the main dance floor.

The following morning I ring the buzzer next to a door leading down to a basement in a quiet square of San Antonio, further up the hill from the West End. Inside is the air-conditioned office of Neil Brittle, Club 18–30's regional manager for the Western Mediterranean. His company, part of Thomas Cook, has become synonymous through TV programmes and newspaper headlines with the notorious, leery excesses of young Britons holidaying in the Mediterranean. Around one thousand Club 18–30 holidaymakers arrive in San Antonio each week in the summer to sample Ibiza's fruits.

'Yes, we still have a strong image within the industry for offering crazy youth holidays, but we have moved away from that now,' insists Neil, now a family man in his early thirties who started with the company as a rep in Turkey in 1997. 'The brand is just so strong still in people's heads. We don't do organized bar crawls any more.'

What kind of people, I ask, come on a Club 18–30 holiday nowadays?

'Our average age is actually nineteen to twenty-one. We get 40 per cent of our guests from the south of England, 30 per cent from the north, and around 15 per cent from the Glasgow area. Some people come back year after year, but most don't. In the 1990s we were famous for our "Beaver España" adverts. That's over now, but we still want people to have fun. Our strategy over the past five years has been to cut out this sort of innuendo and the bar crawls. It used to be that we would offer eight things to do and guests would just have to get used to it. But now we have loads of things to do – between thirty and forty. We call it the "nouveau niche" and it includes things such as spa days and organized team sports. We also do non-competitive sports in the pool and play giant chess and Jenga. But here in Ibiza our biggest thing is the day cruises. We will send out three boats a day with about 550 people on board. They will go out from twelve thirty till four in the afternoon, and for fifty euros you get a buffet and as much drink as you want. On board there will be a Manumission DJ and they will stop off at a secluded beach. Guests can pay for these cruises individually, or more common is to buy them as part of a package of six or seven events. So for €240 for one week, say, they will get a day cruise, four tickets to nightclubs and other stuff. In general, they will only leave San Antonio once a week and only venture out to club nights such as Cream and Manumission. They won't go to Pacha or Space, for example.'

Companies catering to young, usually first-time holidaymakers, such as Club 18–30 and First Choice's 2wentys brand, offer broadly the same destinations across the Mediterranean. For example, 2wentys sends people to San Antonio, but also to Magaluf and Palma Nova on the neighbouring Balearic island of Majorca. In Greece, its destinations are Faliraki, Rhodes; Kardamena, Kos; Kavos, Corfu; Laganas, Zante; and Malia, Crete. Club 18–30 operates out of the same destinations in Greece as well as Majorca, but also offers a wider range of other Spanish resorts such as Playa del Ingles on Gran Canaria and Playa de las Americas on Tenerife.

In addition, it offers Sunny Beach in Bulgaria and Ayia Napa in Cyprus.

'Malia in Crete is a really hot potato at the moment for us,' says Neil. 'But each destination offers something different, especially when it comes to the type of clubs you want. Corfu is better for cheesy chart music, Gran Canaria is best for an R&B and urban sound, whereas for hard house you go to Tenerife. But the serious clubbers come to Ibiza, of course. We also look for new destinations, though. We just need an area of nightclubs, bars and hotels of a certain standard on the coast – remember that we don't actually own any assets at all. Cancún would have been perfect for us, but the hurricane wrecked it. But somewhere like Thailand would be too far away for us.'

It must be a huge responsibility, I say, overseeing hundreds of young holidaymakers intent on partying, often away from home for the first time.

'In Crete, there used to be six hundred people on bar crawls being herded around at one time. It was very difficult to manage so that's why we stopped. Concerned parents do ring me up, though. Fifty per cent of my job is reactive. People run out of money here. If there's an accident or a rape we'll talk to the police, of course. There are ninety thousand people holidaying with us across the Mediterranean each year, so things will happen. People try to jump between the balconies when they're drunk, for example. We've had two deaths this year from this, so we insist that the balconies' railings must be at least one metre high. Someone was run over outside a club, too. And a guy died of heart failure after coming out of a club. But Saga holidays have a worse death rate than us.'

Beyond the more visible problems associated with the often bawdy behaviour of young 'Brits Abroad' are the sexual-health concerns being increasingly expressed by health professionals. A report published in 2004 by the Centre for Public Health at Liverpool John Moores University in the journal *STI*, whose research was based on the same technique as the 2003 drugs study mentioned above of interviewing young British tourists via anonymous questionnaires as they left Ibiza airport, found that 11 per cent of men and 3 per cent of women visiting the island had sex with at least six people during their average ten-day stay. Half of the men did not use condoms, with the research showing there was an increase in unprotected sex from 2000 to 2002. One in four men and one in seven women admitted to having sex with more than one person. One in twelve visitors said they had sex with non-Britons, leading the report's authors to conclude that young Britons visiting Ibiza 'represent a substantial conduit for transmission of sexually transmitted infections between countries'.

'Substantial numbers of individuals visiting international nightlife resorts have unprotected sex with people they meet while abroad,' the researchers added. 'This poses an increasing threat to the sexual health of UK residents, but as yet little attention has been paid to developing interventions that might reduce sexual risk-taking among young people holidaying abroad . . . Without such measures to protect the health of young people abroad, already elevated rates of STIs and unwanted pregnancies in the United Kingdom may continue to climb.'

Melanie Johnson, public-health minister at the time, responded by saying she was concerned by the findings, but added: 'In the summer of 2003, we worked with the three main youth-holiday companies, and "Sex Lottery" materials communicating safe-sex messages were shipped into resorts in Ibiza, Rhodes, Majorca, Cyprus and Corfu. Materials reminding young holidaymakers to these destinations of the importance of using condoms and practising safe sex were also included in their ticket inserts.'

The Department of Health has since worked with both Club 18–30 and 2wentys, handing out over 100,000 free condoms to holidaymakers in Ibiza, Corfu and Majorca. In the summer of 2006, the Terrence Higgins Trust handed out free condoms and lubricants to young tourists at Birmingham airport, after a Foreign & Commonwealth Office survey found that 64 per cent of people surveyed from the West Midlands reported 'having casual sex' as a favoured holiday activity, compared to a national average of 28 per cent.

The way these companies market themselves may have been toned down over the past few years, and their websites now provide links to NHS sexual-health information sites such as Playingsafely.co.uk, but there's still little doubt about what guests should expect at their destinations. For example, this is how 2wentys sells itself on its website: 'Improve your pulling power! Believe us when we tell you, getting involved does wonders for your chances of pulling.'

One of the key components of a positive holiday experience for guests is, of course, the reps. But there have long been reports of reps themselves being the principal catalysts for problems. This reputation was enflamed by the broadcast of *Club Reps* on ITV in the early 2000s, which documented the antics of Club 18–30 reps in Faliraki, Greece (a later series concentrated on reps in Gran Canaria). For example, in 2003 a number of reps were arrested in Faliraki – a resort with a much tougher policing policy than Ibiza – for promoting sex games and striptease competitions in public and for general lewd behaviour. Bar crawls were banned by the resort's authorities and the negative publicity no doubt helped the company decide to change its promotions strategy at all its resorts, despite the programme greatly increasing the number of people booking holidays with the company.

'We have one rep for every sixty guests,' says Neil. 'We recruit them in the winter, when a hundred reps for the whole company are chosen from thousands of applicants. Some leave after only two days in the job because they are homesick, so we over-recruit for this reason. We have a 35 per cent turnover of staff in a season and only 30 per cent come back the next year. They get between one and three weeks of training. They don't do it to make money but to have a good time.

They earn commission on trips, and accommodation is included, though. We certainly don't encourage them to have relationships with guests, but all we ask is that they are discreet.' (Reps use the term 'chickening' to describe having a relationship with a guest.)

I later get the chance to talk to Deborah Milroy, a twenty-one-year-old Club 18–30 rep from Glasgow. She has spent the past three summers repping, including spells on both Majorca and Ibiza, after originally going on a Club 18–30 holiday to Tenerife with friends. 'Majorca is very different,' she says. 'It's more filled with lads and ladettes. It's big groups of boys drinking and trying to meet girls. I prefer Ibiza. I came here to have a good summer. Most of the reps are students. We earn about 5–10 per cent commission on trips booked through us, but it's mostly boat parties. The days when we forced drinks down their throats are over, but it's still good fun. Lots can happen, though, such as balcony falls or lost passports. We play hard and all the reps are like a big family. We have a big reunion party in November back in Britain with the guests, then we come back to the resorts in April to get ready for the new season. It would be difficult to do the nine-to-five back home now.'

Santa Eulalia is Ibiza's third-largest town and lies on the eastern coast about fifteen kilometres north of Ibiza Town, at the mouth of the island's only river. Boasting a smart yachting marina, it is where many of the British ex-pats on the island live, and, due to the fact that the town's burghers have clamped down on nightclubs and bars, it is a popular destination for families. It was the setting for *The Life and Death of a Spanish Town*, the American novelist Elliot Paul's 1937 bestselling account of how the Spanish Civil War so terribly affected the island's community.

Under the awning outside the Royalty Hotel – a place that Paul described as having 'outstanding service' – a waiter brings two glasses of fresh orange juice to the table. Sitting opposite me is Hazel

Morgan, president of Amics de la Terra Eivissa, part of Friends of the Earth's international network of regional environmental NGOs. Hazel is in her early sixties, and has lived permanently on Ibiza since 1974, after leaving her native Sussex for the 'almond trees and little white houses'. She has fully integrated into local life -- she repeatedly greets Spanish friends and neighbours as they pass us on the street -- and often fights on behalf of, or now more usually alongside, the growing number of locals furious with the way tourism is being managed on the island. That she has been nominated to be president of a local group such as Amics de la Terra Eivissa says much about her standing in the community; it could also be symptomatic of the fact that 55 per cent of the resident population of Ibiza and Formentera (the small neighbouring island off the south coast) were not actually born on the islands, according to a local survey conducted in 2006.

'People behave here like they wouldn't do anywhere else in the world,' she says. 'It is sold as a place where you can do anything you want. People used to come here to visit the place. Now people come here to escape the restrictions of their lives back home. They like its laissez-faire feel. But the young here have been very influenced by the clubbers. They are starting to develop their habits, and there is very little debate about it here.'

Ibicencos, as the locals refer to themselves, are famously reluctant to rock the boat, says Hazel. They have an instinctively reserved nature, formed over centuries of quiet, rural island life.

'People only tell you their real opinion with their eyes,' she says. 'They are reluctant to ever go on the record. They won't interfere or even defend anything. They just let other people be. This normally admirable sense of tolerance is having a negative influence on the island. But they are now finally starting to come out and show signs of fight over the issue of road construction here.'

In February 2006, a mass demonstration, involving one-fifth of the island's resident population, against the building of a new €260-million four-lane highway between San Antonio and Ibiza Town rocked the normally laid-back island to its core. The anger tapped into a growing sense of frustration across much of Spain that mass urbanization of the rural landscape is getting out of control, especially in the areas frequented by tourists. The authorities in Ibiza say the new road is needed to help business and tourism develop between the two towns, and that it will also vastly improve the dreadful safety record on the stretch of road by the superclubs near San Rafael, as the British government has requested. But a significant proportion of the local residents claim that the road will cut like a cleaver right through the heart and spirit of the island.

'The construction industry is now actually worth more than tourism on the island – it's got that bad,' says Hazel in an exasperated tone. 'There is a very uneasy relationship between the two at the moment. Bulldozers have been burnt by protestors and 23,000 people marched against the road building. Even some of the truck drivers have complained about how they've been treated by the construction firms they work for. There are archaeological sites being destroyed to make way for the new road, which will have four lanes and a tunnel. Even the tourism association here has started complaining that the island is going to the dogs. Only 50 per cent of visitors now say in surveys that they will come back again to Ibiza. They blame the degraded state of the island – the sewage problems, the traffic, the ports, the lack of public transport and taxis.'

One of the people Hazel blames for this discord – and it's a name that I've heard mentioned repeatedly across the island – is Abel Matutes. There must be few places in the world where a name hangs over a destination with such omnipotence.

El Mundo newspaper has likened the Matutes family to the Kennedys of Massachusetts: a hugely powerful dynasty that casts a formidable shadow over its homeland, with various family members having fingers in many pies, particularly politics. Abel Matutes is the patrician figure of Ibiza today and has been throughout the three decades that Ibiza has thrived on tourism. At the age of twenty-nine, he became the mayor of Ibiza in 1971. In the years since he has founded the conservative Popular Party in the Balearic islands, been the senator of Ibiza and Formentera, a member of the Spanish parliament, a member of the European parliament and a member of the European Commission. From 1996 to 2000 he served as Spain's foreign minister, before finally retiring from politics.

But the Matutes family has an extraordinary range of business interests across the island, too. Perhaps the most significant in terms of tourism is the Fiesta Hotel Group (which includes the Palladium and Fresh hotel brands), of which Abel Matutes is the chairman. As well as owning hotels on Ibiza, it also has hotels elsewhere in Spain, including Barcelona, Menorca, Majorca, Madrid and Fuerteventura. In addition, Fiesta owns hotels in the Dominican Republic, Sicily and Mexico, and in late 2006 announced plans to construct Grand Palladium, a $260-million 1,600-room 'green' resort in Jamaica. Upon the announcement, Matutes said that Bob Marley had personally invited him to invest on the Caribbean island before his death. The Matutes family also has major investments in Space and Privilege nightclubs, as well as ferries, marinas, farms, water works, quarries and a number of other sectors in Ibiza. It is no surprise, then, that Abel Matutes has been labelled the 'Godfather of Ibiza' by the local media. (Matutes responded to being referred to as the Godfather of Ibiza in a 2005 interview with the *New York Times* by saying: 'People know that I do things for them. If I am, then I'm a good godfather.')

'Matutes is the eye of the hurricane,' says Hazel. 'He accused road protestors such as me of being radicals and anti-democracy. He said we were violent and against civilization. He doesn't care about the anger, though, because he has the clubbers and they don't care about the environment and the beauty of the island. This road will just be the beginning, as they must be building it for something big. Matutes now wants to build a marina right next to the sunset strip at San Antonio. He also wants to build a new golf course for his Fiesta hotels. He wants to use his "farming" status to secure water for the course and to use water from the sewage plant, but Amics de la Terra Eivissa are against it because these kinds of projects always end up using well water and our wells are already salinated with four grammes of sodium chloride per litre, because they are being infiltrated by seawater seepage as they become over-exploited. The new course they're starting to build is close to the *salinas* [Ibiza's salt marshes, which are the first stop for birds migrating from Africa], and they are using the spoil from roadworks near the airport to landscape the course, too, which helps them save millions of euros but is causing a lot of truck traffic pollution as it's moved. We have five aquifers under the island, but we're now having to build desalination plants to keep up with demand. It's all madness. There is a golf course here already and it doesn't even make any money – in fact, it was the fight against this golf course that kickstarted the environmental movement on the island and led one party to lose an election here. But golf is still being touted as a way to extend the tourist season, and, of course, golfers want three or four courses to play on during a week's holiday.'

Abel Matutes is an elusive man, but in 2006 he did give an interview to *Pacha* magazine. He stoutly defended himself against accusations from the 'against-everything people' that his business interests have a negative impact on the island. 'We need to look for a kind of tourism that offers more quality and one that is less seasonal in nature,' he told the magazine. 'We don't want more tourists, but instead have them spread throughout the year to produce a greater turnover. This will improve the profitability of the companies and be beneficial to our employees. We must improve the complimentary offer. Ibiza only has one golf course, whilst Majorca offers more than twenty. Ibiza has a great demand for boat mooring. Today we have thousands of boats that anchor in front of our shores, spoiling the Posidonia [seagrass] meadows, yet they don't even buy their mineral water here because they haven't got the chance to moor. I would enlarge [the ports] as much as we could and wherever we could and also create a new marina ... I believe what [Fiesta hotels] have achieved is clearly positive and today Ibiza is a real gem, one of the most-loved tourist destinations in the world. I have never seen a place with the same natural conditions, climate and hospitable people. For all these reasons we have to take care of it and improve it.'

In 2002 the Balearic islands, including Ibiza, became the first major tourism destination in the world to impose an 'eco-tax' on tourists. The plan, conceived by the islands' then left-wing government, seemed sensible on paper: all eleven million visitors staying on the Balearics each year would be levied one euro per night, and the money raised could be used to right the environmental wrongs caused by years of largely unregulated mass tourism on the islands – an industry that produced 84 per cent of GDP. But the tourism industry – both locally and within the main source countries such as the UK and Germany – was outraged by the proposal, fearing that the tax might scare off price-sensitive tourists, and bitterly fought its implementation. The Association of British Travel Agents (ABTA) threatened to move its annual convention away from Majorca in protest; the Federation of Tour Operators warned that 'people will choose to go elsewhere on holiday if this goes ahead'; and companies such as Thomas Cook said they would be 'speaking to government ministers about this'. The proposed tax had coincided with a feeling within the industry that visitor numbers were already falling, and media speculation that Ibiza, in particular, was 'past it' as dance music had begun to lose popularity – there was a 7 per cent drop in the number of Britons visiting Ibiza between 2004 and 2005, with the total falling beneath two million for the first time in many years.

The tax did go ahead, despite the protestations. But from the start it was dogged by red-tape woes and intransigence, as the hotels were handed the task of collecting it. They complained that the tax was higher for more expensive hotels and that families on a two-week holiday were being charged around €50, which was driving away trade. In October 2003, a new right-wing government was elected on a ticket promising to scrap the tax.

Hazel, a key advocate of the tax, simply shakes her head at the mention of it. 'I get tired of fighting sometimes, as we are always losing. Carbon dioxide emissions in Ibiza have risen 53 per cent since 1990, but nothing is being done. The hoteliers just have such a stronghold here. Up to the 1970s I would say it was mainly ignorance about the environment here, but now it seems like wilful inaction.'

I ask Hazel how strict the planning laws are on the island.

'Sure, from 2007 any new building will have to have rain-harvesting facilities, but planning here is still very vague. If you have enough money you can more or less do what you want. There isn't even a tourism plan here. Planning for the mansions where the rich tourists go gets passed very quickly. They put big walls up around these places, even though it is against the local tradition, and they plant palms, even though pine is the truly native tree here. It all helps to erode Ibiza's character. A big issue, of course, is the clubbing: everyone who lives here complains about the nightclubs. People write to the local papers, even the priests. The hospital here receives about ten overdoses a night in season, and it affects the locals as they get delays in their care. But the disco people just don't seem to care. Many locals worry that the families holidaying here will be driven away. It just shouldn't be so cheap for clubbers to be able to pop over here for the weekend. Tourism like this just isn't sustainable. Residents here can't wait for the beginning of October, when the season ends. It all begins again in May, though, with the clubs opening at the end of

June. If Ibiza had concentrated on attracting high-end tourism right from the start, maybe things wouldn't be so bad. But we are all doomed here, I'm afraid. Tourism, I feel, has become an ultra indulgence for some people. Who says it is our human right to go on holiday wherever we want, whenever we want, if we can be allowed to ignore the consequences?' (NB: In late 2007, a new Socialist government was elected to govern the Balearics. One of the first promises made by the new tourism minister was to immediately call a halt to large-scale construction projects and force all nightclubs to close by 6 a.m.)

12
Kamikaze Sex and Kalashnikovs
Tallinn, Estonia

TALLINN HAS BEEN SOMETHING OF A soft touch for invading hordes over the centuries. Just about every nation or clan that borders the Baltic Sea has at one time or another approached the city's imposing, yet clearly breachable walls with menacing intent, keen to secure its strategically located, sheltered harbour for themselves – Vikings, Danes, Swedes, Poles, Nazis and Soviets. Poignant dates litter this small country's history: 1346, when the city was sold by the Danes to the Teutonic Order; 9 March 1944, when the Nazi-held city was bombed remorselessly by the Soviets throughout the night; 20 August 1991, when Estonia finally regained independence from the Soviets after the so-called Singing Revolution.

But a more recent date may come to be noted by historians as a turning point for the city – 31 October 2004. This was the day when the first easyJet flight from the UK landed at Tallinn's airport. Some feel the city has never been the same since.

For around forty pounds each way, the journey to Tallinn's medieval Old Town – a UNESCO world heritage site – became instantly affordable to Britons. The state airline Estonian Air soon dropped its prices, too, in order to compete with easyJet. Before this date, most Britons visiting the city were over fifty and largely interested in the culture and architecture that have long made Tallinn a jewel of the Baltic, challenging the splendours of St Petersburg further to the east. Beyond Tallinn itself, other attractions have also proved popular: the limestone cliffs at Ontika to the east of the capital; the coastal spa town of Pärnu to the south; the forested and bog-filled nature reserves; and the large islands of Hiiumaa and Saaremaa to the west, which during the depths of winter are connected to each other, and to the mainland, by ice roads across the frozen sea. It was perhaps inevitable, though, that once Tallinn became a cheaper destination to reach it would suffer the same fate as Dublin, Amsterdam and Prague, and fall within reach of groups of men travelling from the UK on stag parties. Tallinn has now joined the ranks of former eastern bloc cities, such as Krakow, Bratislava, Budapest, Riga, Vilnius and Warsaw, that have to deal with sometimes hundreds of drunk, leery men each weekend, singing and stumbling their way from bar to strip club in search of alcohol and sex. But of all these cities, Tallinn is seen to be particularly vulnerable to this form of tourism as, unlike the bigger cities that these 'staggers' head to, the downtown area where most tourists congregate is little more than a mile wide. Despite being a relatively small proportion of the total number of visitors to the city, staggers more than make their presence felt.

In the shadow of Toompea Castle, where the Riigikogu, Estonia's parliament, now sits, I enjoy a buffet of ham, cheese and rye bread in my hotel's breakfast room. Studying my tourist streetmap, I see that I'm only ten minutes' walk from the city's medieval heart – a stroll that will take me past the Russian Orthodox cathedral sitting ostentatiously at the highest point of the city, and past a look-out point that offers views right across the city and out towards the giant 314-metre television mast built during the Soviet era, from whose observation deck the Finnish coast is visible.

As I wash my breakfast down with a strong coffee, behind me three British men in their late thirties – the first to emerge from bed out of a group of staggers a dozen strong – talk about the night before.

'You've got a McDonald's, bars and a strip club on one street. What more could you want?' asks one.

Another switches on his digital camera and begins to show his friends some photographs taken the night before. 'She a cracker, isn't she? I'm going to ring her tonight. I think I'm in love.'

A middle-aged couple from Germany sitting at the table next to me tut under their breath.

The tradition of men escorting a groom far away from his bride-to-be's attention to enjoy his last few days of 'freedom' has been taking place for centuries across many different cultures. It is said to date back to ancient Sparta. In the US they are called bachelor parties, and in Australia they're known as buck parties. The common ingredients of beer, laddish banter and sexual innuendo unite them all. But for Britons, what was once nothing more than a long boozy night at a local pub, which at worst would climax with, say, a strippergram disguised as a policewoman, has evolved over the past decade into an altogether different beast. The hen party, the corresponding outing for the bride, has also undergone a similar, if slightly less bacchanalian transformation.

To get a taste of what happens on a typical stag weekend (some, it must be said, are altogether more sedate), all you need to do is look at the websites of any of the many companies that now arrange stag and hen weekends. Take Tallinn Pissup, the company that says it organizes 60 per cent of all the stag, hen and 'divorce' parties travelling to Estonia's capital city. For £29 a person it offers a 'medieval lesbian stripper show and meal' package:

'Enjoy a private meal in a cellar restaurant at one of our pubs in the city centre,' says the website. 'First a slap-up meal – with three free beers, snacks, main course and dessert – then a stripshow from two girls that lasts for 20 min. Each of the girls performs a strip and lapdances, and then one willing victim is chosen as the toy for the girls. Vagitarians are also catered for if you don't eat beef. The perfect way to start a Saturday night!'

For £19, 'tottie tours' of the city are available that allow you to 'visit all three of the top lapdancing bars in one night'. The party continues during the daytime, too. For £34 you can choose a demolition derby, where drivers 'ram into each other and even roll over some fine Soviet cars'. For an extra £100, 'at the end of the event, you can agree with our rep to buy the cars and smash them into a tree, have them blown up, etc'. Or you can learn to fire pump-action machine guns in a wood at 'Dr Death's Military Academy', although Kalashnikov shooting has been banned now that Estonia is a member of NATO.

If that doesn't give you a flavour of a weekend organized by this London-based company, then consider Pissup's ten commandments:

1. Get pissed up on a Leo Sayer [all-dayer]
2. Stare at buffage with ample cha-chas [large-breasted women]
3. Avoid girls looking like a bulldog licking piss off a nettle [ugly women]
4. Also avoid mingers with fried eggs [small-breasted ugly women]
5. Watch two fanny winkers do some carpet munching [lesbian oral sex]
6. Stir the porridge [female masturbation]
7. Use your wood to play into the bunker [anal sex]
8. Burp the worm [male masturbation]
9. Park your breakfast [defecate]
10. Do it all with Pissup

It is hard to pinpoint why stag (and some hen) weekends have descended into such a mindless vortex of lewd euphemism and crude sexism. Is it due to a decade of laddish culture fed on *Loaded*, *FHM* and *Nuts*? Is it down to the huge growth in low-cost airlines, which give us easy access to distant cities where we can 'enjoy' such excesses without recrimination? Or is it because the average marrying age has risen, meaning that most staggers have more disposable income? (The average stag weekend cost £365 a head in 2004, according to a Morgan Stanley survey.) It's probably a combination of all of these factors, compounded by the often suffocating peer pressure that shadows such trips, threatening to ridicule anyone who questions their partici-pation in such activities.

Unsurprisingly, many of these cities are now shunning such trips as they begin to see their largely negative impact. The backlash started in Dublin in the late 1990s, after locals started to complain that the city's Temple Bar area was being ruined by drunken and bawdy stag and hen parties. Similar reactions followed in popular destinations such as Edinburgh, Prague and Barcelona, as residents noticed that the economic benefit of such visitors was short term and often limited to just a few businesses. In 2006, Oskars Kastens, a Latvian MP, branded tourists from the UK as 'savages', saying, 'If somebody is going to another country for sex tourism it is quite different to a person going to another country to visit museums. I'm welcoming people coming to visit my country, but not just for stag parties.' Earlier in the year, officials in Riga said they were considering banning strip clubs from the city centre, due to trouble with street fights. Some in Tallinn are now starting to ask similar questions.

After breakfast, I walk through the cobbled streets of the old town to the tourist office on Vabaduse Väljak (Freedom Square) to meet the office's general manager, Evelin Tsirk. In her early thirties, she has worked in Estonia's fledgling tourism industry for ten years.

'There was just one tourist office when I started,' she says. 'The first place opened in 1992, but it was only in 1998 that we started to market Tallinn internationally. Back then the majority of people coming here were from Finland – 70 per cent of all international visitors, with 70 per cent of them here just for the day. It was cheap for them to come here. They came to buy butter, cheese, vodka and beer. It's not as cheap for them now. It costs about €100 for a return on the ferry to Helsinki.' (The journey takes three hours by ferry, or one and a half hours by hydrofoil.)

Evelin says that within a year of easyJet's arrival, the number of British visitors rose by 67 per cent. The demographic shifted immediately; the majority are now in their twenties and thirties rather than over fifty.

'We now get a bad press about Tallinn,' she says. 'We have to try and market it as a cultural destination, not as a stag-party place. They are causing a disproportionate problem. It is really not good for us at all. They make trouble in the bars and clubs, less so on the streets. But they are very noisy. We have signs in some bars now, saying "No stag parties". We even had an Australian film crew here recently to film the British stag parties. The film crew's arrival made the Estonian TV news.

The British were not the first foreign visitors to misbehave like this, Evelin says. 'We used to have the same problems with drunk Finns. Somehow we in Tallinn are seen to be causing the problem with the stag parties, but how? Ultimately, it is the responsibility of the airlines and the hotels. There has been a discussion in parliament about prostitution and alcohol laws. We now stop alcohol from being sold at some shops and petrol stations. Things are getting a little better as some stag parties are starting to see Tallinn as quite expensive compared to elsewhere. There seems to be a trend that they always look for new places. They are not welcome when they misbehave.'

The city has made great efforts, she says, to attract other markets beyond Western Europe, such as the Japanese and Americans. But even though tourism accounts for about 10 per cent of the country's economy and employs a third of Tallinn's workforce directly or indirectly, tourism is still not being taken seriously enough by the policy-makers.

'Tourism is quite poorly represented here at government level. Enterprise Estonia – which is owned by the government – tries to get businesses to invest here, but only a small part deals with tourism. Our marketing strategy is still largely the same as it's always been – we promote the old town. Tourists love it. But the Finns and Swedes now go all over Estonia. The Britons, though, still mainly go to just Tallinn. Most of our budget goes on promoting Tallinn to Russians and Finns, as they make up about half of our visitors. Germany and Britain are important to us, but they are expensive places to market. An article in a newspaper is more important to us than spending on posters. Riga and St Petersburg are our biggest competitors. We have lost some of the Finns in terms of numbers, but now we are being discovered by the Spanish, French and Italians. Tourism here now is really dependent on airline routes, though. Estonian Air now flies to Barcelona and Paris, which has made a difference.'

Britons, she says, only make up about 5 per cent of Tallinn's visitors. In 2005, 63,000 British tourists travelled to the city. This compares to 540,000 Finns (Tallinn is sometimes mockingly called a 'suburb of Helsinki'), which, she says, shows what a disproportionate impact the stag parties are having on Tallinn. They are not the only type of visitor that can present problems, though.

'We are the third-busiest destination in the Baltic for cruise ships,' she adds. 'About 340 cruises will visit this year. It can be a problem with the public toilets in the city, as many of the passengers want to use them. Coach parking is a problem, too. But the cruisers don't spend any money in the four to six hours that they're ashore. The only real positive is if they talk about Tallinn to friends and persuade them to come. But we have just opened a new dock for the cruise ships and plan another one.'

Evelin adds that Estonia is increasingly being eyed up as a holiday-home destination. 'More and more people are buying holiday homes here. Foreigners also own a lot of hotels, but this isn't a problem. We have the same business rules for foreigners here as for ourselves.'

Later in the day, while being shown around the old town by Tiina Peil, one of the city's official guides, I pass an estate agent's window. Huge country houses within an hour's drive of Tallinn are on offer for under €100,000. Tiina, an academic who supplements her income by being a tour guide, raises her eyebrows with envy as we peer in through the glass and tells me that house prices are rising so fast that foreign investors now see Estonia as one of the world's best places to invest in property. In 2005, the price of properties in Tallinn city centre rose by about 50 per cent, and by 28 per cent across the country as a whole. This helps explain why Estonia's economy is growing at such a fast rate, with 9.1 per cent GDP growth in 2005. This small country, with a population of just 1.3 million people, has been described as the Hong Kong of Eastern Europe due to its current economic verve. Others have labelled it 'E-Stonia', due to it being the home of vanguard internet companies such as Skype and KaZaa. A lot of online gambling is also based in Estonia, and an Estonian émigré established Hotmail. It's a country very much on the up, after a traumatic decoupling from the Soviet Union and then entry into the European Union in 2004. It is understandable, therefore, that many of Estonia's citizens resent the fact that most Britons know it for hosting either stag parties or the Eurovision Song Contest, as it did in 2002.

'The Germans and Scandinavians now go to our five national parks outside Tallinn,' says Tiina. 'But most people still stick to Tallinn if they visit. Personally, I think the cruise ships are a bigger problem here than the stag dos. In the summer months they swamp the town and don't actually do that much for the economy. The cab drivers here love the stag dos, because when British men are drunk they pay in pounds instead of kroons.'

The temperature falls rapidly as the sun drops beneath the city walls, and Tallinn old town begins to swell with tourists looking for an evening meal. Many congregate first in the bars that line the town square, where the only original Gothic town hall in northern Europe still stands, unchanged since 1429. Within a few hundred metres of this geographic and symbolic heart of the city are located most of the bars and clubs frequented by the staggers. A street called Pikk just to the north of the square is the home to a few bars, but the most densely packed area is Suur Karja, a street to the south just one hundred metres long and tightly packed with half a dozen or so bars. Most of the strip clubs and nightclubs are located down side streets near here, or over in the modern area, beyond the tram lines that divide the city centre in two distinct halves.

The city's busiest tourist restaurant is perhaps Olde Hansa, which offers medieval-style cooking served by staff dressed in period costume. It has a long terrace of tables outside on the street, where people sit under blankets eating dried elk meat and bear sausage washed down with mead. When I arrive, a group of twenty-odd men from England – who judging by their shirts could be on a rugby tour rather than a stag party – are rowdily singing bawdy songs, to the obvious discomfort of some families sitting at the far end of the terrace. It's no surprise when you consider the lyrics to their re-interpretation of the music-hall classic 'Daisy Bell':

'Daisy, Daisy,
Give me your answer, do.
I'm half crazy,
Six inches into you . . .'

There are no police in evidence on the street, but along Suur Karja I can see a car with the markings of a private security firm. However, its occupants are clearly being employed to watch over certain bars, and Olde Hansa doesn't seem to be one of them.

The bars along Suur Karja itself, such as Nimeta, Tallin's best-known bar among staggers, are typical of sporting bars the world over – lots of beers on tap supplying many men, and a few women, watching live football on the big screen. One bar has a karaoke stage in its front window, and another has a live band playing. All of them are packed with men shouting at the screens, singing en masse, or sinking pints. Within a few hours many of them will be making their way to the strip clubs and nightclubs near by.

Back over in Vabaduse Väljak, just five minutes' walk away, I meet Dr Nelli Kalikova in the lobby of the 1930s Scandic Palace Hotel. From 1996 to 2003 she was the head of Estonia's AIDS prevention centre, before deciding to enter politics as an ethnic Russian member of parliament for the Res Publica party, which describes itself as promoting 'compassionate conservatism'. She has since been outspoken about the rise of stag parties in Tallinn and, in particular, the fact that part of their itinerary is often a visit to the city's prostitutes.

'The men on stag parties drink like pigs,' she says. 'They come here just to buy sex. It's their last party before marriage. About 30 per cent of the girls' clients refuse to wear condoms here. They pay more for this "privilege", or they do tricks like pulling it off at the last minute. It is kamikaze sex. The first thing we tell the girls is not to be tempted by this "double money". Sadly we can't prevent the violent sex, though.'

Kalikova says there is a 5 per cent infection rate among the prostitutes in the city when it comes to HIV/AIDS, but this is increasing as more and more of the women become drug addicts. She says that they are normally infected by pimps, boyfriends or criminals who use them violently, rather than by tourists, but she's convinced that staggers don't know the risks they are taking by having sex with the prostitutes.

'We ask the girls to take an HIV test every two months,' she says. 'But in the last two to three years we have noticed that more girls are now testing positive because we have a growing population of drug users. If she is a heroin user, she doesn't care about protection. If a client pays for no condom, she will do it. About half their clients are now tourists. But some girls are now starting to leave the trade as the economy gets better. Most girls only do it for one or two years. In the 1990s about 30 per cent of them were under eighteen. That percentage is now down to single figures. Child prostitution does exist, but it is small. There are some street kids, though. It is mostly Finnish paedophiles who come here to look for them near the harbour and market and might pay them as little as 25 kroons (£1) for oral sex.

'In the 1990s, half the prostitutes were Estonians and half were Russians. But many Estonian girls have stopped now as they find it easier to get normal work here. But Russians are still not seen positively here due to the country's history. Better integration here would certainly help these girls.'

Kalikova alludes to the significant divide that still exists within Estonia between the Estonians and ethnic Russians, who are largely treated as second-class citizens and live either in faceless, grey housing estates just outside Tallinn or to the east of the country, near the border with Russia. After decades of Soviet rule, there is still much antipathy among the Estonians towards the Russian families who were encouraged to live in the Baltic region by their leaders in Moscow.

I ask her why she thinks Tallinn has attracted the stag parties.

'We had a stupid politician who helped to cause this problem,' she says quickly. 'In 1999, he said he'd found a good area for a red-light district in the city. It got the whole subject talked about. I think it was a bad idea from the start. The sex industry here has been like an advert for these types of tourists to come. But we have quite a different form of prostitution here than most other places. For example, we don't have street prostitution here. In Latvia they do. Here, you take a taxi and ring the number on the card and the driver takes you there. The taxi drivers get a high price for this. There are strip clubs here where you can get prostitutes, too. Everyone knows them. It would be easy to take away their licence. But there is corruption from the drug criminals. Society here is in the early stages of capitalism and many people are cruel and don't care. And most of the media here seems to support the sex trade. There was sympathy in the press recently for a musician who said he had "accidentally" rented out a house that was being used as a brothel. In the Soviet era, prostitution existed but it was mainly confined to the hotels for the foreigners. It was very corrupt back then, though.'

Is there, I ask her, a way to reduce the impact of the stag parties on Tallinn?

'We have to fight against the economic reasons that create prostitution. We shouldn't be promoting Tallinn's sex industry abroad. We should be promoting our beautiful medieval city. We usually see the English as being polite people – it is awful for us to see them like this.'

Half an hour later, a psychologist who works with prostitutes at an outreach day centre in the city comes to the hotel to meet me. He calls himself 'Roman', saying he prefers not to reveal his professional identity in order to protect the women he and his colleagues try to help. He also refuses to let the whereabouts of the centre be made public, to keep the women safe from potential abuse.

'We go out on to the streets and might meet about twenty women a day,' he says. 'We give them free condoms and lubricants. Some women run brothels in their own flats, but there can be aggression towards them and much fear for the women doing this. We find the women in many ways, but often it is simply by typing "Sex in Tallinn" into Google, as many of the tourists do when trying to find women before they arrive here. About 50 per cent of the business is through the taxi drivers. A man will pay about 500 kroons (£21) for one hour if he organizes it through a taxi driver. The girl will get about 20 per cent of this. All the hotels have contacts, too.'

Roman says that the government is now closing some of the brothels down, which is angering the taxi drivers, some of whom were earning up to 5,000 kroon (£210) a night in commission. 'But there are only four policemen in Tallinn doing undercover investigations into prostitution,' he laments. 'It's already hard enough to get the girls away from prostitution. They have many social and psychological problems. Many have had a poor education, but their ambition is big – to be rich and successful. They often have children but don't want to work in a factory. We try to motivate them to continue their education. We help them secure subsidized education. We try to persuade them to enter the legal job market. They are very brave in their work but are afraid to enter a hospital or normal workplace.'

Most of the women, he says, suffer depression for about two weeks when they first start working as prostitutes, before slowly getting anaesthetized to it. About half are on painkillers. He hands me a survey of prostitutes that was conducted in 2005 by the Estonian Institute for Open Society Research. It paints a picture far worse than even Kalikova suggested. It found, for example, that one in every five prostitutes surveyed tested positive for HIV and one in five also suffered from 'uncured venereal diseases'. Of the women who were addicted to drugs and who had been tested for HIV, 82 per cent were found to be HIV positive. At least 85 per cent of the prostitutes were thirty or under, with 26 per cent aged between nineteen and twenty-one. At least half had become prostitutes before the age of eighteen. Thirty-six per cent had children, 59 per cent were ethnic Russian, 23 per cent had official daytime jobs, and 17 per cent were 'housewives'.

Extrapolating from the data, the report estimated that there were three thousand prostitutes working in Estonia (Kalikova says 1,500 work in Tallinn), meaning that the ratio of prostitutes to the population is twice the European average, three times that of Finland and Norway, and seven times that of Sweden. The authors concluded: 'One could argue that Estonia has become an export and transit state of prostitution and trafficking in women'. They also said: 'The survey shows that many sex buyers practise organized visits to brothels as large groups. The most frequent collective visits to brothels are organized foreign tourists as special male groups, e.g. "British bachelors", as well as businessmen, who are provided with sexual services besides business meetings.'

Roman says that of the women his own centre has surveyed, 47 per cent say they have received an injury from their work, 59 per cent have been 'sexually humiliated' by their clients, 29 per cent hit with fists and 20 per cent have been raped.

'There is a big problem with violence for the women who go to the hotels alone,' he says. 'These ones usually have another job and do it for extra cash. Estonians, Russians, Finns and Latvians account for 89 per cent of the prostitutes' business, but some girls only work with tourists. They can get up to €70 an hour. The girls like to work with tourists because they spend money. In the clubs, they get €10 for a dance, or €50 for a private dance. The internet is now a very popular way to find girls. There's always a middle man, though – even the web designers make money from it. It is sad for me to see Tallinn as the sex capital of Europe. The tourists now come here and only hear about the sex clubs. We need to change our culture. Women have less status here now than they did in Soviet times, they cannot find themselves. We are only starting to adopt a European spirit. We can earn money with our minds, not just our bodies.'

The question of just who is to blame for the stag parties creating a negative impression of Tallinn is being asked with increased frequency in the city. Is it the tourists? Is it the bars? Is it the local politicians? In October 2006, the British Embassy in Estonia convened a seminar to discuss the problem. Among the invited stakeholders were tour operators, bar owners, politicians and tourism chiefs. A British police officer was also invited to explain how rowdy crowds of men are controlled in British town centres each weekend.

'We held the seminar simply to learn more about the issue,' says Nigel Haywood, the British ambassador to Estonia since 2003. 'We've all read about it in the papers and certainly seen it. You just need to take a flight to Tallinn from London on any Friday night. Stags are a pretty major component of the British tourists here. But they don't really have an impact in terms of the embassy. We've had two arrests for drugs in two years. It's too simplistic to think that they just have a drink and want to fight. If you don't want it in your city centre then get rid of the strip joints.'

Haywood says that expanding the range of activities on offer for the staggers might be a solution. 'We need to work on getting tourists out of Tallinn and into the countryside to help develop the supply chain. If you only let people into Tallinn and feed them beer then that's what they'll do. It's in Estonia's interest to get people to actually remember where they've been and to want to come back, maybe even on their honeymoon. At least firing Kalashnikovs in the countryside gets them out of the city. I've been on the odd stag party myself and I would love to have, say, canoed between pubs, or something imaginative like that.'

In 2006, the House of Commons public accounts committee said stag and hen parties abroad should be charged more often when they require British diplomats to bail them out of trouble. This followed research by the Foreign & Commonwealth Office in 2005 which found that 24 per cent of people on stag and hen parties abroad – 70 per cent of such parties now travel outside the UK, including destinations as far off as Las Vegas, Cancún and Dubai – face problems such as theft, assault, injury and arrest. Only a third were adequately supplied with contraception and nearly half did not have any travel insurance.

A report by the Czech tourism office in 2004 also said that the police believe 20 per cent of all weekend crime in Prague involves British men on stag trips. About 500,000 Britons visit the city each year, many for the 'sex clubs and cheap beer', as the report put it. The police also estimate that there are 15,000 'women and child' prostitutes in the Czech Republic, with 65 per cent of demand driven by foreigners. Such stag trips both greatly swell demand and provide a veneer of acceptability to the fact that many of the prostitutes and 'dancers' whose services are secured are women trafficked across borders by criminal gangs.

Haywood says that all the information gleaned at the seminar he held was shared amongst the embassies in other European cities frequented by stag parties. 'The numbers of visitors are much bigger in places such as Prague and Riga. We have maybe two or three flights a day here from the UK, whereas there are twenty to Prague. Here in Estonia, there is a small community and good government. Let's see if we can use this as a testbed. We have to produce leaflets to hand out. All groups have leaders, be they the best man or tour rep. We need to take them aside when they arrive and explain everything to them. But to be honest, very little of my day is taken up with tourism-related matters. Most of my time in 2006 was taken up preparing for the Queen's state visit. A BBC crew was following me for the whole year.' (The Queen spent twenty-four hours in Estonia in late October 2006 during a state visit of the Baltic States.)

At the seminar, however, Haywood was a little more forceful about the impact of stag parties. 'There is potential damage to our image,' he said. '[The stag parties] are generally good-natured, but can be rather loud. We know they can try and dress up as chickens and try and climb the tower in the town-hall square horizontally. It is a very small, confined area. This sort of behaviour can really make a negative impact both on the UK and on Tallinn. None of us wants to be labelled as a nation who just wants to drink and party. We really do have a problem if the police need to be involved.

Superintendent Martin Surl of Gloucestershire Constabulary's Cheltenham and Tewkesbury division, who has twenty years' experience dealing with the British drinking culture, was even blunter in his address to the seminar attendees: 'There's a feeling here that the locals have abandoned the old town now to the tourists, that it's a bit of a Disneyland and they don't care. But Estonia needs to be very clear what it wants. You need the stag parties to have a good time on your terms, without them noticing that they've been controlled. It is the bars' responsibility. They're making the money. They need to think about the wider economy. The police are just the backstop. It may be fine if in bar X there are five hundred people enjoying themselves, but if they get tanked up on beer and there's a riot, then everyone else is disturbed. Don't kick someone out of one bar into another. Make sure he is finished in Tallinn for that night. In Cheltenham if you got kicked out of one nightclub you wouldn't be able to get into another. At home they know the boundaries, but when they come here they don't know them because no one has told them. They are lost. They have not got a clue.

'Stag partiers are not by nature aggressive people. They are not the local villains. They are people from a mixed background who come together once. They could be lawyers, doctors, people who work in factories. Some of them are very naive. The reason they are coming here is because they want to test the boundaries, it is unknown.'

This seems far too lenient a view of staggers, in my opinion. Tallinn itself clearly carries some of the blame for providing a plentiful supply of cheap beer and easy access to prostitution, but these men must surely be responsible for their own actions.

In 2006, the Scottish Executive's 'adult-entertainment working group' published its recommendations on how the adult-entertainment industry in Scotland could be better regulated and workers better protected. It cited stag and hen parties as helping to sustain the demand for sex clubs along Edinburgh's Lothian Road. 'Adult-entertainment activities represent a commodification of sexuality and intimacy, and sexualize male dominance and the denigration of women,' said the group. 'The fact that there is a demand for sexually exploitative activities does not make these activities legitimate.'

Perhaps this needs to be posted up alongside those online listings for medieval lesbian stripper shows in Tallinn?

13

Cleared for Take-Off
Six Miles High

TRAVELLERS HAVE LONG STOOD AT Portsmouth harbour looking out across the Solent, considering their imminent passage to distant shores. From sailors heading to battle to booze-cruisers on their way to France, this maritime city has acted as a gateway for countless voyagers over the centuries. Journeys of adventure, stoicism and deadly duty are etched deep into its – and the country's – rich history.

But if its current inhabitants look into the sky above their heads, instead of out to sea, they can witness firsthand the most important travel story of our age – the boom in air travel. Portsmouth sits directly beneath one of the busiest patches of airspace in the UK, if not the world. Almost seven hundred aircraft pass over the city and the surrounding area every day, many either on their way to, or returning from, Spain, through an air sector known to air-traffic controllers and pilots as 'Hurn'. Imagine a giant road in the sky, slightly wider than the Isle of Wight and 24,500 feet tall, running north to south from Hampshire down across the English Channel towards Normandy's Cotentin Peninsula, busy with planes just a few minutes apart horizontally and 1,000 feet apart vertically. To anyone other than an aviation professional, the sight of this relentless traffic on a radar screen would be likely to evoke a headache, possibly even a palpitation of anxiety. Hurn is just one of the numerous air sectors – many with evocative or mysterious names such as Seaford, Berryhead, Lakes, Dagga, Saber, Willo, Timba, Lydd, Strumble, Talla, Compton and Clacton – that form an invisible patchwork across the UK.

Just a few miles to the west of Portsmouth up the M27 towards Southampton is the town of Swanwick, home to the largest purpose-built air-traffic-control centre in the world. From a room the size of ten tennis courts, 350 air-traffic controllers manage just over half a million square kilometres of airspace above England and Wales, all the time relying on one of the country's most powerful computer systems. On a busy day at the peak of the summer-holiday season, Swanwick's staff can handle more than 6,000 flights. But such is the density of air traffic over the southern half of the UK that Swanwick is not handed responsibility for the skies under 24,000 feet over Greater London or under 21,000 feet above Manchester. Instead, the task of orchestrating all the aircraft taking off and landing from Heathrow, Gatwick, Stansted, Luton and London City airports is given to a dedicated control room known as the London Terminal Control Centre, located at West Drayton, near Heathrow. Similarly, a centre at Manchester airport handles all take-offs and landings in the Manchester area. Combined with the rest of the air traffic over the UK, this all adds up to a phenomenal volume of aircraft traffic, with much of it passing little noticed overhead – unless, of course, you live near an airport. According to the Civil Aviation Authority (CAA), there were 3,654,988 commercial-aircraft movements in and out of the UK's airports in 2005, 1,150,383 of which were via London's airports. Commercial passenger aircraft make up the vast majority of air traffic, with private planes, military aircraft and air freight combined accounting for about 8 per cent of movements. Recreational and training flights from aeroclubs account for a further 21 per cent, although these are typically very small aircraft flying at relatively low altitudes. And these figures do not even include the many thousands of 'overflights' passing high over the UK each year – planes travelling from, say, northern continental Europe out towards the so-called 'North Atlantic Tracks' on which all planes travel when heading to North America. With the possible exception of the skies directly over cities such as Atlanta, Chicago and New York which act as the US's major aviation hubs, the skies of southern England, particularly over London, are the most congested anywhere on the planet.

The Hurn sector has now become symptomatic of the pressures facing our skies. Such has been the scale of the increased volume of traffic passing through Hurn that, like some other busy sectors, it has had to be redesigned to accommodate the extra burden. Historically, Hurn has suffered from a bottleneck caused by the fact that it is sandwiched between two restricted military airspaces that lie over the Channel on either side of the Isle of Wight. According to the National Air Traffic Services (NATS), the organization that provides air-traffic control for the majority of the UK's airspace, the bottleneck at Hurn has been responsible for 13 per cent of all the UK's air-traffic delays. This is easy to believe when you consider that Monarch Airlines, which carried 3.2 million passengers to Spain, Gibraltar, Portugal and Cyprus from the UK in 2006, says that 53 per cent of all its routes pass through this narrow sector. And with one in every fifteen passengers who fly out of the UK heading due south to Spain, according to CAA figures, it is logical that the majority of them will pass through Hurn.

But since 2007, new paths have been added to the sector, as well as new holding stacks designed principally for traffic awaiting clearance to land at Gatwick and Heathrow at times of peak congestion. Gone are the old stacks, named Bewli and Elder, replaced by two new higher-capacity stacks known as Kathy and Bilni. Military-airspace restrictions in the area have been relaxed, too. However, such is the rate of growth in aviation traffic – NATS predicts there will be an 18.7 per cent increase in demand between 2005 and 2012 – that these changes are only designed to last until 2012. After that, few are willing to speculate what the needs will be.

The word 'growth' now hangs heavily over not just the UK's aviation industry, but the rest of the world's too. While airlines, airports and tour operators welcome the financial gain that will naturally come from growth, environmentalists and those living near airports view the prospect with dread. In just a few years, the number of people flying has risen rapidly, and due to the pollution emitted by planes, air travel has become the focus of one of the highest-profile, bitterest climate-change battlegrounds. Just what damage this pollution causes already generates plenty of heated debate, but it is the damage that will be caused in the future if this rate of growth continues that is the real pinch point.

So how much is air travel expected to increase? By any number of measures, growth is predicted to soar. In 2006, for the first time in history, the world's aviation industry carried just over two billion passengers by air, according to the International Civil Aviation Organization, the UN's specialized agency for aviation. With a predicted annual global growth rate of 3.5 per cent, it forecasts that by 2015, 2.5 billion passengers will be travelling annually on scheduled flights alone. Airbus, one of the world's two largest aircraft manufacturers (alongside Boeing), says that in 2005 the number of passenger aircraft in the world with more than one hundred seats stood at 12,676. By 2025, it says that 27,307 such aircraft will need to be in service to meet predicted demand.

In 2003, the UK government published an aviation white paper in which it set out the aviation needs of the country for the next thirty years. It said UK airports should expect to be handling between 350 and 460 million passengers by 2030. But when it updated this forecast just three years later, it said that its mid-range forecast now stood at 465 million, whereas the high end of the range was 490 million. In 2005, the number of passengers stood at 228 million. No wonder the airspace planners are unwilling to draw up plans for our skies beyond 2012.

What is causing this growth? As globalization continues, business, trade and commerce are all going to drive demand, but the main cause will be the increasing aspiration to travel; more precisely, the wish to go on holiday via a plane. 'This increasing desire and propensity to fly can be explained by the growing affordability of air travel,' said the white paper's 'progress report' published in late 2006. 'Rising incomes, lower air fares, a greater choice of ticketing options and a greater range of services from UK regional airports are all contributing to making air travel a more realistic option for people across the UK. Within the growing numbers of journeys taken, the proportion of leisure travellers has risen from 2000 to 2005. In the South East, the proportion has risen from 62 per cent to 65 per cent of all flights from Heathrow, and from 77 per cent to 82 per cent of flights from Stansted.'

In some other countries, of course, growth is much less about holidaying and more about economic development as they play a rapid game of 'catch up' and emulate the transport infrastructure of developed nations. For example, in 2006 China announced that it planned to build forty-eight new airports by 2010. The terminal building under construction at Beijing Capital international airport promises to be the world's biggest airport building. This ambition may seem extraordinarily bold, yet it needs to be put in perspective: even once these new airports are completed there will still be fewer than 500 paved airports in China, compared to more than 5,000 in the US, the most air-dependent nation in the world.

Should we accept the assumption that all this projected growth will actually materialize? After all, the aviation industry is notoriously vulnerable to sudden drops in demand, caused by a range of factors over the years such as SARS, 9/11, the Gulf Wars and high-profile crashes. There is a view, however, that as long as flights are comparatively cheap, then the demand will always be there; the question is how to meet this demand. This is why governments such as the UK's use a 'predict and provide' strategy – consulting widely on what the various interested parties say they both need and expect, then attempting to deliver this. Some see this as simple common sense, whereas others see it as a self-fulfilling prophecy, especially when viewed against the environmental negatives associated with air travel – the unholy trinity of greenhouse gases, poor local air quality and noise pollution. The issue has parallels with road building: to ease a congested road the answer most often put forward is to widen it, or simply to build a bigger and better road. But increased capacity invariably invites further demand, and before you know it the new road is full of traffic and you are back to square one, albeit with much more net pollution. Would concentrating on demand management and investing in alternative forms of transport be wiser? A similar quandary now faces global aviation.

The heart of the issue facing aviation – and tourists deciding whether they should be taking a flight to a destination – is establishing just how polluting aviation actually is, especially set against all this projected growth. But so much noise has been generated about this issue – particularly in the UK – over the past few years that it is easy to lose sight of some of the key facts.

It helps to consider first exactly what it takes to lift a plane full of passengers and luggage 35,000 feet into the air, propel it through the upper limits of the troposphere at speeds of up to 900 kmph, and then land it safely at a destination that can be thousands of kilometres away from its starting point. Conveniently putting aside the physics of aerodynamics, the simple answer is kerosene – and lots of it. In 2005, aviation accounted for 8 per cent of global oil usage – 83 million barrels of oil a day. For example, according to Boeing, one of its 400-tonne 747–400 jumbo jets covering a route 5,630 kilometres in length (equivalent to London–Dubai), carrying almost 57 tonnes of kerosene in its wings and tail, will consume on average 12 litres of fuel per kilometre travelled. If it gets instructed to enter a holding stack while awaiting clearance to land, it will burn 100 kilograms of fuel for every minute that it is being held. (With this in mind, it isn't surprising that there are doubts as to whether aviation can continue to grow if oil supplies soon start dwindling, as peak-oil forecasters believe. In 2006, Campaign for Better Transport, a sustainable-transport campaign group, questioned the assumptions of the 2003 white paper's growth predictions for aviation because they were based on the assumption that oil would remain priced at $25 a barrel in real terms until 2030, whereas they had already risen to at least three times that figure.) It is what happens to this fossil fuel as it is combusted in an aircraft's jet engines, though, that is of most significance in terms of pollution.

The use of hot gas, such as steam, as a propellant has been documented as early as the first century BC, when an Egyptian named Hero invented a toy that used steam to spin a sphere. Others, including Leonardo da Vinci, advanced the idea over the centuries, but it wasn't until the 1930s that the concept was applied successfully to powering aircraft. Frank Whittle in the UK and Hans von Ohain in Germany both developed jet engines for aircraft independently from one another under the shadow of the looming Second World War. Due to the war effort, gasoline was in short supply and so the first jet-powered flights used kerosene, a fuel until then most commonly used for powering lanterns. However, kerosene remained the fuel of choice in the decades that followed, largely because it boasted two key safety advantages over most other alternatives – a low freezing point and a relatively high flash point, meaning it was safer to transport, especially at very high altitude. Today, though, kerosene-based aviation fuels such as the ubiquitous 'Jet A' contain many additives such as antistatic agents, corrosion inhibitors, dyes, icing inhibitors and antioxidants to stop clogging, all of which help improve safety and performance.

Put very simply, a jet engine mixes compressed air drawn in through fans at the front of the engine with the fuel, and then combusts this mixture at a temperature of around 1,500C. The resulting flame and exhaust plume are expelled at a velocity of about 400 metres per second, whereby Newton's third law of motion ensures the plane is thrust in the opposite direction. As the plane pushes through the air – ascending to a high altitude because the air is thinner there and therefore less fuel is required to propel it through the air – it leaves behind it a long trail of polluting emissions, which are often visible from the ground and are known as contrails.

The exhaust from a jet aircraft contains many pollutants. The most commonly discussed is carbon dioxide (CO_2), but in addition to this are water vapour, nitric oxide and nitrogen dioxide (known together as ozone-forming NOx), soot and sulphate particles, and a range of other compounds such as sulphur oxides, carbon monoxide and hydrocarbons. Each causes its own unique problems, but CO_2 and water vapour are thought to have the greatest impact in terms of climate change.

Air travel is the world's fastest-growing source of anthropogenic (man-made) CO_2 emissions, the pollutant that is understood to cause our greatest cumulative impact on the climate. For every kilogram of kerosene burnt, 3.155 kilograms of CO_2 are produced, which means that a jumbo jet flying from London to Dubai would emit 180 tonnes of CO_2 during its one-way trip. That's equivalent to the lifestyle-related emissions -- driving, domestic heating, food, etc. – of eighteen average UK citizens in an entire year.

In 1999, the Intergovernmental Panel on Climate Change (IPCC), a UN-convened panel consisting of around 2,500 of the world's leading climatologists, published a special report on the effect of aviation on the global atmosphere. It said that aviation was responsible for about 2 per cent of total anthropogenic CO_2 emissions in 1992, or about 13 per cent of CO_2 emissions from all transportation sources. But aviation has grown considerably since this date, and even accounting for advances in fuel efficiency over this period, CO_2 emissions from aviation have still increased significantly. In 2006, the EU said that aviation accounted for 3 per cent of Europe's CO_2 emissions. In the UK, the figure is even higher at about 6 per cent. However, these figures are often criticized by environmentalists as being misleading because they can exclude emissions from charter flights and omit some international routes, due to the vagaries of national and regional governments often not collecting data beyond their borders. The confusion is muddied still further by the fact that an aviation lobby group such as the International Air Transport Association (IATA) still quotes the global figure of 2 per cent in some of its literature, even though this dates from 1992 – an age ago in aviation terms, even before the advent of Europe's budget airlines.

The common cry by the aviation industry is that aircraft still only account for a tiny portion of global CO_2 emissions when compared to other polluters such as cars, factories and homes. This isn't denied by environmentalists, but what they point to, as ever, is growth. While these other sectors have enormous opportunities to make significant reductions in their emissions, and some are already doing so, largely through technological advances and efficiency savings, aviation, due to growth, remains almost the only sector within the economies of most developed nations whose emissions will continue to vastly outstrip any efficiencies or technological advances it manages to achieve. Its emissions may be in single percentage figures now, but in just a few decades it could quickly balloon to be one of the major polluting sectors – some predict even the biggest – if all the other sectors manage to achieve their reduction targets.

This theory is best rationalized by the Tyndall Centre for Climate Change Research, the internationally respected independent climate-change research network of scientists across the UK. It has examined the future growth of aviation emissions set against the UK government's own commitment made in 2003 of achieving a 60 per cent reduction in annual carbon emissions by 2050. This target was set to try to stabilize the concentration of CO_2 in the atmosphere at 550 parts per million (ppm), which is seen by the government as a concentration that should spare us from 'dangerous climate change'. The consensus among climate scientists now, however, is that 450ppm is the target we should really be aiming for if we don't want to see global average temperatures rise by more than 2C over this period. If this is the case, then we really don't have much time: in 2006, the concentration stood at about 380ppm – 36 per cent above pre-industrial levels – with a current rise of about 2.5ppm a year. For this reason, many scientists, including those at the Tyndall Centre, are now saying that, no matter how politically unpalatable the message may be, a 90 per cent reduction by 2050 is actually what is required across the developed nations. (Remember, this is not the emotive alarmism of a campaign group: the founding director of the Tyndall Centre, Professor Mike Hulme of the School of Environmental Sciences at the University of East Anglia, has himself spoken out against the 'language of catastrophe' many now use when speaking of climate change. This is the Tyndall Centre's sober, analytical view of the situation we now face.)

But such an ambitious reduction will be next to impossible if aviation is allowed to grow as predicted, says the Tyndall Centre. If all other sectors achieve their 60 per cent reduction targets – a huge task in itself – and aviation continues to expand unchecked, then it would account for between 24 per cent and 50 per cent of the UK's 'carbon budget' by 2050. If the government was to adopt the 90 per cent target many now say is needed to stabilize emissions at 450ppm, and aviation continues to expand unchecked, then aviation would account for 50–100 per cent of the carbon budget by 2050. Worse, the Tyndall Centre notes that the government's own low-range forecasts for aviation published in 2003 are already significantly out of date. We face a worst-case scenario where to avoid the extremes of climate change the rest of the economy would have to be *completely* carbon-free in order to allow us still to fly at the volumes predicted.

'The Tyndall analysis reveals the enormous disparity between the UK's position on carbon reduction and the UK government's singular inability to seriously recognize and adequately respond to the rapidly escalating emissions from aviation,' it said in a technical report published in 2006. 'Indeed, the UK typifies the EU in actively planning and thereby encouraging continued high levels of growth in aviation, whilst simultaneously asserting that they are committed to a policy of substantially reducing carbon emissions . . . Ultimately, the UK and the EU face a stark choice: to permit high levels of aviation growth whilst continuing with their climate-change rhetoric; or to convert the rhetoric into reality and substantially curtail aviation growth.'

The report's message, it seems, must have been drowned out by the roar of jet engines. Just a few months after it was published, the UK government issued its white paper 'progress report' in which it reaffirmed its commitment to greatly expand the country's airport capacity by confirming that it still supported a third runway at Heathrow airport – which would allow an additional five hundred flights a day to pass over London – despite opposition not just from environmental groups and local residents but also opposition parties. Somewhat anomalously, the transport secretary Douglas Alexander defended the announcement, saying that it was the government's intention that aviation 'should meet its climate-change costs', without offering much in the way of explanation. Keith Jowett, the chief executive of the Airport Operators Association, welcomed the news, adding that the aviation industry 'can be green and still grow'. Again, there was no accom-panying evidence for such an extraordinary claim.

The view out of the aircraft window now suddenly seems very bleak indeed, but there is still an important wild card yet to throw into the mix – contrails. These thin trails of ice particles and exhaust fumes left behind a plane as its passes through the sky might have a certain beauty, but there is growing evidence that they may have a more significant climate-change impact than even the aircraft's CO_2 emissions.

When hydrocarbons such as kerosene are combusted, water vapour is produced as a by-product. Burn a litre of kerosene and about 1.1 kilograms of water vapour is produced as a result. When this water vapour is emitted at the sub-zero temperatures found at the highest altitudes commercial planes travel at (28,000–40,000 feet, where temperatures range from -30C to -60C), it condenses on the various nucleating aerosols found in the exhaust, such as soot and sulphuric acid droplets, and then freezes. If the atmospheric conditions are right – low temperatures and high air humidity – a visible contrail of ice particles forms behind the plane and can survive for hours.

It's the impact these contrails then have on the climate that is cause for most concern – and controversy. Whereas the impact of increased levels of atmospheric CO_2 is now well understood by comparison, our knowledge of how clouds – contrails being man-made cirrus clouds – interact and affect the climate is at best patchy and at times contradictory. One certainty is that clouds play a crucial role in determining how much solar radiation – heat –

remains within the atmosphere and how much is reflected back out into space. On a basic level, we notice every day that clouds have an impact: if a cloud masks the sun on a hot day we notice the temperature drop; conversely, a clear night is much colder than one with plenty of cloud cover. But the density and altitude of a cloud appears to have a huge bearing on its impact, too. For example, a thick, low-level cloud such as a cumulus is thought to have an overall cooling effect on the climate because it blocks most of the sun's rays, whereas a thin, high-level cloud such as a cirrus allows much of the sun's radiation to pass through, giving an overall warming effect.

The radiative differences between various types of cloud cover and cloudless skies are collectively known as 'cloud radiative forcing' and are assessed by climatologists using a measure known as *albedo*, which calculates the percentage of radiation a surface reflects back. The *albedo* of snow is 90 per cent (which is one of the main reasons why we don't want the ice caps to melt), whereas the average *albedo* of the Earth's surface is 30 per cent. But the *albedo* of clouds ranges from 0.1 per cent to 80 per cent, which is why clouds create such variables in climate-change analyses.

Establishing the precise impact contrails have on the climate has proved notoriously hard. The most debated study on the subject in recent years was published in the science journal *Nature* in 2002; it examined the skies over the US in the three unprecedented days after 9/11 when all commercial planes were grounded. The event gave climatologists a unique opportunity to study a period, albeit a short one, when the skies were free of contrails; they compared ground temperatures for those three days with the same dates in previous years using meteorological records. The findings appeared to suggest that daytime contrails might reduce ground temperatures, whereas night-time contrails have an opposite effect. Another study, also published in *Nature*, in 2006, looked at the impact of night-time contrails over the UK and concluded that night flights 'are twice as bad for the environment' as daytime flights. Its authors said that night flights only account for 22 per cent of air travel over the UK, but contribute as much as 60–80 per cent of the greenhouse effect attributed to contrails. Flights during the winter also had a greater impact, too.

When the IPCC studied aviation's impact on climate change in 1999 it acknowledged that the influence of contrails is little understood, but it did say that they 'tend to warm the Earth's surface, similar to thin high clouds'. The IPCC noted that satellite photographs from space clearly show the scar-like presence of contrails across the congested skies over Europe and the US. (Astronauts aboard the international space station have also commented on how they can clearly see contrails from their orbiting position 360 kilometres above Earth.)

Possibly of more significance is that contrails can 'seed' much larger cirrus clouds, with their ice crystals acting as artificial nucleating agents. Contrails can also be quickly dispersed by high-altitude winds to form thin cloud cover across many hundreds of square kilometres.

'Extensive cirrus clouds have been observed to develop after the formation of persistent contrails,' said the report. 'Increases in cirrus cloud cover (beyond those identified as line-shaped contrails) are found to be positively correlated with aircraft emissions in a limited number of studies. About 30 per cent of the Earth is covered with cirrus cloud. On average an increase in cirrus cloud cover tends to warm the surface of the Earth. An estimate for aircraft-induced cirrus cover for the late 1990s ranges from 0 to 0.2 per cent of the surface of the Earth.'

The golden bullet from the report, however, was the following sentence: 'Over the period from 1992 to 2050, the overall radiative forcing [artificial impact on the natural climate] by aircraft (excluding that from changes in cirrus clouds) for all scenarios . . . is a factor of two to four larger than the forcing by aircraft carbon dioxide alone.' The so-called contrail 'multiplier' has since been interpreted to be 2.7 times larger than the CO_2 impact. Now think back to what the Tyndall Centre report was saying about aviation's CO_2 impact on climate change and multiply this by 2.7, not forgetting of course that we still don't know what further impact contrail-induced cirrus clouds may have, even though some studies published since the 1999 IPCC report that examined this phenomenon indicate the impact could, indeed, be significant.

Whatever measure you choose to use, it is increasingly obvious that aviation is having a considerable impact on climate change – and is likely to get much worse as we continue to fly more, all the time urged on by the government's obsession with chasing the fool's gold of airport expansion.

Assuming that the idea of padlocking up the world's aircraft hangers is unlikely to take off, there are only two ways to reduce aviation's climate-change impact: demand management, and advances in technology and efficiency. And this isn't an either/or scenario: if emissions are to be reduced, it would seem that all options must be pursued.

The Japanese have a word for the combined inefficiencies in any system – *muda*. Eradicating *muda* is a concept most famously practised by Toyota and involves constantly examining every aspect of a system closely to see if improvements, no matter how small they may seem, can be made. The goal, of course, is to increase profits through improved efficiency. The aviation industry adopts a similar principle, too, for the simple reason that anything that can reduce 'fuel burn' will mean lower fuel bills, which in recent years have become the largest overhead for many airlines as oil prices escalate. (For many US airlines, staffing still remains the largest overhead due to the heavy unionization of the domestic industry – a fact that is often cited when discussing why most US airlines remain in such dire financial straits.)

Any savings in fuel use also carry the enormous bonus of reducing emissions, too. Therefore, airlines now have a double incentive to reduce the amount of kerosene they burn. IATA is boastful of the fact that new aircraft today are 70 per cent more fuel efficient than forty years ago and 20 per cent more efficient than ten years ago. It also claims that the industry is aiming for a further 50 per cent fuel-efficiency improvement by 2020. To date, these savings have been largely achieved through improvements and refinements to design and engineering. For example, engines have become much more efficient over the past four decades, but these efficiencies have now started to tail off and even plateau in some cases. In other words, the low-hanging fruit have already been picked. Each efficiency improvement from now on will be much harder to attain. (And what makes this a true Morton's Fork is that engine technology has reached a point whereby the designers are faced with either reducing noise pollution, as many airports are now demanding of airlines, or reducing NOx emissions and CO_2 emissions.)

The same is true with the fundamental design of the modern aeroplane. The aerodynamic shape of a plane, if it is to retain a basic wing-fuselage-wing design, is near to its optimum now. Wing-design advances such as 'winglets' (upturned wing tips) have helped, but designers say the next step – and this would truly be a paradigm shift – would be to consider futuristic 'blended-wing' designs. But no one in an industry in which a new piece of hardware can cost over £100 million likes to make extravagant leaps of faith in new technology unless it can guarantee the advantages it promises.

More significant, even, is the fact that most airlines are currently investing huge sums in two new aircraft that are expected to remain in service for fifty years or more – the Airbus 380 and Boeing 787

Dreamliner. Therefore, many airlines have committed themselves to a long period of investment, which means they are highly unlikely to be in the market for revolutionary new planes for at least several decades. We now know, then, that the best-case-scenario fuel efficiencies that the industry will be able to offer will be the three litres per hundred passenger–kilometres that IATA says both the A380 and B787 are capable of. (IATA claims that these new planes offer a better fuel efficiency per passenger kilometre travelled than even a hybrid car. However, it's a chalk-and-cheese comparison: it's like arguing that five hundred people are better off flying from London to Sydney in an A380 than all getting into their own cars and driving there, even if it were possible. Given the average fuel efficiencies of the global fleet of planes today, flying anywhere emits broadly the same amount of emissions as if you drove there by car without taking any other passengers with you. Therefore, if you drive the UK average of 12,000 miles a year, you are creating the same amount of emissions as if you had made one London–Los Angeles return trip.)

Reducing the weight of an aircraft still offers potential. Most airframe manufacturers are now experimenting with composite materials that are lighter than the traditional materials used to build planes, such as aluminium. For example, the B787 is 50 per cent composite materials by weight. Beyond the actual design of the plane, many mundane but nonetheless important savings can be made, too – TAP Portugal doesn't hand out newspapers to its passengers any more in order to reduce weight. Passengers could also be required to carry less luggage – a number of airlines, of course, already charge passengers if they wish to place bags in the hold.

It is advances in the design of the fuel itself, though, that many are now pinning their hopes on. The kerosene used in planes has changed little in the past forty years, but a range of alternatives are now being touted, such as liquid hydrogen, bioethanol, hydrogen fuel cells, BTLs (biomass-to-liquids) and hydrotreated vegetable oils, to name a few. However, it will be a very long time indeed before any of these options seriously begin to challenge kerosene's market dominance. (Dr Mike Farmery, the global fuel technical manager at Shell Aviation, whose job includes seeking new alternatives to kerosene, says that kerosene is likely to remain the preferred aviation fuel for at least the next three decades.) Concern about safety is an obvious hurdle for such a risk-averse industry. Before any new fuel could enter the market it would need to undergo at least a decade of trials and safety checks to gain regulatory clearance for use. The last thing any airline would want to risk is using a fuel that carries even the slightest chance of being more dangerous than kerosene.

Another significant hurdle, particularly for alternatives such as liquid hydrogen, is that any new fuel would ideally need to be universally available for international airlines to be able to use it, and preferably distributed by the same method as kerosene is today. Neither airports nor airlines are going to want to bear the cost and inconvenience of needing to build, facilitate or retrofit a brand-new fuel-delivery method. Any airline that has just bought a new A380 or B787, for example, will want to know that the facility to fill it up with fuel will be in place at all the world's major airports for the full life expectancy of their new purchase. (Liquid hydrogen, for example, is four times bulkier than kerosene, which means that most drawing-board designs for hydrogen planes have the passengers in the wings and the fuel in the fuselage!) Put simply, any new fuel would need to be what the industry calls a 'drop-in' replacement.

Currently, the only alternative that could come on to the market in the near future – which Dr Farmery says is now drawing a lot of interest from the US military – is 'synthetic' kerosene, made not from oil but from natural gas, biogas or coal. It has the major advantage of working within existing aeroplanes. In fact, there are already planes flying in South Africa fuelled on this technology – but with fuel made from coal and therefore not offering any significant emissions advantage over kerosene. Another advance being trialled by both Boeing and Airbus at present is the use of hydrogen fuel cells. However, these are not used as a propellant; instead they are being used as potential replacements for the Auxiliary Power Units located in the tail of most planes that provide the onboard electricity.

It is for these reasons that there is now growing expectation that biofuels, such as bioethanol, could provide the solution. In theory, they could power the current global fleet of planes without the need for any major infrastructure changes. In 2006, Sir Richard Branson announced that over the next decade he would invest $3 billion of his transport companies' profits into a new company called Virgin Fuels, which would develop such biofuels. The big advantage they claim to offer is that they would be carbon neutral, because, unlike fossil fuels, they only emit the CO_2 the biofuel crop absorbed when growing. This might well be true, but it doesn't account for the considerable amount of energy it takes to farm monocrops such as corn or rapeseed, principally the energy needed to produce the fertilizer and pesticides they rely on. Also, to produce enough biofuels to feed not just the world's planes but its land-based vehicles too would mean grubbing up just about the whole planet for these crops.

A 2002 report examining aviation's environmental impact, published by the Royal Commission on Environmental Pollution, was dismissive of alternatives to kerosene, particularly biofuels: 'Other possible fuels generally lack the operational benefits of kerosene, or even hydrogen. Of the renewable biofuels, ethanol has been suggested as a possible aviation fuel. However, it has lower energy density than kerosene, requiring aircraft to carry more fuel, and would increase water vapour emissions from aircraft in flight. Moreover it has less attractive combustion characteristics. In particular, under conditions prevailing in some phases of a flight, especially approach, it would be difficult to eliminate formation of formaldehyde as a pollutant in the exhaust gases. We therefore share the view that kerosene will remain the fuel for air travel for the foreseeable future.'

An editorial published in the *New Scientist* in the week of Branson's announcement was more forceful: 'We cannot grow our way out of the twin crises of climate change and energy security. There is a real danger of creating a biofuels bubble that will burst, leaving behind a pungent whiff of chip-fat oil, burning rainforests and rotting fields.'

Ultimately, it seems that the most realistic short-term hope for biofuels is that they can be mixed with kerosene or diesel to produce a composite fuel that offers reduced emissions.

The last main area where efficiencies are possible – and perhaps offer the most immediate hope – are the operational practices of airports and air-traffic controllers. Eurocontrol, the European organization for the safety of air navigation, says that a 6–12 per cent reduction in Europe's aviation emissions could be possible *overnight* if the continent switched to a 'single skies' air-navigation system. At present, each country is responsible for its own airspace and can charge its own rates for planes to fly through it. This means that the majority of planes over Europe do not fly directly to their destination as the crow flies. In fact, there is an average 7 per cent distance inefficiency at present, says Eurocontrol – just a 1 per cent improvement would save the equivalent of 500,000 tonnes of fuel a year. Planes try to avoid overflying certain countries, or get delayed in holding stacks by the inevitable congestion caused by more than thirty-five separate national air-traffic-control centres trying to manage skies that carry more than nine million flights a year. The story is much the same elsewhere in the world: the journey time between Europe and China was recently cut by thirty minutes when the Chinese authorities authorized commercial jets to fly through a previously restricted airspace. Within just a year, 2,860 flying hours – and an enormous quantity of fuel – was saved on these routes alone.

There's considerable discussion within the industry currently about whether fuel burn could be reduced by increasing the number of 'point-to-point' flights (direct A–B flights) and reducing 'hub-and-spoke' routes (A–B, but via C). However, it's a debate that is politically charged: Europe's Airbus has developed the giant A380 (it can carry up to 555 passengers in a traditional three-class configuration, or a rather unsettling 853 if everyone squeezes into economy), because it believes the future to be hub and spoke, whereas the US's Boeing believes its smaller B787 (210–330 passengers, depending on the configuration) will serve a point-to-point future. Airbus says its plane is more efficient because it carries far more people at a time, whereas Boeing claims its plane to be the 'environmentally preferred' choice because it will be flying more direct routes than its rival. In reality, though, both are going to service the growth of aviation in the decades to come. (Airbus's marketing vice-president made a revealing admission at an industry conference in 2007 when he said: 'Climate change is not an element we factor in. We see global aviation growth of 5 per cent a year. There is no constraint in that forecast because of governments' response to climate change.')

Another heated debate within the industry is whether aircraft that are not fully booked should be allowed to cancel and simply transfer their passengers to another convenient flight. Monarch Airlines, for example, has complained that the 'skies are full of half-full aircraft, and the average load factor is only 75 per cent'. It says that one in every four flights within Europe could be cancelled if passengers were allowed to be transferred, but regulations that came into effect in 2005 would mean an airline being fined £5,000 per passenger if it did so. (In March 2007, it was revealed that British Mediterranean Airways was flying an empty plane between Heathrow and Cardiff six days a week just to keep hold of its sought-after Heathrow landing slot.)

One controversial proposal for managing planes once they are in the air is to make them fly at a lower altitude, or even at a slower speed. Flying at a lower altitude would lead to fewer contrails being produced in the sky, but would result in a 5 per cent increase in CO_2 emissions due to planes having to travel through denser air.

Big fuel savings are already being made at airports that make planes use a landing technique known as 'Continuous Descent Approach'. Instead of planes banking hard just before reaching the runway, they are instead ordered to align themselves with the runway much further out. This way the plane descends more smoothly and gradually, thereby reducing noise pollution and saving an average of 200 kilograms of fuel per flight. Eurocontrol is also lobbying that more countries allow planes travelling in their airspace to fly closer to one another by reducing the vertical height separation between them from 2,000 feet to 1,000 feet. This, it says, could offer another 5 per cent fuel saving.

Some airports are now trialling the towing of planes from their stands out to the take-off areas instead of letting them power themselves using their engines. In December 2006, Virgin began towing some of its 747–400 jumbos at Heathrow and Gatwick, claiming it could save up to two tonnes of fuel per flight. Other airports, such as Dallas-Forth Worth in Texas, limit pilots from over-using reverse thrust as a breaking mechanism immediately after landing as this helps to reduce NOx levels at ground level, one of the main health concerns of people living near airports. Manufacturers also say they are considering the possible use of parachutes and spoilers to help reduce the need for reverse thrusters after landing.

Overall, there is an industry assumption that a 1–2 per cent annual increase in fuel efficiency is possible over the coming decades via a combination of all the advances and technologies listed above. But when this is set against IATA's prediction of 3.5 per cent annual growth, it becomes immediately apparent why demand management is now so crucial if aviation's emissions are ever to be reined in.

The opening up of the skies has resulted in one of the biggest lifestyle changes for Europeans of the past decade, particularly for Britons, because many of the budget airlines use UK airports as hubs. Flying at a whim within Europe was always an expensive habit, reserved for the rich or for those able to charge it as a business expense. Many people chose to travel by car and ferry, or train or coach, if they went abroad at all. Long fractious drives to France were the only experience many Britons had of trying to negotiate international travel themselves without the assistance of a tour operator or travel agent, other than the summer charter flights to Spain and Greece. If people did fly abroad for a holiday it tended to be a scheduled flight across the Atlantic to the US, particularly Florida. But in the mid-1990s the monopoly of the state airlines was finally relaxed, leading to the rapid introduction to a stagnant marketplace of a wide range of low-cost carriers. Their philosophy of offering the cheapest flights to those that booked first was instantly successful. It quickly created a fierce, cut-throat industry in which consolidation, take-overs and liquidations became as common as long check-in queues and cramped leg room.

All the leading budget airlines offer extraordinary tales of growth and expansion. But Ryanair is perhaps the most intriguing of the industry's many examples of rapid growth, if only because its founder Michael O'Leary is so colourful a character. Still only in his forties today, the multi-millionaire Dubliner began his airline in 1985, employing just fifty people to shuttle 5,000 business travellers a year between Dublin and London. By early 2007, it was carrying 40 million passengers annually via 454 routes to over 130 European cities, ranging from Aarhus to Zaragoza. O'Leary claims his company to be Europe's cheapest airline, with tickets averaging £28: some flights are 'free', with the passenger only charged various airport and passenger taxes, and insurance levies. With the average short-haul return fare out of the UK costing £73, according to the CAA, it's easy to see how Ryanair and the other budget airlines have achieved such a degree of market dominance in such a short period of time. Price is everything in this market.

O'Leary is as unapologetic about the ruthlessness of his business acumen as he is about his industry's damage to the environment. For example, he claims that climate change has little to do with Ryanair, and if anyone has a problem with his business's impact on the environment his advice is simple: 'Sell your car and walk.' In January 2007, he was the focus of a headline-grabbing spat when Ian Pearson, the UK's environment minister, said: 'When it comes to climate change, Ryanair are not just the unacceptable face of capitalism, they are the irresponsible face of capitalism.' (Pearson also said the attitude of US airlines to emissions reductions was 'a disgrace' and that British Airways was 'only just playing ball' on the issue.) O'Leary responded angrily, saying that Pearson 'hasn't a clue what he is talking about' and that 'being savaged by a dead sheep is like water off a duck's back'. He added that Ryanair was the 'greenest' airline in Europe because it had invested €17 billion in buying the most modern planes available, allowing it to reduce its passenger-per-kilometre emissions by half since 1998.

One environmental group has calculated that more than 16 million trees would need to be planted to absorb just one year's worth of CO_2 emitted from Ryanair's fleet of aircraft. That's as many trees as were blown down across southern England in the hurricane of 1987. The predicted growth of the airline doesn't offer environmentalists much hope either. The number of passengers travelling with Ryanair is growing annually at a rate of about 20 per cent. In 2005, for the first time Ryanair carried more passengers than the total number of British Airways passengers worldwide. In 2006, it was responsible for 2.9 million tonnes of CO_2 being released into the atmosphere, according to analysis by BBC's *Newsnight* of the company's own filings with the US Securities and Exchange Commission – a 700 per cent rise since 1998.

In the face of this kind of growth, tweaks in efficiency here and there are virtually insignificant. In Europe, overall demand for flights is growing 5 per cent a year on average (in hotspots such as Croatia it's as high as 25 per cent), whereas in China it stands at 14 per cent and in India at 15 per cent, albeit from a much smaller base. We've already heard about China's expansion plans, but India is fast playing catch-up, largely driven by its booming new low-cost sector. Its airlines currently have 330 new aircraft on order – its current civil fleet numbers just 200, but by 2020 India's minister for aviation is predicting that up to 2,000 planes could be operating. Every time a domestic flight takes off in India today it is said that half of the passengers on board are flying for the very first time! Only 10 million Indians currently fly, out of a population of about a billion, but this could reach 100 million by 2020. However, this is still nowhere near the aviation penetration levels found in Europe and the US.

So how can all this demand be managed? Can it be slowed, let alone reversed? The most obvious answer would be to increase ticket prices and therefore drive down the appetite to fly. Many feel that ticket prices are currently artificially low due to the fact that aviation has historically enjoyed enormous tax advantages in comparison with most other sectors of the economy, and that the industry therefore doesn't adhere to the 'polluter pays' principle. If ticket prices were to reflect the full cost of the environmental damage wrought by aviation – economists call this 'internalizing the externalities' – then flying would be a far less appealing choice to price-sensitive consumers. Putting a price on environmental damage is notoriously difficult, but the much-heralded Stern Review on the economics of climate change published in 2006 by Sir Nicholas Stern, a former chief economist at the World Bank, at least gave us a broad outline figure to work with. Stern said that the environmental cost of each tonne of CO_2 we emit should be priced at \$85 (£45). If this principle was applied to aviation, one London–Miami return flight emitting two tonnes of CO_2 per passenger, say, would need to cost £90 more than the current price – a hike that might well make many passengers rethink the need to make that journey.

There are many problems with this simplistic course of action, though. First, it would need to be applied nation by nation, because international laws drafted by a fledgling International Civil Aviation Organization towards the end of the Second World War as part of the so-called Chicago Convention, subsequently supported by 4,000 bilateral treaties, prevent certain taxes from being applied to aviation globally. The industry, for example, does not pay duty or VAT on its fuel. In 2003, it was estimated in a report written by a former adviser to the Treasury and commissioned by the Aviation Environment Federation (AEF) that whereas motorists pay 75p a litre for their fuel, airlines pay just 18p, largely due to such tax advantages. Nor is VAT applicable to any other part of the airline industry. Once you pass through passport control everything is zero-rated in terms of tax – a loophole aviation has long enjoyed. Outrageously, this tax break means that flying is deemed to be a social 'necessity', alongside food, books, buses and children's clothes, which also operate under similar VAT exemptions. Many European countries have reversed this anomaly (the UK is one of only four EU states that doesn't apply VAT to domestic flights). But airlines say that if some countries chose to start taxing fuel sold in their airports, they would simply fill up their planes with fuel in another country, even if it meant making a detour which of course would create more emissions.

In 2006, the Environmental Audit Committee, a cross-party group of MPs charged with monitoring the UK government's environmental policies, slammed the way aviation is largely able to dodge any tax liabilities: 'It is scandalous that governments around the world have failed to grasp the nettle of taxing aviation fuel,' it said in its 'Reducing Carbon Emissions from Transport' report. 'It is equally scandalous that no member state within the EU charges VAT on international air tickets. While this would require coordination across the EU, individual states are free to impose VAT on domestic tickets . . . The Government has the power to increase taxes on domestic flights: it should do so, and as soon as possible . . . The Government should study how best to raise public awareness of the climate-change impacts of flying, and of the undesirability – and ultimately impossibility – of ongoing increases in flights within a declining carbon budget.'

Since 1983, in an attempt to address this tax imbalance, air tickets bought in the UK have been liable to Air Passenger Duty (APD). In late 2006 this duty was raised by the Treasury from £5 to £10 for short-haul flights and from £20 to £40 for long-haul flights. It resulted in an enormous hue and cry by both airlines and environmentalists. It had been billed as a 'green tax' aimed at discouraging people from flying, yet the airlines saw it as a cynical way for the Treasury to raise £1 billion, whereas environmentalists complained that the tax was not being ring-fenced for environmental projects and, worse, was far too small an increase to affect demand.

But even with this doubling of APD, the UK aviation industry still benefits hugely from the remaining tax breaks. In fact, the AEF report estimated that it saves £9 billion a year due to its tax advantages. (It is also an open secret that some airlines now receive payments from local councils – in other words, taxpayers' money – for patronizing their regional airports.) The airlines, naturally, are very sensitive to the charge that they are on easy street, saying that they bring huge economic benefits to the nation by allowing international trade to occur, and that they can't absorb any extra costs.

'Airlines have got no money,' says Maurice Flanagan, the vice chairman and group president of Emirates, an airline that pays its owner a £100 million dividend each year. 'In 2005, aviation created just $7 billion profit from a $450 billion global business. Higher tax would reduce demand because it is a very price-sensitive industry. It just can't afford it.'

More compelling, perhaps, is their case that increasing ticket prices to drive down demand would prove to be a regressive tax, in that it would hit the poorest hardest. It's an argument put forward with increasing regularity by the airlines: just as flying has become affordable to the masses, they say, you now want to take it away from them? (There's certainly no doubt about just how much more affordable flying has become: Maurice Flanagan says that in 1947 it cost the average Australian thirty-six weeks' wages to travel from Sydney to London by air. Now it costs one week's wages. Similarly, only a decade ago the average one-way fare from London to Barcelona was £208; now it is £39.)

Sir Stelios Haji-Ioannou, the charismatic founder of easyJet, says he feels passionate about this issue: 'My view about the low-cost airlines being the poster child of pollution is that first it's wrong. Aviation accounts for less than 5 per cent of global CO_2 emissions. Airlines are being targeted unfairly. Taxing gas-guzzling Chelsea tractors is going to have a greater impact on the environment because it will genuinely change behaviour as you have a choice of a big or small car. If you are going to do something about airlines – and fair enough, we have to share our responsibilities – it has to be in a way that is non-discriminatory for lower-income people. If you put a flat £10 tax on every ticket you are not saving the environment, you are taxing the poor because the rich will just continue to travel.'

This raises the question of who exactly is flying and creating all this growth? Have the skies been opened and democratized for all, or are the rich simply flying more than ever before? Despite the airlines' claims, there seems to be very little evidence that the growth is down to the 'poor' now flying in huge quantities. According to a CAA survey conducted in 2003, the average income per household for UK leisure passengers making an international trip from a UK airport ranged from £33,531 at Birmingham airport through to £54,488 at Heathrow. In 2002/3, the UK average household income was £28,704. Data from another CAA survey conducted in 2004 showed that of 62,849 passengers ending their leisure trips at Manchester, Gatwick, Heathrow, Stansted and Luton airports, 76 per cent were from the socio-economic groups A, B and C1, whereas only 24 per cent were from groups C2, D and E. CAA data also shows that between 2000 and 2004, the number of people in the lowest two household-income brackets using Manchester, Gatwick, Heathrow and Stansted airports actually fell, whereas there was a slight increase at Luton airport. A YouGov poll conducted in 2006 found that 49 per cent of those polled from socio-economic groups C2, D and E said they had not flown in the past year at all, compared to 31 per cent of the ABC1s polled. At the other end of the scale, of the ABC1s polled, 6 per cent said that they had flown seven or more times in the past year, compared to 0 per cent of the C2DEs, although the survey included all flights, as opposed to just leisure flights.

A report published in 2006 by the Environmental Change Institute based at the University of Oxford examined this issue: 'Much of the recent expansion in flying has occurred because better-off people are flying more often,' it said. 'There is little evidence that those on low incomes are flying more; flying cannot be regarded as a socially inclusive activity ... The UK is increasingly developing an air-dependent culture. If action to tackle flying is postponed, we will enter an era in which frequent flying is increasingly the norm for better-off households, with lifestyles adapted to this expectation, including far greater ownership of second homes abroad, and more geographically-distant networks of friends and family.'

If not 'green' taxes, would the airlines accept any other measures that would enable them to pay a more proportionate price for the pollution they create? 'It has to be a sophisticated system like emissions trading,' says Haji-Ioannou. 'The industry is actually pretty united behind this idea, so I say let's just get on with it. The impact it ought to have is to encourage more environmentally friendly aircraft. It should reflect the fact that if you fly in business class you are taking up more space on the plane and therefore polluting a lot more proportionately than if you fly in economy or with a low-cost carrier. EasyJet and other low-cost airlines have invested heavily in new fleets, so that's good for the environment. We also fly more people on the same planes. For example, we put 156 people on our planes and there are others flying with just 110 or 120 in the same models, which shows the impact of business class.'

By emissions trading, Haji-Ioannou refers to the so-called 'cap and trade' system whereby an ever-reducing quota of emissions is distributed, priced and then freely traded between sectors in order to use the basic economics of supply and demand to help drive up the price for polluting sectors and reward those making emissions savings. The system has been up and running for many business sectors in Europe for several years, but has been notable by its absence in aviation – another example of the industry's 'special case' international status.

However, in 2006 the European Commission voted to include the aviation industry in the scheme. It now envisages including all flights within the EU from 2011 and all other international flights from 2012. (Incidentally, the industry has said that the US will threaten a trade war with Europe should this happen.) However, yet again, it seems the aviation industry is being treated with kid gloves. Most of its emissions allowance will be given out free of charge, rather than by auction, based on emissions between 2004 and 2006. (Without allowances being auctioned off, the Institute of Public Policy Research predicts that the airlines could stand to make £2.7 billion, simply by passing on the cost of trading these quotas to passengers and pocketing the difference. So now we've gone from polluter pays to polluter earns.) The system also only accounts for CO_2 emissions so doesn't factor in other climate-change impact caused by aviation, particularly contrails. Worse, the predicted price rises are hardly likely to drive down demand: the EC said it expects short-haul tickets to rise by between €1.80 and €9 each by 2020. No wonder most airlines want to pay their industry's environmental costs by emissions trading. (Some campaigners claim that any savings made by emissions trading are likely to be wiped out by EU ministers' approval in March 2007 of the liberalization of transatlantic flights from 2008 onwards, with the resulting drop in prices highly likely to drive up traffic between Europe and the US.)

If governments fail to reduce demand significantly through the mechanisms and policies available to them, what else is left? Carbon offsetting? Offsetting the emissions resulting from your holiday flight by paying, say, £10 to a company to plant a tree or hand out energy-efficient light bulbs in developing nations has become extremely fashionable in recent years. At best it falls into the 'better than nothing' approach to tackling climate change, but at worse it lulls us into a false sense of security. It fails to address the heart of the issue: that we need to reduce emissions, not just neutralize them. Such schemes are also notoriously hard to police, and are of questionable scientific merit. How do you know that the person who received a light bulb from your offset purchase wasn't about to buy one anyway? And being able to guarantee that the tree you paid to be planted won't be cut down for the next hundred years is next to impossible. Where and how you plant the tree seems key, too: research at the Carnegie Institution in Washington suggests that trees planted in tropical forests, and at low altitude, are better able to reduce atmospheric carbon dioxide than those planted in temperate climates. And if only things could be as simplistic and convenient as cancelling out the release of 'mineral carbon' – fossil fuels such as kerosene that have been locked underground for millennia – via the planting of 'biological carbon' – trees – back into the ground.

Concerned about the growing lack of public confidence in offsetting schemes, the government announced in January 2007 that it was to introduce higher standards, with a new 'gold standard': it said that only four companies operating in the UK at that time would have qualified for this, such were the vagaries of the schemes on offer. Friends of the Earth, however, was still scathing of the whole notion of offsetting: 'Carbon offsetting schemes are being used as a smokescreen to avoid real measures to tackle climate change. We urgently need to cut our emissions, but offsetting schemes encourage individuals, businesses and governments to avoid action and carry on polluting.' A few months earlier, the MPs from the Environmental Audit Committee had also urged caution about the use of offsetting schemes: 'The public should not be encouraged to think that offsetting implied that growth in aviation emissions was environmentally tenable.'

Which leaves us with the last resort: self-discipline. Or some might say first resort – the Bishop of London, the Rt Revd Richard Chartres, created headlines around the world in 2006 when he proclaimed that flying is a 'symptom of sin': 'There is now an overriding imperative to walk more lightly upon the Earth and we need to make our lifestyle decisions in that light,' he said. 'Making selfish choices such as flying on holiday or buying a large car are a symptom of sin. Sin ... is living a life turned in on itself where people ignore the consequences of their actions.'

Whatever your beliefs, it does seem that we, as a generation that avidly consumes flights whilst knowing the impact they are having on the environment, do indeed face a difficult choice. Do we continue to take our minibreaks, visit our second homes, holiday on the other side of the world, and partake of all the other forms of what the industry itself describes as 'non-essential' travel? Or do we start to curb this habit, even if others elsewhere in the world will be, metaphorically, quick to take our place on the plane? Is this a sacrifice worth making, or a sacrifice too far?

Haji-Ioannou believes we shouldn't be beating ourselves up over this. 'Most other nations are just not worrying about these things yet,' he says. 'As always, an environmental conscience comes with wealth and having solved all your other problems . . . There is a big constituency of people now who own second homes and flying has become a lifestyle issue for them. People say easyJet is bad because it promotes non-essential travel. Who is going to tell them what essential travel is? Is seeing your loved ones once a week essential or non-essential? My mother and father live in Greece and I see them once a month. If I told my mother I was only going to see her every six months because of environmental considerations, she would commit suicide.'

A man who stands very much on the other side of the debate from airline figures such as Haji-Ioannou is Jeff Gazzard of the Green Skies Alliance, a 'worldwide information network of environmental organizations concerned with aviation's environmental effects'. More than any other campaigner in the world, perhaps, he has been working for years to raise awareness among politicians, the industry and the public about the impact aviation is having on the environment today, but more importantly in decades to come. 'The genie is out of the bottle now,' he says. 'When you look at the maths in terms of aviation's contribution to climate change and its growth, when you look at the solutions that are technology- and operations-based and you see that the growth will always outpace even the very best of those solutions, you know that this leads inexorably to demand management. People know deep down now they have to do something about this, but it's the "hows" and the "whens" that they struggle with.'

Surprisingly, perhaps, Gazzard doesn't believe we should stop flying altogether. 'Ultimately, it means flying *less*. This isn't saying closing airports, or saying don't fly at all. Some environmentalists do advocate this, of course, and in an ideal world I believe this too, but

I also believe you have to be pragmatic about this. My view of campaigning is don't scare the horses. Your voice just wouldn't be heard if you say the Earth is flat. To say to the general public that they should stop flying is just not practical, even if 63 per cent of *Sun* readers polled in 2006 did say they would be willing to give up a foreign holiday to help save the planet.'

The role of governments over this issue will be important, Gazzard believes, but it will be more a case of persuading people to reduce their flying habit themselves, albeit with a bit of a prod and a push. 'I think within a few years we will start seeing health warnings on adverts for flights akin to cigarettes,' he says. 'Nothing complicated about CO_2 emissions or whatever, just a strong government-driven message that says something like, "Is this flight really necessary?" I also think that within about five years there will be a big rethink by the government about expanding airports in the UK and introducing proper green taxation that really does reduce demand.' (In March 2007, the Conservative Party published a consultation paper in which it proposed a 'Green Air Miles Allowance' of one short-haul return flight a year per person before taxes would begin to take effect in order to drive down demand. It also suggested charging fuel duty and/or VAT on domestic flights and replacing APD with a per-flight tax based on CO_2 emissions. The paper was widely condemned, perhaps indicating just how reluctant we are to face the prospect of flying less.) 'The kind of price increasing that my organization would like to see,' says Gazzard, 'is 3.6 pence per kilometre, which I think is fair and linked to the distance travelled. Obviously, if you were flying to Australia it would cost a fortune, which is why I would be happy to see an upper cap. For a typical European flight it would add £60–£90 to the cost of the ticket. Surveys show that once green taxes get to about £75 a flight then they really start to have a real impact on demand. [About half of all flights within Europe are journeys under 500 kilometres.] We've also run these figures through Department of Transport traffic models and it shows that this rise would reduce growth by half. I'm not obsessed as some are over the issue about whether this money should be ring-fenced for environmental projects, but if that helps brings the public on board to the idea then it should be done. The idea quite simply is for a congestion charge for the skies.'

But doesn't he think that this would, as the airlines might say, hit the poorest hardest?

'Who are we describing as "poor" in this argument? There is nothing equitable about the islands of Bangladesh disappearing due to climate change. In some sense, it's the "rich" who are flying now that will be able to protect themselves from the problems. If we all wanted to emulate a low-carbon-footprint lifestyle then it would be the poorer members of our society who we would look to first for inspiration. Flying is not a necessity. It is a luxury. It may be a sign of our lives that we now see it as a necessity, but it is not.

'However, this is not about not flying, it's about flying less. It's about getting all your carbon consumption in line with where it should be. We're told to walk our kids to school, change our light bulbs, etc., to help reduce our carbon footprint, but for me the single most polluting activity you can take over a year is to go to, say, Florida by plane on a holiday. And you have a choice not to do this, whereas in other areas this choice may not exist. We cannot keep saying as a society that the only way we should judge socio-economic progress is by how much we can pollute. Basically, that's what the airlines are saying when they say that raising ticket prices to reduce demand will price the poor out of the skies.

'Our personal carbon footprint in the UK is about ten tonnes of CO_2 a year, but we need to reduce this to about 3–4 tonnes to avoid dangerous climate change, according to climate scientists. Whereas in fast-developing nations such as China their footprint is about 1.2 tonnes now. The fairest solution is to aim for so-called "contraction and convergence": we make reductions in order to allow developing nations to double their emissions so they can try to move towards the levels of development we now enjoy. That's a simple mathematical truth and is morally equitable. I believe, perhaps naively, that the post-Kyoto international emissions agreements will be based along these lines.'

(According to the Association of Asia Pacific Airlines, the aviation-related CO_2 footprint of the average world citizen is currently 0.08 tonnes per year. The average across Asia is half that figure, whereas in Europe it is three times larger than the world average and in the US it is almost seven times larger.)

So what does that actually mean in terms of trying to decide how many holiday flights would be an 'equitable' amount to take? 'My own starter target for people concerned about the impact of their holiday flights is that if they take one holiday flight a year, they should try to cut one of those out every three years and instead holiday locally, or, say, go to Europe by train. In other words, be air-travel-free one in every three years. Whether that is ultimately going to be enough, that's for others to judge, but it's a start and is pragmatic advice.'

Interestingly, some people are already beginning to make such commitments, although the figure is still minuscule compared with the numbers of people flying. An online community called the Flight Pledge Union now encourage anyone to make a personal pledge on their website to reduce their flying. Within a few months of launching in early 2006, it had received almost one thousand pledges. 'There are two pledges – gold and silver,' says the website. 'If you sign the gold pledge, you promise to take no flights in the coming year, except in a personal or family emergency. If you sign the silver pledge, you promise not to take more than two return short-haul flights, or one return long-haul flight, in the coming year – again, except for an emergency.' (In February 2007, the Bishop of London signed up to the gold pledge, following criticism that he wasn't practising what he preached when he admitted that he had been taking flights for his 'diocese work'.)

The important thing to remember, says Gazzard, is that we first need to stabilize emissions, then start reducing them. 'Stabilizing the amount we fly personally for leisure is easy – we just need not fly any more than we do already. But reducing is not difficult either. Just think back to how Britons were holidaying a decade or so ago before the budget airlines became established – we'd go on one trip abroad a year maximum in general and some of those trips would be by ferry, car or train. The rest of the time we'd holiday within our own shores. For example, one problem today that's causing growth is that there are now an enormous amount of people flying multiple trips a year to France to visit their second homes or to take minibreaks. But France is the one country in Europe where you can get just about everywhere seamlessly by high-speed train.' (A survey in 2003 by HACAN ClearSkies, a campaign group against airport expansion in the UK, found that people with second homes abroad take an average of six flights a year, whereas half the population do not fly at all.) 'I cannot see any reason why many of those with second homes in France, particularly those that live in southern Britain, don't go by train. I understand the cost arguments, but these are people who can afford second homes. Is it really that outrageous a notion for someone to go to France by train instead of by plane? We are simply all going to have to be more disciplined about the amount of CO_2 we're responsible for.'

The Final Call

Conclusion

IN 1971, THE GREEK ORTHODOX CHURCH adopted a new prayer in an attempt to seek divine intervention for a problem that was beginning to trouble its followers deeply. So many tourists were now visiting the monasteries located in the dramatic limestone rocks at Meteora in Thessaly that the monks were starting to leave for the relative sanctuary of the monasteries two hundred kilometres east on the thin peninsula underneath Mount Athos. The short prayer was entitled, 'For Those Endangered by the Touristic Wave'. It read:

> Lord Jesus Christ, Son of God, have mercy on the cities, the islands and the villages of our Orthodox Fatherland, as well as the holy monasteries, which are scourged by the worldly touristic wave. Grace us with a solution to this dramatic problem and protect our brethren, who are sorely tried by the modernistic spirit of these contemporary Western invaders.

Over three decades on from this prayer of despair, a huge disconnect still remains between the visited and the visitor. Furthermore, the 'touristic wave' is breaking with ever more force on the shores of the world's destinations. In 1971, there were 170 million 'international tourist arrivals', according to the UNWTO. By 2006, this figure had risen to 840 million and in 2010 it is predicted to pass the one billion mark for the first time. And the UNWTO says that by 2020 it expects the figure to have reached 1.6 billion – almost ten times the number of tourists that travelled abroad in the year when prayers were first being said in Greece for 'this dramatic problem'.

If concerns were being aired about the impact of tourism as far back as the early 1970s, then where does that leave us today, let alone in a future destined for further relentless growth? How does the world's largest service industry – which, according to the WTTC, directly or indirectly employs one in every 11.5 workers on the planet and generates just over 10 per cent of the world's economic wealth each year – answer the lengthening charge sheet laid before it?

My travels through some of the world's major destinations did not reassure me that the industry has a full grasp on how tourism can so often be a negative force. It still clings to the convenient myth that the good ship *Tourism* brings economic bounty to all that sail in her. And it is still making some other extraordinary claims – that, for example, tourism nurtures world peace, love and understanding. There seems to be little evidence to me that tourists and those that serve them engage with each other on a balanced, harmonious footing.

What seems to be all too obvious is that the bounty is carved up between an extremely select few – often located in a country other than the destination – and that far too many of the industry's workers, particularly in developing nations, are no more than wage-slaves scratching a pitiful living. The assumption often made by the industry that these workers' lives are automatically of a better quality now that they are employed within tourism appears to be remarkably far from the truth, as I witnessed repeatedly from Thailand through to Cancún. And there is plenty of evidence that many locals have been displaced to make way for tourists, often at a considerable cost to the local environment. Tourism generally appears to be a one-sided transaction whereby the buyer – the tourist – comes off much the better from the deal than the sellers at the destination. To apply the same ruthless, often exploitative business logic and practices to tourism employed by other sectors seems to be one of the key problems. Lord Marshall, the former CEO and chairman of British Airways, got it right when he said that tourism is 'essentially the renting out for short-term lets of other people's environments, whether that is a coastline, a city, a mountain range or a rainforest'. Tenants, as any landlord will know, have little reason to care about the upkeep of a property for the period beyond their let.

This is not to say, though, that the future is one of total despondency – far from it. Encouragingly, there does seem to be growing acceptance and understanding by some within the industry that it is in grave danger of trashing the very assets on which it depends to survive; that it could become the slapstick cliché of the man up a tree sawing through the branch he is sitting on.

Upon announcing the latest runaway growth figures for tourism in February 2007, Francesco Frangialli, the UNWTO's secretary-general, issued a cautionary note amid the self-satisfaction. 'It is increasingly apparent that tourism is falling victim – but also contributing – to climate change and the reduction of biodiversity. The path ahead is therefore marked by a different type of growth: more moderate, more solid and more responsible ... A heavier responsibility now lies on our shoulders, the responsibility to make this new phase of growth more economical in its use of energy and natural resources, more sustainable, and lastly, more in keeping with the spirit of solidarity.'

A similar cry went out in 2006 in an editorial published in *Travel Weekly*, the UK trade publication: 'This industry needs to set out where it stands on the environment. Polite notices about putting out towels to clean in hotel rooms don't wash with an increasingly green public ... This issue is not going to go away. Tobacco firms knew for twenty years that advertising and smoking bans were inevitable and fought to ensure they came out the best they could. What is travel's strategy to protect itself? We might make people's dreams come true, but there are those who argue travel contributes to future nightmares.'

This realization that tourism operates in a world of finite resources is timely, but the difference between spotting the hazard in the water and actually turning the tanker around is huge. For all the corporate social responsibility reports that the major tour operators and hotel chains now wave in the air to show they care, more of them need to start showing meaningful leadership on the issue of environmental stewardship. Otherwise, accusations that their efforts are simply 'greenwash' will continue to be justified.

Take Airtours as an example. In February 2007, it began offering the UK's first-ever round-the-world package holiday – a twenty-three-day whistlestop tour of ten countries at a cost of £4,499. The package begins in Manchester and the charter flight – with its 239 passengers, twelve cabin crew, ten holiday reps and accompanying doctor – then flies westward to New York, before continuing on to Las Vegas, Hawaii, Sydney, Borneo, Beijing, Agra, Dubai, Cape Town and Cairo. (With an average stay of two nights at most destinations, there might seem to some little time to experience the culture and peoples of each stopover. 'The airline is currently tailoring a special in-flight menu for the trip, with meals reflecting the local dishes of the countries visited,' said an Airtours spokeswoman.) During the course of the holiday, the plane is in the air for a total of seventy-three hours and is responsible for 2,289 tonnes of CO_2 – almost seven tonnes per passenger – entering the atmosphere, according to Friends of the Earth, who described the package upon its announcement to the press as 'one of the most polluting package holidays possible'. A company spokesperson responded to Friends of the Earth's comment, saying: 'According to the Stern Report, aviation accounts for only 1.6 per cent of global greenhouse gases. As a responsible tour operator, we operate a modern fleet of fuel-efficient aircraft and any customer who chooses to offset their carbon debt can do so via a link from our websites.'

But does this round-the-world package really chime with the company's stated commitments to the environment? Airtours is owned by MyTravel, one of the UK's largest tour operators. It says its group of companies is 'in the business of responsible leisure travel': 'The board and executive management recognize that the scope, nature and scale of the group's operations have a direct effect on the environment and we are committed to offering our products and services through a framework of controls, systems and procedures which seeks to minimize negative impacts.' It evidently believes that the Airtours package – and the offer to its customers to voluntarily offset their flights – falls within this vow. Additionally, since January 2007 all MyTravel charter-tour-operator customers have been asked if they would like to make an opt-out donation at the time of booking of 40p per person to the Travel Foundation, a charity largely funded by the UK tourism industry, to help support its sustainable tourism projects around the world. But is a 40p donation to charity really enough to help salve a tourist's conscience? It's the kind of question the industry needs to be asking itself with increasing regularity and volume, it would appear.

But what of the destinations? Surely they bear significant responsibility for the plight many of them now find themselves in? A cocktail of political ineptitude and developer greed seems to have been served up at far too many tourist resorts across the world, leading to the same mistakes being repeated time and again. I was struck by just how many places – Cancún, Costa Blanca, Thailand, Kerala, Ibiza – say that water supply has become one of their biggest concerns now that they rely so heavily on tourism. And the cause is always the same: unplanned, rapid over-development. Many are now so desperate to cling on to the business they have that they are resorting to ever-more-desperate short-term measures that can only exacerbate their plight. So, for example, we now see helicopters being used in the Alps to ferry snow to pistes melting under the pressures of climate change. Likewise, marine scientists in Australia are now proposing the 'hosing down' of vulnerable parts of the Great Barrier Reef during periods of high temperatures, as well as the building of floating pontoons to provide shade, all to protect the corals from being damaged from bleaching as a result of climate change.

Every destination has faced the same choice: should it invest in tourism, or not? The temptation must be great, particularly for those in developing nations. Tourism is often presented to potential desti-nations by prospective developers and investors as a benign, clean industry that will bring much-needed foreign currency into the economy. No need for big polluting factories in your midst to earn a living, they are told, just a hotel full of happy tourists. Once destina-tions were able to fend off such advances, or at least nurture their own home-grown investors to ensure that more of the profits could remain within the local economy. But now international trade rules, such as the General Agreement on Trade in Services (GATS), which all member states of the UNWTO must adhere to, mean that market liberalization has become the mantra and so-called 'self-protectionism' is frowned upon (even though the rules seem to be quite different for the developed nations and their heavily protected and subsidized farmers). International trade treaties such as GATS are the life-force of globalization and allow, for example, the multi-national hotel conglomerates to set up in most countries; if a government favours a local investor it can do little to resist. Coupled with this is the pressure placed on destinations and their governments from organizations such as the UNWTO and big-business lobbyists such as the WTTC to view tourism as a 'development tool' and to therefore open up further to international investment as well as build or improve transport infrastructure such as airports. But who does this relentless expansion and development really benefit? Many destinations are now beginning to wonder.

I began my travels for this book with some questions circling in my head. Is tourism a force for good in each destination? How vulnerable are these destinations to tourism's all-too-often heavy hand? It's obviously impossible to turn back the clock for the most distressed destinations, which are surely now in terminal decline. The urgent task for many destinations is to identify where they now stand on tourism's bell curve of development formulated by Dr Stanley Plog over three decades ago, and to make sure they stay on its rise as opposed to its fall. Maintaining and cherishing the unique characteristics that first drew visitors to a destination seems to be the key to success. In contrast, trying to match a rival destination by building similar facilities seems to have been a mistake made the world over. For any would-be destination contemplating turning to tourism, the advice must surely be to view the prospect with the utmost caution and only proceed with a considered and strict plan. And always diversify – tourism is extremely vulnerable to the whims of external forces, and should never be the only industry. Many in the past have viewed themselves as King Canute, able to repel the worst excesses of the 'touristic wave', only to be soon inundated.

From what I saw, the concept of tourism 'hubs' or 'clusters' seems to offer the best model for reducing the risk to the environment and offering a sustainable future for the resident community, due to the simple fact that the impact is concentrated in one relatively small area. Both Benidorm and Cancún appeared to have adopted this model early on, but the discipline required to resist over-development was lost somewhere along the way. It's the creep of tourism that appears to lead to the most damage, and the first shoots of this spread are invariably, if inadvertently, nurtured by backpackers. The beaches of Thailand bear testament to this. In quick time, the pressure to increase bed capacity inevitably means that developers turn to neighbouring areas, with often negative results, as is now so evident on the Riveria Maya south of Cancún. Likewise, in Spain it is the green carpet of golf courses and villas now spreading out in concentric circles from the main beaches of the costas that are creating the greatest pressures on water supply, not the towers of Benidorm.

One of the best remedies being offered to relieve the symptoms of this pressure seems to be quotas. The communities living in the shadows of the Taj Mahal and Machu Picchu, for example, have long urged a cap on visitor numbers to help limit damage. Nearly everywhere I went, the local community expressed the desire to see fewer tourists paying more for their visit. Quality not quantity. Most felt they were being constantly forced to undersell themselves due to pricing pressure from the tour operators. A simple cap on the number of visitors to an area each year does not seem to be the answer, however. It is inequitable, as it acts to artificially strangulate supply, which inevitably drives up prices. The result is that the destination becomes the sole preserve of more affluent tourists. This is what has happened in places such as Bhutan, the tiny kingdom in the Himalayas which limits access by charging tourists about $200 a day. A much smarter idea – one suggested by the British thinktank the Centre for Future Studies – is a lottery-based entrance system. Starting with the most sensitive destinations – reefs, mountains, small tropical islands and vulnerable heritage sites – an annual cap would be agreed. A lottery would be held online, say, so that anyone in the world could apply for a ticket. The lucky ticket-holders would then be allowed to enter, according to a range of price bands and available calendar slots. Spare tickets could be bought and sold, but the important thing would be that the number of visitors wouldn't exceed a sustainable level. The system would also offer the important psychological advantage that the ticket-holder would feel lucky to have been granted entrance to such a special site, and therefore would be more likely to act with care and respect once there.

The idea is endorsed by Tricia Barnett, the director of Tourism Concern: 'I do think lottery-based quotas are a good idea if they are organized well in advance. It's very, very simple and a really intelligent way to manage places. If more places did this I think the future could be much brighter for a lot of destinations. The tour operators would have to apply for tickets just like everyone else. It's not dependent on wealth, which I think is important. The internet allows carrying capacity to be better managed in vulnerable places. It is important, however, that the local people are able to access these places for free, or at least at a much cheaper rate during times when tourists are barred.'

Tourism is a notoriously fickle business, leaving destinations ever vulnerable to the winds of change, whether these be the changing tastes of tourists or sudden natural disasters, and with the levers of patronage and power often now lying beyond their shores, many destinations have largely lost control of their destiny. If you don't control the supply pipeline then you leave yourself extremely vulnerable, as the nations of Europe reliant on gas from Russia are now realizing.

And, finally, what of us, the tourists? Not many of us are likely to dwell on this as we lie on our beach towels or peruse the souvenir stands, but it is our unshakeable human right to be a tourist. Under Article 13 of the Universal Declaration of Human Rights – the historic document adopted by the UN General Assembly in Paris on 10 December 1948 – 'everyone has the right to freedom of movement and residence within the borders of each state; everyone has the right to leave any country, including his own, and to return to his country.' Combine that with Article 24 – 'everyone has the right to rest and leisure, including reasonable limitation of working hours and periodic holidays with pay' – and you have international tourism.

But it took the UN General Assembly more than fifty years to acknowledge formally that, while the opportunity to travel abroad as a tourist is a sign of an enlightened age, this right also carries with it a huge burden of responsibility. In 2001, the UN General Assembly voted to recognize officially the UNWTO's 'Global Code of Ethics', a document that includes this sentence with its extraordinary final stanza: 'The prospect of direct and personal access to the discovery and enjoyment of the planet's resources constitutes a right equally open to all the world's inhabitants; the increasingly extensive participation in national and international tourism should be regarded as one of the best possible expressions of the sustained growth of free time, and obstacles should not be placed in its way.'

The code also includes articles that reflect the foundations of all responsible tourism: 'tourism should be conducted in harmony with the attributes and traditions of the host regions and countries and in respect for their laws, practices and customs'; 'tourists and visitors have the responsibility to acquaint themselves, even before their departure, with the characteristics of the countries they are preparing to visit'; and 'tourism infrastructure should be designed and tourism activities programmed in such a way as to protect the natural heritage composed of ecosystems and biodiversity and to preserve endangered species of wildlife.'

It might appear unnecessary to labour these points, but amid the frenzy of the check-in queue at the airport or hotel it is easy to forget that being an international tourist is a rare privilege in this world. After all, only 5 per cent of the world's population have ever travelled by plane. And while leisure and travel are our human right, we often seem to assume these rights without remembering the rights of others.

Whilst on holiday it can be very easy conveniently to suppress the level of sensitivity we might display at home about issues such as the environment. For example, we tend to deny or mask the tensions that so clearly often exist between 'us', the visitor, and 'them', the visited.

This is our leisure time, after all. We have worked hard for our two weeks away in the sun. And we haven't come on holiday to worry.

But the motivation behind some of our holidays often doesn't bear up well to scrutiny when placed under the spotlight. For example, how many of our holidays are status driven; less about the experience than about how others might see us once they know where we've been? 'Where are you going this year?' is just as important a social signifier to some as 'What car do you drive?', 'Where do you work?', or 'Where do you live?' And how many of our holidays, if we're honest with ourselves, truly offer us the rest, wellbeing and meeting of cultures we crave?

Are we now, as consumers desensitized by a blinding blizzard of choice, expecting too much from our holidays, so much so that destinations are pressurized into taking negative measures just to sate our desires? About twenty years ago a Japanese psychiatrist working in France noticed a strange phenomenon: a small number of Japanese female tourists, mainly in their thirties, were fainting in the streets of Paris, even though they appeared to be otherwise healthy. Upon interviewing some of the women, he established that they were suffering a psychiatric breakdown caused by the fact that Paris did not meet their high expectations. Instead of finding the charm and romanticism of Paris projected in so many movies, they were shocked by the rudeness of some Parisians and collapsed. About a dozen Japanese tourists a year suffer from what is now called 'Paris Syndrome'. The Japanese embassy now provides a helpline for its tourists and the only known cure is for sufferers to be repatriated.

It's a flippant example, perhaps, but it illustrates the way we can project our aspirations and desires on to a destination. Whereas the average Parisian might shrug their shoulders at such an attitude, many destinations are so desperate for our custom that they try to provide everything they think we might need -- golf courses, constant air conditioning, large swimming pools. Everywhere I travelled I saw identikit hotels offering exactly the same 'international-standard' facilities, because 'that's what our guests expect'. Must we always pack our Western-orientated aspirations and demands alongside the novel and sun cream? A holiday is by its very nature a self-centred act, but that needn't mean it wreaks the damage of a selfish act.

Equally, the pressures we often bring to bear on destinations by always seeking the lowest prices cause many problems. As with flying, the price we pay for our holidays today does not in any way reflect the lasting impact our visit can have on a destination. If we demand ever-cheaper holidays, we can't then be surprised that costs are cut at the destination, with obvious negative effects. It was heartbreaking to see the living conditions workers have to endure in Cancún. Our demand for cheap winter sun inevitably means low wages for the waiters, chambermaids, gardeners, taxi drivers and other service staff that make our holidays possible.

As the trend for experiential holidays increases – we now have a generation raised on gap years and minibreaks, as well as fit, well-off babyboomers entering retirement, none of whom are sated by two weeks on a sun lounger – so our destination footprint increases further still. In contrast to the last-minute, have-it-all tourism that we enjoy today, we must surely develop a mindset in which we appreciate that it is an honour to visit another country and that, as guests, we must tread with tentative, respectful steps.

There is, of course, a whole new market rapidly growing up to meet the needs of tourists with this mentality. They go by a range of names: ecotourists, responsible tourists, ethical tourists, etc. Just as many of us are now waking up to the truth about cheap food, cheap clothes and many other aspects of our corner-cutting consumer culture, so more of us are now thinking about what lies behind the façade of our holiday. It is, after all, the very motivation that made me set off to research this book. But it struck me during my travels how important it is that this form of tourism doesn't remain in the small niche it currently occupies. It is surely wrong to draw a line in the sand and put ethical/responsible/ecotourism on one side, and the rest on the other. If so, the former will forever remain a small sector of the market. There seems to be a grave danger, too, that it has become an aspirational badge of honour to go on such holidays, to help set us apart from 'other' tourists, whereas for ethical tourism to have any true significance it must be absorbed into mainstream thinking, both by tourists and the industry itself. This leaves us with a thorny dilemma: do we support these niche operators, or do we instead try to influence the mainstream operators by demanding change from within, through relying on the sometimes flawed logic that companies always listen to their customers?

Certification schemes for tourists seeking guarantees have proved to be notoriously blunt tools destined for the fringes of tourism, as is discussed in the Costa Rica chapter, but one scheme does offer genuine hope that it could achieve wide recognition across the industry, certainly within Europe. Within the next year or two, the Fairtrade label, which guarantees that workers have been paid a fair wage, is set to become a common sight in holiday brochures and websites, alongside the names of accredited hotels.

'We don't approve of certification in general, but we do believe there could be a Fairtrade label because there's a market for it,' says Tricia Barnett of Tourism Concern, which has spent three years working with the Fairtrade Labelling Organization based in Germany to develop the label for tourism. 'People already understand the concept of Fairtrade. We never originally thought a label would work really, but we noticed that other types of "fair" labels were starting in Europe and we were worried that the Fairtrade brand would be diluted. The industry seems to be genuinely excited about it, especially the Association of British Travel Agents (ABTA).'

However, Barnett believes that due to the climate-change impact of aviation, all tourists now face an extra, almost crippling dilemma.

'Tourism Concern's message has always been a tough one to get across: how do you let people know that going on holiday can help to continue to impoverish people? However, now you have this double bind that if you don't fly you could help to further impoverish people. The current environmental debate about aviation concerns me. There are legitimate concerns, of course, about its impact, but at the same time there is a no less legitimate concern about people who have become over-dependent on tourism. Whether we like it or not, it's a fact that too many countries are now over-dependent on tourism and if we were not to fly, their poverty would be exacerbated. We have to find a balance and that's incredibly difficult. What we would like to do is find a way of working out destination footprints too, not just for the journey, so we can use that as a tool to guide travellers and holidaymakers. This footprint would include what it took to build the hotel, to import all the goods and the food, the transport when you're there, etc. It would help tourists make a decision, but would also help to incentivize the destination to reduce its footprint in order to be more attractive. It would help us move away from the current situation, where guests are simply told to switch off their light, and would better contextualize their stay within the framework of their carbon footprint.'

Barnett suggests one solution to the vexed issue of whether or not to fly is to stay longer at a destination. 'What's been happening in the past decade is the growth of very short-term holidays, such as trips to India or Dubai for a weekend. This is insanity. We must try to stay in one place longer, as opposed to having lots of short trips. If we had a future where we each had our own annual carbon budget, we could make the decision about how we used our carbon accordingly.'

It's an idea shared by Tony Wheeler, the co-founder of the Lonely Planet guidebook empire. In 2006, Lonely Planet joined forces with rival publishers Rough Guides to announce they would be urging their readers to 'fly less and stay longer', as well as to carbon-offset their flights. 'We're now saying think before you go,' says Wheeler, 'but I do worry about it all, you know. You go to so many places these days and you see the aircraft lined up at the airports and you see the amount of stuff being built, and talk of 100 million Chinese travellers coming on to the market, and I just don't know if it can be sustained. I'm beginning to doubt that this is all possible. It's scary in all sorts of ways. I really feel this. But everything we do has negatives. With tourism, we have to look at the positives and minimize the negatives.'

The travel I undertook to research this book represents this double bind we now face as tourists – should we travel to these places at all, knowing the impact it can have? I took the journalistic decision to go to each destination to listen and speak to the protagonists, so that I could witness their circumstances first-hand and try to tell the wider story. In an attempt to keep my transport-related emissions down, I did attempt to conduct some interviews by telephone when I thought it was appropriate, but in reality there can never be a substitute for looking into people's eyes when asking them painful questions – and, sadly, too many of the questions that arose from what I saw and heard on my travels were uncomfortable both for me and the interviewees to face, be it the sex workers in Thailand, the hotel builders in Dubai, or the villagers in Kerala concerned about water depletion.

Due to a number of constraints, ranging from financial and family considerations to more physical barriers such as vast expanses of water to cross, like the majority of long-haul tourists I was heavily reliant on planes. It's no consolation, but all that time spent waiting in airport lounges did at least give me the chance to tot up the total emissions of the travelling undertaken to research this book. I calculated that the sum of my journeying broadly represented the total amount of travelling the average Western tourist enjoys over a four-to-five-year period, if you include all the short breaks as well as the traditional two-week summer holidays. Including the various flights, hire cars, taxis, buses and trains that I took – my short rides by horse and camel were mercifully carbon neutral – my travels were responsible for just under ten tonnes of CO_2 entering the atmosphere. Almost nine tonnes of that was down to the flights alone. And then there's the all-important 'contrails multiplier' to consider. It's an awful lot of extra baggage to carry.

Overall, I had to weigh up the environmental negatives of conducting this research against what I hoped would be the positive impact of giving a new platform to the all-too-often muffled debate about the impact of our holidays. I did initially consider 'offsetting' my travels, as is now so popular, but I believe this only acts to disguise the damage being done. Carbon offsetting is like a strong cough medicine: something that suppresses the symptoms – in this case, guilt – without actually addressing the cause of the ailment. The offsetting being sold to us today is little more than the equivalent of the indulgences sold to sinners by medieval churchmen – a way to pay off your sins. While I would never go so far as to claim, as the Bishop of London has done, that flying is a 'symptom of sin', I think we as tourists are now morally obliged to consider the full environmental impact of our holidays with as much, if not more, vigour than we apply to their price and personal rewards. If we still want to make that trip, then we need to offset it, not by paying a company to plant a tree on our behalf, but by viewing it in the context of our personal carbon budget and trying to make cutbacks in other areas of our lives, such as the amount we drive and the amount of energy we use in our homes. For this reason, I now consider myself to be carrying a considerable carbon debt, with a long period of repayment in the form of personal carbon cutbacks looming before me. This I believe to be the way to approach all carbon consumption, not just that related to our holiday habits – everything we do or buy, certainly 'non-essentials' such as holidays, must have a carbon cost embedded in its price tag. As our carbon literacy increases over time – be it through self-awareness or, as some are arguing, through a regulated 'cap and trade' carbon-trading system for citizens, not just for big business as is the case now – our holidays will become a key part of our constant carbon balancing act. The most equitable system by far would be one where everyone was handed the same sustainable quota of, for want of a better term, 'carbons' each year. If a far-off holiday tipped you over your annual carbon allowance, then you would have to buy carbons off someone who hadn't used up their quota. The polluter would pay, whereas the person who had been thrifty with their carbons would be financially rewarded. Ideally, this logic could also extend to holiday destinations, too, whereby we would need to pay the appropriate carbon price for the activities we do and accommodation in which we stay. On an even more sophisticated level, water use could also be priced into our holidays, as could all other uses of resources. All of this would help us step back from the current damaging trend of impulse-buy holidays, where little consideration is given to their environmental impact. And if the predictions are correct about the huge increase in the number of international tourists travelling from countries such as China and India, then consuming a more equitable slice of the pie will become ever more imperative if the world's tourism destinations are not to be rapidly overwhelmed and ulti- mately destroyed by the 'touristic wave' so feared by the Greek Orthodox monks.

A more considered, thoughtful style of holidaying is already being widely practised without many of its practitioners even being aware of its fashionable new moniker – 'slow travel'. The term was inspired by the founding principles of the slow-food movement that origin- ated in Italy, which promotes the understanding and enjoyment of food by celebrating local, artisan produce rather than the main- stream, homogenized food served up by international restaurant chains or found on most supermarket shelves. Fundamentally, the slow-food movement is about taking back control of the food we eat and consuming it on terms that we believe to be dear both to us *and* the original producer, be it environmental sustainability, taste, or fair pay. Similarly, slow travel is a mindset in which tourists 'downshift' by stepping back from the impulses and temptations they would normally succumb to without due consideration, and instead focus on the quality as opposed to the quantity of the experiences offered by their holiday. Therefore, the journey itself becomes just as important as the destination, with trains, say, being preferred over planes, both for environmental reasons and for reasons of enjoyment and experience. Small hotels, guesthouses or homestays are preferred over large hotel chains, enabling more money to 'stick' to the destination, as well as allowing the tourist to experience the destination and its communities in a more truthful and rewarding manner. This isn't about the tourist suffering for the cause, but about rediscovering the real reasons why we instinctively wish to holiday abroad – to give ourselves temporary sanctuary and rest from the mundane routines of our daily lives by jumping into a plunge pool of different cultures and landscapes. In German, there is a word for the stress endured during holidays – *freizeitstress*, literally meaning 'free-time stress' – and in Germany courses are now available to help you learn how to enjoy your holiday more. Likewise, we must relearn why it is we crave travel. A good test is to recall the highlight of your last holiday. Invariably, it won't be the speedy room service, the all-weather tennis courts at your hotel, or the fact that your hire car had a more powerful engine than your car at home – in other words, the kind of things you may have sought before you left home. Perhaps it was a walk up to a viewpoint, a memorable meal at a restaurant discovered by chance, an idle conversation with a local about their life, or something as simple as just getting lost for a few hours.

The slow traveller might, say, draw up a three-year holiday plan which factors in both their own desire to enjoy wonderful holidays, but also a desire to travel with as soft and considered a footfall as possible. I call this 'Goldilocks' holidaying, whereby to reduce your travel emissions you alternate between taking a taste from the big bowl, the medium bowl and the baby-sized bowl. In other words, in year one you might travel long-haul by air. The next year you would travel to a nearby country or region by rail within a 1,000-kilometre radius. And in the third year, you would holiday locally within your own country or region. If we were all to adopt this approach it would dramatically reduce our combined holiday-related emissions. For example, a train trip to the Lake District from London produces *one-fortieth* of the CO_2 emissions per passenger of a flight from Heathrow to Florida. Are we really saying that, in order to warrant such an extravagance of emissions, a trip to Orlando is forty times better than a holiday in the Lakes? The Goldilocks method still allows us to travel to far-off places and therefore support the communities that have become, for right or wrong, reliant on tourism, but it also means that these trips become ones to savour and cherish, as opposed to being so regular and routine they are at risk of becoming as disposable an experience as any other product in our throw-away culture.

The onus must now be on all of us to approach our holidays with fresh imagination; to encourage tourism to be a positive force, and not the pernicious disease that I have sadly witnessed afflicting so many places in so many diverse ways. There seem to be many ideas and approaches to reduce its negative impacts, but the one thing this mighty industry lacks is time. For many of the destinations we love, this surely is the final call.

Sources

The majority of this book draws on first-person testimony from the dozens of people I interviewed during my travels. Below is a chronological list of source material I referred to, or quoted, in the order that they are referenced throughout each chapter. I also hope it is useful as a source of further reading.

General news

There were numerous ways I tracked the fast-moving tourism industry whilst researching this book. I found a combination of the following helped to keep me abreast of most developments:

Travel Weekly (www.travelweekly.co.uk; for print subscriptions call +44 (0)1444 445566)

Tourism Concern (www.tourismconcern.org.uk; for membership call +44 (0)20 7133 3330)

www.travelmole.com

www.eturbonews.com

www.travelwirenews.com

www.nationalgeographic.com/news

www.planeta.com

www.worldhum.com

www.lonelyplanet.com

Introduction

'Travel Trends: International Passenger Survey 2005', Office of National Statistics, November 2006
www.statistics.gov.uk/pdfdir/ttrends1106.pdf

'The Future of Air Transport' white paper, Department for Transport, December 2003
www.dft.gov.uk/about/strategy/whitepapers/air

'The Future of Air Transport' progress report, Department for Transport, December 2006
www.dft.gov.uk/162259/165217/185629/progressreport

'About the World Tourism Organization', World Tourism Organization website
www.world-tourism.org/aboutwto/eng/menu.html

'Tourism in London', Government Office for London website
www.gos.gov.uk/gol/Culture_leisure/Tourism

1. Two Degrees from Meltdown

Swiss Federal Institute for Snow and Avalanche Research
www.slf.ch

WWF Alpine Programme
www.panda.org/about_wwf/where_we_work/europe/what_we_do/alps/index.cfm

'High Ski Runs Fuel Habitat Fears', BBC News Online, 17 January 2007
http://news.bbc.co.uk/1/hi/sci/tech/6268403.stm

'Scientists Grouse at Eco-unfriendly Ski Resorts', *Guardian*, 7 March 2007
http://environment.guardian.co.uk/conservation/story/0,,2028354,00.html

International Commission for the Protection of the Alps (Cipra)
www.cipra.org

Ski Club of Great Britain
www.skiclub.co.uk

US National Ski Areas Association
www.nsaa.org

L'Association du Service des Pistes des Grands Montets (in French)
www.pisteurs.com

Compagnie du Mont Blanc
www.compagniedumontblanc.fr

World Glacier Monitoring Service
www.geo.unizh.ch/wgms

'"Major Melt" for Alpine Glaciers', BBC News Online, 4 April 2006
http://news.bbc.co.uk/1/hi/sci/tech/4874224.stm

'Many Ski Resorts Heading Downhill as a Result of Global Warming', United Nations Environment
Programme press release, 2 December 2003
www.unep.org/Documents.Multilingual/Default.asp?DocumentID=363&ArticleID=4313&l=en

'Climate Change in the European Alps: Adapting Winter Tourism and Natural Hazards Management',
Organisation for Economic Co-operation and Development report, 18 January 2007
www.oecd.org/document/45/0,2340,en_2649_34361_37819437_1_1_1_1,00.html

Mountain Wilderness
www.mountainwilderness.org

Neil McNab
www.mcnabsnowboarding.com

'Ski Industry Report 2006', Crystal Ski report, 11 July 2006
http://destinations.thomson.co.uk/devolved/about-thomson/press/the-ski-industry-report-2006.html

In addition, www.pistehors.com is an excellent source of news and background
information about the winter sports industry in the French Alps.

2. A Line in the Sand

Palm Jumeirah
www.thepalm.ae

Nakheel
www.nakheel.ae

'Dubai's Man-Made Islands Anger Environmentalists', Reuters, 27 October 2005,
www.planetark.com/avantgo/dailynewsstory.cfm?newsid=33190

'Huge Artificial Islands Destroy Dubai's Coral Reefs', Salt Lake Tribune, 27 February 2005
www.cdnn.info/news/eco/e050227.html)

Sheikh Mohammed bin Rashid Al Maktoum
www.sheikhmohammed.co.ae

Department of Tourism and Commerce Marketing, Dubai
www.dubaitourism.ae

Burj Al Arab
www.burj-al-arab.com

Dubai Holding
www.dubaiholding.com

Emaar
www.emaar.com

Jumeirah Group
www.jumeirah.com

Emirates
www.emirates.com

'United Arab Emirates: Country Reports on Human Rights Practices 2005', report by the US Bureau of
Democracy, Human Rights and Labor, 8 March 2006
www.state.gov/g/drl/rls/hrrpt/2005/61701.htm

'Asian Workers Protest Lack of Pay in Dubai', Agence France Presse, 19 September 2005
www.iran-daily.com/1384/2381/html/ieconomy.htm

'No Water to Have a Shower after Work', Gulf News, 21 September 2005
http://archive.gulfnews.com/articles/05/09/21/182800.html

'Disgruntled Labourers Win the First Round', Gulf News, 21 September 2005
http://archive.gulfnews.com/articles/05/09/21/182799.html

'Dubai Workers Taste Blood', Calcutta Telegraph, 22 September 2005
www.telegraphindia.com/1050922/asp/nation/story_5269715.asp

Al Naboodah Laing O'Rourke
www.alnaboodah.com/html/naboodah-rourke.htm

'Strike Halts Work at Dubai Tower', BBC News Online, 23 March 2006
http://news.bbc.co.uk/1/hi/business/4836632.stm

'Building Towers, Cheating Workers: Exploitation of Migrant Construction Workers in the United
Arab Emirates', Human Rights Watch, November 2006
http://hrw.org/reports/2006/uae1106

Ski Dubai
www.skidxb.com

'Global Deserts Outlook', United Nations Environment Programme, June 2006
www.unep.org/geo/GDOutlook

'A Big Feat', Gulf News, 31 August 2006
http://archive.gulfnews.com/articles/06/08/31/10064003.html

Al Maha
www.al-maha.com

3. The Model State

Kerala Human Development Report 2005, United Nations Development Programme, March 2006
http://hdr.undp.org/reports/detail_reports.cfm?view=1102

'Kerala: The Impact of Travel and Tourism on Jobs and the Economy', World Travel and Tourism
Council, 2003
www.wttc.org/regProg/pdf/KERALA%20FINAL.pdf

'Tourism Policy of Kerala 1995', copy archived at
www.indiainbusiness.nic.in/indian-states/kerala/TourisFinal.htm

Kerala Tourism Development Corporation
www.ktdc.com

Kabani
www.kabani.org

'Kerala Tourism Refutes Report of Child Sex Tourism in India', eTurboNews, 19 January 2006
www.travelindustryreview.com/news/7

'Travel and Tourism in India', Euromonitor International report, September 2006
www.euromonitor.com/Travel_and_Tourism_in_India

'Airbus Announces 138 Jet Orders at Air Show', USA Today, 16 June 2005
www.usatoday.com/travel/news/2005-06-16-airbus-update_x.htm

'Airbus Flies High at the Paris Air Show', Airbus press release, 18 June 2005
http://events.airbus.com/A380/EVENTS/lebourget2005/articleDetail.aspx?ArtId=466

Zero Waste Kovalam Project
www.zerowastekovalam.org

'Statement Against Police Firings on Adivasis in Muthanga', People's Union for Civil Liberties, 7 March 2003
www.pucl.org/Topics/Dalit-tribal/2003/wayanad-statement.htm

'Hunting Down the Hunter: a Dying Breed', Independent, 12 April 2006
http://news.independent.co.uk/environment/article357245.ece

The Blue Yonder
www.theblueyonder.com

'Cape Town Declaration', Cape Town Conference on Responsible Tourism in Destinations, August 2002
www.icrtourism.org/capetown.html

'Tourism and the Human Right to Water', Tourism Watch presentation, March 2005
www.tourism-watch.de/fix/files/eed_tw_tourism_and_water_06_eng.pdf

Kallancherry Retreat
www.kallancheryretreat.com

4. A Pitching Wedge Away from the Sand Trap

I am indebted to the advice of Giles Tremlett, the Guardian's *Madrid correspondent and author of* 'Ghosts of Spain: Travels Through a Country's Hidden Past', *London: Faber & Faber, 2006*

Hotel Don Pancho
www.don-pancho.com

Matías Pérez Such quote: 'Benidorm Estilo', Ayuntamiento de Benidorm, 2003

Ayuntamiento de Benidorm (Benidorm's Mayor's office)
www.benidorm.org

'Plan Bleu', United Nations Environment Programme
www.planbleu.org

'A Sustainable Future for the Mediterranean: the Blue Plan's environment and Development Outlook', edited by Guillaume Benoit and Aline Comeau, Earthscan, 2005

'From Dream Home in the Sun to Pile of Rubble: How Costa Boom Turned Sour', *Guardian*, 29 December 2005
www.guardian.co.uk/spain/article/0,2763,1674659,00.html

'Destruction at all Cost(a)s 2006', Greenpeace report, July 2006
www.greenpeace.org/raw/content/espana/reports/destruction-at-all-co-a-sts-20.pdf

'Illegal Water Use in Spain: Causes, Effects and Solutions', WWF Mediterranean programme report, May 2006
http://assets.panda.org/downloads/illegal_water_use_in_spain_may06.pdf

'Freshwater and Tourism in the Mediterranean', WWF Mediterranean programme report, June 2004
http://assets.panda.org/downloads/medpotourismreportfinal_ofnc.pdf

Global Anti-Golf Movement
www.antigolf.org

Chee Yoke Ling quote: 'A Rough Deal: Golf Displaces People', *Tourism in Focus*, Tourism Concern newsletter, Issue 15, Spring 1995

R.A. Tanner and A.C.Gange, 'Effects of Golf Courses on Local Biodiversity', *Landscape and Urban Planning* 71: 137–146, 2005

'Is it OK . . . to Play Golf?', *Guardian*, 24 January 2006
http://lifeandhealth.guardian.co.uk/experts/leohickman/story/0,,1693590,00.html

Key Resorts
www.thekey.es

Fytofoam at Mosa Trajectum
www.fytoplus3e.com

5. A Massage for Mr Average

Empower Foundation
www.empowerfoundation.org

The Sex Sector: The Economic and Social Bases of Prostitution in Southeast Asia', edited by Lin Lean Lim, International Labour Office, Geneva, 1998
www.ilo.org/public/english/bureau/inf/pr/1998/31.htm

The Task Force to Protect Children from Sexual Exploitation in Tourism, World Tourism Organization website
www.world-tourism.org/protect_children

Travel Trade Guide 2006, Tourism Authority of Thailand
www.tourismthailand.org

J. O'Connell Davidson, 'British Sex Tourists in Thailand', in M. Maynard and J. Purvis (eds.), *(Hetero)sexual Politics*, London: Taylor & Francis, 1995

Jacqueline Sánchez Taylor, 'Dollars are a Girl's Best Friend? Female Tourists' Sexual Behaviour in the Caribbean', *Sociology*, vol. 35, No. 3, pp. 749–764. Cambridge: Cambridge University Press, 2001

'Profiting from Abuse', Unicef report, December 2001
www.unicef.org/publications/index_5623.html

Ecpat
www.ecpat.net

'The Extent and Effect of Sex Tourism and Sexual Exploitation of Children on the Kenyan Coast', UNICEF report, December 2006
www.unicef.org/infobycountry/kenya_37817.html

'"Sex Tourism" Rapist Jailed in France', CNN.com, 21 October 2000
http://archives.cnn.com/2000/WORLD/europe/france/10/20/france.trial

'Tightening the Law', *Guardian*, 28 November 2005

'Chuwit Kamolvisit News', 2Bangkok.com
www.2bangkok.com/chuwit.shtml

'Chuwit Avoids Conviction', *The Nation*, Bangkok, 14 July 2006
www.nationmultimedia.com/2006/07/14/national/national_30008667.php

Ambassador City Jomtien
www.ambassadorcityjomtien.com

'MP Says Water Crisis in Pattaya May Hit Tourism', AsiawaterBusiness, August 2005
www.asiawaterbusiness.com/news_show.php?language=english&n_id=575

'The People's Paradise', *Time*, 7 August 2005
www.time.com/time/magazine/article/0,9171,501050815-1090819,00.html

Pattaya Today
www.pattayatoday.net

6. The Trail on Trial

Alex Garland, *The Beach*, Viking, 1996

China Williams, Matt Warren and Rafael Wlodarski, *Thailand's Islands and Beaches*, Lonely Planet Publications, 2005

Wordsworth's 1844 letter to the *Morning Post*, reprinted in *The Prose Works of William Wordsworth*, edited by W.J.B. Owen and Jane Worthington Smyser, vol. 3, Oxford: Clarendon Press, 1974

John Ruskin, *Praeterita*, Everyman's Library Classic, 2005

David Nicholson-Lord, 'Against the Western Invaders', *New Statesman*, 9 December 2002
www.newstatesman.com/200212090011

Michael Elliott, 'Must the Backpackers Stay Home?', *Time*, 8 December 2002
www.time.com/time/magazine/article/0,9171,1101021216-397505,00.html

Dr Stanley C. Plog, 'Why Destination Areas Rise and Fall in Popularity: An Update of a Cornell Quarterly', *Cornell Hotel and Restaurant Administration Quarterly* (24) pp. 13–24, © 2001

WWF Thailand
www.wwfthai.org

'Chiang Mai Safari: Rare Animals on the Menu at Zoo', *The Nation* (Bangkok), 17 November 2005
http://nationmultimedia.com/2005/11/17/national/index.php?news=national_19180026.html

'Night Safari Unplugged: Boom or Bust', *Chiang Mai City Life*, vol. 14, no. 4, April 2005
www.chiangmainews.com/ecmn/viewfa.php?id=1036

'Post-Tsunami Reconstruction and Tourism: A Second Disaster?', Tourism Concern report, 10 October 2005
www.tourismconcern.org.uk/pdfs/Final%20report.pdf

'Phuket Action Plan', World Tourism Organization website, 1 February 2005
www.unwto.org/tsunami/Phuket/Draft%20Phuket%20Action%20Plan-A%20Rev.3.pdf

Danny Boyle quote: 'The Heart of Whiteness: The Allure of Tourism in *Vertical Limit* and *The Beach*', by Mahwash Shoaib, *Bad Subjects*, Issue 54, March 2001
http://bad.eserver.org/issues/2001/54/shoaib.html

The Adventure Club, Koh Phi Phi
www.phi-phi-adventures.com

'The Future of Travel', The Centre for Future Studies report, 22 September 2006
www.futurestudies.co.uk and www.churchill.com/pressReleases/220906.htm

7. The Dragon and the Mouse

'China To Top Charts As Global Tour Mecca', *People's Daily*, China, 20 October 2003
http://english.people.com.cn/200310/20/eng20031020_126404.shtml

'Chinese Outbound Tourism', World Tourism Organization report, 2003
www.world-tourism.org/publications/pr_1302-1.html

'Fact and Figure', China National Tourism Administration website
www.cnta.gov.cn/lyen

'Outbound Travelling Jumps Fifty-fold in Twenty Years', *China Daily*, 4 February 2006
http://news.xinhuanet.com/english/2006-02/04/content_4133422.htm

'Chinese Tourists Flock to UK in Search of Clarks, Fog and the "Big Stupid Clock"', *Guardian*, 27 June 2005
www.guardian.co.uk/uk_news/story/0,,1515396,00.html

'VisitBritain Welcomes Landmark Tourism Agreement with China', VisitBritain press release, 21 January 2005
www.visitbritain.com/corporate/presscentre/presscentrebritain/pressreleasesoverseasmrkt/jan-mar2005/VBwelcomeslandmarktourismagreement.aspx

'Chinese Tourists Behaviour in "Elsewhereland"', by Wolfgang Arlt, paper presented at the Tourism in Asia conference at Leeds University, 10–12 June 2006
www.china-outbound.com/Newsletter/2006_07_conference_paper_elsewherland

China's Outbound Tourism, by Wolfgang Arlt, Oxford: Routledge, 2006

'Chinese Tourism', *The Economist*, 22 June 2006

'China, China Hong Kong SAR and China Macau SAR: The Impact of Travel and Tourism on Jobs and the Economy', WTTC report, 24 April 2006
www.wttc.org/publications/pdf/FINAL%20WTTC_China%20English.pdf

'MyTravel to Offer Tours to Madame Mao's Holiday Spot', *Guardian*, 22 March 2006
www.guardian.co.uk/china/story/0,,1736577,00.html

'China Agrees to Ban Transplant Tourism', *New Scientist*, 2 December 2006
www.newscientist.com/article.ns?id=dn10711&feedId=online-news_rss20

'The Tourism Boycott', Burma Campaign UK website
www.burmacampaign.org.uk/action_holiday.html

'Tourism in Burma', Voices for Burma website
www.voicesforburma.org/tourism

'To Go or Not To Go? Burma Update', Tourism Concern press release, 7 June 2006
www.tourismconcern.org.uk/media/2006/Burma%20update%20June%2006.htm

'Gormo–Lhasa Railway: Take Action', Free Tibet Campaign website
www.freetibet.org/campaigns/railway/railwayaction.html

'Interesting Facts and Figures', Hong Kong International Airport website
www.hongkongairport.com/eng/aboutus/facts.html

Hong Kong Disneyland
www.hongkongdisneyland.com

'Database on Particular Policy Issues – Economic Services: Hong Kong Disneyland', Hong Kong Legislative Council website
www.legco.gov.hk/database/english/data_es/es-hk-disneyland.htm

'Decommissioning of Cheoy Lee Shipyard at Penny's Bay', Legislative Council Panel on Environmental Affairs report, 23 June 2003
www.tourism.gov.hk/resources/english/paperreport_doc/legco/2003-06-23/ea23june03_eng.pdf

'Disney's Hong Kong Headache', *Time*, 8 May 2006

www.time.com/time/magazine/article/0,9171,1191881,00.html

'Disney Hong Kong: Magic is Missing', *Asia Times*, 18 July 2002
www.atimes.com/atimes/China/DG18Ad01.html

'Miscues Mar Opening of Hong Kong Disney', *USA Today*, 9 November 2005
www.usatoday.com/money/companies/2005-11-09-hong-kong-disney-usat_x.htm

'Cleaning the Magic Kingdom', *San Francisco Chronicle*, 23 January 2001
www.sfgate.com/cgi-bin/article.cgi?file=/chronicle/archive/2001/01/23/MN89901.DTL

'Green Groups Rap HK Over Toxic Mud at Disney Park', Reuters, 22 April 2002
www.planetark.org/avantgo/dailynewsstory.cfm?newsid=15584

'Disney Magic a Long Wait Away in Hong Kong', *New York Times*, 3 February 2006
www.iht.com/articles/2006/02/03/news/disney.php

'Disney Takes Shark's Fin Off Menu', *The Standard*, Hong Kong, 10 June 2005
www.thestandard.com.hk/stdn/std/Metro/GF10Ak01.html

'HK Disney Answers Soup Critics', BBC News Online, 9 June 2005
http://news.bbc.co.uk/1/hi/world/asia-pacific/4076408.stm

'Disney Hong Kong Knocked Over Pay', BBC News Online, 9 April 2006
http://news.bbc.co.uk/1/hi/business/4893448.stm

'Disney Listens to Workers', Associated Press, 21 May 2006
www.disneylandparkfans.com/News/DisplayPressRelease.asp_Q_id_E_5226Listen

'Crowds Try to Storm Hong Kong Disneyland', *USA Today*, 2 June 2006
www.usatoday.com/travel/news/2006-02-06-hongkong-disney_x.htm

'Group Slams Disney Over Labor Abuses in Factories', *The Standard*, Hong Kong, 11 September 2006
www.thestandard.com.hk/news_detail.asp?pp_cat=11&art_id=27031&sid=9824599&con_type=1

'Hong Kong Disneyland Faces Calls to Reveal Attendance', Bloomberg.com, 12 September 2006
www.bloomberg.com/apps/news?pid=20601088&sid=abgV0NmhSwzI&refer=muse

8. All at Sea

Cruise Lines International Association
www.cruising.org

Royal Caribbean
www.royalcaribbean.com

Freedom of the Seas
www.freedomoftheseas.com

'The Future of Cruising – Boom or Bust? A Worldwide Analysis to 2015', by Tony Peisley, Seatrade Research report, March 2006
www.seatrade-global.com/cruise_report/cruise_report_home.htm

'International Convention for the Prevention of Pollution from Ships, 1973, as modified by the Protocol of 1978 relating thereto (MARPOL 73/78)', International Maritime Organization website
www.imo.org/Conventions/contents.asp?doc_id=678&topic_id=258

Cruise Junkie
www.cruisejunkie.com

Ross A. Klein, *Cruise Ship Squeeze: The New Pirates of the Seven Seas*, New Society Publishers, 2005

'Marine Pollution: Progress Made to Reduce Marine Pollution by Cruise Ships, but Important Issues Remain', US General Accounting Office's Report to Congressional Requesters, February 2000
www.epa.gov/owow/oceans/cruise_ships/gaofeb00.pdf

'Carnival Pleads Guilty; Fined $18 Million for Lying about Ocean Pollution', The Office of Inspector General investigation report, US Department of Transportation, 19 April 2002
www.oig.dot.gov/item.jsp?id=770

International Council of Cruise Lines
www.iccl.org

'A Shifting Tide: Environmental Challenges and Cruise Industry Responses', Conservation International report, 2003
www.celb.org/xp/CELB/downloads/Cruise_Interim_Summary.pdf

'Cruise Pollution Update: More Cruise Ships, More Passengers, More Pollution', Bluewater Network report, 2006
www.bluewaternetwork.org/reports/cv/Cruiseship_MiniReport_06.pdf

Responsible Cruising in Alaska
www.responsiblecruising.org

'Cruise Industry's Economic Impact on the Caribbean', Florida-Caribbean Cruise Association report, May 2001
www.f-cca.com/downloads/carib_impact.pdf

'The Impact of Cruise Ships on Small Bahamian Islands', by Sir Arthur Foulkes, *Nassau Tribune*, 16 May 2006
www.bahamapundit.com/2006/05/the_impact_of_c.html

'Making All-Inclusives More Inclusive', Travel Foundation report, February 2004
www.thetravelfoundation.org.uk/assets/project%20summaries/allinclusives%20final%20report.doc

'Sweatships: What It's Really Like to Work On Board Cruise Ships', War on Want and International Transport Workers Federation report, 2002
www.waronwant.org/download.php?id=71

'Exploring Cancún', Planeta.com
www.planeta.com/ecotravel/mexico/yucatan/cancun.html

'Ship Harms Major Coral Reef off Yucatan', *New York Times*, 21 December 1997

Galápagos Conservation Trust
www.gct.org

Charles Darwin Foundation
www.darwinfoundation.org

International Association of Antarctica Tour Operators
www.iaato.org

9. Turtles and Towers

Hotel El Rey del Caribe
www.reycaribe.com

Inter-American Development Bank
www.iadb.org

National Trust Fund for Tourism Development (FONATUR)
www.fonatur.gob.mx/_Ingles/index.html

'Summary of Project Information: 20211 Occidental Mexico', International Finance Corporation website, 13 January 2003
www.ifc.org/ifcext/lac.nsf/Content/SelectedProject?OpenDocument&UNID=2EEA8B7142AEA41F8525 6CAD007BFD3D

'Investment Summary: Sunset Beach Resort and Spa Hotel Limited', Inter-American Investment Corporation website, 24 October 2003
www.iic.int/projects/view.asp?ID=28&origin=results&QS='union=AND&viewby=50&startrec=1&top_ parent=151

'Mexico: World Bank Approves \$200.5 Million for Sustainable Development', World Bank website, 6 September 2005
http://web.worldbank.org/WBSITE/EXTERNAL/TOPICS/EXTENERGY/0,,contentMDK:20637199~menuP K:64615830~pagePK:166745~piPK:459740~theSitePK:336806,00.html

'Tourism: An Opportunity to Unleash. Shared Growth in Africa', World Bank, Note Number 16, July 2006
http://siteresources.worldbank.org/EXTAFRSUMAFTPS/Resources/note_16.pdf

'Tourism and Development: Red Flags Being Ignored', *Jamaica Gleaner*, 24 September 2006
www.jamaica-gleaner.com/gleaner/20060924/cleisure/cleisure2.html

'MIF Supports Tourism Development in Mexico's Tequila Region', Inter-American Development Bank press release, 10 March 2006
www.iadb.org/news/articledetail.cfm?font=2&artid=2877&language=English

'Alcohol-Soaked Spring Break Lures Students Abroad', *USA Today*, 5 January 2003
www.usatoday.com/news/nation/2003-01-05-spring-break-usat_x.htm

'Cancun Spring Break', StudentSpringBreak.com
www.studentspringbreak.com/dests/cancun.shtml

Riu Hotels and Resorts
www.riu.com

'Not So Inclusive', *Geographical,* February 2004
www.geographical.co.uk

Polly Pattullo, *Last Resorts: Tourism in the Caribbean,* London: Cassell and Latin American Bureau, 1996

'Paying a High Price for Paradise', *Observer,* 28 February 1999

'Montezuma's Revenge: How Sanitation Concerns May Injure Mexico's Tourist Industry', *Cornell Hotel and Restaurant Administration Quarterly,* vol. 45, no. 2, pp.132–144, 2004
http://cqx.sagepub.com/cgi/content/abstract/45/2/132

Cancún Convention and Visitors Bureau
www.cancun.info

Riviera Maya
www.rivieramaya.com

Community Tours Sian Ka'an
www.siankaantours.org

World Heritage Alliance
www.worldheritagealliance.org

10. Green Gold

Beatrice Blake and Anne Becher, *The New Key to Costa Rica,* Berkeley, California: Ulysses Press, seventeenth edition, 2004

Arenal Mundo Aventura
www.arenalmundoaventura.com

ACTUAR
www.actuarcostarica.com

Arenal Oasis
www.arenaloasis.com

Puentes Colgantes del Arenal
www.puentescolgantes.com

Costa Rica Tourism Board
www.visitcostarica.com

'The Ecoclub Interview with the "Architect of Ecotourism"', *Ecoclub,* issue 85, October 2006
http://ecoclub.com/news/085/interview.html

'Tourism: 2020 Vision', World Tourism Organization, vol. 1, no. 1, December 1998

The International Ecotourism Society
www.ecotourism.org

International Year of Ecotourism 2002
www.world-tourism.org/sustainable/IYE-Main-Menu.htm

Third World Network media releases, 2002
www.twnside.org.sg/title/iye1.htm
www.twnside.org.sg/title/iye3.htm

Green Globe
www.greenglobe21.com

Martha Honey, *Ecotourism and Sustainable Development: Who Owns Paradise?,* Washington, DC: Island Press, 1999

Sustainable Tourism Stewardship Council
www.stscouncil.org

Ron Mader posting to Planeta.com forum, 14 January 2004
http://forum.planeta.com/viewtopic.php?t=58

'Goodness Sells: A Modest Proposal for the Rebranding of Ecotourism in the United States', by Frances Figart, Planeta.com, September 2005
www.planeta.com/planeta/05/0509goodness.html

'Taking the Natural Path: in 2002, the International Year of Ecotourism, Will We Set New Standards for Green Travel?', *E/The Environmental Magazine*, 1 July 2002
www.encyclopedia.com/doc/1G1-90191344.html

Erlet Cater, 'Ecotourism as a Western Construct', *Journal of Ecotourism*, vol. 5, no. 1&2, pp. 23–39
www.multilingual-matters.net/jet/005/jet0050023.htm

Richard Sharpley, 'Ecotourism: A Consumption Perspective', *Journal of Ecotourism*, vol. 5, no. 1&2, pp. 7–22
www.multilingual-matters.net/jet/005/jet0050007.htm

Rosaleen Duffy, *A Trip Too Far: Ecotourism, Politics and Exploitation*, London: Earthscan, 2002

'Exclusive Interview with Wade Davis', *Courier*, August 2005
www.greentravel.biz/pdfs/E0805WadeDavisInterview.pdf
www.ntaonline.com

'Massive Growth of Ecotourism Worries Biologists', *New Scientist*, 4 March 2004
www.newscientist.com/article.ns?id=dn4733

Hotel Punta Islita
www.hotelpuntaislita.com

F. Gary Stiles and Alexander Skutch, *A Guide to the Birds of Costa Rica*, Cornell University Press, 1989

'IDB Approves $20 Million Loan to Costa Rica for Sustainable Tourism in Protected Wilderness Areas', Inter-American Development Bank press release, 18 December 2006
www.iadb.org/NEWS/articledetail.cfm?Language=En&parid=2&artType=PR&artid=3541

11. Party Politics

I am indebted to Stephen Armstrong, author of The White Island: The Extraordinary History of the Mediterranean's Capital of Hedonism *for his advice.(London: Black Swan, 2005.)*

'The Shock Death Toll on Ibiza's Roads', *Mail on Sunday*, 8 July 2003

Pacha
www.pacha.com

Mark A. Bellis, Karen Hughes, Andrew Bennett, Roderick Thomson, 'The Role of an International Nightlife Resort in the Proliferation of Recreational Drugs', *Addiction*, 2003, 98 (12):1713–1721
http://pt.wkhealth.com/pt/re/addi/fulltext.00008514-200312000-00014.htm

'British Gangs and Guns Bring Terror to Ibiza', *Independent*, 14 August 2006

Club18–30
www.club18-30.com

Mark A. Bellis, Karen Hughes, Andrew Bennett, Roderick Thomson, 'Sexual Behaviour of Young People in International Tourist Resorts', *Sex Transm Infect*, 2004; 80:43–47

'Holiday Sex Fuels Disease Fears', BBC News Online, 4 February 2004
http://news.bbc.co.uk/1/hi/health/3454119.stm

'Condom Campaign to Target Young People Heading for the Sun at Birmingham Airport', Terrence Higgins Trust press release, 25 July 2006
www.tht.org.uk/mediacentre/pressreleases/2006/july/condomcampaignatbirminghamairport.htm

2wentys
www.firstchoice.co.uk/2wentys

'Confessions of a Club Rep', *Guardian*, 20 August 2003
http://travel.guardian.co.uk/article/2003/aug/20/travelnews

Amics de la Terra Eivissa
www.amics-terra.org

'Ibiza Rises Up Against Blight of Tourism', *Observer*, 26 February 2006
http://observer.guardian.co.uk/world/story/0,,1718122,00.html

'Fiesta Breaks Ground for "Green Holiday" Resort', *Jamaica Gleaner*, 13 November 2006
www.jamaica-gleaner.com/gleaner/20061112/news/news1.html

'Six-Lane Highways for the Mediterranean Island of Ibiza', *New York Times*, 11 July 2005
www.nytimes.com/2005/07/11/international/europe/11spiegel2.html?ex=1173157200&en=8cb16b805aea015c&ei=5070

'The Godfather: Part II', *Pacha Lifestyle Magazine*, No. 16, October 2006

'Why Is the UK Tourism Industry Scared of the Balearic Eco-tax?', Tourism Concern press release, 20 February 2002
www.tourismconcern.org.uk/media/2002/Balearic%20ecotax%20press%20release%2012%20Feb%202002.htm

12. Kamikaze Sex and Kalashnikovs

Tallinn Pissup
www.tallinnpissup.com

'Is It OK . . . to Go on a Stag Weekend?', *Guardian*, 25 July 2006
http://money.guardian.co.uk/ethicalliving/story/0,,1828342,00.html

'Latvian Brands Tourists "Savages"', BBC News Online, 4 August 2006
http://news.bbc.co.uk/1/hi/england/merseyside/5245684.stm

Tallinn City Tourist Office
www.tourism.tallinn.ee

'Eek! Baltic Goldrush as Britons Make Estonia Europe's Property Hotspot', *Guardian*, 11 March 2006
www.guardian.co.uk/international/story/0,,1728752,00.html

Iris Pettai, Helve Kase and Ivi Proos, 'Prostitution in Estonia: A Survey of the Situation of Women Involved in Prostitution', Estonian Institute for Open Society Research, 2006

'British Group Tourism to Tallinn', British Embassy (Estonia) seminar held with Enterprise Estonia, 3 October 2006. DVD of seminar supplied to author by the British Embassy in Estonia.
www.britishembassy.gov.uk/servlet/Front?pagename=OpenMarket/Xcelerate/ShowPage&c=Page&cid=1161593073956

'Adult Entertainment Working Group Report and Recommendations to Ministers on the Adult Entertainment Industry in Scotland', Scottish Executive, vol. 1, April 2006
www.scotland.gov.uk/Publications/2006/04/24135036/0

13. Cleared for Take-Off

Much of the research conducted for this chapter was undertaken at the Second Aviation and Environment Summit (www.environment.aero), held on 25–26 April 2006 at Geneva Airport, which I attended on behalf of the Guardian *resulting in the following two articles:*

'Is it OK to Fly?', *Guardian*, 20 May 2006
http://travel.guardian.co.uk/article/2006/may/20/ecotourism.guardiansaturdaytravelsection

'How Could Planes Be Less Damaging?', *Guardian*, 20 May 2006
http://travel.guardian.co.uk/article/2006/may/20/ecotourism.guardiansaturdaytravelsection4

'CAA Approves Hurn Airspace Change Proposal', Civil Aviation Authority press release, 21 February 2007
www.caa.co.uk/application.aspx?categoryid=14&pagetype=65&applicationid=7&newstype=n&mode=detail&nid=1416

'Swanwick Factfile', National Air Traffic Services website
www.nats.co.uk/text/80/london_area_control_centre.html

'Table 03, Aircraft Movements 2005', CAA Statistics website
www.caa.co.uk/docs/80/airport_data/2005Annual/Table_03_1_Aircraft_Movements_2005.pdf

'Executive Summary: HURN TCSW Stakeholder Design Development Workshop', NATS website, 11 July 2005
http://nats-airspace.hosting.alchemydigital.com/1public/Hurn/data/TCSW_HURN_exec_summary.pdf

'The Future of Air Transport' white paper, Department for Transport, December 2003
www.dft.gov.uk/about/strategy/whitepapers/air

'The Future of Air Transport' progress report, Department for Transport, December 2006
www.dft.gov.uk/162259/165217/185629/progressreport

'Airbus Global Market Forecast for 2006–2025', Airbus website
www.airbus.com/store/mm_repository/pdf/att00008552/media_object_file_AirbusGMF2006-2025.pdf

'Fears for Environment as China Plans 48 new airports', *Guardian*, 10 May 2006
www.guardian.co.uk/international/story/0,,1771219,00.html

'747 Fun Facts', Boeing website
www.boeing.com/commercial/747family/pf/pf_facts.html

'Environmental Audit – Ninth Report', House of Commons' Environmental Audit Committee,
19 July 2006
www.publications.parliament.uk/pa/cm200506/cmselect/cmenvaud/981/98102.htm

'Aviation and the Global Atmosphere', Special Report of Intergovernmental Panel on Climate Change
Working Groups I and III in collaboration with the Scientific Assessment Panel to the Montreal
Protocol on Substances that Deplete the Ozone Layer, 1999
www.grida.no/climate/ipcc/aviation/index.htm

'Air Transport's Environmental Track Record', International Air Transport Association website
www.iata.org/pressroom/facts_figures/fact_sheets/Environment.htm

Alice Bows and Kevin Anderson, 'Policy Clash: Can Projected Aviation Growth Be Reconciled with the
UK Government's 60% Carbon-Reduction Target?', Tyndall Centre for Climate Change transport
policy research paper, 22 November 2006
http://dx.doi.org/10.1016/j.tranpol.2006.10.002

Alice Bows, Kevin Anderson and Paul Upham, 'Contraction and Convergence: UK Carbon Emissions
and the Implications for UK Air Traffic', Tyndall Centre for Climate Change Research technical report,
no. 40, February 2006
www.tyndall.ac.uk/research/theme2/project_overviews/t3_23.shtml

'Chaotic World of Climate Truth', BBC News Online, 4 November 2006
http://news.bbc.co.uk/1/hi/sci/tech/6115644.stm

'Airport Expansion Plans Confirmed', BBC News Online, 14 December 2006
http://news.bbc.co.uk/1/hi/uk_politics/6177543.stm

Gavin Pretor-Pinney, *The Cloudspotter's Guide*, 'Chapter 12: Contrails', Sceptre, 2006
www.cloudappreciationsociety.org/cloudspotters-guide

Nicola Stuber, Piers Forster, Gaby Rädel and Keith Shine, 'The Importance of the Diurnal and Annual
Cycle of Air Traffic for Contrail Radiative Forcing', *Nature*, 441, 864–867, 15 June 2006
www.nature.com/nature/journal/v441/n7095/abs/nature04877.html

David J. Travis, Andrew M. Carleton and Ryan G. Lauritsen, 'Climatology: Contrails Reduce Daily
Temperature Range', *Nature*, 418, 601, 8 August 2002
www.nature.com/nature/journal/v418/n6898/abs/418601a.html

'Branson Pledges $3bn Transport Profits to Fight Global Warming', *Guardian*, 22 September 2006
www.guardian.co.uk/frontpage/story/0,,1878589,00.html

'The Environmental Effects of Civil Aircraft in Flight', Royal Commission on Environmental Pollution
special report, 29 November 2002
www.rcep.org.uk/avreport.htm

'Editorial: Biofuels – a paler shade of green', *New Scientist*, issue 2570, 26 September 2006
www.newscientist.com/channel/opinion/mg19125702.200-editorial-biofuels--a-paler-shade-of-green.html

Eurocontrol
www.eurocontrol.int

'The Heat Is On', *Travel Weekly*, 23 March 2007

'Phantom Flight Service Grounded', *Guardian*, 12 March 2007
www.guardian.co.uk/airlines/story/0,,2031727,00.html

'Virgin Atlantic Move to Save Fuel', BBC News Online, 3 December 2006
http://news.bbc.co.uk/1/hi/business/6203636.stm

'Worried About Airline Pollution? Sell Your Car, Says Ryanair Boss', *Guardian*, 22 June 2005
www.guardian.co.uk/uk_news/story/0,3604,1511753,00.html

'Labour Targets Airlines Over Carbon Emissions', *Guardian*, 5 January 2007
http://environment.guardian.co.uk/travel/story/0,,1983334,00.html

'Ryanair Hits Back in "Green" Row', BBC News Online, 5 January 2007
http://news.bbc.co.uk/1/hi/uk_politics/6233019.stm

'Ryanair Retracts Emissions Claim', BBC News Online, 29 January 2007
http://news.bbc.co.uk/1/hi/business/6310571.stm

'Stern Review on the Economics of Climate Change', HM Treasury and Cabinet Office review,
30 October 2006
www.hm-treasury.gov.uk/independent_reviews/stern_review_economics_climate_change/
sternreview_index.cfm

'Convention on International Civil Aviation (also known as the Chicago Convention)', ICAO,
7 December 1944
www.icao.int/icaonet/dcs/7300.html

Brendon Sewill, 'The Hidden Cost of Flying', Aviation Environment Federation report, February 2003
www.aef.org.uk/downloads/HiddenCost.pdf

Sally Cairns and Carey Newson, 'Predict and Decide: Aviation, Climate Change and UK Policy',
Environmental Change Institute report, University of Oxford, 17 October 2006
www.eci.ox.ac.uk/research/energy/downloads/predictanddecide.pdf

'BATA YouGov Survey Full Results', British Air Transport Association, 13 October 2006
www.yougov.com/archives/pdf/BATA.pdf

'Airlines Stand to Make £2.7 Billion Profit from EU Climate Scheme', Institute of Public Policy
Research press release, 18 December 2006
www.ippr.org.uk/pressreleases/?id=2488

'Open Skies Deal Will Undo Curbs on CO_2, Say Greens', *Guardian*, 24 March 2007
http://politics.guardian.co.uk/green/story/0,,2041876,00.html

'Care Needed with Carbon Offsets', BBC News Online, 15 December 2006
http://news.bbc.co.uk/1/hi/sci/tech/6184577.stm

'A Smoke-Screen Against Action to Cut Emissions', Friends of the Earth press release, 18 January 2007
www.foe.co.uk/resource/press_releases/carbon_offsetting_18012007.html

'It's a Sin to Fly, Says Church', *Sunday Times*, 23 July 2006
www.timesonline.co.uk/tol/news/uk/article691423.ece

Green Skies Alliance
www.greenskies.org

'Greener Skies: A Consultation on the Environmental Taxation of Aviation', Conservative consultation
paper, 12 March 2007
www.conservatives.com/pdf/greenerskiesconsultation.pdf

Flight Pledge Union
www.flightpledge.org.uk

'Facts and Figures', Transport 2000 website
www.transport2000.org.uk/factsandfigures/Facts.asp

Conclusion

'Exodus 1971: New Bargains in the Sky', *Time*, 19 July 1971
www.time.com/time/magazine/article/0,9171,905388-1,00.html

'Another Record Year for World Tourism', World Tourism Organization press release, 29 January 2007
www.unwto.org/newsroom/Releases/2007/january/recordyear.htm

'Tourism 2020 Vision', World Tourism Organization website
www.unwto.org/facts/menu.html

'Blueprint for New Tourism', World Travel and Tourism Council report
www.wttc.org/blueprint/WTTCBlueprintFinal.pdf

'Visitor Payback in the Outbound UK Tourism Industry', Responsible Tourism Partnership website
www.responsibletourismpartnership.org/payback.pdf

'Editorial: How Green Do We Want To Go?', *Travel Weekly*, 28 April 2006
www.travelweekly.co.uk

'Around the World in 23 Days – and One Jet', *Guardian*, 21 October 2006
www.guardian.co.uk/uk_news/story/0,,1927864,00.html

'Corporate Social Responsibility', MyTravel PLC website
www.mytravelgroup.com/AniteNextPage.asp?p=PLCCSR

'Australia Mulls Hosing the Great Barrier Reef', TravelWireNews.com, 7 November 2006
www.travelwirenews.com/cgi-script/csArticles/articles/000101/010125.htm

'The Future of Travel', The Centre for Future Studies report, 22 September 2006
www.futurestudies.co.uk and www.churchill.com/pressReleases/220906.htm

'Universal Declaration of Human Rights', UN General Assembly, 10 December 1948
www.un.org/Overview/rights.html

'Global Code of Ethics for Tourism', World Tourism Organization website
www.unwto.org/code_ethics/eng/global.htm

'"Paris Syndrome" strikes Japanese', BBC News Online, 20 December 2006
http://news.bbc.co.uk/1/hi/world/europe/6197921.stm

'Fair Trade in Tourism', Tourism Concern website
www.tourismconcern.org.uk/fair-trade/fair-trade.html

'Oops, We Helped Ruin the Planet', *Guardian*, 4 March 2006
http://travel.guardian.co.uk/article/2006/mar/04/travelnews.climatechange.environment

'Anywhere But Here?', *Guardian*, 13 January 2007
http://travel.guardian.co.uk/article/2007/jan/13/saturday.green

'Evangelists of "Slow Travel" Hurry to Spread Their Gospel', *Observer*, 28 January 2007
http://observer.guardian.co.uk/uk_news/story/0,,2000543,00.html

Declaration

Travel journalism is often blighted by the fact that journalists do not declare to their readers when they have been the guest of a company. Travel is an expensive business and much of the travel writing we enjoy simply would not occur without this sometimes awkward relationship. However, as long as it is openly declared, I don't feel that it should compromise the bond of trust between a reader and writer.

Whilst researching this book I did attempt to pay my way whenever possible, but there were occasions when – either to gain access as a journalist to interviewees or to reduce otherwise crippling costs – I accepted the hospitality of companies. These were those occasions . . .

Burj Al Arab, Dubai
Al Maha, Dubai
Ski Dubai
Disneyland Hong Kong
Freedom of the Seas, Royal Caribbean
Hotel Punta Islita, Costa Rica
Hotel Don Pancho, Benidorm
Pacha, Ibiza

In addition, the *Guardian* covered my costs when reporting from the WTTC summit held in Washington DC from 10–12 April 2006. This trip was crucial in giving me unparalleled access to some of the industry's leading figures, many of whom were interviewed for this book.

And finally...

In many ways, I hope this book is just the start of a journey. For debates and updates about the future of tourism, please visit www.leohickman.co.uk